Making Projects Critical

Edited by

Damian Hodgson
and
Svetlana Cicmil

First published 2006 by
PALGRAVE MACMILLAN
Houndmills, Basingstoke, Hampshire RG21 6XS and
175 Fifth Avenue, New York, N.Y. 10010
Companies and representatives throughout the world

PALGRAVE MACMILLAN is the global academic imprint of the Palgrave
Macmillan division of St. Martin's Press, LLC and of Palgrave Macmillan Ltd.
Macmillan® is a registered trademark in the United States, United Kingdom
and other countries. Palgrave is a registered trademark in the European
Union and other countries.

ISBN-13: 978–1–4039–4085–8
ISBN-10: 1–4039–4085–1

This book is printed on paper suitable for recycling and made from fully
managed and sustained forest sources.

A catalogue record for this book is available from the British Library.

Library of Congress Cataloging-in-Publication Data
Making projects critical / Damian Hodgson and Svetlana Cicmil (eds.).
    p. cm.—(Management, work and organisations)
  Includes bibliographical references and index.
  ISBN 1–4039–4085–1 (paper)
    1. Project management. I. Hodgson, Damian E. II. Cicmil, Svetlana. III. Series.
HD69.P75M355 2006
658.4′04—dc22   2005056131

10 9 8 7 6 5 4 3 2 1
15 14 13 12 11 10 09 08 07 06

Printed and bound in China

MANAGEMENT, WORK AND ORGANISATIONS

Series editors: **Gibson Burrell**, The Management Centre, University of Leicester
Mick Marchington, Manchester Business School
Paul Thompson, Department of Human Resource Management,
University of Strathclyde

This series of new textbooks covers the areas of human resource management, employee relations, organisational behaviour and related business and management fields. Each text has been specially commissioned to be written by leading experts in a clear and accessible way.

The books contain serious and challenging material, take an analytical rather than prescriptive approach and are particularly suitable for use by students with no prior specialist knowledge.

The series is relevant for many business and management courses, including MBA and post-experience courses, specialist masters and postgraduate diplomas, professional courses and final-year undergraduate courses. These texts have become essential reading at business and management schools worldwide.

Published

Peter Boxall and John Purcell
STRATEGY AND HUMAN RESOURCE MANAGEMENT

Paul Blyton and Peter Turnbull
THE DYNAMICS OF EMPLOYEE RELATIONS (3rd edn)

Karen Legge
HUMAN RESOURCE MANAGEMENT: anniversary edition

Hugh Scullion and Margaret Linehan
INTERNATIONAL HUMAN RESOURCE MANAGEMENT

Damian Hodgson and Svetlana Cicmil
MAKING PROJECTS CRITICAL

Sharon C. Bolton
EMOTION MANAGEMENT IN THE WORKPLACE

Keith Grint
LEADERSHIP

Jill Rubery and Damian Grimshaw
THE ORGANISATION OF EMPLOYMENT

Marek Korczynski
HUMAN RESOURCE MANAGEMENT IN SERVICE WORK

J. Martin Corbett
CRITICAL CASES IN ORGANISATIONAL BEHAVIOUR

Helen Rainbird (ed.)
TRAINING IN THE WORKPLACE

Harry Scarbrough (ed.)
THE MANAGEMENT OF EXPERTISE

Diana Winstanley and Jean Woodall (eds)
ETHICAL ISSUES IN CONTEMPORARY HUMAN RESOURCE MANAGEMENT

Adrian Wilkinson, Mick Marchington, Tom Redman and Ed Snape
MANAGING WITH TOTAL QUALITY MANAGEMENT

For more information on titles in the Series please go to www.palgrave.com/business/mwo

Invitation to authors

The Series Editors welcome proposals for new books within the Management, Work and Organisations series. These should be sent to Paul Thompson (p.thompson@strath.ac.uk) at the Dept of HRM, Strathclyde Business School, University of Strathclyde, 50 Richmond St Glasgow G1 1XT

Series Standing Order

If you would like to receive future titles in this series as they are published, you can make use of our standing order facility. To place a standing order please contact your bookseller or, in case of difficulty, write to us at the address below with your name and address and the name of the series.

Please state with which title you wish to begin your standing order.

Customer Services Department, Macmillan Distribution Ltd
Houndmills, Basingstoke, Hampshire RG21 6XS, England

For Jude and for Kay
D.H.

For Johannes
S.C.

Contents

Notes on the contributors

Neil Alderman is Senior Lecturer at the University of Newcastle-upon-Tyne Business School. His background is as a geographer. Neil spent 19 years as a contract researcher in the Centre for Urban and Regional Development Studies before joining the Business School as Senior Lecturer. His research interests include innovation and technology management, product development in engineering (with particular reference to engineer-to-order companies), innovation in large-scale projects and the management of complex projects. Neil is a member of the British Academy of Management, the European Academy of Management and is a fellow of the Royal Geographical Society (with the Institute of British Geographers).

Mike Bresnen is Professor of Organisational Behaviour at the University of Leicester Management Centre. He holds a first-class degree in Industrial Economics and a PhD from the University of Nottingham and has previously worked at Warwick Business School, Cardiff Business School and Loughborough University. He is co-editor of *Organization* and a founding member of the Innovation, Knowledge and Organisational Networking research unit (ikon) based at Warwick Business School, where he is also an Associate Fellow. He is the author of *Organising Construction* (1990) and has researched and published widely on the organisation and management of the construction process, as well as on inter-organisational relations, project management, leadership and professionals. He is principal investigator on a number of recent EPSRC/ESRC projects investigating knowledge management and project-based learning in construction, manufacturing and service sectors, as well as innovation in the biomedical field.

Svetlana Cicmil is Senior Lecturer in Project Management and the Director of MBA Programmes at Bristol Business School, University of the West of England. Svetlana has been involved in a number of research projects and has published widely on the topics of project management, the international transfer of management knowledge and management education. Her particular interests lie in processual perspectives on the complexity of project-based work and in the application of organisational social theory to broaden the intellectual foundations of the project management field.

Stewart R. Clegg is Professor and Director of ICAN Research at the University of Technology, Sydney. He has made many contributions to several literatures, including those of project management, organisation theory, the sociological and political theory of power, and management. He has published a great many books, articles, chapters, handbooks, encyclopedias and such like, the most recent of which is *Managing and Organization: An Introduction to Theory and Practice*, with Martin Kornberger and Tyrone Pitsis (2005).

Stuart Green is Professor of Construction Management within the School of Construction Management and Engineering at the University of Reading. Prior to entering academia, he worked for a national construction company and also gained design experience with an engineering consultancy. He is currently Director of the Innovative Construction Research Centre and is responsible for an extensive research programme funded by the UK Engineering and Physical Sciences Research Council (EPSRC).

G. Harindranath is Senior Lecturer in Information Systems at Royal Holloway, University of London. Hari holds a doctorate from the London School of Economics, and his research interests include ICT use in small and medium enterprises, information infrastructure policy and e-government initiatives in transition economies, and ICT and economic development. He is an Associate Editor of the *Journal of Global Information Management*, and he has published in a range of journals including *Decision Support Systems, European Journal of Information Systems, Human Relations, The Information Society* and *Information Technology for Development*.

Charles Harvey is Dean and Professor of Business History and Management at Strathclyde Business School, UK. He has twice won the prestigious Wadsworth Prize for Business History and is joint editor of the journal *Business History*. He has published extensively in leading business journals, including the *Journal of Management Studies, Human Relations* and *Organization Studies*.

Damian Hodgson is Senior Lecturer in Organizational Analysis at Manchester Business School at the University of Manchester. His work is broadly located within the field of critical management studies, and focuses on the evolution of self-disciplinary forms of control over expert labour, with a particular interest in project working and project management. He has published in a range of journals including *Organization*, the *Journal of Management Studies* and *Gender, Work and Organization*.

Chris Ivory is Lecturer at the University of Newcastle-upon-Tyne Business School. His background is as a social scientist. Before coming to the Business School Chris was a research associate in the Centre for Urban and Regional Development. Chris's research interests include innovation, the media, critical management approaches to project management and the management of complex projects. He is a member of the British Academy of Management and the European Academy of Management.

Donncha Kavanagh is Senior Lecturer in Management at University College Cork, the National University of Ireland, Cork, Ireland. He has published in the fields of management, organisation studies, engineering, and marketing. His research interests include the history of management thought and the sociology of knowledge and technology. He is currently researching the translation of management technologies into higher education. Vita and full list of publications is at http://www.ucc.ie/academic/mgt/dk/.

Anneli Linde is Lecturer and Research Fellow at Umeå School of Business (USBE), Sweden. Her research interests focus on IT-mediated change processes and the strategic use of management systems in multi-project organizations.

Henrik C.J. Linderoth holds a position as Assistant Professor at Umeå School of Business (USBE), Sweden. His research interests focus on IT-mediated change processes, and the relations between temporality and permanency in change processes.

Monica Lindgren is Associate Professor and Senior Lecturer at the School of Industrial Engineering and Management, Royal Institute of Technology, Stockholm, and Research Associate with the Centre for Entrepreneurship and Business Creation, Stockholm School of Economics. Monica teaches courses in management, research methodology and entrepreneurship. Her research – often departing from a critical perspective – includes areas such as competence development, identity theory, gender, project work, entrepreneurship and collective leadership.

Carol Linehan is Lecturer in Management at University College Cork. Her interests bridge organisational analysis and human resource management.

Marton Marosszeky holds the Multiplex Chair for Engineering Construction Innovation in the School of Civil and Environmental Engineering at the University of New South Wales. He is co-author with John Oakland of *Total Quality in the Construction Supply Chain.* He is internationally recognised for his research into construction process management and technology. He has developed management tools for safety, quality and waste management in construction and he has a special interest in the drivers of technological change and the strategic use of IT within construction. He is a Fellow of the Institution of Engineers, Australia and a Fellow of the Australian Institute of Building.

Nick Marshall is Research Fellow in the Centre for Research in Innovation Management (CENTRIM) at the University of Brighton. He researches and publishes in the areas of organisational knowledge, learning and communication, project-based organisations, and inter-organisational relations. His current research is exploring the nature and effects of cognitive diversity in multi-functional engineering teams.

Ian McLoughlin is Director of the University of Newcastle-upon-Tyne Business School and Co-Director of the Centre for Social and Business Informatics at Newcastle. He has held visiting positions at the University of Adelaide, the University of Wollongong and the Danish Technical University. His research interests include technology and organisation; new forms of work; organisation and employment relationship; managing change and project management; social informatics and socio-technical systems; development and deployment of the technologies of e-government. He is a member of the British Academy of Management Council and a member of the Executive Committee of the Association of Business Schools.

Eamonn Molloy is University Lecturer in Operations and Technology Management, Saïd Business School, University of Oxford, and Fellow of Green College, Oxford. Eamonn has also worked at the University of Warwick and the University of Bath since completing his PhD in Science and Technology Studies at Lancaster University. Eamonn's research focuses on interactions between work, technology and organisation in both public and private sector organisations, particularly in the context of organisational change.

Peter Morris is Professor of Construction and Project Management at University College London and Executive Director of INDECO Limited, a projects-based management consultancy. He is a Fellow of the Institution of Civil Engineers, Chartered Institute of Building, and Association for Project Management. He was until 1996 a Main Board Director of Bovis Limited. Between 1984 and 1989 he was a Research Fellow at the University of Oxford. He has written many papers on project management as well as the books *The Anatomy of Major Projects* (1988) and *The Management of Projects* (1994); he is the editor, with Jeffrey Pinto, of *The Wiley Guide to Managing Projects* (2004).

Manuela Nocker is completing her (part-time) PhD in Organisational Psychology at the London School of Economics. Her doctoral research focuses on the generation of social space, team processes, practices of knowledge creation and of organising in the context of projects of professional service firms. She worked for a decade as careers adviser in a local institution in South Tyrol/Italy. She has extensive experience as trainer and consultant in the areas of organisational behaviour, management development and organisational change, in applied research of organisational change, and in executive coaching for the private and public sector. Her current research interests are ethnographies in organisations, the narrative approach, practice-based studies of collective knowing/learning and strategising, project teams and collaborative work, identity construction, and the role of improvisation for collective action.

Johann Packendorff is Associate Professor and Senior Lecturer at the School of Industrial Engineering and Management, Royal Institute of Technology, Stockholm, where he is responsible for course programmes in project management and industrial operations. His main research areas are project work and entrepreneurship, both studied from non-mainstream perspectives, and he has also inquired into management control, organization change and identity theory. Together with Monica Lindgren, he is currently starting up a research programme on leadership as a collective process.

Tyrone S. Pitsis is Senior Research Associate at the Innovative Collaborations, Alliances and Networks Research Center in the Faculty of Business, University of Technology, Sydney. He teaches within the School of Management on the MBA program. His research interests are in the phenomenology of project-based organising, wisdom and positive organizational scholarship.

Thekla Rura-Polley received her PhD in Business Administration from the University of Wisconsin-Madison. She currently works in the faculty at the University of St Thomas in St Paul, Minnesota. Her research focuses on virtual collaboration, innovation and non-profit organisations.

John Sillince is at Aston Business School. He has undertaken empirical studies of rhetoric, change and innovation in organisations using interviews, observations and qualitative, inductive, discourse-based methodology. The research included studies of: changing strategising in line with e-business; the discursive methods that managers use to get new working practices accepted; and the negotiation of change. He has also theorised about contingency and persistence of rhetoric in the form of a concept of organisation as constituted by rhetorical processes, and of discourse coherence and institutionalised argumentation repertoires.

Charles Smith qualified originally as an engineer and worked on projects for 30 years. During that time he transferred his management interest from engineering construction to organisations and change, supporting this new focus with an additional degree, in psychology, from the Open University. He now consults on management and projects, recently acting as coordinator of a major international project management research network.

Jörg Sydow earned his doctorate in business administration at the Free University of Berlin where he is now Professor of Management at the School of Business and Economics and Director of the doctoral programme 'Research on Organizational Paths'. Before, he held a chair for planning and organisation at the University of Wuppertal, Germany, and was a Visiting Professor at Bentley College, the Universities of Innsbruck and Vienna, and the University of Arizona. Currently he is an International Visiting Fellow of the Advanced Institute of Management Research (AIM), London. He is a founding co-editor of two leading German journals, *Managementforschung* and *Industrielle Beziehungen – The German Journal of Industrial Relations*, and a member of the editorial boards of leading journals, including *Organization Studies, Organization Science* and the *Scandinavian Journal of Management*. His research interest include: management and organisation theory, strategic partnering and interfirm networking, technology and innovation management, and industrial relations.

Janice Thomas is Associate Professor at Athabasca University and Programme Director for its Executive MBA in Project Management. Before becoming an academic she was a practising project manager. Her research interests centre on providing both academia and practice with clearer understandings of how project management influences organisational activities. Theoretical influences include critical theory, complexity theory and sense-making theories.

Roger Vaughan was Managing Director of A&P Appledore Ltd, which designed and project-managed new shipbuilding facilities around the world. After a spell as Director of Productivity at British Shipbuilders, where he led the production technology development programme, he became joint Chief Executive of Swan Hunter, the warshipbuilder. He then became Director of the Newcastle University School of Management and was part of the research team exploring the project management of service-led projects in both the engineering and public sectors. He is a Fellow of the Royal Academy of Engineering and a Visiting Professor at the University of Newcastle-upon-Type Business School.

Richard Whittington is Professor of Strategic Management at Saïd Business School and Millman Fellow at New College, University of Oxford. He has authored or co-authored several books, including *The Handbook of Strategy and Management* and *The European Corporation*, and has published in leading academic journals such as *Organization Science, Organization Studies* and the *Strategic Management Journal*. He is on a number of editorial boards, including the *Academy of Management Review*, the *Journal of Management Studies* and *Organization Studies*. His current research interest is in the changing nature of strategy work.

1

Making projects critical: an introduction

Svetlana Cicmil and Damian Hodgson*

> Concepts developed by the academic community ... must be recovered from operational and textbook definitions and reconnected to ways of seeing and thinking about the world. In the dialectics of the situation and the talk of individuals with different perspectives, the emergence of new ways of talking becomes possible.
>
> Alvesson and Deetz, 2000: 146

Beyond the mainstream

It is always tempting at this point in a text to 'jump straight into defining' (Stacey, 2000: 2) what a 'project' is and what it is not – and to move swiftly on to how it is therefore to be modelled and managed, as is the case with almost all seminal texts in the field. The purpose of this introduction is to show the potential problems with such haste; specifically, that it often results in the obscuring of what lies behind the definitions and prescriptions. This cautionary note at the very outset encapsulates the mission of this text: to provide space outside of the tightly defined and densely populated conceptual landscape of mainstream project management, space where other perspectives, other concerns and other agenda may be articulated and explored. In this sense, the collection continues the mission of two workshops organised and held at Bristol Business School in the UK in 2003 and 2004, with the explicit aim to 'Make Projects Critical'. These workshops brought together a diverse community of researchers and practitioners from Europe, North America and Australasia with a common interest in considering vital issues and values which are both ignored and obscured by 'mainstream' project management.

* The authors wish to thank Johann Packendorff, Monica Lindgren and Janice Thomas for their helpful and constructive comments on an earlier draft of this chapter.

1

Framing these workshops and this text, therefore, is the notion of *mainstream* project management literature and research. By *mainstream*, we particularly mean the prescriptions related to managerial skills and competencies that are offered to practitioners in the vast number of project management texts in existence. This mainstream literature, in general, uses the language of design, regularity and control to propose models and prescriptions as a route to increasing the ability of humans to control complex worlds (Wood, 2002; Stacey, 2001), to the exclusion of other approaches or ways of reasoning. As a rule, mainstream research into projects and project management remains heavily reliant on the functionalist, instrumental view of projects and organisations, where the function of project management is taken to be the accomplishment of some finite piece of work in a specified period of time, within a certain budget, and to an agreed specification. Most mainstream textbooks and professional associations for project management promote this normative view of the field as practice, which can be summarised as the application of knowledge, skills, tools and techniques to project activities to meet project requirements.

The limitations and challenges to this view of projects are widely recognised across the field, and increasingly within the mainstream project management community itself. In recent years, project management has attracted significant attention from an increasing number of researchers and practitioners, coincident with the increased 'adoption' of project-based work across industrial sectors (Kreiner, 1995; Packendorff, 1995; Cicmil, 2001; Hodgson, 2002). At the same time, the foundations and practical application of a once-glorified managerial technology, embodying the scientific achievements of operational research in work scheduling and control under specific constraints of time, cost and a unique outcome, have been seriously questioned by both the academic and the practitioner communities. Several important writers in this field maintain that little radical examination of the intellectual foundation of project management has been done within this stream of research, arguably since the 1960s (Morris, 1997; Koskela and Howell, 2002). In the same vein, writers such as Frame (1994, 1995, 1999), Morris (1997) and Maylor (1999, 2001), among others, have called for a reexamination of the dominant doctrines in project management for their failure to deliver on their promises. Nonetheless, the tendency in the field is still to treat the basic framework of project management as compelling and essentially sound. Most such efforts have been directed towards searching for *improvements* in traditional models and skills (see, for example, Young, 1999, 2003; Maylor, 2003; Meredith and Mantel, 2003) towards a model which better represents the 'true' nature of projects, and for a method of project management based on 'critical success factors' (Stallworthy and Kharbanda, 1985; Belassi and Tukel, 1996; Kharbanda and Pinto, 1996; Belout, 1998; Boddy and Paton, 2004), with the assumption that such an ideal model objectively exists in the world of practice. There is little evidence that the resulting torrent of competing streams of thought, methods of enquiry and best-practice claims and propositions has creatively contributed either to constructive debate in the field or to resolving the difficulties encountered in practice.

To readdress this situation, we intend through this text to create an opportunity to stand back and problematise that which seems known and accepted about projects. Taking this concern as its point of departure, this edited collection aims at opening up new trajectories within the research agenda in the field of studies relevant to projects, project performance and project management. The starting objective is to critically evaluate the intellectual foundations of project management as a field of study and a practising discipline, to expose and understand the key obstacles to innovative research and the creation of knowledge communicable and relevant to practitioners, and to broaden the research agenda by encouraging a more critical approach in this area of organisational life. In particular, the collection will explore the potential of critical research to enhance the intellectual basis of the project management subject area.

As a tentative starting point, therefore, we would pose some fundamental questions which might guide our reflection on how projects are conceived and how they could be conceived:

- Is there a universal explanation of what projects are and how projects evolve?
- What is the meaning behind the concepts in use, that is, the terms such as 'project', 'project management' and 'project success'?
- What are the implications of the 'mainstream' definitions of 'project' and 'project management' for the nature of knowledge and the intellectual foundations of studies of project-based organising, work and management?
- What are the consequences of project organising as currently prescribed, both for project managers and project workers?
- What alternative perspectives upon projects exist beyond the mainstream?
- Whose interests are being served by the reproduction of the status quo in the field?

To understand why we have highlighted this sort of concern (and, equally importantly, why we feel such concerns are not routinely considered in the vast 'mainstream' literature on projects), we will need to locate our discussion within a reexamination of the evolution of project management. In doing so, we aim to underline why projects merit such serious attention, and to account for their rising popularity and importance in contemporary organisations.

A history of project management

Project management emerged as a social practice in the post-second World War development of technology and infrastructure. Despite various streams of praise and criticism, project management and projects have been accepted by many both within and outside the field as natural, self-evident and indispensable. The emergence of project management is described in some detail by Morris (1997) and Engwall (1995), highlighting its development in practice through a number of major projects which can be traced back to the Manhattan Project in the 1940s. While the US oil and chemicals industry played a major role in this period, the majority of the groundwork was done in US defence and aeronautics in the 1950s, including widespread use in the Apollo space programmes (Harrison, 1981). As is evident from contemporary writings (Gaddis, 1959), the Cold War acted as a significant driver on project management development in the USA throughout this period. The intellectual activity in developing the field until the 1960s was based almost exclusively on quantitative techniques within operational research (OR). During the 1960s and 1970s, the predominantly technicist approach was criticised and the theoretical foundations of the field expanded (Packendorff, 1995; Winch, 1996) to encompass traces of organisational research and theories largely concerned with project organisation structures (that is, the matrix form), project leadership, the role of human resource management in facilitating project work and advice on project team-building. In the 1980s and 1990s there was a revival of the OR-based project management research driven by the developments of computer-based technology, which resulted in the creation and promotion of sophisticated expert systems for project planning, control and risk analysis, and an increased use of terminology such as project information systems, project communication networks and so on. This was in no small measure due to the awakening of public sector clients, including government agencies, in their search for robust management models and procedures to minimise disasters of budget and time overruns and questionable quality associated with the project work and outcomes delivered by contractors. A variety of project control methodologies (for example the PRINCE family) and risk management schemes have been developed against such a background. Despite the increased sophistication of these models for project planning and monitoring, researchers found that only the most basic ones are actually used by practitioners and that they are not always used as intended (Packendorff, 1995; Besner and Hobbs, 2004).

The 1990s saw an expansion of the project management field of study from its engineering heartlands into what became widely accepted as a 'multidisciplinary subject', significantly engaging business and management researchers and educators (Winch, 1996). This coincided with the promotion and acceptance of project-based work, organising and management across industries and sectors, as a powerful and universal organisational response to the challenges of managing in a complex world. As Clarke (1999: 139) states: 'In a world where change is becoming increasingly important, tools such as project management, if used properly, can provide a useful way for organisations to manage that change effectively.' It is usually based on the introduction of a set of procedures, or on a new model of administration with the strategic aim to enhance competitiveness through a more effective intra-organisational integration and optimal utilisation of scarce resources (Cleland, 1997).

The contemporary surge in interest in 'project management' is typically explained by reference to the increasing recognition of 'the project' as a versatile, flexible and predictable form of work organisation. Its image as a universal solution to organisational problems has been established through the promotion of specific techniques for planning, monitoring and control, tried and tested in the operations of traditionally project-oriented industries such as defence, aerospace and construction (see, for example, Young, 1999; Frame, 1999; Maylor, 2001). Projects and project teams have emerged in the practitioners' and academic discourses as unique economic and social processes on which the emerging 'knowledge economy' heavily relies (Frame, 1994, 1995; Briner and Hastings, 1994; Cleland, 1997; Cleland and Ireland, 2002; Clarke, 1999; Young, 2003; Meredith and Mantel, 2003). They are promoted as universally applicable templates for integrating, by design, diverse functions of an organisation that enable concentration of flexible, autonomous and knowledgeable individuals in temporary project teams, for the focused accomplishment of goals efficiently, timely and effectively, for customer satisfaction and company benefits.

The created myth about projects and project management continues to expand as knowledge-intensive firms increasingly based on project models are hailed as the organisation of the future (Weick, 1995; Frame, 1999). Thus Frame, for example, claims confidently that the underlying reason for the projects becoming the central focus of management activity in many organisations can be stated 'in a single word: *competition*' (1999: 4, italics original). The literature of the 1990s and in the recent years has drawn attention to the centrality of project-based organising and project working in the processes of information-sharing and knowledge management in organisations (Wiig, 1997; Davenport and Prusak, 1998; Hansen *et al.*, 1999; Silver, 2000; DeFillippi, 2001). Cleland (1997) points out that as project teams evaluate new technologies and resources, they gain insights into the need for making changes. Projects supposedly provide, according to Cleland, a central point where new knowledge, skills and atti-tudes can be developed. The received wisdom of this kind has resulted in a widespread adoption of 'the project' in contemporary organisations as the focal unit of their operations. Not only are projects considered suitable ways to control endeavours in a turbulent environment (Ekstedt *et al.*, 1999), but, more importantly, they are regarded as the appropriate way to stimulate a learning environment and enhance creativity so as to deliver complex products (Hobday, 2000). Despite the inherent contradiction between these two arguments for project-based organising (Tjaeder and Thomas, 2000), it is precisely upon this ambitious promise to deliver both 'controllability and adventure' (Sahlin-Anderson and Söderholm, 2002) that the attraction of organisa-tional 'projectification' is founded.

In certain academic circles, the expanding influence of 'project-based work' has been referred to as the *projectification of society* (Midler, 1995; Lundin and Söderholm, 1998; Jessen, 2002; Sydow and Staber, 2002). In essence, this notion attempts to capture the growing colonisation of all quarters of life by project-related principles, rules, techniques and procedures, aspiring to form a new 'iron cage' of project rationality (Hodgson and Cicmil, 2003). As more and more organisational members are consequently being redefined as *project workers* and *project managers* across industrial sectors, both schol-arly and practitioner communities are experiencing the implications of this shift for employees and organisations (Packendorff, 1995; Hodgson, 2002). The emerging concerns are related to the impact on identity, reshaped intersubjective interaction, and increased control over the individual through ideologies of efficiency and performativity (Fournier and Grey, 2000). These mechanisms are actualised in a number of 'project-related' contemporary tendencies including the use of information technology (IT) in business process restructuring, the promotion of self-managing teams, the ideology of 'knowledge society' and 'knowledge worker', and the emergence of project-based organisation. The resulting drive towards the professionalisation of the project management discipline has been accompanied by the struggle and the tensions involved in conceptualising, promoting and agreeing on the universally acceptable document which should outline the formal body of project management knowledge. This struggle reflects and encapsulates the competition between the nationally embedded professional associations of project management, with distinct bodies of knowledge proposed by the (US-based) Project Management Institute (PMI), the (UK-based) Association for Project Management (APM), the International Project Management Association (European in origin) and the numerous corporate models such as Ericsson's 'PROPS' model (see Linde and Linderoth, this volume).

Accounting for the failure of project management

Concurrently with these developments encompassing the management of projects, project management as an innovative method of effective organising and efficient operation and the phenomenon of 'projectified society', mainstream research into projects and project management continues to rely heavily on the prescriptive and the instrumental. Despite a high level of research enthusiasm against the background of instrumental rationality in decision-making and control, it is increasingly apparent that accepting and applying such orthodoxy does not eliminate project failures, nor does it guarantee project success (Williams, 2004). Although the project management body of thought has been substantially modified since the 1990s, the core concerns continue to shape academic enquiry and practitioners' discourses about projects and project management. Simultaneously, a growing body of literature, as well as a growing body of empirical evidence and the voices of numerous practitioners, supports the view that the very reason for using projects and project management as a methodology for organisational innovation and change is at the heart of project failures (Clarke, 1999; Thomas, 1999, 2000; Maylor, 2001). These concerns will be discussed in more detail below, as they are central to the aims and the approach taken in this collection.

In the closing decade of the twentieth century, project management was challenged more seriously than in any previous period. Contemporary studies of project performance continue to indicate the disparity between the maturing body of project management know-how and the effectiveness of its application (Baker et al., 1983; Williams, 1995; Belassi and Tukel, 1996; Atkinson, 1999; Morris et al., 2000), as an increasing visibility is being given to the claims about project and project management failures, and about dissatisfaction with project performance and outcomes by affected stakeholders.

A glance at the content of recent public reports and those recorded in previous studies (for example, Morris and Hough, 1987; Standish Group, 1995; Winch, 1996; Ewusi-Mensah and Przasnyski, 1997; Williams, 1999; Atkinson, 1999; Flyvbjerg et al., 2002, 2003) provides an insight into frequent cost overruns, delays and underperformance in terms of quality and user satisfaction, which seem to have become the rule and the reality of contemporary projects. In 1995, for instance, it was estimated by the Standish Group that American companies and government agencies spent $81 billion on cancelled IT projects (Ewusi-Mensah and Przasnyski, 1997). In addition, the same source reports that, in total, 31 per cent of IS/IT projects were deemed complete failures, 53 per cent were late, over budget and did not meet expectations, that only 9 per cent of IT projects are delivered on time or within budget, and a mere 16 per cent in total were considered successful. The average time overrun has been identified as being 222 per cent of the original estimate. The question often raised in public about this issue is, generally, how the IT/IS project risk (both financial and service risk) is shared and transferred among the public sector and private sector participants.

In January 2000, the *Financial Times* (*FT*, 2000) reported, for example, on the 'fiascos' of the major government information technology projects in the UK 'stemming from basic project errors' which 'highlighted the need for greater professionalism in project management ... The government's track record in project management has been, to say the least, poor.' Here, the blame was attributed to a lack of specialist project management knowledge among some civil servants and ministers, and to different approval systems, which have, according to some observers, resulted in unrealistic project deadlines. A growing body of evidence shows that similar observations and conclusions have been made in relation to IT/IS in other sectors and types of organisations. It is not only the poor performance of IS/IT projects that has come under public scrutiny. Bowen et al. (1994) reported that nearly 30 per cent of product development projects never live up to business objectives. According to Winch (1996), UK government-procured construction projects ranging from hospitals to roads, suffer from, on average, 14 per cent cost overrun and 11 per cent time overrun. More recently, the £214 million refit project of the Royal Opera House in Covent Garden resulted in a cancelled opening performance, and the remaining shows being run at huge technical risks associated with the operation of newly installed but not properly tested and learned backstage equipment (*FT*, 1999). The Jubilee Line extension project for the London Underground, for example, has been characterised as having been 'a long saga of overshot deadlines and overspent budgets' (Winder, 1999: 8). In the USA, the belated opening of Denver International Airport after four embarrassing postponements, various scandals and a final cost of $5 billion against the budgeted $1.5 billion, has been held up as another yet example of project failure (Dempsey et al., 1997). More recently, the much-derided construction of the Scottish Parliament Building was described by the Fraser Report in September 2004 as being two and a half years behind schedule with costs running approximately ten times more than the original estimate of £40 million. The conclusion drawn about the destiny of such projects as a rule inherent in their very nature is simple: 'These projects never go according to plan' (*FT*, 1999b).

In light of this, it is unsurprising that governments are taking a greater interest than ever before in project management, in an attempt to address this apparently perennial failing of project management techniques. As noted above, governments, and in particular the US government, have been closely involved in the development of project management models and techniques for over half a century. The UK Office of Government Commerce (OGC) within the British Treasury, for example, has developed and promoted the well-established PRINCE and PRINCE2 models, and is currently taking the lead in setting up Centres of Excellence for Project and Programme Management throughout the UK. Similar initiatives by government agencies in North America and elsewhere indicate the seriousness with which project management models and practices are now considered in the public sector. Meanwhile, the ongoing professionalisation of the field of project management, and the increased influence of professional associations through accreditation of training and credentialism, draws significant support and gains moral legitimacy from this perceived role in protecting public interests and ensuring the effective use of public funds.

Diagnoses and prescriptions

While the existence of a crisis of some kind in the field of project management is recognised in many (although not all) quarters, the diagnoses in the field are unsurprisingly varied. For many established project management writers, the failings of project management are to be expected in a maturing field – as techniques are further honed, and models are perfected through longitudinal and cross-sectoral research, it is assumed that the field will one day settle upon a reliable and basically effective model and array of techniques. Others, both within the mainstream and beyond, see the problem as far more deeply rooted in the fundamental principles upon which the field of project management has been established. In this section, we will look at each of these accounts in turn, considering first the attempts by the mainstream of project management to confront the very real failings in the discipline, before turning to a more critical diagnosis of the current state of project management.

It is not our claim then that project management as a disciplinary area is unaware of or unconcerned by the limitations and continued failings of project management models and methods. There is a long-standing debate on the international scene about the formulation of the formal, professional project management body of knowledge, in which important questions are posed by the proponents of mainstream project management about the boundaries of the project management subject area, its purpose, practical application, and relationship with other aspects of organisational and managerial reality (Meredith and Mantel, 1995, 2003; Walta, 1995; Wideman, 1995; Frame, 1999; Morris *et al.*, 2000, among others). Despite the significant presence of project-based working and organising across industrial sectors and the problematic qualifications of project outcomes as success or failure, a number of authors note that the development of project management knowledge remains unstable and fragmented. As a consequence, the dream of establishing project management as an exemplary field of management science is becoming increasingly remote. Questions have been raised about the underlying belief system which exhibits a strong bias towards functionalist/unitarist tradition, reductionism, operational research and 'how-to-do' prescriptive forms of intellectual output (Kreiner, 1995; Packendorff, 1995; Buchanan and Badham, 1999; Thomas, 1999). It was mainly in the 1990s that critical analysis of social and political power associated with projects as organisational and social arrangements, and project management as a practice and as a social grouping emerged in an explicit form (Buchanan and Boddy, 1992; Kreiner, 1995; Packendorff, 1995; Thomas, 1997; Lundin and Midler, 1998; Buchanan and Badham, 1999; Lundin and Hartman, 2000).

In summary, as a result of the assumptions that have guided the development of project management over the decades, its knowledge system has evolved to now encompass a variety of popular concepts following (at some delay) trends in the broader field of management studies:

- *Controlling the performance of projects* – that is, enforcing the particular set of actions project actors are required to undertake in order to produce the desired outcome by managing the motivations and the actions of people
- *Managing relationships among people* – that is, managing the whole 'system' of interrelated roles and tasks and their interconnectedness
- *Managing the project team culture through project leadership* – that is, designing and controlling the system of values and believes in order to motivate people to subscribe to identified project goals
- *Designing and managing the learning process of project members*
- *Capturing, managing and transferring knowledge in project environments.*

Nonetheless, the response to this crisis has so far been a yet greater emphasis on technicist solutions, quantitative methodologies, positivist methodologies and a stronger reliance on instrumental rationality. In one attempt to move the field forward, Atkinson (1999) asserts that it has become an impossible, and, most likely, non-'value-adding' endeavour to define project management in terms of the traditional 'iron triangle' principles, emphasising the achievement of time, cost and quality objectives as the major justification of the role of project management. According to Atkinson, the attention should be refocused from these efficiency measurements, which are being questioned as appropriate measures of project success (see also Belassi and Tukel, 1996; Baldry, 1998; Chapman, 1998; Maylor, 2001), to the nature of the project as a complex organisational arrangement, the 'good management of which is a flexible attribute which could be a strength for achieving project success' (Atkinson, 1999: 339). Exploration of performance characteristics of public initiatives such as large-scale engineering projects expanded these performance measures to include a discussion of the role of institutions, risks and governance in project success (Miller and Lessard, 2000). For others, it is paradoxical feedback which hinders the effective adoption of project-based working and organising as a structural innovation in complex business environments. Where project management has been mobilised as a blueprint for structuring and coordinating organisational change, according to Clarke (1999), 'People often do not see project management as something to help them but rather something which is mandatory, serving little useful purpose' (Clarke, 1999: 144). Clarke identifies the following as problematic in the application of project management as a vehicle of change: the rigid 'standardisation' of project management as the mode of change management which often causes cultural clashes; project management, or 'managing by projects' or becoming a 'project-based' organisation, is often regarded as another control mechanism, a 'corporate reporting' tool; the inadequate formal completion of change projects; project overload syndrome; individual resistance to imposed procedures and practice; and a lack of confidence and motivation. It becomes obvious that the very principles of the effective, structured project management methodology are simultaneously seen as its major causes of failure.

Another influential attempt to address the malaise comes from what is known as the 'Scandinavian School' of project studies (Lundin and Söderholm, 1995; Lundin and Midler, 1998; Ekstedt *et al.*, 1999; Lundin and Hartman, 2000; Sahlin-Andersson and Söderholm, 2002; Söderlund, 2004). In the 1990s, Packendorff succinctly summarised the concern shared by a group of Scandinavian scholars, arguing that contemporary propositions for the improvement of project management knowledge and practice were ill-conceived, reflecting fundamental misconceptions within the field. He identified three major deficiencies which are ingrained, maintained and reproduced across the research field through certain ontological, epistemological and methodological assumptions: (1) the assumed universality of project management theory, (2) the lack of empirical studies of projects, and (3) the lack of alternative representations of 'projects' (summarised in Table 1.1).

Emerging from this school are a number of vital themes which move beyond traditional understandings of projects and their management: the conceptualisation of projects as temporary organisations (Lundin and Söderholm, 1995), the recognition of the historically embedded nature of projects (Kreiner, 1995; Engwall, 2003) and the shift in focus from single to multiple project management (Engwall and Jerbrant, 2003). While this introduction of sociological perspectives to the field of projects is clearly welcome, indeed long overdue, the more conservative current work in this tradition remains strongly wedded to a functionalist viewpoint, focusing upon improving project performance through attention to social (that is, human) factors. Equally, within this perspective, the inclusion of power and power relations tends to be limited to the introduction of a form of micropolitics, separated from the larger power differentials inherent in modern, capitalist society. While there is much to be drawn from the Scandinavian School, and much which improves upon the narrow mechanistic

Table 1.1 Common and alternative assumptions on project management

	Common assumptions	Alternative assumptions
Project management theory	General theory for all kinds of projects, generic concept collecting different theories applicable to projects under one umbrella	Middle-range theories on different sorts of projects, classified according to different selection criteria
Aim of research on projects	Prescriptive, normative theory, grounded in ideal models of project planning and control. Research undertaken as survey studies of large samples of projects	Descriptive theory, grounded in empirical narrative studies on human interaction in projects. Research undertaken as comparative case studies
Research metaphor for the project	A tool, a means for achieving higher-level ends	A temporary organisation, an aggregate of individuals temporarily enacting a common cause

Source: Adapted from Packendorff (1995: 326)

instrumentalism of traditional project management, we would argue that the school remains too conservative in its ambitions and does not take its argument to its logical conclusions. It does, however, open the space of project studies to more explicitly 'critical' currents, and some of the strongest critical work on projects to have emerged so far has its roots in the advances made by the Scandinavian School (see, for example, Lindgren and Packendorff, 2001, 2003).

Critical perspectives on projects

Governed by the tradition of 'natural sciences' (for example, systems theory), the project management body of knowledge emphasises the role of project actors and managers as 'implementers', narrowing down their role to the issues of control (time and cost) and content (planned scope of work) and marginalising their wider potential role as competent social and political actors in complex project-labelled arrangements. Dissemination of 'best practice' carries a message about the possibility of the progressive rationalisation of action and a belief in the progressive and cumulative character of knowledge. This typically assumes rationality, universality, objectivity and value-free decision-making, and the possibility of generating law-like predictions in knowledge.

More recently, work has emerged which takes a more fundamentally critical position towards mainstream project management, its nostrums and methods (see, for example, Packendorff, 1995; Bresnen, 1996; Metcalfe, 1997; Thomas, 1997; Lindgren and Packendorff, 2001; Bredillet, 2002, 2004; Gill, 2002; Hodgson, 2002; Buckle and Thomas, 2003; Cicmil, 2003; Hodgson and Cicmil, 2003; Hodgson, 2004; Cicmil and Hodgson, 2004). The belief system underpinning the definition and reification of the 'project', project organising and project work in contemporary organisations is reproduced and sustained in most of the mainstream literature through a set of assumptions which emphasise certain problems and voices and silence others. Propositions to 'project manage' a particular business affair, strategic problem, political issues or change initiatives imply invoking a 'technical' solution through *expert* management. Project managers are thus depicted as having privileged knowledge of the *real world*. Their managerial status is legitimised on such ontological and epistemological grounds. Consequently, the normative/rational prescriptions offered to practitioners about managing projects and creating managerial knowledge tend to dominate organisational discourses.

Critical authors suggest the need for a wider picture of what goes on in projects and project management by focusing on who is included in and who is excluded from the decision-making process, analysing what determines the position, agendas and *power* of different participants, and how these different agendas are combined and resolved in the process by which the *decisions* are arrived at. Much of this work derives from the diversity of positions collectively referred to since the mid-1990s as 'Critical Management Studies', which has taken issue with numerous elements of managerial knowledge, technologies and techniques. The work of, for example, Reed (1992), Alvesson and Willmott (1996) and Thompson and McHugh (2002), among others, critiques the dominance of functionalism and positivism in management. Such work takes issue with positivist epistemology in the field of management, in so far as it perpetuates the belief that *managers face an objective reality* which they can control by applying suitable methods for a *rational* assessment of the problematic situation in order to come up with the correct solution. The consequence of this is a proliferation of methods, tools, analytical techniques and applied instruments with which management itself becomes identified. Management skills and knowledge are reduced to *value-neutral competence*, ignoring the political aspect of organisations, and ethical and moral issues, reinforcing the belief that management can be conceptualised in a technical way by agreeing on *terminology and meaning*. Managers are seen as rational technicians, dealing with technical issues that are resolvable through the application of superior knowledge of the planning and control techniques. Alvesson and Deetz have commented on the problems with narrow, conventional approaches to studying the phenomenon of management and the need to adopt a much more critical stance and varying theoretical lenses:

> There is considerable agreement that conventional, universal statements of what management is about and what managers do – planning, organizing, coordinating and controlling – do not tell us very much about organizational reality, which is often messy, ambiguous, fragmented and political in character. (Alvesson and Deetz, 2000: 60)

It is argued that conventional approaches to organisational and management research have exposed managers and other employees involved in problem-solving and decision-making to an overwhelming amount and range of techniques (empowerment, teamwork, flexibility) which can be interpreted as 'covert tools of manipulation and exploitation' (Huczynski and Buchanan, 2001: xxi). The most important requirement for the development of critical project management studies is the inclusion of critical social theory into the research process. Central to it is the need to explore how the relationships between individuals and collectivities are being constituted and reproduced in the context of project management, and how asymmetrical power relations create and sustain the social reality of projects. In this context, we argue that the main issue for the project management research community should not be what form of critical analysis is best suited for enhancing the intellectual basis of critical management studies. Drawing on Critical Theory and particularly the contribution of Jürgen Habermas, Alvesson and Willmott (1996) suggest that intellectual efforts should be focused on encouraging inspiration from a variety of theories and ideas, as a counterforce to technicist and instrumental forms of rationality in project environments. From a Habermasian perspective, it might be argued that the objective, abstract and universal body of knowledge claimed in a number of authoritative sources as proprietary to project management fails to live up to the challenges of the embodied and power-laden realities of its operation. 'Project management', as created by this school of thought, exhibits the characteristics of what Alvesson and Willmott (1996) call *management as colonising power* and *management as distorted communication*. From this perspective, the possibility of critical project management will depend on the extent to which a social theory about the nature of projects provides concerned actors with authentic insights into their position in project environments, leading to their enlightenment, changed attitudes and emancipatory action.

Another major influence on critical work with implications for understandings of project management is the wide and varied oeuvre of Michel Foucault, drawn upon by writers such as David Knights, Stewart Clegg, Barbara Townley and Stanley Deetz, among others. Work on project management which continues this tradition (Hodgson, 2002; Lindgren and Packendorff, 2003; Thomas, 2003) tends to highlight the implied calculability and formality of project management methodology, embodying a strong functionalist commitment to ensuring the effective control of workers. These and similar voices remain under-represented in the general debate about project management. A key challenge for critical work from this perspective is thus to draw attention to the power relations maintained by project management technologies. In particular, a key research theme is a focus on the consequences of those techniques of observation, measurement and performance control central to project management methodologies for both the management and the self-management of workers within project settings.

To advance such critical work, we would argue that the scope for critical research into projects and project management, and in particular the emancipatory aspect of such research, needs to be expanded. This means a more radical acknowledgement of voices from practitioners in project environments, such as Balck's:

> Practitioners, in particular we as project managers, are well advised to rid ourselves of the
> constricting historical background of a mechanistic world image and rationalism. Without

question the best method to help us correct our way of traditional thinking is 'on-the-job training'; that is, experiencing the real success and failures in dealing with our everyday business endeavours. (Balck, 1994: 2–)

We would argue that taking this seriously means moving beyond the narrow instrumentalism which bedevils yet largely defines the 'iron triangle' approach to project management. Our hope is that this collection may constitute a first step towards creating a vocabulary and a resource for a critical engagement between practitioners and academics beyond the confines of the existing language, concepts and assumptions of mainstream project management.

Making projects critical: new trajectories

At this point, it is opportune to return to the intentions behind this collection. As stated in the very introductory sections of this introduction, this edited book aims at opening up new trajectories within the research agenda in the field of studies relevant to projects, project performance and project management in order to address the persisting and prevailing concerns articulated in literature and practice which we attempted to briefly illuminate above. We hope that the voices from critical researchers who contributed to this book signpost possible routes towards a critical evaluation of the intellectual foundations of project management as a field of study and a practising discipline and to broaden the research agenda by encouraging a more critical approach in this area of organisational life. Explicitly we take up the challenge offered by Flyvbjerg (2001: 166) to conduct research that 'contributes to society's capacity for value-rational deliberation and action', in essence to make social science matter in the context of project work.

For the sake of clarity of presentation, we have grouped their work to resemble the key concerns identified in this introduction. One is the issue of epistemological and ontological assumptions behind the legitimised definitions of projects and project management which in turn have shaped most of the mainstream research in the field and the nature of knowledge created in the research process. Building on some of these alternative theoretical approaches and concepts which will be discussed in Part 1, the remaining two sections present the work that explores the implications of critical theories and methodologies for our understanding of social action and management skills in everyday practice in organisational arrangements labelled 'projects'. We consider, first, those arrangements which have resulted from 'applying' project management within specific organisations as a structural solution to effectively accomplishing discrete organisational goals and efficiently utilising available resources (Part 2). Then, a consideration is given to the body of work which critically looks at the complex processes of relating that go on in the landscapes labelled 'projects' where multiple parties (representing discrete organisations and groupings) interact (Part 3).

And finally, what might it mean for both the scholarly and the practitioner community to encourage a different way of viewing and thinking about projects and project management as social phenomena through critical studies? How might a consideration of lines of reasoning and practice other than those promoted by mainstream project management thinking respond to the identified crisis in the field? We believe that one of the ways of responding to these questions is to emphasise the importance of looking at projects and project management as social phenomena which are not neutral, but socially constructed in the interaction among people. Such interaction is simultaneously power and conversational relating among individuals and groups through the medium of symbols and artefacts which form and are formed by one another. Asymmetries of power that are part of intersubjective relating inevitably invoke the issues of control, domination and ideology and their implications for the identity and well-being of individuals and society. Therefore, another important aspect of critical approaches to project management is to reexamine the currently dominant imperative of performativity in relation to how this shapes the development of the body of knowledge and best practice in the field (particularly related to 'critical factors for project success') and illuminate the importance of considering other indicators of 'project success' beyond time, cost and quality performance, to encompass the environment, health and safety and ethics. And third, critical project management research appeals directly to practitioners as it, in terms of methodology, is interested in specific local situations and in lived experiences of various project actors with an aim of initiating some transformative redefinition (Alvesson and Deetz, 2000) of actors' own perception of self, their voice and their influence in shaping their own social roles and place.

Several prominent mainstream authors (Winch, 1996; Morris et al., 2000; Maylor, 2001; Koskela and Howell, 2002; Morris, 2002) have raised the need for introducing alternative theoretical approaches to studying projects and for identifying the implications that they may have for how we talk about and conceptualise our understanding of knowledge creation about projects. The first chapters in the opening section take this fundamental need for a new theory of the project as their starting point.

Part 1: new theoretical perspectives

In Chapter 1, Hodgson and Cicmil take issue with the 'naturalisation' of the project as a universal and pervasive organisational object. They draw parallels between the foundations of project management and an enduring theme of management theory: the belief that its study is analogous to natural science, that is, discovering universal laws and fundamental properties of objects which (pre)exist 'out there', in the 'real world'. From this naive realist perspective, many writers on project management feel able to present their field as gradually converging on a generic model of the project management process, complete with common ontology and a standardised terminology globally recognised by professional project managers. Many texts and documents in the field, from textbooks and manuals to academic articles, are implicated in this naturalisation, engaging both explicitly and implicitly in the reification of 'the project'. They argue that the debate within project management thus exhibits the trait termed by Robert Chia as the phenomenon of 'false concreteness'. Their concern with this tendency centres upon the consequences of an epistemological position which insists upon the reality of its focus, that is, the systematic preclusion of alternative representations/classifications of the phenomena of interest.

In the next chapter, Linehan and Kavanagh (2003) draw on Chia's (1995) work to make an important distinction between two ontologies of projects – *ontology of being* and *ontology of becoming*. From the perspective of a 'being' ontology, they argue, 'primacy is given to objects, things, states, events and nouns. In the context of projects, a "being" ontology leads us to talk and think about organisation structure in an objectified manner' (Linehan and Kavanagh, this volume). This perspective underpins most of the mainstream approaches to project working (as a 'template' of effective organising and creativity), as noted above. In contrast, an alternative approach, a 'becoming' ontology, emphasises process, verbs, activity and the construction of entities. The latter emphasises the role of language, conversational relating, intersubjective understanding and interpretation as key to making sense of arrangements labelled projects in contemporary society. By clarifying the different ontologies which may be employed with regard to projects, they seek to set out alternative ways to approach the understanding of projects in context. Instead of thinking about the project as a temporary endeavour undertaken to create a unique product or service, they posit an alternative position in which a project is considered as an emergent outcome of disparate and ambiguous political practices.

The next contributor, Mike Bresnen, shares the previous chapter's concern with the limitations of the ontology and epistemology of contemporary project management theory. Bresnen develops a critique of mainstream project management by drawing attention to the differences in epistemic culture which exist between the fields of mainstream project management on the one hand, and organisational change and learning on the other. The chapter opens with a consideration of the increasing influence of project management thinking across sectors, detailing how mainstream project management embodies a particular way of seeing organisations that reflects the characteristic problems of projects. Several tendencies within mainstream project management are critiqued: in particular, the dominance of mechanistic models of management theory in the field, the focus upon the project and project organisation as the unit of analysis and the narrow, sector-specific nature of emphasis placed on research in project management. Contrary to current work which sees project organising as a powerful source of change and innovatory practice in organisations, the chapter brings into question the easy concatenation of learning and project-based work, and challenges project management's ability to deliver in this dimension.

In the next chapter, Thomas initiates a wider debate about project management practices, focusing in particular upon their operation in the realm of power/knowledge.

Adopting a Foucauldian approach, she examines how project management influences what is 'knowable' and therefore 'doable' in the field of projects by tracing the history of project management discourse and making some initial steps towards an archaeology of the field. Focusing on current practices in project management, she then reviews some of the 'truths' of project management as detailed in best-selling project management texts, disseminated through mainstream project management training and repeated by practising project managers. Making the clear link between the shortfalls of project theory and the practical deficiencies of the field, she argues that it is the fundamental contradictions evident in project management knowledge that lead to implementation failures. Problematising the concept of the project, she argues, is a vital starting point in the development of a different fundamental understanding of the function of projects in organisations.

Collectively, this first section takes a necessarily broad view of project management as a field, as a discipline, as a knowledge community and as a profession in the making. The next sections look in more empirical detail at project management as implemented in contemporary organisations mobilising critical lenses to understand the evolution of projects, their success and failure.

Part 2: projects within organisations

The next chapter, by Lindgren and Packendorff, starts by questioning the stereotypical distinction made in many descriptions of projects that contrast challenging and exciting project work and mundane and routine 'ordinary work'. Drawing on a variety of empirical cases, they underline that from the perspective of the project worker (as opposed to simply the project manager), projects are both stimulating but also sources of stress, loneliness, disrupted family lives and superficial workplace relations. They explore stories from two very distinct projects, one theatre project implemented in the Baltic Opera House and one IT consultancy project implemented by the software company Compute. Mobilising Foucault's analysis of the modern prison system as a metaphor for project work and its consequences in society, they interpret project work in each case as an explicit expression of the disciplinary principles upon which all modern organising is built. From this perspective, project work implies disciplining people and 'souls' in space and time. Unlike the traditional Weberian bureaucracy, they argue that projects are less open and less formal technologies for disciplining their subjects, which transfer many of the traditional management responsibilities to the individual personally. Instead, drawing on the personal accounts and reflections of project workers, they argue that the sources of discipline within projects have become hidden, informal and individualised.

In an original and challenging chapter, Manuela Nocker challenges the association of project-based organising with flexibility, speed and adaptability, criticising the reliance of project management methodologies on 'how-to' manuals, prescriptive recipes and critical success factors. She argues that this reflects an underlying ontology which reifies both 'the project' and by implication project management practice, and takes 'the project' as a given, separated from the people who sustain, reproduce and renew it. As an alternative to this approach, her chapter examines the possibility of expanding our understanding of the nature of projects by exploring the process through which participants momentarily crystallise a project definition, in terms of meaning and potential for action. Her analysis centres upon the shaping of a project's shifting boundaries through the enactment of *physical, mental* and *social spaces.* Drawing on an ethnographic case study of an ICT project team from a global management consulting firm working in information systems design, she illustrates how these various forms of space relate to each other and to the particular emergence of the overall project configuration. By tracing different narratives, Nocker uses the multiple voices of the team and other stakeholders in framing what she refers to as the emerging 'project horizon', and considers how this concept offers a radically different understanding of the formation and transformation of a project.

Anneli Linde and Henrik Linderoth draw inspiration from the work of Latour in their analysis of three IT-mediated change projects and their contexts. In this chapter, they explicitly adopt an Actor Network Theory (ANT) lens, understanding society as a seamless socio-technical web which interconnects heterogeneous actants (both human and non-human) through mutual inscriptions and enrolments. From this position, projects are considered as ongoing translations of the project vision, whereby various participants attempt to enrol others through problematisation and interessement to establish and stabilise a network. Their empirical studies indicate how the interpretative flexibility of the technology in each case gave rise to conflicting translations, causing continuous realignments of competing networks enacted through battles of wills and face-saving strategies. They argue pragmatically that a socio-technical lens is necessary if we are to understand and even foresee the complex interactions between heterogeneous actor groups and drifting technologies.

Molloy and Whittington take a rather different interpretation of the work of Latour in their analysis of two reorganisation projects, which they understand through Lundin and Söderholm's (1995) definition of 'temporary organisations'. Drawing on Bruno Latour's 'sociology of association', they analyse the reorganisation projects through the understandings of the practitioners themselves in an attempt to uncover how such actors 'construct society'. In doing so, they, like their research subjects, refuse to accept and thereby reinforce taken-for-granted distinctions between the social and the technical, and arrive at an original and challenging interpretation of everyday practice in project settings. In particular, they argue that 'the skill to recognise, accept and manage uncertainty about groups, agency, objects, matters of fact and epistemological assumptions is a key feature of reorganisation practice' (this volume). The outcome of this methodological orientation is a remarkable shift in our understanding, which sees project workers as 'savvy engineers' of diverse organisational objects, encompassing the human and the non-human, mobilising an array of artefacts, technologies and categories in pursuit of their goals.

Taking a reflexive approach to his own experiences as project manager, the next chapter by Charles Smith analyses the evolution of a two-year project to reengineer and downsize a financial services organisation. As he explains, the project was undertaken in the context of a variety of power–knowledge communities with significant and diverse interests in its outcome. In an empirically focused chapter, the main stages of the project are summarised, noting its perceived objectives and attributes at each stage, and describing the relationship to the project of the main parties. In terms of a 'rational scientific' model of projects, characterised by a specified intended outcome achieved through completion of a planned set of tasks, the project can be seen to have passed through a series of significant shifts in that rationality. Smith examines the changes in the project aims and expectations, the plan to complete, the meaning of success or failure, and the parties' identification with or dissociation from the project. Smith considers and rejects one possible and common interpretation, which would be to dismiss the rational scientific model as being an entrenched paradigm that has 'failed'. Instead, he sets out an alternative view, treating rational project management, and the related concepts of success and failure, as a resource deployed by the various parties, at critical stages, to defend their interests by reinterpreting the evolving project.

Part 3: inter-organisational projects

The final section, as noted above, deals primarily with the issues which arise in relation to projects in which multiple parties interact. This section opens with a detailed and rich study of a multi-agency civil engineering project, through which Nick Marshall explores the complexities of notions of power. In doing so, he critiques the failure to address power in mainstream project management writings beyond limited considerations of interpersonal influence and 'politicking'. Instead, he argues, it is necessary to understand power as relational, productive and constantly renegotiated in the process of 'doing' project work. Given the marginal status of projects, as phenomena which are to an extent both unique and repetitive, they provide an ideal location to consider the interplay between enduring power structures and voluntary activity. In this chapter, Marshall makes full use of this opportunity and, drawing upon writers such as Foucault, Clegg and Law, develops a persuasive position to illustrate the operation of power beneath the overarching discourse of 'partnering' in the UK construction industry.

Drawing on case studies from the same sector, the following chapter by Stuart Green highlights the disparity between the literature on project management, the models and prescriptions which characterise much mainstream writing and the 'lived realities' of the management of projects. He interprets project management as a form of discourse promoted and circulated across industries, which cannot be understood separately from the context in which it is enacted and from the individuals who enact and thus reproduce project management in their daily lives. His primary interest is therefore in a 'critical evaluation of how the discourse of project management shapes the lived realities of "project management" for the construction industry's workforce'

(Green, this volume). He therefore focuses upon the enactment, or rather the dramaturgical 'performance' of project management scripts, in a variety of contractors and subcontractors involved in construction in London's Canary Wharf. In contrast to other chapters which understand project management as an effective form of control, Green paints a compelling picture of the anarchic employment relationship that typifies construction projects in the UK, in the shadow of enterprise culture, casualisation of labour, lean construction and partnering. Despite the dominance of project working in construction, he challenges accounts of the discursive dominance of project management in this sector, arguing that career progression is dependent on leaving behind the tools and techniques of project management at an early stage and learning new and better scripts passed down by management fashion.

In the next chapter, Jörg Sydow challenges the static and technocratic approach which has dominated the field of project management for half a century, to the neglect of the social contexts in which projects exist. Focusing attention instead upon the embeddedness of projects in such networks, he argues that it is this embeddedness which enables projects to straddle and to profit from both fluidity and continuity. This argument is supported by an analysis of a sector dominated by project working, that of television production, drawing upon the concept of project networks. Adopting a structuration perspective, his approach is distinctive in that it pays equal attention to social practices and structures at the level of both the single project and the project network. Moreover, the perspective allows the incorporation of temporal embeddedness, a concept he utilises with regard to the understanding of project boundaries and paths. Through such an approach, he argues, vital issues of perception, process and power in the establishment and operation of projects may be addressed.

In their analysis of one of the highest-profile projects of recent years, Clegg, Pitsis, Marosszeky and Rura-Polley develop an innovative interpretation of project management practice drawing on their understanding of the future-oriented nature of all projects. They frame their chapter with a critique of current mainstream project management, drawing attention to the weak conceptual framework underpinning project management theory as it stands. In particular, they take issue with the linear and unbounded rationality implicit in many of the current bodies of knowledge and project management methodologies. Drawing on a more reflexive and temporal notion of the project, based on the work of Alfred Schutz and Karl Weick, they examine the successful completion of a key project in the preparations for the 2000 Olympics in Sydney. They argue that a vital component of the successful project was the understanding by the project team of the project in the 'future perfect': seeing the work to be accomplished as 'simultaneously past and future', as a cognitive and strategic shift which allows for a radically different conception of how projects can be managed.

In the next chapter, Sillince, Harvey and Harindranath take the contrasting case of a PFI-(Private Finance Initiative) governed IT project failure, examining the development of the project through the use of discourse and rhetoric. They interpret the project in this chapter as a multi-organisation network, and as socially interpreted and socially constructed discourse analysis. This is in stark contrast to mainstream approaches to analysing (and advising on the best practice of managing) the conception, initiation and high-level planning stage of the project life cycle, where it is seen as a discrete chunk of reality where rational decision-making, evaluation and risk management play the key role in the successful negotiation of the contract and formation of the project organisation.

In the final chapter in this section on complex and multi-organisational projects, Ivory, Alderman, McLoughlin and Vaughan draw upon the related resources of symbolic interactionism and sense-making, allied to arguments from the literature on innovation, to shed light upon the development of a long-term engineering project. Rather than adopting a unitary perspective on this phenomenon, their analysis is based around the 'significant discontinuities' which characterise complex and long-term projects and which create a need for sense-making by different 'social groups' (customers, clients, contractors, suppliers, engineering and other technical disciplines). They develop this perspective through a rich and detailed analysis of the interior design of new railway rolling stock in the UK, a project with significant distinguishing features. They argue that this project could be better understood as an arena in which 'conventional assumptions, processes and procedures were challenged' rather than a rational and self-evident shared reality. They expand upon this position by highlighting the conflicting discourses of different groups in their separate but related attempts to 'make sense' of needs, requirements and the context of the project itself.

The collection concludes with an afterword and commentary by Peter Morris, who over thirty years has guided and advanced the core debates within the field of project management and the management of projects. His work to date reflects an abiding concern with the foundations and 'boundaries' of project management in its various incarnations, and has been particularly influential in the composition and evolution of the Association for Project Management's body of knowledge. His considered and constructive comments will, we hope, help to initiate a productive dialogue between the critical contributions incorporated within this collection and the large number of committed practitioners, consultants and academics involved in projects and their management.

References

Alvesson, M. and Willmott, H. (1996) *Making Sense of Management: A Critical Introduction.* London: Sage.

Alvesson, M. and Deetz, S. (2000) *Doing Critical Management Research.* London: Sage.

APM (Association for Project Management) (1995) APM *Body of Knowledge*, Version 2, High Wycombe: APM Publishing.

Atkinson, R. (1999) 'Project Management: Cost, Time and Quality, Two Best Guesses and a Phenomenon; It's Time to Accept Other Success Criteria', *International Journal of Project Management*, 17(6): 337–42.

Baker, B.N., Murphy, D.C. and Fisher, D. (1983) 'Factors Affecting Project Success', in D.I. Cleland and R.W. King (eds), *Project Management Handbook*. New York: Van Nostrand Reinhold, 669–85.

Balck, H. (1994) 'Projects as Elements of a New Industrial Pattern: A Division of Project Management', in D.I. Cleland and R. Gareis (eds), *Global Project Management Handbook*. New York: McGraw-Hill International Editions, 2–11.

Baldry, D. (1998) 'The Evaluation of Risk Management in Public Sector Capital Projects', *International Journal of Project Management*, 16(1): 35–41.

Belassi, W. and Tukel, O.I. (1996) 'A New Framework for Determining Success/Failure Factors in Projects', *International Journal of Project Management*, 14(3): 141–51.

Belout, A. (1998) 'Effects of HRM on Project Effectiveness and Success: Toward a New Conceptual Framework', *International Journal of Project Management*, 16(1): 21–6.

Besner, C. and Hobbs, B. (2004) 'An Empirical Investigation of Project Management Practise: In Reality, Which Tools do Practitioners Use?', in D. Slevin, D. Cleland and J. Pinto (eds), *Innovations: Best Papers from the PMI Project Management Research Conference*. Newtown Square, PA: PMI.

Boddy, D. and Paton, R. (2004) 'Responding to Competing Narratives: Lessons for Project Managers', *International Journal of Project Management*, 22: 225–33.

Bowen, H.K., Clark, K.B., Holloway, C.A. and Wheelwright, S.C. (1994) *The Perpetual Enterprise Machine*. New York: Oxford University Press.

Bowker, G.C. and Star, S.L. (1999) *Sorting Things Out: Classification and Its Consequences*. London: MIT Press.

Bredillet, C.N. (2002) 'Beyond the Positivist Mirror: Towards a Project Management "Gnosis"', paper presented at the IRNOP conference in Rotterdam, Amsterdam.

Bredillet, C. (2004) 'Beyond the Positivist Mirror: Towards a Project Management "Gnosis"', paper presented at the IRNOP conference in Turku, Finland.

Bresnen, M. (1996) 'Traditional and Emergent Professions in the Construction Industry: Competition and Control over the Building Process', in I. Glover and M. Hughes (eds), *The Professional-Managerial Class: Contemporary British Management in the Pursuer Mode*. Aldershot: Avebury.

Briner, W. and Hastings, C. (1994) 'The Role of Projects in the Strategy Process', in D.I. Cleland and R. Gareis (eds), *Global Project Management Handbook*. McGraw-Hill International Editions.

Buchanan, D. and Badham, R. (1999) *Power, Politics, and Organisational Change: Winning the Turf Game*. London: Sage.

Buchanan, D. and Boddy, D. (1992) *The Expertise of the Change Agent*. London: Prentice-Hall.

Buckle, P. and Thomas, J. (2003) 'Deconstructing Project Management: A Gender Analysis of Project Management Guidelines', *International Journal of Project Management*, 21(6): 433–41.

Chapman, R.J. (1998) 'The Role of System Dynamics in Understanding the Impact of Changes to Key Project Personnel on Design Production within Construction Projects', *International Journal of Project Management*, 16(4): 235–47.

Chia, R. (1995) 'From Modern to Postmodern Organizational Analysis', *Organization Studies*, 16(4): 579–604.

Cicmil, S. (2001) 'Reconstructing the Project Management Knowledge System: A Multiple-Perspective Agenda', paper presented to Critical Management Studies Conference, UMIST, Manchester, 11–13 July 2001.

Cicmil, S. (2003) 'Knowledge, Interaction and Project Work: The Perspective of Complex Responsive Processes of Relating', paper presented at the 19th EGOS Colloquium, subtheme 'Project Organizations, Embeddedness and Repositories of Knowledge', Copenhagen, Denmark, 3–5 July 2003.

Cicmil, S. and Hodgson, D.E. (2004) 'Knowledge, Action, and Reflection in Management Education – The Case of Project Management', paper presented at the 20th EGOS Colloquium, Ljubljana, Slovenia, July 2004.

Clarke, A. (1999) 'A Practical Use of Key Success Factors to Improve the Effectiveness of Project Management', *International Journal of Project Management*, 17(3): 139–45.

Cleland, D.I. (1997) 'New Ways to Use Project Teams', in D. Cleland (ed.), *Field Guide to Project Management*. New York: Van Nostrand Reinhold.

Cleland, D.I. and Ireland, L.R. (2002) *Project Management – Strategic Design and Implementation*, 4th edn. New York: McGraw-Hill International Editions.

Davenport, T.H. and Prusak, L. (1998) *Working Knowledge*. Boston, MA: Harvard Business School Press.

DeFillippi, R. (2001) 'Project Based Learning, Reflective Practices and Learning Outcomes', *Management Learning*, 32(1): 5–10.

Dempsey, P.S., Goetz, A.R. and Szyliowicz, J.S. (1997) *Denver International Airport: Lessons Learned*. New York: McGraw-Hill.

Ekstedt, E., Lundin, R.A., Söderholm, A. and Wirdenius, H. (1999) *Neo-Industrial Organising*. London: Routledge.

Engwall, M. (1995) *Jakten på det Effektiva Projektet*. Stockholm: Nerenius & Santérus.

Engwall, M. (2003) 'No Project is an Island: Linking Projects to History and Context', *Research Policy*, 32: 789–808.

Engwall, M. and Jerbrant, A. (2003) 'The Resource Allocation Syndrome: The Prime Challenge of Multi-Project Management', *International Journal of Project Management*, 21(6): 403–9.

Ewusi-Mensah, K. and Przasnyski, Z.H. (1997) 'Critical Issues in Abandoned IS Development Projects', *Communication of the AMC*, 40(9): 74–80.

Financial Times (1999) 'Royal Opera House Cancels Performance', 24 November: 5.

Financial Times (2000) 'Whitehall Counts the Costs of IT Projects', 14 January: 13.

Flyvbjerg, B. (2001) *Making Social Science Matter*. Cambridge: Cambridge University Press.

Flyvbjerg, B., Bruzelius, N. and Rothengatter, W. (2003) *Megaprojects and Risk: An Anatomy of Ambition*. Cambridge: Cambridge University Press.

Flyvbjerg, B., Holm, M.S. and Buhl, S. (2002) 'Underestimating Costs in Public Works Projects – Error or Lie?', *Journal of American Planning Association*, 68(3): 279–95.

Fournier, V. and Grey, C. (2000) 'At the Critical Moment: Conditions and Prospects for Critical Management Studies', *Human Relations*, 53(1): 7–32.

Frame, J.D. (1994) *The New Project Management*. San Francisco, CA: Jossey-Bass.

Frame, J.D. (1995) *Managing Projects in Organisations*. San Francisco, CA: Jossey-Bass.

Frame, J.D. (1999) *Project Management Competence: Building Key Skills for Individuals, Teams and Organisations*. San Francisco, CA: Jossey-Bass.

Gaddis, P.O. (1959) 'The Project Manager', *Harvard Business Review*, 32(May–June): 89–97.

Gill, R. (2002) 'Cool, Creative and Egalitarian? Exploring Gender in Project-Based New Media Work in Europe', *Information, Communication and Society*, 5(1): 70–89.

Hansen, M.T., Nohria, N. and Tierney, T. (1999) 'What's Your Strategy for Managing Knowledge?', *Harvard Business Review*, March–April, 1999, 77(2): 106–16.

Harrison, F.L. (1981) *Advanced Project Management*. Aldershot: Gower.

Hobday, M. (2000) 'The Project-Based Organisation: An Ideal Form for Managing Complex Products and Systems?', *Research Policy*, 29: 871–93.

Hodgson, D.E. (2002) 'Disciplining the Professional: The Case of Project Management', *Journal of Management Studies*, 39(7): 803–21.

Hodgson, D.E. (2004) 'Project Teams: The Legacy of Bureaucratic Control in the Post-Bureaucratic Organisation', *Organization*, 11(1): 81–100.

Hodgson, D.E. and Cicmil, S. (2003) ' "Setting the Standards": The Construction of "the Project" as an Organizational Object', paper presented to the 3rd Critical Management Studies Conference at Lancaster University, July 2003.

Huczynski, A. and Buchanan, D. (2001) *Organizational Behaviour: An Introductory Text*, 4th edn. Harlow: FT Prentice Hall.

Jessen, Svein Arne (2002) *Business by Projects*. Oslo: Universitetsforlaget AS.

Johnson, P. and Duberley, J. (2000) *Understanding Management Research – An Introduction to Epistemology*. London: Sage.

Kharbanda, O. and Pinto, J. (1996) *What Made Gertie Gallop? Lessons from Project Failures*. New York: Van Nostrand Reinhold.

Koskela, L. and Howell, G. (2002) 'The Underlying Theory of Project Management is Obsolete', *Proceedings of the PMI Conference, July 2002*. Seattle: Project Management Institute.

Kreiner, K. (1995) 'In Search of Relevance: Project Management in Drifting Environments', *Scandinavian Journal of Management*, 11(4): 335–46.

Lindgren, M. and Packendorff, J. (2001) 'What's New in New Organizational Forms? On the Construction of Gender in Project-based Work', paper for the Gender, Work and Organisation conference 'Rethinking Gender, Work and Organisation', 27–29 June, Keele University, UK.

Lindgren, M. and Packendorff, J. (2003) 'Deconstructing Projects: Towards Critical Perspectives on Project Theory and Projecticised Society', paper presented to Making Projects Critical workshop, April 2003, Bristol Business School.

Linehan, C. and Kavanagh, D. (2003) 'Creating Contexts for Knowing: Contrasting Project Ontologies', paper presented at the 19th EGOS Colloquium, subtheme 'Project Organizations, Embeddedness and Repositories of Knowledge', Copenhagen, Denmark, 3–5 July 2003.

Lundin, R.A. and Hartman, F. (eds) (2000) *Projects as Business Constituents and Guiding Motives*. Boston, MA: Kluwer Academic Publishers.

Lundin, R.A. and Midler, C. (eds) (1998) *Projects as Arenas for Renewal and Learning Processes*. Boston, MA: Kluwer Academic Publishers.

Lundin, R.A. and Söderholm, A. (1995) 'A Theory of the Temporary Organization', *Scandinavian Journal of Management*, 11(4): 437–55.

Lundin, R.A. and Söderholm, A. (1998) 'Conceptualising a Projectified Society: Discussion of an Eco-Institutional Approach to a Theory on Temporary Organizations', in R.A. Lundin and C. Midler (eds), *Projects as Arenas for Renewal and Learning Processes*. Boston, MA: Kluwer Academic Publishers.

Maylor, H. (1999) *Project Management*, 2nd edn. London: Pitman.

Maylor, H. (2003) *Project Management*, 3rd edn. London: Pitman.

Maylor, H. (2001) 'Beyond the Gantt Chart – Project Management Moving On', *European Management Journal*, 19(1): 92–100.

Meredith, J.R. and Mantel, S.J. (1995) *Project Management – A Managerial Approach*, 3rd edn. New York: John Wiley & Sons.

Meredith, J.R. and Mantel, S.L. (2003) *Project Management – A Managerial Approach*, 5th edn. New York: John Wiley & Sons.

Metcalfe, B. (1997) 'Project Management System Design: A Social and Organisational Analysis', *International Journal of Production Economics*, 52: 305–16.

Midler, C. (1995) ' "Projectification" of the Firm: The Renault Case', *Scandinavian Journal of Management*, 11(4): 363–73.

Miller, R. and Lessard, D.R. (2000) *The Strategic Management of Large Engineering Projects*. Boston, MA: MIT Press.

Morris, P.W.G. (1997) *The Management of Projects*, 2nd edn. London: Thomas Telford.

Morris, P.W.G. (2002) 'Science, Objective Knowledge and the Theory of Project Management', *Proceedings of the Institute of Civil Engineering*, 150(May): 82–90.

Morris, P.W.G. and Hough, G.H. (1987) *The Anatomy of Major Projects*. London: Major Projects Association.

Morris, P.W.G., Patel, M.B. and Wearne, S.H. (2000) 'Research into Revising the APM Project Management Body of Knowledge', *International Journal of Project Management*, 18: 155–64.

Packendorff, J. (1995) 'Inquiring into the Temporary Organisation: New Directions for Project Management Research', *Scandinavian Journal of Management*, 11(4): 319–33.

Reed, M.I. (1992) *The Sociology of Organisations: Themes, Perspectives, and Prospects*. Hemel Hempstead: Harvester Wheatsheaf.

Sahlin-Andersson, K. and Söderholm, A. (eds) (2002) *Beyond Project Management: New Perspectives on the Temporary–Permanent Dilemma*. Copenhagen: Liber.

Silver, C.A. (2000) 'Where Technology and Knowledge Meet', *Journal of Business Strategy*, 21(6): 28.

Söderlund, J. (2004) 'Building Theories of Project Management: Past Research, Questions for the Future', *International Journal of Project Management*, 22: 183–91.

Stacey, R. (2000) *Strategic Management and Organisational Dynamics – The Challenge of Complexity*, 3rd edn. Harlow: FT Prentice Hall.

Stacey, R. (2001) *Complex Responsive Processes in Organisations: Learning and Knowledge Creation*. London: Routledge.

Stallworthy, E.A. and Kharbanda, O.P. (1985) *International Construction and the Role of Project Management*. Aldershot: Gower.

Standish Group (1995) 'Chaos', paper on line at http://www.standishgroup.com/, accessed March 2005.

Sydow, J. and Staber, U. (2002) 'The Institutional Embeddedness of Project Networks: The Case of Content Production in German Television', *Regional Studies*, 36(3): 215–27.

Thomas, J. (1997) 'Problematizing Project Management Practices to Shed Light on Implementation Problems', paper presented to the Organization and Management Theory Division of the Academy of Management Conference (AoMC) in Boston.

Thomas, J. (1999) 'It's Time to Make Sense of Project Management', paper presented to the Western Academy of Management Conference in Redondo Beach, California.

Thomas, J. (2000) 'Making Sense of Project Management', in R.A. Lundin and F. Hartman (eds), *Projects as Business Constituents and Guiding Motives*. Boston, MA: Kluwer Academic Press.

Thomas, J. (2003) 'Problematizing Project Management', paper presented to Making Projects Critical Workshop, April 2003, Bristol Business School.

Thompson, P. and McHugh, D. (2002) *Work Organisations*. London: Palgrave.

Tjaeder, J. and Thomas, J. (2000) 'On Learning and Control – Competing Paradigms or Co-existing Requirements for Managing Projects in Ambiguous Situations?', paper presented to International Research Network on Organizing by Projects (IRNOP) Fourth Bi-annual Conference held in Australia in January.

Walta, H. (1995) 'Dutch Project Management Body of Knowledge Policy', *International Journal of Project Management*, 13(2): 101–8.

Weick, K. (1995) *Sensemaking in Organisations*. Thousand Oaks, CA: Sage.

Wideman, R.M. (1995) 'Criteria for a Project Management Body of Knowledge', *International Journal of Project Management*, 13(2): 71–5.

Wiig, K.M. (1997) 'Knowledge Management: An Introduction and Perspective', *Journal of Knowledge Management* 3(2): 155–66.

Williams, T. (1995) 'A Classified Bibliography of Research Relating to Project Risk Management', *European Journal of Operational Research*, 85: 180–8.

Williams, T.M. (1999) 'The Need for New Paradigm for Complex Projects', *International Journal of Project Management*, 17(5): 269–73.

Williams, T. (2004) 'Assessing and Building on the Underlying Theory of Project Management in the Light of Badly Over-Run Projects', paper presented to PMI Research Conference, London, 2004.

Winch, G. (1996) 'Thirty Years of Project Management – What Have We Learned?', *British Academy of Management Conference Proceedings*, Aston Business School, September 1996, 8.127–8.145.

Winder, R. (1999) 'A Grand Departure Goes Uncelebrated', *Independent on Sunday*, 16 May 1999: 8.

Wood, M. (2002) 'Mind the Gap? A Processual Reconsideration of Organisational Knowledge', *Organization*, 9(1): 151–71.

Young, T. (1999) *How to be a Better Project Manager*. London: Kogan Page.

Young, T. (2003) *The Handbook of Project Management – A Practical Guide of Effective Policies and Procedures*. London: Kogan Page.

part 1

New theoretical perspectives

2

Are projects real? The PMBOK and the legitimation of project management knowledge

Damian Hodgson and Svetlana Cicmil

Introduction

Numerous commentators have noted the contemporary explosion of interest in project organising and project management outside of its traditional heartlands in construction and engineering (Winch, 1996; Young, 1998; Frame, 1999; Maylor, 2001; Meredith and Mantel, 2003). While this increased influence has been noted since the 1960s (Bennis and Slater, 1968), some commentators have more recently begun to speak of the 'projectification of society' (Midler, 1995; Lundin and Söderholm, 1998): the growing colonisation of all quarters of life by project-related principles, rules, techniques and procedures to form a new 'iron cage' of project rationality. This shift is explained by many of its proponents by reference to the increasing recognition of 'the project' as a versatile, flexible and predictable form of work organisation, offering a distinctive break with bureaucratic modes of organising. Our argument in this chapter is that the expansion of project organising is dependent upon concerted efforts to *reify* 'the project', so as to establish projects and more importantly associated project management techniques as a fundamental building block in organisations. We wish in this chapter to start to question the ontological foundations of 'the project', drawing on perspectives which would instead see 'the project' as a constructed entity, with powerful and often unrecognised consequences for the governance of what we label as 'projects' in contemporary organisations.

For most project management writers, 'the project' is a universal and transhistorical phenomenon – from the construction of the pyramids at Giza to the Allied landings in Normandy in 1945, 'projects' have always existed; so for instance, prominent authors argue:

Although some may argue that the construction of the Tower of Babel or the Egyptian pyramids were some of the first 'projects', it is probable that the caveman formed a project to gather a raw material for mammoth stew. It is certainly true that the construction of Boulder Dam and Edison's invention of the light bulb were projects by any sensible definition. (Meredith and Mantel, 2003: 8)

Of course there is nothing new about undertaking projects in organisations. Anyone who doubts this need merely visit Machu Picchu in the Andes or the Hangzhou canal in China or the Coliseum in Rome. (Frame, 1999: 3)

Whenever and wherever civilizations took root, there were projects to manage: buildings to erect, roads to pave, laws to write. Without the advanced tools, techniques and methodologies we have today, people created project timelines, located materials and resources and weighed the risks involved. (PMI, 2001: 9)

In an offhand manner, typical of introductory paragraphs of textbooks, such statements emphasise that what the authors take so much for granted is hardly worth mentioning; that projects have always been with us; that the human race has only achieved all that it has achieved through 'projects'; even that 'the project' is a universal feature of human existence.[1] From this perspective, the only difference today is that we are now in a position to study projects systematically and scientifically so as to develop a cogent and reliable 'Body of Knowledge' regarding the *real* nature of projects – and how they can, indeed must, therefore be managed.

At the same time, a minority of writers have begun to dig at the foundations 'beneath' the discourse of project management (see, for example, Kreiner, 1995; Packendorff, 1995; Cicmil, 2001; Räisänen and Linde, 2001; Hodgson, 2002, 2004; see also Lundin and Midler, 1998; Lundin and Hartman, 2000; Sahlin-Andersson and Söderholm, 2002). In one of the earliest contributions of this nature, Kreiner makes explicit queries over the ontological status of 'the project', arguing forcefully that

> [Projects] do not exist ready-made for us to scrutinise and classify. They are of course enacted, and thus 'constituted by the actions of interdependent actors' (Weick, 1969: 27). (Kreiner, 1995: 344)

Packendorff, in a similar vein, states:

> Project Management has become a scientific field in its own right, a field defined not by its theories or its origins, but by the habit of human beings to label a variety of co-ordinated, time-limited undertakings as 'projects'. The field is obviously held together by certain conceptions on process rationality; differences in outcome and process are disregarded in favour of alleged similarities in the planning and implementing of projects. But is there really a single, consistent, unambiguous empirical phenomenon that can be labelled 'the project'? (1995: 324)

It can be argued that the efforts of the field of project management to discover the 'true' nature of projects serve instead to further the 'reification' of the project, and thus the reification of the models and techniques of project management which stem from this foundational concept, 'institutionalized conceptions of what a "project" really is, conceptions that influence what happens in project organizations' (Packendorff, 1995: 329). These 'institutionalised conceptions' of the project invoke and carry with them notions of project life-cycle models, Gantt charts, critical paths, work breakdown structures, resource allocation, PERT, and many other associated techniques and concepts familiar to project managers.

Our argument is that the creation of such fixed standards leads to the establishment of a 'Body of Knowledge' which embodies particular political imperatives: in particular, a technicist and instrumental rationality which focuses upon means–ends logic and an ideology of control. This therefore has vital implications for project governance within work organisations, that is, for the rules and regulations under which a project functions, the mechanisms put in place at an organisational or inter-organisational level to ensure compliance with certain standards within, between and across projects. In so far as project governance implies the standardisation of practices between projects, it is reliant upon a conception of projects as 'real' and of the practices by which projects are managed as universal and consistent. Our intention in this chapter is to challenge this conception by 'unravelling' the project as it has been gradually constituted, reified and naturalised over time. We do this in the first instance through an analysis of the Project Management Body of Knowledge (henceforth, the PMBOK) of the largest professional organisation, the Project Management Institute (PMI). We start with a brief discussion of the formulation of the PMBOK before highlighting the PMBOK's role in constructing 'standards' and 'infrastructure' for the field of project management (PM). By doing so, we intend to take a first step towards bringing into question the specific forms of project management knowledge based around the standards and the infrastructure which the PMBOK invokes and legitimises. In particular, we have concerns about the premature 'black-boxing' of PM knowledge, the elevation of universal, abstract rationality over embodied and reflexive rationality, and the constraining effects this has upon the action of individuals who work within and manage projects. Through a critical examination of the construction of 'the project' itself, we hope to open the way to alternatives to technicism and instrumentalism, a wider integration of ethical concerns and a shift towards an embodied and enacted rationality in the management of projects.

Making 'the project' a reality: discovery or invention?

Comforting visions of project management as another scientific quest of discovery are seriously undermined by a range of developments in the philosophy of knowledge and social studies of science and technology. Since *The Archaeology of Knowledge* (Foucault, 1972), it has become increasingly difficult to maintain that objects of all kinds precede the emergence of a field of study; rather, it is argued that objects of knowledge are constructed by and through the creation of a body of knowledge. Foucault argues forcefully that objects of knowledge do not consist of a 'silent, self-enclosed truth'; instead, an object of knowledge is *constituted by* 'all that was said in all the statements that named it, divided it up, described it, explained it, traced its developments, indicated its various correlations, judged it' (Foucault, 1972: 35). Thus objects as diverse as 'madness', 'intelligence', 'leadership', 'quarks', 'gender' and 'homosexuality' have been analysed in terms of their construction by discourse, rather than their 'discovery' by a field of knowledge. This reverses the taken-for-granted order of events: rather than a discourse emerging *because of* the existence of an object of interest, it is argued instead that the discourse *brings the object into existence*. In this light, the study of projects and of their management is not a question of discovery, it is one of invention. In the place of a self-evident 'project' to be explored, we are interested in the ongoing discursive construction of what is to be understood and accepted as 'the project'. To summarise the foundation of the chapter, then, rather than asking 'what is a project?', we would pose the question in these terms: 'What do we do when we call something "a project"'?

From this perspective, the fundamental step in the creation of a discipline is the 'naturalisation' of the object around which it is based as a universal and pervasive object; thus project management relies upon the naturalisation of 'the project' itself as both focus and *raison d'être*. Many texts and documents in the field of project management, from textbooks and manuals to academic articles, are thus implicated in this naturalisation, engaging both explicitly and implicitly in the *reification* of the project. Reification is succinctly defined by Berger and Luckmann as 'the apprehension of the products of human activity *as if* they were something other than human products' (1966: 106). Many aspects of the debate within project management thus exhibit what Robert Chia describes as the phenomenon of 'false concreteness'. False concreteness, according to Chia, is an inheritance of positivism which

> often begins with the production of documents speculating on notions about … the existence of a particular object which then forms the legitimate focus of investigation. At this stage a speculated object begins to take on a life of its own (reification) and is increasingly perceived as being separate and independent of our apprehension of it. Next … the impression is given that it is in fact the existence of the object which first stimulated our attention towards it. Finally researchers become so accustomed to talking in these inverted terms that the initial stages of conceiving, reifying and inverting of the observer/observed relationship are forgotten or strongly denied. (Chia, 1995, in Johnson and Duberley, 2000: 99)

A typical effect of the reification of a discipline's focus is the systematic elimination of alternative representations/classifications of the phenomenon in question. The establishment of 'the project' as a reality, and the suppression of conflicting definitions of 'the project', is thus for many a vital foundation for the discipline of 'project management'. In this sense, 'the project' may be seen to be akin to the 'epistemic object' of

Knorr-Cetina (1997), acting as a generator of new conceptions and new solutions in the area. So, for instance, Meredith and Mantel assert that it is possible to investigate and agree on the nature of the projects for which project managers are responsible, and therefore on 'the skills that must be used to manage projects, and the means by which the manager can bring the project to a successful conclusion in terms of the three primary criteria: performance, time, and cost' (Meredith and Mantel, 2003: 8). There is a recognition here that the establishment of boundaries for project management as a discipline currently relies upon the definition of what the project *really is*:

> This all is possible if we succeed in clarifying the nature of a project and determining how it differs from the other activities that are conducted in organisations. (Meredith and Mantel, 2003: 8, emphasis added)

This realist and reifying perspective of many in mainstream project management reflects an enduring theme of management theory: the belief that its study is analogous to natural science, that is, discovering universal laws and fundamental properties of objects which (pre)exist 'out there', in the 'real world'. From this realist perspective, many writers on project management feel able to present their field as gradually converging on a generic model of the project management process, complete with common ontology and a standardised terminology globally recognised by professional project managers:

> The general assumption underlying the PMBOK and subsequent ambitions to create a project management profession, is that project management knowledge is applicable to all sorts of projects in all sorts of industries and environments. (Packendorff, 1995: 324)

This quest for a 'universal' model of project management is reflected in the increasing focus on a quantitative analysis developing 'cross-industry' comparisons. Morris, for instance, depicts the field closing in on this goal, claiming that

> It was only in the mid-to-late 1980s that sufficient inter-industry exchange of project management expertise and practice had occurred for a multi-industry, universal model of best project management practice to emerge in any kind of robust form. (Morris, 1997: 307)

The first danger we wish to highlight relates to the power effects of this reification: that the notion of 'false concreteness' extends beyond definitions of the project and serves to establish current understandings of project management as *laws*, inevitable and universal. Bowker and Star (1999) cite Bloor, Douglas and Latour as contributing to our understanding of how objects have material and political consequences upon the world as experienced. Latour sums up the recursive effect of this reification process: 'if [such objects] are *out there in the world* then they must be real and so we must model our society accordingly' (Latour, 1993, quoted in Bowker and Star, 1999: 60 italics in original). They cannot be questioned or resisted – they must instead be accommodated. It is noted in much of the emergent critical literature that such 'project management best practices' contained and promoted by the PMBOK tend to reflect principles of job fragmentation, intensive surveillance and enhanced accountability, based upon inter-locking systems of ideational, system and structural control (Metcalfe, 1997; Hodgson, 2002). We will return to the techniques and technologies of project management in our discussion below; for the moment it is enough to highlight that the legitimation of these techniques relies upon reification, locating 'the project' and 'project manage-ment' as 'things/objects' existing 'out there' in reality.

Project, standards and infrastructure

It is important to recognise that for reification to be effective, it requires institutional support (Douglas, 1986) – an *infrastructure* of relationships with the historical devel-opment of tools, routines of work practice, organisational arrangements and technol-ogy which forms a 'negotiated order' (Bowker and Star, 1999) across diverse communities of interested parties. In particular, this is attempted (and occasionally achieved) through concerted efforts to institutionalise *standards* (Brunsson and Jacobsson, 2000) which define and stabilise what an object 'is'. In the case of project management, the most influential attempt to establish standards *vis-à-vis* 'the project' is through the creation and dissemination of a coherent and universal body of knowledge. One of the aims of this chapter is to analyse the construction of such standards so as to identify 'the traces of bureaucratic struggles, differences in world view and systematic erasures' (Bowker and Star, 1999: 55) which remain in the PMBOK. Our broader goal is analyse the infrastructure linked to such standards and objects to provide an insight into 'how standard narratives that appear universal have been constructed' (Bowker and Star, 1999: 41).

In order to do this, we have drawn heavily on the work of Bowker and Star (1999) and in particular the tools that they offer for analysing the creation of standards and infrastructure and the means by which such infrastructures are made invisible through naturalisation. In the next section we will explain in more detail the evolution of the PMI PMBOK itself. We will then look at the notions of standards and infrastructure in turn, to demonstrate how the PMBOK attempts to provide standards for the field of project management, foundational definitions of the object of enquiry, and based upon this an infrastructure for the future of the discipline. In light of these processes, we will consider the implications of this reification of the project for communities of practice and the implications for power relations within and between organisations and industries. We will conclude by underlining the political and ethical implications of this invisible infrastructure.[2]

The PMBOK and the naturalisation of the project

While there exist numerous documents, texts, guides and so on in the field of project management which attempt to define and classify projects, our focus in this chapter will be *The Guide to the Project Management Body of Knowledge* (PMI, 1996, 2000). The PMBOK forms the cornerstone of the largest professional association in the field of project management, the US-based Project Management Institute (PMI). The increasing influence of the PMI is partly indicated by the increase in PMI membership in recent years, from 8,817 in 1992 to over 100,000 by 2003. The PMBOK was first developed and published in 1987, and has since been revised and republished twice since, in 1996 and 2000; in this time, through extensive dissemination, the PMI PMBOK has established itself as 'the *de facto* standard in the field' (Blomquist and Söderholm, 2002: 35).

A prevailing position within the debate over the nature of the PMBOK (see Wideman, 1995; Morris, 1999; Turner, 1999; Morris *et al.*, 2000) is that the PMBOK should be a stand-alone concept based on 'objective, publicly-testable knowledge based on facts', although opinions differ about how it is to be achieved. For the 1996 version, the title changes from *The Project Management Body of Knowledge* to *The Guide to the Project Management Body of Knowledge*, to reflect the acceptance that while the knowledge contained may be objective and based on facts, one document cannot contain 'all those topics, subject areas, and intellectual processes which are involved in the application of sound management principles to … projects' (PMI, 1996: vii). Instead, the PMBOK from 1996 onwards claims to 'identify and describe that subset of the PMBOK that is generally accepted', that is, knowledge and practices 'applicable to most projects most of the time [with] widespread consensus as to their value and usefulness' (PMI, 1996: 3). The notion that there exists a core to PMBOK knowledge and practices which is more or less universal is a key component in arguments for standardisation across projects which underpin the concept of project governance.

While the various revisions entail slightly different contents, sections and emphases, the fundamental structure of the PMBOK remains the same, establishing standard concepts and practices grouped in nine knowledge areas[3] (see Table 2.1). The goals also remain broadly the same: to provide a common lexicon, to put in place a structure for professional development programmes, to provide a framework for the refereeing and selection process for the *Project Management Journal*, and to facilitate knowledge transfer and management technology transfer across industries and national borders, with the overarching mission of promoting the professionalisation of project management. However, the PMI's definition of the PMBOK is not merely a definition, description and model of 'the project'. In defining 'the project' it incorporates knowledge of related techniques (such as Activity Duration Estimating, Qualitative and Quantitative Risk Analysis and so on) deemed necessary for the manipulation of the project.

Given the importance of standard-setting, it is no surprise to see that the PMBOK is officially authored by a collective entity known as the PMI Standards Committee. In common with most official documents and guides, it is delivered in an impersonal

Project Integration Management	Coordination of the various elements of a project, including coordination of all changes
Project Scope Management	Understanding of project life cycle, construction of WBS, change control
Project Time Management	Scheduling with Gantt charts, milestone charts, PERT/CPM networks, tracking schedule variances
Project Cost Management	Employment of cost estimating methodologies, budgeting process, tracking cost variance
Project Procurement Management	Understanding contract and procurement processes, resolving disputes
Project Quality Management	Identifying internal and external customer–supplier chains, doing things right first time, monitoring quality
Project Risk Management	Identifying and modelling risk, planning for risk
Project Human Resources Management	Managing conflict, motivating matrix resources, team building, appraisal
Project Communication Management	Understanding different forms of PMIS, maintaining formal and informal communication channels

Source: PMI (2000)

passive tone which both effaces the author and thereby guarantees the 'objectivity' of the knowledge contained therein; as Silverman indicates, 'anonymity is part of the official production of documentary reality' (1997: 58). This rhetorical device is necessary (but of course not sufficient) to establish that the contents accurately reflect 'a reality that exists independently of any individual observer, interpreter or writer' (Silverman, 1997: 59). In doing so, it can be seen as an attempt to rise above the petty interpersonal differences which exist between writers and provide an authoritative definition of the disciplinary area. That said, the PMBOK is not, however, an entirely anonymised document: although the authorship is credited to a committee, there is some recognition that the PMBOK exists as a collective effort. For the sake of transparency and in recognition of their efforts, the membership of the Standards Committee is also listed in an appendix to the 1996 edition, as well as a full list of 96 reviewers and their institutions, which is dominated by names of corporations such as AT&T. In a similar way to academic referencing, this appendix can be seen to be invoking a network of allies (Latour, 1987) to strengthen the truth claims of the document itself. This can be seen as the co-production of the authority and the object: through their involvement in the composition of the document, the reputation of academics and organisations is built at the same time as the contents are legitimised as the verdict of 'the great and the good', the expert authorities in this field.

It is our contention in this chapter that the PMBOK as described above, in collaboration with a range of ancillary documents and the wider efforts of a network of agencies, is a key element in the ongoing naturalisation of 'the project' as a taken-for-granted object through the institutionalisation of *standards*. As such, the PMBOK constitutes a key step in the establishment of an invisible infrastructure built upon and around a specific notion of 'the project'. The naturalisation of categories or objects is a process of 'stripping away the contingencies of an object's creation and its situated nature. A naturalized object has lost its anthropological strangeness' (Bowker and Star, 1999: 299). As a consequence of this naturalisation, it often requires intensive work to recapture and reestablish the contingency of such objects, and even just to maintain an awareness of other possibilities, of choices not taken in the construction of the object.

Our aim in the next two sections, then, is to highlight and to some extent to problematise the efforts of the PMBOK to establish incontrovertible standards across communities of practice with regard to the 'recognition' and existence of projects (and associated concepts, such as sub-projects, programmes, and so on). This leads us into a consideration of the way in which the PMBOK contributes to the construction of an infrastructure for the discipline of project management, which will be evaluated in the light of Star and Ruhleder's (1996) properties of infrastructure. We will then return to the notions of membership, naturalisation and the politics of the project as an object.

Standards, standardisation and the PMBOK

According to Bowker and Star (1999), standards are 'idealised' in that they are never perfectly realised – they exist as a Platonic ideal to be aspired to in the imperfections of everyday practice, and a healthy awareness of their unattainability is often a key criterion of membership of professional and expert communities. Nonetheless, they are also a vital element for classification in that 'every successful standard imposes a classification system, at the very least between good and bad ways of organizing actions or things' (Bowker and Star, 1999: 15). While it is far from clear that the PMBOK has successfully established a universal classification system, it is evident that the foundation of universal standards is a key goal of the document. It is stated in the 1996 PMBOK that

> PMI was founded in 1969 on the premise that there were many management practices that were common to projects in application areas as diverse as construction and pharmaceuticals. By the time of the Montreal Seminar/Symposium in 1976, *the idea that such common practices might be documented as 'standards' began to be widely discussed.* (PMI, 1996: 139, emphasis added)

The PMI Project Management Standards Program was later established to advance this standardisation, with a clear vision and mission reflecting the perceived importance of standardisation (see Box 2.1). The American National Standards Institute (ANSI) approved the PMBOK as a standard on 21 September 1999. Our argument is that the creation of such 'standards' enables the establishment of an object which embodies the political and managerial imperatives that underpin its discursive construction. In particular, the technicism and instrumental rationality which characterises the PMBOK has vital implications for how projects are implemented and judged throughout work organisations. To illustrate the role of the PMBOK in establishing standards for the

---

Box 2.1   The PMI Project Management Standards Program

The PMI Standards Program holds a position of preeminence among countless professional communities. Its purposes are to develop standards for the profession that are valued by PMI members and the global marketplace and to assist in improving the understanding and competency of both new and experienced project management practitioners worldwide.

PMI is recognized as a Standards Development Organization by the American National Standards Institute (ANSI) and the *PMBOK® Guide* has been approved as an American National Standard by ANSI (ANSI/PMI 99-001-2000). The *PMBOK® Guide* also is recognized by the Institute of Electrical and Electronics Engineers (IEEE) as an IEEE standard. In addition, it is used as an underlying reference in an International Organization for Standardization (ISO) Technical Report on managing software projects.

Vision

Worldwide Excellence in the Practice of Project Management through Standards which are Widely Recognized and Consistently Applied

Mission

To Assist in Improving the Understanding and Competency of Experienced and New Project Management Practitioners and Customers Worldwide

To Accomplish This We Will Identify, Define, Document and Champion Generally Accepted Project Management Approaches and a Common Project Management Lexicon

Purpose

To Develop Standards for the Project Management Profession That Are Valued By PMI Members, The Marketplace and Other Stakeholders

Source: PMI website (www.pmi.org).

---

project management field, we will examine it in the light of six characteristics of standards set out by Bowker and Star (1999: 13–14).

1   Standards as 'agreed-upon rules for the production of (textual or material) objects'

A key objective of the PMBOK is the establishment and reinforcement of a globally accepted terminology, indeed ontology, for the field of project management. As Morris *et al.* perceptively note, 'The Body of Knowledge ... reflects the ontology of the profession; the set of words, relationships and meanings that describe the philosophy of project management' (2000: 156). Clearly, the PMBOK is based upon the key question 'What is a Project?', defined on the second page of the document, as well as core definitions of the associated concepts of the 'Program' and the 'Sub-Project'. More broadly, though, the 15-page PMBOK Glossary provides a 'complete' lexicon for the discipline, a legend to the PMBOK's map of the project management terrain. Hence rules for the production of objects such as the 'critical path', 'project scope', 'milestones' and so on may be found within the PMBOK, and such objects have considerable power within the operation of projects and organisations.

As Wood (2002: 162) notes, any model is 'a symbolic representation of reality but can also be seen as part of a wider political struggle' as terminology, implied meaning and choice of representational symbols are the privilege of the powerful.

2 Standards 'cover more than one community of practice, over time'

A community of practice (Lave and Wenger, 1991) is a unit of analysis that cuts across formal organisations and contains a set of relations among people doing things together, including their activities, objects, routines and exceptions. The PMBOK itself defines its readership as 'Project Managers and other team members; Managers of project managers; Project customers and other project stakeholders; Functional managers with employees assigned to project teams; Educators teaching project management and related subjects; Consultants and other specialists in project management and related fields; Trainers developing project management educational programs' (PMI, 1996: 3). Part of the mission of the PMI is to expand its formal membership, drawing on all of these groups to build the core 'community'. However, within and beyond these categories, there is greater diversity; by their very nature, projects are intended to draw together and coordinate/control the activities of a heterogeneous group of actors, and interdisciplinarity is the rule rather than the exception. Indeed, it is to overcome this heterogeneity that the PMBOK exists – to provide/impose a common language and common conceptual apparatus across a huge diversity of participants, from electrical engineers and IT specialists to research scientists and builders, to school administrators and social workers.

3 Standards 'enable action/cooperation over distance and heterogeneity'

As Harvey argues in *The Condition of Postmodernity* (1990), a key dimension of globalisation is the establishment of universal standards: in terms of international law, the metric and imperial systems, the Gregorian calendar, Greenwich Mean Time and so on. As noted above, an explicit aim of the PMBOK is to 'standardise' the communications, interpretations and actions of participants regardless of background, profession or nationality. As explained by one member of the PMI Standards Member Advisory Group, 'PMI standards are critical to the survival of companies marketing to multiple nations' (Holtzman, 1999: 3). Thus, global conformity to these standards represents a criterion of success for the PMBOK and for the PMI more generally, and is certainly central to the notion of standardised project governance.

4 Standards 'tend to be enforced by legal bodies'

In recent editions, the theme of professionalisation has come to the fore in the PMBOK and the PMI's associated activities. While the recognition of the PMBOK by the

American National Standards Institute (ANSI) in 1999 was a key step, the long-term goal is institutionalisation, primarily through certification, such that membership of a professional body (such as the PMI) is required to practise as project manager. This would entail affording legal status to the standards embodied within the PMI's PMBOK (and arguably the reverse, laying legal obligations and liabilities upon the profession and its representative body, the PMI).

5 Standards 'do not reflect any natural law that the "best" will win'

Counter to the naive realist view of certain proponents of the various PMBOKs, standards do not prevail because of their innate superiority, in terms of greater accuracy, simplicity or other qualities. As convention rather than natural law predominates here, it is the combined effect of a network of agencies which enforces standards upon a population. This is particularly evident where standards are central to a specific and ubiquitous infrastructure for a discipline or community of practice, a point we will return to in the discussion of infrastructure in the next section.

6 Standards 'possess inertia and are therefore difficult/expensive to change'

Related to the previous point, it is argued that the long-term goal of the PMI is the *naturalisation* of such standards, through their embedding in the subjectivities of the association's membership, related documents or IT applications such that they eventually constitute an invisible foundation to the disciplinary area, tied intimately to techniques, procedures and other arrangements. Again, this leads us into a fuller consideration of the relationship between standards and a wider network of influence, which may be addressed through a more comprehensive examination of the infrastructure associated with 'the project' and the PMBOK.

While the establishment of 'standards' is thus a key objective of the PMI in creating the PMBOK, merely writing and distributing such a document is a small step in the naturalisation and reification of a particular understanding of 'the project'. A more effective next step is the establishment of an infrastructure, and the gradual effacement of this infrastructure into the everyday practices, rules and institutions which affect activity in a given area. In the next section we will highlight various properties of infrastructure to highlight its role in the reification of projects.

The PMBOK and the infrastructure

Just as standards are implicit in the construction/classification of objects, so both standards and objects are instrumental in and at the same time reliant upon the establishment of an accepted infrastructure within and beyond a certain community. Bowker and Star's key argument is that classification and standardisation are made possible by, and at the same time enable, the establishment of a taken-for-granted, transparent and boundary-spanning infrastructure. The effect of infrastructure is to merge the technical/scientific theory of categorisation with the commonsensical approach to classification, which in modern societies tends to be based upon three premises (Lakoff, 1987, in Bowker and Star, 1999: 33):

1 Things come in well-defined kinds.
2 The kinds are characterised by shared properties.
3 There is one right taxonomy of the kinds.

Where the convergence is effective, the consequence is that it becomes difficult to question or analyse workability, complexity and lack of transparency of the resulting system of infrastructure, its architecture and its use. The process of establishing an infrastructure around an object is 'buried in implicit common sense assumptions about the actor, concrete persons, and the observer's own views about everyday life' (Cicourel, 1964, in Bowker and Star, 1999: 320). In this process, everyday life categories thus disappear into institutions, into habit, into the taken-for-granted, and become no longer available for consideration and challenge.

As a counter to this, and as part of the 'struggle against the tendency of infrastructure to disappear' (Bowker and Star, 1999: 34), Bowker puts forward the methodological approach of infrastructural inversion (Bowker, 1994). Infrastructural inversion means learning to look closely and acknowledge the depths of interdependencies of technical networks, arrangements and standards, on the one hand, and the interrelated process of politics and knowledge production, on the other. To attempt this infrastructural inversion, we will consider the wider linkages and implications of the PMBOK in the light of nine properties of infrastructure proposed by Star and Ruhleder (1996).

Embeddedness

First of all, it is argued that '*infrastructure is sunk into, inside of, other structures, social arrangements, and technologies*'. The 'embeddedness' of the PMBOK can be seen reflected in the increasing number of businesses/organisations adopting PMBOK-based training and certification courses to create a pool of professional project managers to manage projects and project-based arrangements. The PMBOK is also built into other business procedures – HRM, operations, the adoption of information systems and software installations, management standards, prescriptions, checklists and documentation, evaluation and audit practices. Thus the use of the PMBOK in the International Organisation for Standardisation (ISO) Technical Report on managing software projects, and its adaptation by the Institute of Electrical and Electronics Engineers (IEEE), indicates the interpenetration of infrastructure. More subtly, the terminology and language standardised through the PMBOK permeates into other documents and discourses within individual organisations and networks of organisations. The infrastructure as defined by the PMI (2000) aspires to gradually 'invading' wider social environments by targeting project stakeholders, the education sector and consultancy activities.

Transparency

'*Infrastructure is transparent to use in the sense that it is always there in a universal, stable format to invisibly support tasks irrespective of the variety of local contexts.*' In the preceding discussion we attempted to illuminate how through the standardisation of 'the project' in the PMBOK, the debates and disagreements over the nature of projects are made to disappear behind powerful, impersonal and ahistorical claims about how projects should be accurately defined – and how they therefore should be effectively managed. The kind of schemata given in Table 2.1 articulates the implied stability and universality (both commonsensical and technical/scientific) and is presented to diverse communities of practice as the objective and universal knowledge require-ments for all kinds of activities categorised as project-based. The transparency of the infrastructure is enhanced to the extent to which it reflects broader modernist con-ceptions of knowledge particularly in the area of management – that it should reflect a form of rationality which is linear, reductivist, unambivalent and instrumental (see Townley, 2002, for a fuller discussion).

Reach or scope

'*Infrastructure has reach (either spatial or temporal) beyond a single event or one-site practice*'. This is precisely what is claimed by the PMI as the key purpose of the PMBOK: 'to identify and describe that subset of [knowledge within the profession of project management] that is ... *generally accepted* ... [which] means that the know-ledge and practices described are applicable to most projects most of the time, and that there is widespread consensus about their value and usefulness' (PMI, 2000, ch. 1: 3, italics original). Thus an article of faith is that an effective PMBOK can (and should) be used by different communities of practices, across different organisations, sectors and nations, as a guide for standard practice. In practice, this means a certain ambi-guity in the composition of the PMBOK, and the tensions between the diverse com-munities and their perceived requirements count for much of the debate within the mainstream project management field over the PMBOK (see, for example, Curling, 1995; Walta, 1995; Wideman, 1995; Pharro, 1997; Morris, 1999; Turner, 1999; Morris *et al.*, 2000; Turner, 2000).

Learned as part of membership (in a community of practice)

'*The taken for grantedness of artefacts and organizational arrangements is a sine qua non of membership in a community of practice.*' Infrastructure sets a form of membership hierarchy within the relevant communities of practice based upon familiarity with naturalised objects within the field – to belong, one must be conversant and comfortable with elements of infrastructure to the extent that they become 'taken for granted', self-evident and thus both fundamental and beyond debate. The PMI and other national bodies condition the individual joining in the profession by establishing training, examination and certification processes, procedures and mechanisms, based on PMBOK infrastructure. Organisations and their senior management, in turn, use such a prescription to differentiate, rank and exercise power over individuals aspiring to the membership of the PM community of practice. This is related to the subsequent aspect of Bowker and Star's definition of infrastructure.

Links with conventions of practice

'Infrastructure both shapes and is shaped by the conventions of a community of practice.' Clearly, in any given field the constant evolution of conventions of practice, habits and norms will outstrip the development of formal infrastructure. An illustrative example would be the importance given to standardised terminology and language proprietary to the project management discipline. It is stated in the PMBOK that the document provides a 'common lexicon within the profession and practice for talking and writing about project management' (PMI, 2000: 3), compiled on the basis of agreement over terms that are either unique to project management discourse or else carry specific meaning in the project management context compared with everyday usage. Emergent empirical work in this area (see, for example, Hodgson, 2002) indicates the way in which standardised terminology and vocabulary penetrate conventional communication in practice and enable the distinction between professional and illegitimate/incompetent speech to be made.

Embodiment of standards

'Infrastructure takes on transparency by plugging into other infrastructures and tools in a standardised fashion.' In the case of the PMBOK this is achieved in relation to other infrastructures, including among other things educational material/textbooks (see Frame, 1999; Meredith and Mantel, 2000, 2003), professional certification schemes, management development programmes, project management consulting and tendering protocols. Via these channels, it further penetrates official organisational policies, strategic change initiatives, reorganisation programmes and operating procedures.

Built on an installed base

'Infrastructure does not grow de novo, but wrestles with the inertia of the installed base and inherits strengths and limitations from that base.' Notwithstanding the opening comments on the anachronistic view of projects espoused by many project management writers, clearly the current infrastructure related to the PMBOK inherits many elements from its historical precursors; the influence of scientific management is reflected in the continued use of techniques of job fragmentation and work study in work breakdown and Gantt charts. As Barley and Kunda point out, the Critical Path Method (CPM) and the Program Evaluation and Review Technique (PERT), 'popularised by operations researchers in the 1960s, were direct extensions of the Gantt Chart developed by Henry Gantt in the early 1900s' (Barley and Kunda, 1992: 379). More recently, the influence of Total Quality Management and Business Process Re-engineering methodologies is implicit in the process-based focus since the 1996 version of the PMBOK.

Becomes visible upon breakdown

'*The normally invisible quality of working infrastructure becomes visible when it breaks.*' While in many fields, infrastructures are so embedded and transparent that they are all but imperceptible other than in crisis situations, this cannot be said for the field of projects; instead, many of the workings are clearly visible and remain to some extent open to challenge. The 'disappearing' infrastructure in project management is constantly hampered by the inability of its elements to capture the variety of practice, to transfer seamlessly across contexts and to achieve the efficacy claimed by its proponents.

Is fixed in modular increments, not all at once or globally

'*Because infrastructure is complex and layered, and because it means different things locally, it is never changed from above.*' This is exemplified in two ways in the case of the PMBOK, with some tension between the two factors. On the one hand, that the PMBOK is constructed as a central, overarching document listing *all* accepted principles, processes, tools, techniques and standards underpinning best practice for project management implies a centralising authority which has the right to legitimise or reject change. On the other hand, it is accepted in later versions of the PMBOK that although knowledge and practices described in the document are generally accepted, they should not 'be applied uniformly on all projects; the project management team is always responsible for determining what is appropriate for any given project' (PMI, 2000: 3). There is also the less than transparent process of adaptation within the PMI committee responsible for revising the PMBOK and its constituent elements.

What we have tried to do in the preceding two sections, therefore, is to trace the relationship between the PMBOK, standards and infrastructure – in particular, to indicate how far the PMBOK can be seen to be implicated both in the establishment of standards which construct the project as an object and in the promotion and development of an infrastructure based around this object. The intended consequence can be summarised as the reification of the project and the naturalisation of an infrastructure built around this concept. As an early step in opposition to this 'false concreteness', we have attempted to begin the process of undoing the invisibility of the infrastructure by highlighting the processes of reification in operation and the contingent nature of the project itself as currently defined. In the next section we wish to underline the political and ethical importance of reification, naturalisation and invisibility, in particular by considering the impact of such standards and infrastructure upon the community of practice in question.

The dangers of invisibility

While it is interesting and perhaps thought-provoking to consider the ways in which the PMBOK as a document attempts to establish standards and an infrastructure for an increasingly popular sub-topic of management, this would be of little more than idle interest were it not for the powerful material consequences of such entities. The consequences of throwaway statements regarding the existence of pyramids as evidence of the universal importance of projects are serious, as they invoke an ahistorical concatenation of prehistorical work organisation, Adam Smith's division of labour, Taylorism, Cold War project methodologies and the contemporary techniques and technologies associated with the discipline of project management. Such statements serve as a subtle legitimation of contemporary formulations of project management, in its principles and techniques, as somehow universal and timeless and thus encourage uniform and universal systems of project governance. Implicitly, we argue, this hinders critical debate over the specific nature of project management as it is constituted today, and 'black-boxes' both techniques and practices in the discipline. In particular, there is the clear danger that the 'black-boxing' of knowledge in this area, as definitions, techniques and procedures become set in stone, effectively removes the ethical and political questions from the agenda. Second, we would argue that the establishment of universal knowledge of this kind implies a loss of a reflexive and embodied rationality in favour of abstract principles and blind faith in universal techniques (Townley, 2002).

As is the case in similar fields such as accounting and quality management, we would concur with Bowker and Star that the establishment of standards, categories and infrastructure 'should be recognised as the significant site of political and ethical work that they are' (1999: 319). Bowker and Star argue that infrastructure has become now the great inner space, a landscape in, on and around which we act, which influences and frames our moral, scientific and aesthetic choices:

> It is politically and ethically crucial to recognize the vital role of infrastructure in the 'built moral environment'. Seemingly purely technical issues like how to name things and how to store data in fact constitute much of human interaction and much of what we come to know as natural. (Bowker and Star, 1999: 326)

Where such standards take on an unassailable 'reality' and form the basis for systems of project governance, their power effects become unmistakable. Following Bowker and Star (1999), we would underline the political and moral significance of the PMBOK by returning to the issue of membership of communities of practice and the importance of naturalisation here.

As discussed above, Bowker and Star describe 'membership' as the experience of encountering objects and being in an increasingly naturalised relationship with them. Thus, the creation of 'naturalised objects' is central to the creation of *communities of practice* (Lave and Wenger, 1991) for whom membership is dependent on familiarity with and acceptance of such objects and categories as self-evident and self-evidently important. Membership in such communities of practice 'has as its *sine qua non* an increasing familiarity with the categories that apply' (Bowker and Star, 1999: 294), that is, familiarity with the classes of action, tools, symbols and so on proprietary to the given community of practice. It is in that process of learning-as-membership and participation that 'you forget the strange and contingent nature of its categories seen from the outside' (Bowker and Star, 1999: 295). This is an explicit aim of the PMBOK (see Frame, 1999; Morris *et al.*, 2000; Meredith and Mantel, 2003): to establish an ontology for the field and more specifically for a broad community of practice. Through the establishment of standards for categorisation and classification of phenomena, objects assume an unchallengeable status within a community or indeed across multiple communities of practice. Where this is achieved,

> The more naturalized an object becomes, the more unquestioning the relationship of the community to it; the more invisible the contingent and historical circumstances of its birth, the more it sinks into the community's routinely forgotten memory. (Bowker and Star, 1999: 299)

Naturalisation is not a natural process – in this case, it takes place as a result of the significant efforts of the PMI to institutionalise the PMBOK as a 'basic reference about project management knowledge and practices for its professional development programs' (PMI, 2000: 4), forming the basis for *certification* of project management professionals and *accreditation* of educational programmes in project management. The implications of the institutionalisation of this position on projects are significant; the cost of membership to a professional community may well be the acceptance of the PMI's conception of the nature of a project, as well as associated technologies and assumptions. As noted elsewhere (Metcalfe, 1997; Hodgson, 2002), the technologies within the PMBOK show a distinct tendency towards a Taylorist direct control, intensive surveillance and heightened visibility and accountability. Similarly, the effects of professionalisation upon project managers themselves, as is the case with many other occupational groups, can often involve increased self-disciplinary control (Grey, 1998; Hodgson, 2002). Bowker and Star argue that classification 'tie[s] a person into an infrastructure – into a set of work practices, beliefs, narratives, and organizational routines' (1999: 319). The dangers of membership and the difficulties of transforming such technologies are therefore exacerbated by the naturalisation of the project as conceptualised by the PMBOK and its embedding in an infrastructure as described above.

On the other hand, this naturalisation is far from an accomplished fact, and rarely if ever occurs without struggle. Given the diversity of communities engaged in projects of some kind, in public and private sectors, it is unsurprising that the PMBOK is forced to leave certain terms open for multiple definitions across different social worlds; hence the notion of a 'negotiated order' (Bowker and Star, 1999). We should therefore not make little of the difficulty facing the institutions behind the PMBOK in their attempt to establish 'universal characteristics' across different types of projects, industries, structures, societies and so on. Current PMI policy seems to be to leave the interpretation of and application to varying environments ambiguous while standardising knowledge areas, competencies, tools and techniques on a scientific basis. We should also reiterate that establishing classification, standardisation and required infrastructure surrounding 'the project' as an organisational object with the desired implications for affected communities of practice through the construction of the PMBOK continues to encounter problems. In fact, a debate around the key issues is still heated, a global synchronisation of 'local'/national versions of PMBOKs has not been achieved, and essential questions remain unanswered. As a final vignette on this topic, it is instructive to consider the recent study (Morris *et al.*, 2000) of responses generated within the UK communities of practice (academics and practitioners engaged in the field of management of projects) on the efforts to professionalise the project management discipline. Morris and his colleagues note that 'valid questionnaire returns were only received from 6% of those polled: many stated that they were unable to respond adequately because they did not really understand what the purpose of a BOK was' (Morris *et al.*, 2000: 158). Such a response indicates the painful path towards establishing infrastructure, classification and standardisation and more fundamentally the danger of institutionalising such frameworks as the foundation for systems of project governance.

Conclusion

Our question in the title of this chapter, 'Are projects real?', represents a deliberate attempt on our part to draw attention to the significant efforts continually put into the reification of the project in the field of project management, particularly on the part of professional associations. The processes of representing, naming and modelling that constitute such reification can be seen as the prerogative of the powerful (Wood, 2002), with significant yet often unrecognised implications for the management and, especially, the governance of projects. We have therefore in this chapter started to question the ontological foundations of 'the project', drawing on perspectives which would instead see 'the project' as a constructed entity which tends to evolve, in practice, into a system of rules with centralised control and coordination, with powerful and often unrecognised consequences for the governance of what we label as 'projects' in contemporary organisations. We have tried through this chapter to highlight instead the contingent and constructed nature of both projects and the infrastructure which accompanies our current conception of projects. We believe there are significant dangers and problems resulting from existing positions taken, and have tried through this and other work (Cicmil, 2001; Hodgson, 2002) to high-light these hazards. As Bowker and Star note:

> We have a moral and ethical agenda in our querying of these systems. Each standard and each category valorizes some point of view and silences another. This is not inherently a bad thing – indeed it is inescapable. But it is an ethical choice, and as such it is dangerous – not bad, but dangerous. (Bowker and Star, 1999: 5–6)

We perceive two specific dangers implicit in the reification of the project and the naturalisation of the related infrastructure. In the first instance, the 'black-boxing' of knowledge in this area, as definitions, techniques and procedures become set in stone, is an effective way of removing the ethical and political questions from the agenda. A cursory reading of the main journals and proceedings from major conferences in this area provides a striking example of the consequences when everyday categories become 'seamlessly interwoven with formal, technical categories and specifications ... The moral questions arise when the categories of the powerful become the taken for granted' (Bowker and Star, 1999: 319–20). In particular, the disciplinary effects of project management as a field become yet more difficult to challenge and overturn. Second, we would argue that the establishment of universal knowledge of this kind implies a loss of a reflexive and embodied rationality in favour of abstract principles and blind faith in universal techniques (Townley, 2002). For both of these reasons, we would wish to articulate a concern about the standardising effects of a uniform system of project governance based upon a universal and reified object, and a real need to reflect and reconsider the foundations upon which current knowledge and practices are being built.

On the other hand, we would also emphasise that 'any given classification provides surfaces of resistances (where the real resists its definition), blocks against certain agendas, and smooth roads for others' (Bowker and Star, 1999: 324). To build on this position and encourage more critical perspectives to be developed by those implicated in projects, we are arguing for the necessity to maintain 'open spaces' where alternative or locally situated knowledge can be created. While this is clearly a difficult challenge, given the tendency of infrastructures to become embedded and to disappear from sight, one possible way out is through denaturalisation, by making clear the contingency and political nature of all categorisations, and the constructed nature of all objects:

> A key for the future is to produce flexible classifications whose users are aware of their political and organizational dimensions and which explicitly retain traces of their construction. (Bowker and Star, 1999: 326)

It is in this spirit that this chapter is intended: as an attempt to open up the project to alternative perspectives by problematising the basis of current technologies and techniques, by highlighting the political and ethical imperatives embedded within current 'taken-for-granted' conceptions of the project. In doing so, we hope to provide further discursive resources for dissenting voices both within and outside the field in addition to the growing body of critical work in this area.

Notes

1. As Meredith and Mantel proudly assert, 'We are able to achieve goals through project organization that could be achieved only with greatest of difficulty if organized in traditional ways' (2003: iii).
2. This analysis of generative documents and texts involved in the constitution and reification of the project deliberately excludes the issue of the consumption of and interaction with such documents on the part of 'users' of all kinds. It also involves postponing a thorough examination of techniques in practice (although for the reasons cited above, it is impossible to draw a line between definitions of the project and descriptions of techniques for its measurement and management). This decision does not imply that we see such documents as a perfectly accurate reflection of what takes place in organisations, or as objects with the power to determine what takes place – indeed, quite the opposite. We see this chapter as an early step in a broader critical analysis of the range of technologies, techniques, formulae, rules, IT applications and so on embodied in the PMBOK and intimately linked to the project as a taken-for-granted entity in everyday organisational life. This will clearly involve a much more substantial examination of how a range of individuals interpret and enact the PMBOK in distinct ways, and this work has been commenced in other publications by the authors (see, for example, Cicmil, 2001; Hodgson, 2002, 2004). For the purposes of this chapter, however, we will focus as far as possible on the object which legitimises and gives the field its coherence, the project itself, and its construction and reification as a 'documentary reality' (Silverman, 1997).
3. The nine areas in the 2000 PMBOK include one addition to the eight areas in the 1996 PMBOK: 'Project Integration'.

References

Barley, S.R. and Kunda, G. (1992) 'Design and Devotion: Surges of Normative and Rational Ideologies of Control in Managerial Discourse', in *Administrative Science Quarterly*, 37: 363–99.

Bennis, W.G. and Slater, P.E. (1968) *The Temporary Society*. New York: Harper & Row.

Berger, P.L. and Luckmann, T. (1966) *The Social Construction of Reality*. Harmondsworth: Penguin.

Blomquist, T. and Söderholm, A. (2002) 'How Project Management Got Carried Away', in K. Sahlin-Andersson and A. Söderholm (eds), *Beyond Project Management: New Perspectives on the Temporary–Permanent Dilemma*. Copenhagen: Liber.

Bowker, G.C. and Star, S.L. (1999) *Sorting Things Out: Classification and Its Consequences*. London: MIT Press.

Brunsson, N. and Jacobsson, B. (2000) *A World of Standards*. Oxford: Oxford University Press.

Cicmil, S. (2001) 'Reconstructing the Project Management Knowledge System: A Multiple-Perspective Agenda', paper presented to Critical Management Studies Conference, UMIST, Manchester, 11–13 July 2001.

Curling, D.H. (1995) 'Editorial', *International Journal of Project Management*, Special Issue on PMBOK, 13(2): 67.

Douglas, M. (1986) *How Institutions Think*. Syracuse, NY: Syracuse University Press.

Duncan, W.R. (1995) 'Developing a Project-Management Body-of-Knowledge Document: The US Project Management Institute's Approach, 1983–94', *International Journal of Project Management*, Special Issue on PMBOK, 13: 89–94.

Foucault, M. (1972) *The Archaeology of Knowledge*. London: Tavistock.

Frame, J.D. (1999) *Project Management Competence: Building Key Skills for Individuals, Teams and Organizations*. San Francisco, CA: Jossey-Bass.

Grey, C. (1998) 'On Being a Professional in a "Big Six" Firm', *Accounting, Organizations and Society*, 23(5–6): 569–87.

Harvey, D. (1990) *The Condition of Postmodernity*. London: Blackwell.

Hodgson, D.E. (2002) 'Disciplining the Professional: The Case of Project Management', *Journal of Management Studies*, 39(7): 803–21.

Hodgson, D.E. (2004) 'Project Teams: The Legacy of Bureaucratic Control in the Post-Bureaucratic Organisation', *Organization*, 11(1): 81–100.

Holtzman, J. (1999) 'Getting Up to Standard', *PM Network*, December: 1–4.

Johnson, P. and Duberley, J. (2000) *Understanding Management Research: An Introduction to Epistemology*. London: Sage.

Knorr-Cetina, K. (1997) 'Sociality with Objects: Social Relations in Postsocial Knowledge Societies', *Theory, Culture and Society*, 14(4): 1–31.

Kreiner, K. (1995) 'In Search of Relevance: Project Management in Drifting Environments', *Scandinavian Journal of Management*, 11(4): 335–46.

Latour, B. (1987) *Science in Action: How to Follow Scientists and Engineers Through Society*. Buckingham: Open University Press.

Lave, J. and Wenger, E. (1991) *Situated Learning: Legitimate Peripheral Participation*. Cambridge: Cambridge University Press.

Lundin, R.A. and Hartman, F. (eds) (2000) *Projects as Business Constituents and Guiding Motives*. Boston, MA: Kluwer Academic Publishers.

Lundin, R.A. and Midler, C. (eds) (1998) *Projects as Arenas for Renewal and Learning Processes*. Boston, MA: Kluwer Academic Publishers.

Lundin, R.A. and Söderholm, A. (1998) 'Conceptualising a Projectified Society: Discussion of an Eco-Institutional Approach to a Theory on Temporary Organizations', in R.A. Lundin and C. Midler (eds), *Projects as Arenas for Renewal and Learning Processes*. Boston, MA: Kluwer Academic Publishers.

Maylor, H. (2001) 'Beyond the Gantt Chart – Project Management Moving On', *European Management Journal*, 19(1): 92–100.

Meredith, J.R. and Mantel, S.J. (2000) *Project Management – A Managerial Approach*, 4th edn. New York: John Wiley & Sons.

Meredith, J.R. and Mantel, S.J. (2003) *Project Management – A Managerial Approach*, 5th edn. New York: John Wiley & Sons.

Metcalfe, B. (1997) 'Project Management System Design: A Social and Organisational Analysis', *International Journal of Production Economics*, 52: 305–16.

Midler, C. (1995) '"Projectification" of the Firm: The Renault Case', *Scandinavian Journal of Management*, 11(4): 363–73.

Morris, P.W.G. (1997) *The Management of Projects*. London: Thomas Telford.

Morris, P.W.G. (1999) 'What Project Managers Need to Know', *IEEE Review*, July: 173–5.

Morris, P.W.G., Patel, M.B. and Wearne, S.H. (2000) 'Research into Revising the APM Project Management Body of Knowledge', *International Journal of Project Management*, 18: 155–64.

Packendorff, J. (1995) 'Inquiring into the Temporary Organization: New Directions for Project Management Research', *Scandinavian Journal of Management*, 11(4): 437–55.

Pharro, R. (1997) 'In Search of the Holy Grail', *Project Manager Today*, April: 10.

PMI (Project Management Institute) (1996) *A Guide to the Project Management Body of Knowledge*. Newtown Square, PA: Project Management Institute.

PMI (Project Management Institute) (2000) *A Guide to the Project Management Body of Knowledge*. Newtown Square, PA: Project Management Institute.

PMI (Project Management Institute) (2001) *The PMI Project Management Fact Book*, 2nd edn. Newtown Square, PA: Project Management Institute.

Räisänen, C. and Linde, A. (2001) 'Constructing Project Management: A Critical Analysis Perspective on Project Management Models', paper presented at EGOS Colloquium in Lyon, France, July.

Sahlin-Andersson, K. and Söderholm, A. (eds) (2002) *Beyond Project Management: New Perspectives on the Temporary–Permanent Dilemma*. Copenhagen: Liber.

Silverman, D. (ed.) (1997) *Qualitative Research: Theory, Method and Practice*. London: Sage.

Star, S.L. and Ruhleder, K. (1996) 'Steps Towards an Ecology of Infrastructure: Design and Access for Large Information Spaces', *Information Systems Research*, 7(1): 111–34.

Townley, B. (2002) 'Managing With Modernity', *Organization*, 9(4): 549–73.

Turner, J.R. (1999) 'Project Management: A Profession Based on Knowledge or Faith?', editorial in *International Journal of Project Management*, 17(6): 329–30.

Turner, J.R. (2000) 'The Global Body of Knowledge, and its Coverage by the Referees and Members of the International Editorial Board of this Journal', *International Journal of Project Management*, 18: 1–5.

Walta, H. (1995) 'Dutch Project-Management Body of Knowledge Policy', *International Journal of Project Management*, 13(2): 101–8.

Wideman, R.M. (1995) 'Criteria for a Project-Management Body of Knowledge', *International Journal of Project Management*, 13(2): 71–5.

Winch, G. (1996) 'Thirty Years of Project Management – What Have We Learned?', *British Academy of Management Conference Proceedings*, Aston Business School, September 1996: 8.127–8.145.

Wood, M. (2002) 'Mind the Gap? A Processual Reconsideration of Organisational Knowledge', *Organization*, 9(1): 151–71.

Young, T. (1998) *The Handbook of Project Management – A Practical Guide of Effective Policies and Procedures*. London: Kogan Page.

3

From project ontologies to communities of virtue

Carol Linehan and Donncha Kavanagh

Introduction

Story 1 The king and the cartographer

The story goes that a king employed a cartographer to produce a map of his territory. The king found the map most useful and was so captivated by the power of representation that he asked the cartographer to producer a better map, to a larger scale. The cartographer complied, but after some time the king asked for an even better map. And so on, until eventually the cartographer produced a one-to-one map, which of course was the *territory* and was therefore a useless *map*.

Story 2 The paper mountain

The PCS project was a two-year, $16 million project to replace a process control system in a pharmaceutical plant. The main players in this complex project were the pharmaceutical firm, the software development company and a project management company. In one month, the project management organisation produced 40,000 sheets of A4 paper as part of their work on the project.

An important first step in considering the future of projects and of project management is to consider our understanding of what a 'project' is. What do we assume about the nature of projects? Addressing such a question is to reflect on our understanding of ontology, that is, our understanding of the nature of the world and of existence. This is important because ontological assumptions underpin the set of practices that go under

51

the umbrella term 'project management'. Put differently, what is the 'it' that project managers presume to manage?

In this chapter we introduce the term 'project ontologies' as a way of distinguishing different ways of thinking about what projects are. These project ontologies might also be described as world views, paradigms or cognitive codes. We draw on Robert Chia's (1995) distinction between what he refers to as 'being' and 'becoming' ontologies (and elsewhere, but less usefully, modern and postmodern styles of organisational analysis). For us, a becoming ontology seems to better describe the empirical reality of projects, though we recognise that each ontology is necessarily partial. More important, perhaps, an excessive attachment to one or the other leads to a privileging of some questions, methods and interventions, and a marginalisation of others. What one person sees as a 'problem' others may see as a 'nuisance', an 'opportunity', a 'disaster', a 'storm in a teacup' or a 'joke'. In other words, problems and issues are *interpretations*, and interpretations are always based and consequential on our world view or ontology.

Not only are 'problems' outcomes of retrospective interpretative processes, but they may also be *generated* by dysfunctional interventions. By this we mean interventions that, while they seek to deal with a potential problem, are actually the *source* of the problem in so far as both the 'problem' and 'intervention' are consequences of a dominant ontology. The old story of the king and the cartographer (story 1 above) helps illustrate this point. Similarly, story 2 illustrates how a belief in representationalism – representing the world as it is perceived to be, and then working with those representations – allows us to (project) manage, but that paradoxically an excessive belief in this paradigm leads to overmanagement and ultimately poor management. The general point of the stories is that *excessive* attachment to one world view may actually *create* problems that the world view purports to eliminate. In short, world views are important.

We begin this chapter by exploring what is meant by a being and a becoming ontology of projects, and what kinds of questions and interventions these ontologies prompt. This is developed by reflecting on the implications a shift in language from 'project teams' to 'communities of practice' brings to our questions about project management. We go on to consider how a shift in language should also be considered in the light of its ethical concomitants and potential consequences for participants in project contexts.

Being and becoming ontologies

Following Chia, we present a being ontology as the dominant ontology of organisational analysis. In this world view, primacy is given to objects, things, states, events and nouns. In the context of projects, a being ontology leads us to talk and think about organisation structure in an objectified manner. In other words, our descriptions privilege static accounts of group structuring – for instance, the common discussion in project management texts and practice about the taxonomic distinctions between functional, weak matrix, balanced matrix, strong matrix and projectised structures.

Mistaking abstractions for concrete realities
— tendency for reification

Moreover, these are seen as planned elements of the project organisation, preexisting the actual activities of the project group. This style of thinking leads us to consider project organisations as things, as entities, akin to elephants and other organisms, with functions, parts and structure, and relationships with similar entities in the 'environment' be they parent organisations, client organisations, subcontractors or state institutions. And of course this is all good, not least because it provides stability and structure in a complex, ambiguous and indeed chaotic world. Moreover, it is a world view that infuses the discourse of project management, and its hegemony in that domain speaks eloquently of its practical value.

Story 3   The fortress of files

At the weekly project management meeting of the PCS project (story 2 above), the software company was represented by its project manager and senior project engineer. They brought about a dozen box and lever-arch files to each meeting, and they formed these into a three-sided fortress of files on the table before the meeting commenced.

But a being ontology is not without problems. Story 3 reminds us that while the representationalist technologies of management might be good, necessary and helpful, their limitations must also be recognised. Whitehead's fallacy of misplaced concreteness – wherein 'we have mistaken our abstractions for concrete realities' (Whitehead, 1925: 69) – reminds us of the ever-present tendency towards reification that comes with a being ontology. In many cases the language of 'being' is applied, not only to projects, but also on a macro scale to organisations, which, when viewed in an entitative fashion, treat the organisation as a rational, performance-driven agent (Cooper and Burrell, 1988). Thus the organisation is spoken about as having goals, knowledge, plans and so on. This is not necessarily a problem since one must for pragmatic reasons often assume that entities are real, stable and static. But in at least some instances – and we argue that project-organising is one such instance – a being ontology fits very uneasily with the phenomenon or issue of concern. In particular, focusing on the formal representations of structure and relationships risks missing out on the dynamic, fluid relationships in project groups which are at the heart of their creative potential (Brown and Duguid, 2000). Akin to trying to eat soup with a fork, the gaps and inadequacies mean that it can often fail to adequately capture or engage with the phenomenon.

An interesting dimension to this point is that the discipline of project management has traditionally set itself up as an alternative paradigm to *production* management, arguing that while the latter provides a satisfactory world view and set of techniques in the relatively stable world of production, it is inadequate in a project environment where the focus is on change. The mantra, in short, has been to use production management in stable contexts (for example, running a cheese factory) while using project management to manage change (for example, building a new cheese factory). The irony is that the effort to professionalise and institutionalise the discipline of project management since the 1980s has been founded on an ontological paradigm that is already populated by production management. This has had important consequences. First, the distinction between production and project management has been blurred, partly because the former has found it quite easy to expand into what is now constituted as a closely related territory. Second, the standardisation and codification of knowledge, which are bedfellows of professionalisation and institutionalisation, threaten to sap a deeper understanding of working, managing and knowing that is especially pertinent to the projectised domain (Tsoukas, 1998).

This pragmatic and epistemological issue is perhaps of less import than the ethical problems that are potential consequences of the tendency towards reification that occurs within a being ontology. In a project context, this reification operates at the level of a project goal and at the level of the specific techniques of project management – for example, earned value analysis, the critical path method, risk assessment. Both the goal and the techniques are depicted as inviolable, 'natural', and beyond deconstruction or critique. Thus, project management technologies can be applied to the building of a new school, the development of a new software system, the launching of a new product – but also to setting up a slave-trafficking network or a human-cloning project – with little or no engagement with the ethical value of the specific projects. In other words, project management technologies embody what Weber ([1921] 1968) called 'instrumental rationality' – the continual calculation of means in relation to ends – with little reflection on the ends themselves. In short, a being ontology tends to evacuate values and ethical considerations out of the situation.

Another ethical criticism is that a being ontology is excessively instrumental, tending to see humans as simply a means to an end (the project goal). This is consequential on the tendency towards reification that is inherent within a being ontology. Following Kant, the issue is not that humans cannot be used as a means to achieving an end, but that it is morally wrong to treat them *only* as a means. Here, Habermas's (1971) distinction between 'work' (instrumental action 'governed by technical rules based on empirical fact') and 'interaction' (communicative action that generates and enforces reciprocal norms) is compelling and speaks to the empirical reality that project management has tended to privilege the former over the latter. This is an important point but one that tends to be glossed over in, for instance, the Project Management Body of Knowledge (PMBOK), which purports to offer a doctrinal understanding of the discipline.

Our point is not that a being ontology is wrong or unhelpful; rather that it is partial and that it may blind us to other, perhaps more useful and more human, ways of thinking about and seeing the world.

In contrast to a being ontology, a becoming ontology emphasises process, verbs, activity and the construction of entities. With respect to structure and organisation, a becoming ontology calls attention to the dynamics of how such structural and procedural issues are made relevant and played out within specific project contexts. It focuses

excessive instrumentalism

our attention on situations in which members negotiate their use of governing principles and structural arrangements in actual practice. Thus, rather than speaking about
structure and roles, we instead speak about structuring and sense-making (Giddens,
1984; Weick, 1995). Instead of seeing structure as something that exists prior to the
project, we see structure (that is, order) as an emergent outcome of structuring and
sense-making processes (which is not to belittle or ignore the path-dependency power
of existing technologies and structures embedded within them).   legitimacy.

In the world of projects, this is altogether compelling. Projects are centrally about
change and movement, and a philosophical basis that is founded on these concepts
seems to make most sense. It also clarifies the practical difficulties that confound
practitioners as they seek to implement the representationalist technologies that are
consequential on a being ontology. How, for instance, can one draw an organisation
chart when the 'organisation' is continually changing in terms of membership, roles
and responsibilities?

A becoming ontology demands that we continually question categories and divisions
that are routinely seen as fixed. Paradoxically, a becoming ontology is more secure
intellectually since it provides a kind of 'concreteness check' on the tendency towards
reification that Whitehead warns us of. It is an antidote to what one might term the
'hardening of the categories'. Setting an agenda around ontology means that we must
think about and question our understanding of the nature of the world, and the nature
of the entities that make up the world. To hold a becoming ontology is to demand that
we question boundaries on the basis that these are always human constructions and
mere 'empirical' manifestations of conceptual categories. In this sense, a becoming ontology is fundamentally critical, continually driving us to ask basic questions, to question
received wisdoms, and to be impatient with ready answers. However, this is not to say
that it celebrates cynicism or nihilism. Rather, it demands that we not only question
what is, but that we also construct imaginative answers to the questions that we pose.

What is a project? Project as language and practice

In the context of projects, the most immediate question centres on the nature of projects.
In short, what is a project? Usually, we tend to think of a project as a temporary
endeavour undertaken to create a unique product or service and we recognise its existence in the spoors of managerial technologies – budgets, organisation charts, bar
charts and so on. A becoming ontology compels us to think differently, to consider a
project as an emergent outcome of disparate, ambiguous, political practices. Specifically,
it moves us away from the metaphor of the project as an organism, with a defined goal
or function, embedded in an environment populated by other organisms. Instead, we
find it much better to think of a project first as a language, and second as a practice.
In this section we will explain why we find this valuable.

First, we assert that a project is a language, competing in a set of language games. The project comes to be, as it were, as the language of the project is created; it continues to exist and 'expand' as more and more individuals participate, use and invent the project's language. And it ceases to be – its 'unwelcome' – as the language of the project and of the particular community (as an idiosyncratic network of relations) in which it is embedded dies and is forgotten. Here, we draw on Wittgenstein's (1953) notion that language is always situated and can only be understood in terms of specific 'forms of life'. Associated with each form of life is a 'language-game', consisting of a vocabulary and a set of language rules that are developed and modified in the course of ongoing social practice.

Thinking of a project as a language provides an interesting and ironic perspective on the discourse of project management. One of the reasons why this discourse has flourished is because of the 'silo mentality' in organisations wherein there are perceived communication barriers between departments or functional units. In language terms, the departments are isomorphic with distinct languages – hence we have a sales language, a production language, an accounting language and so on. Project management has been proffered as a potent integrating mechanism to counter the (linguistic) fragmentation that is rampant in the contemporary organisational setting. Ironically, however, the solution has been to impose yet another language into the mix – namely the language of project management, with its vocabulary of bar charts, resource histograms, work breakdown structure, project life cycle, balanced matrix, project risk analysis, critical path method and so on. Underpinning the promulgation of project management is an ideology that project management does provide a unifying language, a kind of organisational Esperanto, that desperately needs to be learned and used across the organisation. While there may be some merit in this argument, it is essentially no different from the arguments previously used by languages that are now indigenous to the organisational context, such as the language of accounting, marketing, quality and so on.

A becoming ontology also reminds us of language's undecidability and inherent ambiguity – *différance* in Derrida's lexicon. The very success of project approaches is that they expect and enable ambiguity, uncertainty and risk, conditions that perhaps underpin their success in creating contexts for innovation and learning. In contrast, the potential difficulty with a being ontology is its intolerance for ambiguity – akin to the king's intolerance for inaccuracy in maps – that ultimately may cause as many problems as it solves.

This celebration of ambiguity and of difference leads us to change the vocabulary and images we use when speaking about projects. In particular, the concept of a project team seems excessively rigid from this perspective, since teams, axiomatically, have a well-defined, singular goal.

As story 4 indicates, projects are complex, ambiguous, confusing phenomena wherein the idea of a single, clear goal is at odds with the reality, most especially in the earlier stages of a project. Hence we need a metaphor that recognises that goals (plural) are

Story 4   It's all Greek to me

One of us spent over a year observing a project team at work, sitting in on project meetings in a quasi-ethnographic manner. Despite having experience in software development, project management and the pharmaceutical industry (the domains of the team's activities), the researcher understood very little of what was said at the meetings. In conversation with members of the project team afterwards, it became clear that many team members shared this feeling, although nobody was willing to admit this publicly.

emergent, provisional outcomes rather than preexisting, fully formed and singular. For us, the metaphor of 'community' is appropriate because communities are necessarily heterogeneous, containing many different points of view and different values. Also communities are emergent. They are extremely difficult to 'engineer' to fit a given task, since their membership and values emerge in the flow of work activity. Furthermore, thinking about the project as a community rather than as a team is important because it reminds us that political skills are the crucial skills in the realm of community organisation (note that we tend not to speak about communities being 'managed'). In centring on the political domain, the key role of the manager shifts to one of identifying and reconciling difference in a context where difference, and changing difference, is axiomatic. These changes are significant, because if the world is an effect produced by language, then changing our language does, in fact, change our world. Community also offers the potential to develop a more sophisticated understanding of the nature of (project) work, learning and identity, especially when it is articulated with the concept of practice, to which we now turn.

In this section, we draw on recent work by Andreas Reckwitz (2002), who outlines the characteristics of a 'practice theory', building on and connecting the works of diverse authors including Bourdieu, Garfinkel, Giddens, Latour, late Foucault and Weber. The vocabulary and perspective of these practice theorists – and Reckwitz is quick to acknowledge the dangers of merging such a diverse group into one category – is that they are opposed to purpose-orientated (*homo economicus*) and norm-orientated (*homo sociologicus*) models for explaining action. Instead, they highlight the importance of shared or collective symbolic structures of knowledge in understanding both action and social order. For instance, Giddens (1984) stresses that an agent's ability to act is best understood by recognising the agent's skill in drawing on a shared cultural stock of knowledge which both constitute and give accounts of an agent's action. For Giddens, the agent's knowledge is more practical than theoretical (or, to use Polyani's terms, it is tacit rather than explicit knowledge). In this sense, the social is thoroughly located in 'practices' which Giddens defines as 'a routinised form of behaviour which consists of several elements, interconnected to one another: forms of bodily activities, forms of mental activities, "things" and their use, a background knowledge in the form of understanding, know-how, states of emotion and motivational knowledge' (1984: 249).

An especially influential strand within practice theory has been Lave and Wenger's work on 'communities of practice' (Lave and Wenger, 1991; Lave, 1993; Wenger, 1998). They take a unified approach to work practices (which are routinely portrayed as stable, routine and regulated by procedures) and learning (which is usually seen as a creative activity, inimical to work practices). In their view knowing is not about abstract, objective information; rather it is about engaging with, and learning to function in, a community. This functioning is not restricted to explicit, formal, expert skills but also encompasses learning about the community's viewpoints, the language it uses, the relations of importance and so on. 'If context is viewed as a social world constituted in relation with persons acting, both context and activity seem inescapably flexible and changing' (Lave, 1993: 5). In a similar vein, Brown and Duguid (1991) argue that many ethnographic studies of work have shown that actual work practices often diverge from the ways organisations 'describe that work in manuals, training programs, organizational charts and job descriptions'. Their work is rich in evidence that routinely highlights the situated nature of work, and knowing in practice. From their perspective, structural and procedural arrangements may facilitate or constrain work, but not determine it. Similarly 'learning' and 'generating knowledge' are thought to be separate from work practice, perhaps even requiring special arrangements – such as project groups – or protected areas (like an off-site training workshop) to occur. However both of these assumptions rest on a being ontology of work and knowledge coupled with a desire to represent both in terms of formal abstractions from practice, the result being that the fluidity and detail of working and knowing get lost in the abstraction.

Lave treats 'community' as a network of relations from which forms of participation emerge. Her use of this metaphor is rich in messy stuff, in conflict and contradiction and dilemmas of participation that can only be resolved in situated local practice. Her view of learning attempts a synthesis of the individual and the structural, which recognises each element's co-constructive role:

> Activities, tasks, functions, and understandings do not exist in isolation; they are part of broader systems of relations in which they have meaning ... Learning thus implies becoming a different person with respect to the possibilities enabled by these systems of relations ... learning involves the construction of identities. (Lave and Wenger, 1991: 53)

Her relational account of interaction expands the view of learning as 'cognitive change' to include a sense of the person 'becoming' as they engage with community activities. The 'community of practice' metaphor can be drawn on to develop an account of what it is project members are participating in. The aim is to use the metaphor in a generative manner to explore the ways of being/possible selves that are constrained or facilitated through people's participation in work practice. Rather than seeing 'individual' or 'community' as the primary focus for analysis, the assumption here is that both are mutually constituted through language in action.

This is a social constructionist view of participation in project contexts in which, as Bateson (1972) suggested, the map is not the territory. This shifting view of language

handwritten: Language is action
handwritten: – legitimacy.

from representation to construction, from a container of knowledge to a constructer of realities, moves us from asking 'what do we know about the world?' to 'what language games do we participate in and what are the consequence and prizes attached to such games?' Language is seen as action, not as a precursor to it:

> As Wittgenstein (1963) proposed, language gains its meaning not from its mental or subject-ive underpinnings, but from its uses in action (language games). Or again emphasizing the significant place of human relatedness in postmodern writings, language gains its meaning within organized forms of interaction. (Gergen and Joseph, 1996: 370)

handwritten: 2.30
handwritten: 4.80

The community of practice metaphor serves as an exemplar of a language of 'becoming' (and indeed a 'becoming of language') to understanding project activities. It moves away from a purely instrumental (modernist?) understanding of projects to highlight the constructed, and often contested, nature of participating in projects. While we believe that such a perspective on projects is generative, it would be folly to suggest that our goal should be to strive for, for example, the 'creation' or 'engineering' of communities of practice in actual project networks. Though the language of 'community' and 'learning' often connotes positive environments it could equally be likely that through participation in particular project contexts members learn to withdraw from risk, resist change and become positioned as marginalised from further project activities. To return for a moment to themes addressed in the call for papers for the second 'Making Projects Critical' workshop[1]:

> there are strong arguments that project working typically leads to the removal of discretion and autonomy from skilled and committed employees and a tendency to deskill project workers of all levels.

Through involvement in project contexts participants may experience negative impacts. The value of a community of practice lens is not that, if used 'properly' in empirical contexts, it somehow avoids such outcomes, but rather that through its emphasis on how project activities and members identities are co-constructed it allows us to consider the many possible emergent features and consequences in project contexts.

So far, so critical (echoing the 'making projects critical' theme), we have identified some of the limits of a 'being' perspective on project activity, highlighted an alternative 'becoming' ontology of projects, and elaborated on how this may help us to view projects differently – through the exemplar of the community of practice metaphor. Yet if we are sincere about our claim that activities, identities and consequences are emergent from particular language games then is it not incumbent on us to reflect also on the possible consequences of our 'becoming' language game? In the remainder of the chapter we attempt to move beyond the dichotomy of being and becoming to consider the epistemological and ethical concomitants of a becoming ontology.

Epistemologising

Our first point relates to an ever-present danger in all dichotomies, namely that each pole is in one sense constituted and defined by its opposite. For example, the concept of 'black' only has meaning because we understand its opposite, 'white'; 'black' is in 'white' and vice versa. While we may seek to privilege one end of a dichotomy, the mutual indwelling of the two poles means that we necessarily highlight the other end as well. Something akin to a dog chasing its tail, the net effect of any attempt to privilege one pole of a dichotomy is that the *dichotomy* (or perhaps dualism is a better term) is privileged over other potential interpretative frames. Similarly, Law's (1994: 15) point that we should have a 'sociology of verbs rather than a sociology of nouns' – a classic statement of a becoming ontology – may be alluring but it is also unrealistic and naive, since one could hardly dispense with nouns *tout court*. (It might be churlish to add that, since every transitive verb requires a noun, Law should really have been arguing for a sociology of *intransitive* verbs.)

Another issue is that the desire to celebrate a becoming ontology – which may partly be inspired by professional and career aspirations – may lead us to an unwarranted demonisation of a being ontology. Things really do come to be; artefacts are made; things are constructed; sometimes a concrete floor is just a concrete floor. The twist to Whitehead's fallacy of misplaced concreteness is that it is just as much a fallacy to mis-place the *absence* of concreteness. A related point is that the valorisation of a becoming ontology may only superficially mask a deeper epistemological two-timing. A particular instance of this is when a becoming ontology is touted as a better, more improved form of representationalism (see Woolgar, 1986, for development). Moreover, in staying at the level of debating ontological positions in a dichotomous fashion we run the risk of forgetting that even 'co-constructed communities' create consequences for those involved in practice. There is a danger that we simply embrace a 'becoming' ontology as a cleverer and better representation of organising and project work without fully reflecting on some possible consequences of our shift in language either for the study of project contexts or for those who work in such contexts.

A related criticism of the postmodernist/constructionist position is that ultimately it is based on some form of relativism. The common argument is that social construc-tionists tend to be interested in construction processes and are more or less mute on questions such as whether 'true' or 'false' knowledge is manufactured or who loses and who wins in the construction processes (Star, 1991). These are important criticisms.

The ethics of becoming

The path of postmodern criticism of the modernist, instrumental, objectification of organisations, projects, knowledge and so on has been well-trodden. We have argued here that a 'becoming' ontology avoids this instrumental objectification with its language of process, fluidity and co-construction. But while this language is beloved of critical academics (ourselves included), are there any ethical considerations around its use? It seems to us that the language of projectification underpinned by a *being* ontology can clearly exhibit the kind of instrumental rationality that legitimises the entitative and objectified treatment of projects, project goals, outcomes and participants (both in academic and practitioners' language games). But so too can a *becoming* ontology, with its emphasis on language of emergent properties, ambiguity, fluidity in relations and so on. At this point we can focus the issues around a number of questions that, for us, seem pertinent and important.

The first issue relates to identity. From a becoming/practice perspective, work, learning and *identity* are co-produced through language in action. Hence, perceived changes in work and organisational environments will lead to changing accounts of 'possible selves'. For instance, the pervasiveness of information and communication technologies in the contemporary organisation has given much credence to Foucault's ideas of the 'disciplined individual', wherein one governs oneself by performing actions in which one is oneself the object of those actions (Foucault, 1977, 1979, 1988). Recently, Gabriel (2002: 176) has spoken about the 'glass cage' – reworking Weber's famous metaphor of the iron cage – within which people now work, under continual (self-)surveillance and discipline, through 'total exposure to the eye of the customer, the fellow-employee, the manager'. An important consequence of this, for Gabriel, is that the self becomes 'fragile'. This echoes Richard Sennett's (1998) examination of the personal consequences on contemporary work forms (where projects hold almost iconic status). An important consequence is the creation of a 'pliant self, a collage of fragments unceasing in its becoming, ever open to new experience – these are just the psychological conditions suited to short-term work experience, flexible institutions, and constant risk-taking' (Sennett, 1998: 133). Also in 1998, Wallulis (1998) wrote about the demise of the 'secure individual', contrasting the current uncertainty about work and family life with a previous generation where there were career ladders, long-term marriages, and incessant and transparent progress in the standard of living. Drawing on earlier work by Kotter (1995) and Capelli (1999), Cadin (2004) has recently contrasted the 'classical' and 'boundaryless' career to exemplify the shifts in work practices, contexts, language games and identity (see Table 3.1).

Table 3.1 Classical and Boundaryless Careers

	Classical career	Boundaryless career
Environment	Stable	Turbulent
Organisational structure	Bureaucratic	Project-based
Career progression benchmark	Objective	Subjective
Favoured career path	Standard and scaled	Idiosyncratic

Source: Cadin (2004: 1)

What interests us, and what we think is apposite to this collection, is the conjunction and mirroring of the language games between critical academics of a constructionist/ postmodern persuasion and that of project practitioners. For instance, Sennett reports that an IBM executive once told the sociologist Walter Powell that the flexible corporation 'must become an archipelago of related activities'. Powell, in turn, speaks of how 'networklike arrangements are lighter on their feet ... than pyramidal hierarchies ... they are more readily decomposable or redefinable than the fixed assets of hierarchies' (Sennett, 1998: 23). This language of becoming echoes a similar lexicon propounded by other academics, gurus and intellectuals in the late 1980s and early 1990s. Kanter – who sought to teach giants how to dance – and Peters – who helped us live with chaos – are exemplars of the period:

> It is better to view economic activity in terms of clusters of activity sets whose membership composition, 'ownership', and goals are constantly changing. Projects rather than positions are central. (Kanter, 1991: 85)

> The new 'bestest' will probably be alternative outfits that consist of *networks* of small, medium, and large firms gathered to do today's (and not necessarily tomorrow's) task as best they can ... the surviving organisation will resemble a floating crap game of projects embedded amid networks of multiple organisations. (Peters, 1990: 75)

This projectised approach to work was taken up with gusto during the 1990s, reflected most noticeably in the growth in membership of the professional bodies. The Project Management Institute (PMI), founded in 1969, now has 200,000 members worldwide, while the International Project Management Association (IPMA) has 30,000 members. Most of this growth occurred during the 1990s (in 1990, the PMI had only 8,500 members).

If the language games of critical academics and practitioners converge more around the temporary and uncertain, do we (as critical academics) simply further legitimate the proliferation of ambiguous, risky, short-term alliances in project contexts with the possibly negative and fragmentary consequences for those working in such contexts? At heart, the issue is whether critical management academics are unwitting participants, providing much of the vocabulary for a new language game, a new point of view that is appropriated by some for particular political interests. This language provides a justification for an abandonment of stability and provides a rhetoric that people will buy into, even though these may be the very people who would most benefit from and need stability.

The ideas of Antonio Gramsci, while formulated in a different time and context, go some way towards explaining and understanding this connection between academics and practitioners. The question that Gramsci (Gramsci *et al.*, 1971; Gramsci and Forgacs, 1988) addressed was simple: 'Why/how do the exploited willingly consent to and accept a conception of the world that belongs to the rulers?' For us the question relates to how and why those working in a project environment – which is characterised by insecurity, anxiety, unstable careers, fragile and corroded identities – accept the world view of the elite, in this case the (project) managerial elite and the owners of capital. In answering this question, Gramsci identified three central processes. First, *universalism* describes the way in which the dominant group manages to portray its parochial interests and obsessions as the common interests of all people. Second, *naturalism* describes how a given way of life is reified to the point where it is equated to nature. In turn, this leads to quietism on the basis that it is pointless to seek to counter that which is natural. Third, *rationalism* describes how the ruling group gives rise to a class of intellectuals who theorise and thus justify/perpetuate the existing way of life. While Gramsci was seeking to understand events in Italy in the 1930s, at least for us his ideas resonate with contemporary phenomena. In particular, his articulation of the relationship between intellectuals – including academics – and an elite group is especially apposite.

Building communities of virtue

Practice theory and particularly the literature on communities of practice provide a valuable and insightful way of thinking about organisational life and identity. Our objective in this final section of the chapter is to retain much of this theoretical scaffolding of practice theory but to reorient it towards issues of value, virtue and ethics. We flag this shift by speaking about communities of virtue rather than communities of practice. (Our understanding of virtue draws especially on the writings of Alasdair MacIntyre (1984).)

Our first point is perhaps aimed at ourselves. We have presented a becoming ontology as a more authentic and more human paradigm, which does not suffer from the instrumentalism and inhumanity of a being ontology. But, and we alluded to this at the outset of the chapter, a being ontology only becomes problematic *in excess*; a map that is the territory is useless, but that does not mean that all maps are useless. One can and indeed must implement and operate the representationalist technologies of management but one must always be alive to the danger that this may lead one to seeing humans as simply and *only* a means to an end. Here, Martin Buber's (1970) distinction between I–it (instrumental) relationships and I–thou (human) relationships provides a useful and clear way of remembering and repeating this important point.

Our second point seeks to address the 'spiritual' crisis in project work head on. Virtue, ethics and morality have a place in projects and this must be reflected in the discourse of project management. Perhaps the best-known distillation of this discourse is the Project Management Body of Knowledge (PMBOK), published by the Project Management Institute (PMI, 2004). It is telling that this document is silent on these topics.

We are not necessarily calling for a new entry to be added to the PMBOK list of its current knowledge areas: integration, time, quality, human resource, communications, risk and procurement. Neither would we like to see ethics in a project domain reduced to instruction in the application of philosophical approaches – for example, utilitarianism versus Kantian ethics – to ethical dilemmas confronting the project manager. Rather, we would advocate an approach founded on the concept of virtue, which was perhaps best described by Aristotle as a character trait that manifests itself in habitual action. Consistent with our earlier discussion on practice theory, both Aristotle and MacIntyre see virtues as being fundamentally grounded in *practice*, which the latter defines as

> any coherent and complex form of socially established cooperative human activity through which goods internal to that form of activity are realized in the course of trying to achieve those standards of excellence which are appropriate to, and partially definitive of, that form of activity, with the result that human powers to achieve excellence, and human conceptions of the ends and goods involved, are systematically extended. (MacIntyre, 1984: 185)

Central to this definition is MacIntyre's distinction between 'internal' and 'external' goods. The former relates to the type of reward that is *exclusively* obtained through the activity itself while external goods relate to rewards, for example money, that may be obtained through a variety of means. This leads him to define a virtue as '*an acquired human quality the possession and exercise of which tends to enable us to achieve those goods which are internal to practices and the lack of which effectively prevents us from achieving any such goods*' (MacIntyre, 1984: 191, original emphasis). Obedience to rules, standards of excellence, tradition and community play an important role in MacIntyre's theoretical architecture: 'To enter into a practice is to enter into a relationship not only with its contemporary practitioners, but also with those who have preceded us in the practice, particularly those whose achievements extended the reach of the practice to its present point' (1984: 194). At the same time, a practice is not an institution (the latter being primarily concerned with external goods).

MacIntyre's ideas are important, even if the implications are not always clear, and when they are clear they tend to be uncomfortable. Related to the project domain, one would suspect that he would *not* see project management as a practice, on the basis that 'Tic-tac-toe is not an example of a practice in this sense, nor is throwing a football with skill; but the game of football is, and so is chess. Bricklaying is not a practice; architecture is' (MacIntyre, 1984: 187). He would likely bemoan the spread of decontextualised educational programmes such as the MBA and, in the domain of project management, PMI certification. These programmes create a managerial class whose members stand outside practice, since they are concentrated on external goods (which can be pursued and obtained in a variety of domains). He might also assert that the fact that (project) management is not a practice is consistent with the spiritual emptiness of the domain.

What then should one do? In these last few paragraphs we will merely outline an agenda for practitioners and, in particular, academics. First, we believe that the concept of virtue needs to be brought back into the discussion and, in particular, into the questions we ask. What do we mean by virtue and why is it important? Which particular virtues should we celebrate and why? Are there universal virtues (history would shed some doubt on this)? What is the relationship between virtue and practice, between virtue and community, and between virtue and tradition? Are there specific virtues associated with the project domain? Does the notion of the 'project domain' run counter to a theory of virtue? How might an orientation towards virtue change academic research and teaching?

The second theme relates to how MacIntyre's notion of practice – one that is grounded in community and tradition – might change our understanding of education, and management education in particular. For MacIntyre, education does not stand outside of practice and it is certainly not a practice on its own. Instead, it is a derivative aspect of particular practices. For MacIntyre, 'teaching is involved in a variety of practices and … teaching is an ingredient in every practice … [but] teaching is never more than a means … it has no point and purpose except for the point and purpose of the activities to which it introduces students' (MacIntyre and Dunne, 2002: 9). Again, this does not sit easily with our current understanding of education. It does, however, provide an intriguing basis for re-imagining pedagogy. One educationalist who has engaged with MacIntyre's ideas is John Roberts, whose experiences with alternative modes of teaching in Cambridge provide a very useful pedagogical prototype (Roberts, 1996).

Finally, the ideas worked through in this chapter provide a basis for a new form of engagement by academics with the institutions of project management, such as the IPMA and PMI. Contrary to MacIntyre's position, these institutions are equally concerned with internal as well as external goods, in so far as they are very much involved in regulating and defining practice. Bearing in mind Gramsci's warning that academics may (unwittingly) provide a legitimating language for new elites, we have a role to play through directly engaging with such institutions. Akin to Socrates who plied his trade in the middle of the marketplace, we need to be in *media res*, in the middle of things, not just sitting idly by concocting better representations of the world 'out there'. Our language moves from capturing knowledge to techniques for engaging participation in project groups – participation aimed at generating unforeseen relationships, encouraging dialogue and stimulating multiple inputs. It is important to point out that our aim is not to supplant practitioners' voices with new trendy postmodern terms, but rather to listen carefully to what practitioners have to say – to draw on vivid stories to highlight challenges, useful techniques or crises that practitioners have experienced:

praxis / phronesis

> An account of a company's venture into overseas markets, how the basic structure of the organization was changed, how people lost and gained jobs, and the attendant excitements and frustrations, may be vivid and empathically absorbing. The specific details cannot be generalized across time and organizations. However, in these concrete detailings, others can more easily locate relevant analogies. In this sense, the language of the circumscribed theory can have greater use-value than the highly general and abstract offering. (Gergen and Joseph, 1996: 374)

justifying case

studies that contextualise lived experience

What is the role of researchers and commentators on project management in this becoming ontology? To draw on Gergen's (Gergen and Joseph, 1996) image, under the modernist assumptions we were polishing mirrors to better reflect the world to those who didn't have our educated eyes to see reality as it was. Now perhaps we are better cast as crystal ball gazers – we present a view of the world in the hope that it may be 'to tell it as it might become'. The point of our story is not to abandon other ontologies or forms of knowing (such as techniques for project groups) but to recontextualise them (and their questions) in a manner that creates more generative possibilities for theory and practice.

Note

1. The second 'Making Projects Critical' workshop, with the theme 'Projectification and its Discontents', was held at Bristol Business School, University of the West of England, on 13–14 December 2004.

References

Bateson, G. (1972) *Steps to an Ecology of Mind*. New York: Ballantine Books.
Brown, J.S. and Duguid, P. (1991) 'Organizational Learning and Communities-of-Practice: Toward a Unified View of Working, Learning and Innovation', *Organization Science*, 2(1): 40–57.
Brown, J.S. and Duguid, P. (2000) *The Social Life of Information*. Boston, MA: Harvard Business School Press.
Buber, M. (1970) *I and Thou*. Edinburgh: Clark.
Cadin, L. (2004) 'Are "Boundaryless Careers" Worthwhile', *ESCP-EAP News*, 8(Autumn): 1.
Capelli, P. (1999) *The New Deal at Work: Managing the Market-Driven Workforce*. Boston, MA: Harvard Business School Press.
Chia, R. (1995) 'From Modern to Postmodern Organizational Analysis', *Organization Studies*, 16(4): 579–604.
Cooper, R. and Burrell, G. (1988) 'Modernism, Postmodernism and Organizational Analysis: An Introduction', *Organization Studies*, 9(1): 91–112.
Foucault, M. (1977) *Discipline and Punish: The Birth of the Prison*. Harmondsworth: Penguin.
Foucault, M. (1979) 'Governmentality', *Ideology and Consciousness*, 6: 5–21.
Foucault, M. (1988) 'Technologies of the Self', in L.H. Martin, H. Gutman and P.H. Hutton (eds), *Technologies of the Self: A Seminar with Michel Foucault*. London: Tavistock, 16–49.
Gabriel, Y. (2002) 'Glass Palaces and Glass Cages: Organizations in Times of Flexible Work, Fragmented Consumption and Fragile Selves', *Ephemera*, 3(3): 166–84.
Gergen, K.J. and Joseph, T. (1996) 'Organizational Science in a Postmodern Context', *Journal of Applied Behavioral Science*, 32: 356–78.
Giddens, A. (1984) *The Constitution of Society*. Cambridge: Polity Press.
Gramsci, A. and Forgacs, D. (1988) *The Gramsci Reader: Selected Writings, 1916–1935*. London: Lawrence & Wishart.
Gramsci, A., Hoare, Q. and Nowell-Smith, G. (1971) *Selections from the Prison Notebooks of Antonio Gramsci*. London: Lawrence & Wishart.
Habermas, J. (1971) *Toward a Rational Society*. London: Heinemann.
Kanter, R.M. (1991) 'The Future of Bureaucracy and Hierarchy in Organizational Theory: A Report from the Field', in P. Bourdieu and J.S. Coleman (eds), *Social Theory for a Changing Society*. Boulder, CO: Westview Press, 63–87.
Kotter, J.P. (1995) *New Rules: How to Succeed in Today's Post-Corporate World*. New York: Free Press.
Lave, J. (1993) 'The Practice of Learning', in S. Chaiklin and J. Lave (eds), *Understanding Practice: Perspectives on Activity and Context*. Cambridge: Cambridge University Press, 3–32.
Lave, J. and Wenger, E. (1991) *Situated Learning: Legitimate Peripheral Participation*. Cambridge and New York: Cambridge University Press.
Law, J. (1994) *Organising Modernity*. Oxford: Blackwell.
MacIntyre, A. (1984) *After Virtue*, 2nd edn. London: Duckworth.

MacIntyre, A. and Dunne, J. (2002) 'Alasdair MacIntyre on Education: In Dialogue with Joseph Dunne', *Journal of Philosophy of Education*, 36(1): 1–19.

Peters, T. (1990) 'Prometheus Barely Unbound', *Academy of Management Executive*, 4(4): 70–84.

PMI (Project Management Institute) (2004) *A Guide to the Project Management Body of Knowledge (PMBOK Guide)*, 3rd edn. Newtown Square, PA: Project Management Institute.

Reckwitz, A. (2002) 'Toward a Theory of Social Practices: A Development in Culturalist Theorizing', *European Journal of Social Theory*, 5(2): 243–63.

Roberts, J. (1996) 'Management Education and the Limits of Rationality: The Conditions and Consequences of Management Practice', in R. French and C. Grey (eds), *Rethinking Management Education*. London: Sage.

Sennett, R. (1998) The Corrosion of Character: The Personal Consequences of Work in the New Capitalism. London: W.W. Norton.

Star, S.L. (1991) 'Power, Technologies and the Phenomenology of Conventions: On Being Allergic to Onions', in J. Law (ed.), *A Sociology of Monsters: Essays on Power, Technology and Domination*. London: Routledge, 26–56.

Tsoukas, H. (1998) 'The Word and the World: A Critique of Representationalism in Management Research', *International Journal of Public Administration*, 21(5): 781–817.

Wallulis, J. (1998) *The New Insecurity: The End of the Standard Job and Family*. Albany, NY: SUNY.

Weber, M. ([1921] 1968) *Economy and Society*. Totowa, NJ: Bedminister Press.

Weick, K.E. (1995) *Sensemaking in Organizations*. Thousand Oaks, CA: Sage.

Wenger, E. (1998) 'Communities of Practice: Learning, Meaning and Identity', in R. Pea, J.S. Brown and J. Hawkins (eds), *Learning in Doing: Social, Cognitive, and Computational Perspectives*. Cambridge: Cambridge University Press.

Whitehead, A.N. (1925) *Science and the Modern World*. New York: Macmillan.

Wittgenstein, L. (1953) *Philosophical Investigations*. Oxford: Blackwell.

Woolgar, S. (1986) 'On the Alleged Distinction between Discourse and Praxis', *Social Studies of Science*, 16: 309–17.

4

Conflicting and conflated discourses? Project management, organisational change and learning

Mike Bresnen

Introduction

Project management as a field of study has, until comparatively recently, been dominated by a discourse in which the effective achievement of specific time, cost and quality objectives has been the driving concern (for example, Cleland and King, 1975; Lock, 2000; Meredith and Mantel, 2000). With continuing observations that project performance across a range of activity often still fails to meet expectations (for example, Winch, 1996), the search continues for more and more effective systems of planning, organisation and control to improve project performance. One result of this is that there now exists a very extensive literature on the problems and challenges of project management which contains a wide range of tools and techniques that managers can apply to their projects in order to achieve more effective project performance (for example, Maylor, 2002). Another result is the increasing visibility and impact of institutions associated with the field of project management – such as the Project Management Institute in the USA and the Association for Project Management and the International Project Management Association in Europe (Grabher, 2002a; Hodgson, 2002: 807–8). Together, these developments signify a much greater prominence of the field than hitherto as well as greater buoyancy in the market for knowledge regarding the use of management techniques for improved project performance.

At the same time as this proliferation of work on project management tools and techniques, there has been increasing interest in the possibilities for cross-fertilisation of knowledge and practice between project-based and non-project-based settings. Part of this interest has centred upon the implications for project management of new management ideas. In some project-based sectors, such as construction and aerospace, the attempt to draw upon, absorb and exploit new management thinking in non-project settings such as manufacturing has been explicit and used to underscore programmes of research (for example, Gann, 1996). Elsewhere, the incorporation of new management ideas and techniques has been more implicit and ongoing as such ideas and techniques have inevitably spread into new areas of application outside of where they first originated. The field of project management has of course long drawn upon mainstream management and organisational theory to provide recipes for project management success – in the areas of motivation, leadership and organisational structure, for example (see Boddy and Buchanan, 1992; Briner et al., 1996).

The traffic, however, is not all one-way. What is particularly interesting about current developments in management theory and practice is the extent to which project management has become part of a more mainstream management discourse focused around the changing nature of organisations and management (Hodgson, 2002). This partly reflects the continuing diffusion of project management concepts and theories from the 1970s onwards from sectors – such as construction, defence and aerospace – with which they were traditionally associated into a wider range of management activity (Morris, 1994). It also reflects perceptions of a greater alignment between the complex and dynamic circumstances in which contemporary organisations are said to operate and the presumed benefits of project management as a more flexible and innovative way of working (Gann and Salter, 2000; Hobday, 2000). However, the increasing importance attached to project management also importantly reflects the greater ubiquity in recent years in the use of the idea of the project as a vehicle of organisational change and development and of the increasingly widespread use of project management methodologies for the implementation of new organisational practices.

Project management has therefore become something of a leitmotif in discussions and debates about organisational design and innovation (Lundin and Midler, 1998; Ekstedt et al., 1999; Lundin and Hartman, 2000). On the face of it, project organisation is a way of working that ought to facilitate, or at least be consistent with, processes of organisational change and learning. After all, projects are inherently developmental in nature and often have built into them the flexibility and fluidity needed to respond to changing circumstances. Moreover, specific task objectives provide a clear focus for the integration of knowledge from diverse sources (functional, organisational). At the same time, however, it could just as well be argued that the ephemeral and transitory nature of projects makes it more difficult to embed new management initiatives or new organisational learning in well-established, generic routines, practices and systems. Critics of the role of project management in organisational change point to the inherent contradiction between a project's emphasis on short-term task objectives and the longer-term developmental aspects of organisational learning (Grabher, 2002a). Increasing attention has also been directed towards examining the problems faced by project organisations in being able to capture and diffuse cross-project learning (DeFillippi, 2001; Prencipe and Tell, 2001; Newell et al., 2003). Furthermore, it is clear that, in many project settings, the infrastructure within which new initiatives can be embedded is often not that of the single organisation, but rather one which encompasses networks of inter-organisational and institutional relationships within which projects are undertaken (Gann and Salter, 2000; DeFillippi, 2001; Grabher, 2002a; Sydow and Staber, 2002).

It is with this potential (dis)association between project management and organisational change and learning processes that this chapter is centrally concerned. Given the constraints and contradictions noted above, the idea that there is a syllogistic relationship between project management and organisational change and learning, in which the one is intimately and positively interconnected with the other, becomes deeply problematic. Instead, it becomes more appropriate to assume that there may be basic contradictions and antagonisms between project-basing as a mode of operation and longer-term processes of organisational change, innovation and learning (Grabher, 2002a). Furthermore, the development of project management as a discipline – to the extent that it involves the increasing refinement of instruments of planning, organisation and control (Hodgson, 2004) – may exacerbate this tendency. The divergent production of knowledge often associated with creative thinking, new knowledge production and organisational learning may increasingly depend upon new forms of cross-professional, cross-organisational and cross-sector working that tend to be project-based (for example, Gibbons et al., 1994). However, the tools and techniques increasingly being made available to project managers are primarily those designed for convergent problem-solving activity and for achieving closure and conformance to specific task requirements (Morris, 1994; Maylor, 2002).

Having said that, there are many different kinds of project activity and many different types of setting in which projects are undertaken, which suggests the need for sensitivity to the contingencies that are likely to affect the interplay of project management and organisational change and learning processes (Prencipe and Tell, 2001). Projects themselves are often creative entities, involving the generation and application of new knowledge, some of which can undoubtedly be captured and applied elsewhere (for example, Faulkner and Anderson, 1987; Grabher, 2002b). Conversely, organisational change often implies the implementation of new processes that are themselves not unduly innovative or complex and therefore comparatively easy to make routine within the organisation. Consequently, it becomes important to understand the factors and circumstances likely to facilitate or inhibit project-based organisational change and learning.

The aim of this chapter is, therefore, to attempt to move towards a more refined critical awareness of the relationship between project management processes, on the one hand, and organisational change and learning processes, on the other. To achieve this aim, the chapter draws upon existing research on project management in many fields. This includes many of the author's own recent research on project-based organisation and learning – based mainly, but not exclusively, on research in the construction sector. The chapter sets out to examine project organisation and management not only as a *vehicle* for organisational change and learning, but also as a primary *location* for such processes – where attempts to introduce new management practices have major implications for ways of working within project organisations. In differentiating between project and non-project settings, the argument is developed that, in many important ways, project management discourse represents the antithesis of the discourse surrounding broader themes of organisational change, innovation and learning. This is not meant to suggest that change, learning and innovation do not occur within projects, but rather that the wider diffusion of managerial ideas within project-based organisations is inherently problematical (DeFillippi, 2001).

The chapter proceeds by first examining the increasing influence of project management thinking and how it embodies a particular way of viewing the organisational realm that reflects the characteristic problems of projects. In doing so, project management is found to incorporate certain epistemic assumptions that differ from those found in discourses surrounding organisational change and learning (Knorr-Cetina, 1999). These revolve in particular around the emphasis in the field upon more mechanistic versions of management theory (Hodgson, 2002), the focus upon the project and project organisation as the main unit of analysis for study and the emphasis placed upon sector-specific research. The main part of the chapter then systematically contrasts several key features of project and non-project organising in so far as they impact upon processes of innovation, change and learning.

Project management, organisational change and learning

Project organisation and project management have not only become mature fields of study in their own right in recent years (Morris, 1994), but have increasingly become part and parcel of mainstream management thinking about the problems of organisational change and learning. At one level, project organisation is becoming an increasingly common phenomenon in organisations, to the extent that it is even held up as a metaphor or model for organisation in late modernity (Drucker, 1993). The features of project organisation that make it particularly appealing to those interested in new modes of organisation are its task orientation and team-based mode of operation, combined with its presumed flexibility and adaptability. These 'adhocratic' elements of project organisation appear to align well with changing environmental circumstances and offer, it would seem, an alternative to more rigid and inflexible bureaucratic forms of organisation. Critical commentators are quick to point out, however, that far from being antithetical to bureaucracy, project management is itself an apparatus of quite explicit and mechanistic control – albeit output-based (Cammack, 2000; Hodgson, 2004). Instead of representing a shift to more decentralised, flexible forms of organisation, therefore, project management in many ways embodies bureaucratic rationality and positivistic thinking.

A second, more modest claim for project management is that it is increasingly becoming an important way of organising complex products and/or linking cross-functional tasks within functionally differentiated bureaucratic organisations (Gann and Salter, 2000; Hobday, 2000). Consequently, project management structures and management techniques become grafted onto what are essentially bureaucratic organisational forms in order to facilitate the achievement of specific, localised task objectives. In some circumstances, working relationships may be formalised and constituted in an explicit team-based structure or matrix organisation (see Galbraith, 1973). In other circumstances, relationships may be much more short-term, task-focused and informal. Whatever the arrangement, the presumption is that project-basing is an important mode of organising in its own right and/or that it can form a useful corrective to the fragmentation commonly found in functional hierarchies. The main issue then becomes how to align the needs of temporary project organisations with those of the established organisation(s) in which they are embedded (Lindkvist *et al.*, 1998; Lundin and Midler, 1998; O'Dell and Grayson, 1998; Ekstedt *et al.*, 1999; Gann and Salter, 2000; Hobday, 2000; Grabher, 2002a).

A third way in which project management is becoming more important in understanding the dynamics of contemporary organisations is in how it relates to processes of knowledge creation, sharing and learning within and between firms (Ayas, 1996; DeFillippi and Arthur, 1998; Hobday, 2000; Prencipe and Tell, 2001; Bresnen *et al.*, 2003). The link between project organisation and knowledge creation is not new, as evidenced in the extensive literature available on the organisation and management of R&D activity. What is new is the broadening out of the debate concerning processes of knowledge creation, sharing and learning to encompass a wider range of intra-organisational and inter-organisational circumstances in which project management also happens to be the norm (DeFillippi, 2001; Grabher, 2002a).

New product development is one important arena in which project-basing has always been the mode of organisation for activities that are centrally concerned with knowledge creation, sharing and learning (Tidd, 1995). Sectors such as construction and aerospace provide archetypal examples of a potentially more complex situation, in which new product development coincides not only with the use of non-routine production or assembly processes, but also with complex patterns of project-based, inter-organisational relationships (Sayles and Chandler, 1971; Cherns and Bryant, 1984; Gann, 2000). The extreme challenges facing project organisation are perhaps typified in sectors such as biotechnology. Here, the development of new products in a rapidly changing technological and competitive environment relies upon complex webs of relationships joining together a range of actors, including scientists and medical practitioners, biotechnology firms, pharmaceutical corporations, medical institutions and venture capitalists (Powell *et al.*, 1996, 2002; Oliver and Liebeskind, 1998; Murray, 2002).

At the same time, project organisation as a mode of working is not without its difficulties and commentators regularly highlight the main features of projects and project organisation that make achieving satisfactory performance a perennial problem (for example, Grabher, 2002a: 207–8). These include the one-off, often unique nature of project tasks and objectives; the finite and often short duration of project life cycles; and the subdivision of work into distinct project stages (such as conception, design and implementation). Added to this, project tasks – whether they involve engineering projects, R&D activity, film-making, advertising campaigns or other project-based activity – are also often complex and uncertain. Projects are therefore seen as having specific requirements that make them difficult to embed neatly within routine organisational processes and which require the development of specific modes of organisation and management techniques, practices and routines. The organisational and managerial features that project task characteristics give rise to include a reliance on temporary, project-based teams and modes of organisation (Goodman and Goodman, 1976; Bryman *et al.*, 1987); extensive inter-functional, inter-professional and often inter-organisational team working (Bresnen, 1990); and the establishment of project-based systems of management and information flow (Hobday, 2000).

Exploring differences in epistemic culture

The response from within the discipline of project management has been the development and refinement of methodologies, tools and techniques for project management that are designed to achieve greater closure, finality and certainty in the achievement of project objectives. Prescriptions for the effective management of projects now abound and an extensive body of knowledge, backed up by the development of supporting institutional mechanisms, now exists to support project organisation and management (for example, Cleland and King, 1975; Bergen, 1986; Love, 1989; Wearne, 1993; Morris, 1994; Lock, 2000; Meredith and Mantel, 2000; Maylor, 2002).

What is particularly noticeable about the field of project management, however, is the way in which it conceptualises organisation and management, drawing extensively upon operational research and systems theory applications and rather less perhaps upon behavioural and social theory (for example, Cleland and King, 1975). An exception that proves the rule here is Boddy and Buchanan's (1992) identification of 'participative' and 'political' perspectives on project management that counterbalance what they see as the overwhelming influence of a 'rational–linear' perspective. Despite this and similar contributions, however, the field continues to be dominated by a discourse that is firmly rooted in more mechanistic versions of management theory (Seymour and Rooke, 1995; Hodgson, 2002). In contrast, the study of organisational change and learning has always been significantly informed and shaped by work within the fields of organisational theory and behaviour, psychology, sociology and related disciplines (for example, Levitt and March, 1988; Cohen and Sproull, 1996). Although strategic management and management of change concerns often drive the agenda for the exploration of issues, there is a clear recognition of the importance of the social and the psychological that permeates work in these fields (Collins, 1998; Argyris, 1999; Dawson, 2003).

These differences in the nature and emphasis in the knowledge bases of project management and organisational change and learning perhaps reflect, at a deeper level, differences in epistemic cultures between the two fields (Knorr-Cetina, 1999). The idea of epistemic cultures refers to differences in the mechanisms and arrangements used within given fields that help constitute 'how we know what we know' (Knorr-Cetina, 1999: 1). Different methodologies used in practice to conduct research and develop theory constitute different sets of practices and routines that reflect the impact of individual agency and socially established norms and conventions. Important differences in the 'machinery of knowing' between fields within a discipline (in this case, management) therefore have important implications for the articulation and validation of knowledge and suggest that there may be important incommensurabilities that exist between diverse knowledge bases. The relevance of this type of analysis to the two fields of study of interest here is that both derive from 'knowledge-in-action', rather than from a predefined body of knowledge which is located within clear disciplinary parameters (as is the case with medicine, law and accountancy). Both bodies of knowledge therefore constitute an amalgam of knowledge that is drawn from various disciplines and, crucially, informed by practice as well as theory.

One subtle but important difference in the 'machinery of knowing' between the two fields can be seen in the way in which projects and their organisational settings are superimposed upon one another in the study of project management and organisational change processes (Bresnen and Swan, 2002). Most analyses of project management naturally bring projects themselves to the foreground – often depicting the project as essentially dynamic and set within a more or less static organisational context. This can be of benefit in drawing attention to the systemic needs of projects. However, it can also tend to create a false sense of order and stability in the organisational background and thereby obscure an understanding of how project-based systems dovetail with those within the wider, changing lattice of organisational relationships in which they are embedded.

Conversely, the organisational change and learning literature naturally brings the organisational context as a whole to the fore. Again, this is crucial in understanding organisation-wide complexities. However, particularly in organisations in which organising by project is the norm (for example, in aerospace, construction, engineering and parts of the media), it can downplay the constraints imposed by project-based systems on wider organisational change processes. It may, for example, be the case that project management processes within such organisations are so well-developed that they act as stultifying influences on attempts to introduce more broadly based managerial initiatives. The problem this reduces to is the commonly encountered methodological quandary of whether to adopt the project or the organisation as the unit of analysis. Significantly, the tendency within the project management field is to opt for the former.

Another important epistemic difference is in the tendency for research on project management to be highly sector-specific – a tendency that contrasts with work on organisational change and learning that is concerned more with understanding generic learning processes. One implication is that industry-based analyses tend to present views of the field that reflect narrower institutional assumptions and perspectives. In the construction industry, for instance, work has highlighted the engineering slant put on the reproduction of knowledge (Seymour and Rooke, 1995; Bresnen and Marshall, 2001). Another implication is that the comparative analysis of project management across industry sectors is very rare indeed.

Although these points emphasise important differences in epistemic culture between the two fields of study, it also needs to be recognised that there are epistemic similarities too, suggesting some common ground between the two fields of study. For example, both fields are heavily oriented towards practice and dependent upon the influx of knowledge from a range of actors, including academics, consultants and practitioners. In other words, 'Mode 2' knowledge production is well-established (Gibbons *et al.*, 1994). Moreover, certain perspectives (for example, systems theory) and methodologies (for example, action research) have been highly influential in the development of each field. Within this broader range of differences and similarities in epistemic culture, it therefore becomes useful to assess the more precise differences between processes of project management, on the one hand, and organisational change, innovation and learning, on the other. It also becomes important to understand the extent to which these differences are influenced by variation in the characteristics of different types of project task.

Contrasting project management and organisational change/learning processes

There are a number of ways in which one would expect project management processes to differ markedly from organisational change and learning processes. These are identified and discussed under the seven thematic headings below.

Project objectives and life cycles

One well-established feature of mainstream theories of organisational learning and change is the distinction between single-loop and double-loop learning (Argyris and Schon, 1978; Argyris, 1999). Whereas single-loop learning involves the identification of mismatches between intentions and outcomes, double-loop learning is a more profound form of learning that derives from a deeper questioning of underlying values and assumptions built into existing routines and practices. As such, it resonates strongly with organisational change initiatives in which the transformation of existing norms and values is considered important (Argyris, 1999).

The connection here with project management is simply that project goals, objectives, systems and processes are designed precisely to achieve single-loop learning.

Project objectives are second-order derivatives of broader organisational goals and, even in the unusual circumstances where the project constitutes the organisation (for example, in the case of a major charity event such as Live Aid), the underlying values and norms that underpin the project are expected to remain intact. This does not of course mean that projects cannot develop their own momentum that leads to the pursuit of new goals and objectives. Nor does it mean that there is no possibility of innovation and learning within the parameters set for the project. However, it does mean that, for the most part, the rethinking of goals and objectives is antithetical to the effective management of projects, which operate according to a logic of finality and closure and the monitoring of performance against preestablished, well-defined goals and objectives. This can, of course, lead to the escalation of commitment in pursuit of those objectives (Staw, 1981) – a phenomenon sometimes observed in military and civil aviation projects. However, such escalation provides evidence in its own right of the driving logic of single-loop learning.

The finite duration of projects and their cyclical nature also have significant implications for the capture of knowledge and the embedding of learning associated with organisational change. Rather than being able to presume that the organisational context surrounding the introduction of change can be taken more or less as given, the nature of projects means that it is necessary to take into account their inherent variability and dynamism. One implication is that the actual duration of the project may affect the ability to introduce and embed new management practices within existing arrangements for the management of projects. A longer-duration project may allow more opportunity for the sedimentation of new practice and the routinisation required that there is simply not enough time for on shorter-duration projects. If the organisation's activities as a whole consist of short-duration projects, then this may have wider implications for the ability to introduce and embed new systems and procedures.

A second implication is that the pace of project working may have an impact upon the introduction of new practices. On the one hand, it might be difficult for new practices to be embedded where there is a lack of rhythmic synchronisation with wider organisational systems (Brown and Eisenhardt, 1997). On the other hand, the use of deadlines, milestones and other time-based controls can provide the 'coupling' that supports the inter-functional communication and reflection necessary for wider organisational learning (Lindkvist et al., 1998).

A further implication of project life cycles relates to the separation of work into stages. Although staged implementation is common in organisational change initiatives as well, there may be more opportunity for fresh iterations that take into account feedback on the effects of change. In project environments, although the overlap of stages may be commonplace, such overlaps pose major problems of integration (for example, Morris, 1973; Bresnen, 1990) and perhaps provide less opportunity for feedback and adjustment, as the overwhelming necessity becomes the drive towards completion.

Sharing knowledge and learning through social networks

Another key feature that has important implications for the ongoing sharing of knowledge and learning is the existence of organisational fragmentation and discontinuity (Bryman *et al.*, 1987; Bresnen, 1988). Research more generally has emphasised the importance of social networks for understanding flows of knowledge and learning within and across organisations (for example, Brown and Duguid, 1991, 2001; Lave and Wenger, 1991; Hansen *et al.*, 1999; Wenger, 2000; Hansen, 2002). Social networks are also important for underpinning the development of social and intellectual capital within organisations (Nahapiet and Ghoshal, 1998; Adler and Kwon, 2002). Such an emphasis on the social transmission of knowledge and learning echoes a long-standing focus in the management of change literature on the importance of social interaction in the change process (for example, Kotter and Schlesinger, 1979; Pettigrew, 1985; Dunphy and Stace, 1988; Collins, 1998).

Understanding the diffusion of knowledge in project settings also depends upon understanding social interaction (DeFillippi and Arthur, 1998; Hansen, 2002; Bresnen *et al.*, 2003). However, the key point about projects is that, in a number of important ways, they create problems for the development and consolidation of the types of social relations that have been shown to enable the diffusion of knowledge and learning throughout the organisation. First, there is the simple difficulty of forming and sustaining knowledge-sharing entities, such as 'communities of practice' (Brown and Duguid, 1991; Lave and Wenger, 1991) in conditions characterised by discontinuities in staffing and constant team-building and rebuilding focused around specific project tasks. Practitioner experience suggests that developing and sustaining communities of practice is a difficult enough exercise (Wenger, 2000), without the added complication of regular and frequent breaks in working relationships. Discontinuity in organisation and the regular reconstruction of new teams are, however, the norm in project environments (Bryman *et al.*, 1987; DeFillippi and Arthur, 1998). The author's research into partnering in the construction sector, for example, has highlighted how the diffusion of knowledge and experience of inter-firm partnering is not only crucially dependent upon, but also constrained by, staff availability and associated secondment practices (Bresnen and Marshall, 2000, 2002).

Second, research has consistently indicated that knowledge creation and dissemination are made easier when the actors involved in the process are more homologous (for example, McPherson and Smith-Lovin, 1987). However, two key features of many forms of project organisation – extensive inter-professional and inter-organisational working – suggest that heterogeneity is more likely to be the norm. Inter-organisational and inter-professional relationships may of course configure in complex ways: it is not uncommon, for instance, to find very close working relationships between similar professionals operating in different organisations (Bresnen, 1990; Bouty, 2000). Regardless of this complexity, however, it is apparent that different cognitive schemas and relational norms – associated with different professional and/or organisational values, codes and norms (see Nahapiet and Ghoshal, 1998) – are likely to act as impediments to the diffusion of knowledge and learning.

Team-building and socialisation processes

The above discussion draws attention to the importance of team-building and socialisation processes in the transmission of knowledge and learning. It could, of course, be argued that the recurrent dismantling of teams and the redistribution of staff with experience of new ways of working helps create a network of weak ties that aids the sharing and diffusion of knowledge and new practice (Granovetter, 1973). However, it has also been shown that, although weak ties may enable the transmission of knowledge that is more explicit, they tend to be less effective than strong ties in enabling the transfer of more complex, tacit forms of knowledge (Hansen, 1999; Hansen et al., 1999; Hansen, 2002). Yet, it is precisely such more tacit forms of knowledge and the need to 'enculture' new ways of working (Blackler, 1995) that are often central to longer-term processes of organisational change and learning. Consequently, to the extent that they involve the break-up and reconfiguration of teams, project team assignment practices work against the wider consolidation and sharing of knowledge through social networks.

Project team-building can, of course, promote the development of strong, local ties centred upon the achievement of specific project objectives. Moreover, such ties may be of the non-redundant type (for example, inter-professional), which may be important in the generation of new knowledge or innovative practice (Hansen et al., 1999). However, such ties may also, as a result, be so strong that they promote an isolation and insulation of the team from wider organisational and environmental influences, thus effectively inhibiting organisational change and learning (Uzzi, 1997; Portes, 1998; Gargiulo and Benassi, 2000; Bresnen et al., 2004). In other words, one possible scenario (where inter-professional and inter-organisational differences are not so acute) is that strong project subcultures become so loosely coupled from the wider organisation that they militate against broader processes of organisational change and learning (O'Dell and Grayson, 1998; Dubois and Gadde, 2002).

A more likely scenario, however, is simply that lack of staff availability constrains the development of project teams and the socialisation needed to inculcate new norms and values. Research on project organisation tends to report the common experience as being one in which project teams are given relatively little time to form and yet face an imperative to reach optimum performance levels as quickly as possible (for example, Bryman et al., 1987; Bresnen and Marshall, 2000, 2002). This puts a premium on the development of 'swift trust', rather than the resilient trust that is able to develop over a longer period of time as partners interact more and more with one another (Meyerson et al., 1996; Ring, 1997). There may of course be 'idle time' during the course of a project that provides extra scope for closer within-team interaction and bonding (DeFillippi and Arthur, 1998). However, this may be offset by the regular turnover of team members as the project progresses from one stage to the next and the recurring need to incorporate and socialise new members is experienced (Bryman *et al.*, 1987). All in all, such conditions can create an instability that complicates processes of socialisation and disrupts patterns of legitimate peripheral involvement that are important for knowledge-sharing and diffusion (Lave and Wenger, 1991).

Diffusing knowledge and learning

Research on the diffusion of knowledge and learning more generally has emphasised the situated nature of knowledge and the difficulties in capturing and transferring learning from one context to another (Lave and Wenger, 1991; Cook and Brown, 1999). This is because the widespread diffusion of innovations in practice (across projects, organisations and sectors) depends on their abstraction from context and their re-embedding in potentially quite different circumstances (for example, Swan and Clark, 1992). Not only does this create a tension between formal tools and techniques available and actual management practice (Hislop *et al.*, 1997), but the resultant translation can distort ideas as they are being applied, with new knowledge being reinterpreted and reconstructed to suit operating and organisational conditions (Røvik, 1998).

In other words, management ideas and practices have some 'interpretative flexibility' (Bijker *et al.*, 1987) and the implementation process itself can have significant implications for how such initiatives are made sense of and enacted (see Weick, 1995; Orlikowski, 2002). In the case of projects, the problem is enormously magnified, to the extent that 'each project is different'. Knowledge obtained from one project becomes difficult, if not impossible, to transfer to the next as it depends crucially upon task and context. In the case of engineering, construction and aerospace projects, for example, variation in client requirements, product specifications, geospatial conditions and performance criteria are all likely to make the extrapolation of learning from one project to the next extremely difficult.

On the face of it, knowledge that is more concerned with changes in management process should be more easily diffused as it involves an abstraction from context. Film-making or advertising, for example, can lead to the generation of new ways of producing, directing and editing work that is artistically highly variegated (Grabher, 2002b). However, it is clear that the greater opportunity for contingent application is precisely what creates scope for the reinterpretation and translation of new ideas into practice. Moreover, recent research has demonstrated how the diffusion of new process knowledge across projects is as much, if not more, dependent upon the social learning processes involved (Newell *et al.*, 2003). 'Reinventing the wheel' may therefore be an inevitable and essential part of the process of embedding new ways of working in such conditions. Film-making again offers a good example of the learning processes that producers, writers and actors sometimes face when confronted with the different ways that film directors use to direct and manage their projects (Morley and Silver, 1977).

A further problem arises when one considers that it is the inherent ambiguity of management ideas that is often considered to be the key to their diffusion within and across organisations (Bijker *et al.*, 1987; Clark and Staunton, 1989). In project settings, however, it is not at all clear how ambiguity in management practice squares with a discourse that emphasises precise objectives and targets and the management (and reduction) of risk and uncertainty. In other words, the ambiguity of management ideas might be more of a barrier to implementation in project environments than it is elsewhere.

Embedding knowledge and learning in organisational routines

Such impediments to the diffusion of knowledge and learning in project environments have broader consequences for the ability of the organisation to strategically develop its core competencies and dynamic capabilities (Dosi *et al.*, 2000; Zollo and Winter, 2001). Learning in business units, including projects, always faces the prospect of being too localised (Levinthal and March, 1993). In a context in which projects are the norm, there are also considerable problems in developing any kind of longer-term 'organisational memory' (DeFillippi and Arthur, 1998). These problems reflect the basic tension between the success of the project, on the one hand, and the viability of the organisation, on the other (DeFillippi and Arthur, 1998; O'Dell and Grayson, 1998).

It has long been recognised that a key challenge facing those introducing organisational change is the need to embed new knowledge and learning in organisational systems, practices and routines that support and reinforce the change and which habituate members of the organisation to different ways of working. In a project setting, however, there is a potential mismatch between the systems and routines available to support longer-term learning and those dedicated to the pursuit of shorter-term, more specific project objectives (Dubois and Gadde, 2002). Studies of post-project reviews, for example, demonstrate how routine project management processes can fail to encourage or, at worst, inhibit, cross-project learning (Busby, 1999; Kotnour, 1999). Indeed, many commentators have highlighted the very standardised nature of project management systems and routines that effectively recreate the self-reinforcing tendencies of bureaucratic mechanisms (for example, Cammack, 2000; Hodgson, 2002).

Prencipe and Tell (2001) develop this theme by exploring the constraints on learning within project-based firms that stem from different combinations of mechanisms for experience accumulation, knowledge articulation and codification (what they label different 'learning landscapes' within project-based firms). Although their analysis is used specifically to suggest that different learning landscapes may help develop project-based firms' dynamic capabilities (see Teece *et al.*, 1997; Zollo and

Winter, 2001), their work shows first and foremost the problematic nature of project-based learning. Their analysis supports other work, more specific to the construction sector, which also demonstrates how project-basing militates against organisational learning and the diffusion of new management ideas through its effects on the firm's 'absorptive capacity' (Winch, 1998; Gann and Salter, 2000; Gann, 2001; Dubois and Gadde, 2002).

Although it receives comparatively less attention, there is also a potential mismatch between human resource management practices within the firm and project management performance requirements. In some project settings, such as the performing arts, the relationship between individual development and organisations is highly attenuated, as individuals gain work and develop their careers by building a portfolio of project-based work and accomplishments, rather than through in-house career development (Faulkner and Anderson, 1987). Early, prominent studies of project management in other settings were quick to recognise that the structures and systems devised for project organisation and management do not necessarily dovetail well with the job and career plans of individuals. Sayles and Chandler (1971), for instance, highlighted the dangers of 'professional obsolescence', as individual experts in the aerospace sector devote too much time to project-based working – a problem at the individual level for which matrix organisation was proposed as a possible solution. The conflict between project management and organisation-wide, human resource management practices is a perennial one. Recent research has demonstrated, for instance, the difficulties of developing pan-organisation training, communication and career development activities for professional staff against a backdrop of project-based working and operational performance requirements (Bresnen *et al.*, 2003).

Change management practices

Embedding new learning in organisational routines also involves consideration being given to change management practices. Strategic management perspectives emphasise the importance of factors such as the scope and depth of change and the style of implementation as having an important bearing upon the appropriateness and effectiveness of organisational change (Dunphy and Stace, 1988). Kotter and Schlesinger (1979), for example, stress the importance of the acceptance of change and identify alternative implementation strategies whose application depends upon particular circumstances. Similar prescriptions can be found in other management of change models that place an emphasis upon the importance of internal context and process (for example, Pettigrew and Whipp, 1991; Dawson, 2003).

There are a number of ways in which these ideas sit uneasily with the requirements of project working. First, there are the constraints, already identified, which inhibit the development of double-loop learning and which, by the same token, significantly diminish the likelihood of radical (that is, widespread and deep) change. Second, project timescales and deadlines may again have implications by seriously curtailing any attempt to develop wide-ranging consultative or participative implementation strategies (Kotter and Schlesinger, 1979). Moreover, not only may there be insufficient 'slack resources' in the form of time to devote to discussion of new changes, but time taken in implementing new ideas may also be seen as a distraction from more pressing project demands. Clearly, there will be differences between projects in the amount of 'idle time' available that acts as an extra resource and/or in the urgency attached to project deadlines (DeFillippi and Arthur, 1998). Moreover, milestones and deadlines may act as important coupling mechanisms linking project and wider organisational systems and goals (Lindkvist et al., 1998). However, for the most part, one would expect time constraints on projects to act as a major impediment to the social processes involved in the implementation of organisational change.

Third, project environments are quite often those in which interaction is governed as much, if not more, by formal, commercial contracts between individuals and organisations, as opposed to internal, hierarchical relationships (Bresnen, 1996a). Where formal contracts are the norm, strategies for implementing change will therefore inevitably require more in the way of negotiation and formal agreement. It may be the case that levels of trust have developed sufficiently in the relationship to enable interaction and the negotiation of change to become more flexible and informal (Ring and Van de Ven, 1994). However, this will depend upon a number of factors, including prior experiences of benefits obtained from the relationship. Research undertaken by the author in the construction sector suggests a further paradox: namely, that it is precisely in those circumstances where greater flexibility is needed (for example, when dealing with more complex and uncertain tasks) that organisations are predisposed to adopt a more conservative, contractually based approach (Bresnen, 1990). Consequently, the introduction of change may engender even more caution in project settings than elsewhere.

Supporting institutional norms and practices

A final important theme is the impact of broader institutional-level effects on the development of knowledge, learning and capabilities in project-based working. Institutional settings can have an important direct impact upon the diffusion of new ideas through processes of mimetic and normative isomorphism that help spread and embed new organisational and management practices and which thereby play an important part in legitimating change and benchmarking practice (Powell and DiMaggio, 1991).

One problem with project environments, however, is the lack of firm and consistent institutional reference points. Project management techniques and practices constitute a body of knowledge that takes a particular slant on the problems of project organisation and whose origins are based in a very specific type of project environment (that is, large-scale engineering work). The professional bodies that articulate and promote this body of knowledge are also more diverse and not as well-established as those in other management disciplines (such as accountancy). Another problem with project environments is that they often occur at the conjunction of diverse institutional interests and perspectives that promote different and conflicting views of the same phenomenon. Project management in construction, for instance, can be viewed as a contested terrain, in which different professional norms and values compete for dominance (Bresnen, 1996b; see also Grabher, 2002b, on advertising).

Given these tendencies towards institutional fragmentation, it becomes important to understand the more complex ways in which knowledge is diffused and legitimated within project environments. Crucially, the spread of new management initiatives and their sedimentation in project management practices and routines occur within a complex web of inter-organisational and inter-professional relationships (Grabher, 2002b; Sydow and Staber, 2002). Windeler and Sydow (2001), for example, in their exploration of the German television industry, have examined how change occurs through the co-evolution of forms of production organisation with new industry practices. The biomedical sector similarly acts as a good example of the development of scientific knowledge within networks of relations between firms that are embedded in a wider institutional context (Powell et al., 1996, 2002; Oliver and Liebeskind, 1998; Murray, 2002). Such complex interactions between institutional processes and emergent practices are also found in construction and engineering, where Winch (1998), for example, has argued that institutional-level effects (diverse professions and institutions) and operational circumstances (project-basing, complex products) combine to militate against the spread of innovative practices (see also Gann, 2000, 2001; Gann and Salter, 2000).

One further crucial difference between project management and organisational change with regard to the effects of context is in the locus of power and influence involved in the implementation and legitimation of change. Organisational change has long been shown to depend upon internal (political) support and a supportive internal climate for change (for example, Pettigrew, 1985; Pettigrew and Whipp, 1991). The context of project management, however, is rather different and it is clear that the legitimation of change depends also upon key external characteristics (for example, whether initiatives conform to contractual requirements). Given these differences in context, it is likely then that initiatives which embody sector idiosyncrasies will be more readily accepted and implemented – in particular, to the extent that they reflect the existing balance of power and influence between groups and institutions within the sector (Elg and Johannson, 1997). In other words, agreement on appropriate performance criteria and metrics, appropriate benchmarks and best practices may depend as much upon conformity to wider project, network and institutional needs as it does upon the needs of the single organisation (Pavitt, 1984; Spender, 1989; Bresnen, 1996a). The downside to this, however, is the encouragement of inward-looking tendencies and the reinforcement of a 'not-invented-here' syndrome within the sector, based on strong project-based subcultures and/or a distinctive industry recipe for change (Katz and Allen, 1982; Bresnen and Marshall, 2001).

Conclusion

This chapter has set out to explore the differences and contradictions between project management as a developing body of knowledge and practice and the wider discourses of organisational change and learning with which it is frequently associated. The main argument that has been developed is that the treatment of the two perspectives as syllogistic is problematic. There are many areas in which the processes that contribute towards the effective management of projects are antithetical to those that

Table 4.1 Summary of key differences between PM and OC/OL discourses

Factors	Project management	Organisational change/learning
Project task characteristics	• Precise task objectives • Finite duration, milestones and deadlines • Clear progression from planning to implementation • Difficulty in routinising processes	• Retain flexibility and adaptability • Extended duration and time to consult and embed changes • Feedback and iteration between planning and implementation • Emphasis on routinising processes
Project team characteristics	• Discontinuities in staffing and team relationships • Project-focused team-building • Minimisation of slack resources, idle time; reliance on 'swift trust'	• Continuity of staff and relationships • Development of organisation-wide communities of practice • Importance of social interaction, training, 'resilient trust'
Wider organisational context	• Project-based management systems • Clearly defined processes and standards for projects • Decentralisation of control for project performance • Limited wider intra-organisational communication and interaction	• Organisation-wide management systems • Organisation-wide processes and standards • Centralised implementation of new management practices • Extensive intra-organisational communication and interaction
Wider network characteristics	• Extensive inter-professional relations across organisations • Inter-organisational contractual relations • Shaping of practices via external referents (contracts, standards)	• Extensive inter-unit relationships within organisations • Intra-organisational authority relations • Shaping of practices by internal policies
Nature of the change	• Incremental change within fixed project parameters • Specific changes made to improve short-term project performance • Clarity and precision in nature of change required	• Wider change in broader organisational arena • Generic changes made to improve long-term performance • Ambiguity allowable to assist diffusion of change

are conducive to the spread of organisational change and learning. Understanding the relationship between the two fields of study therefore requires a greater critical awareness of underlying differences (as well as similarities) in epistemic culture that influence the production and social construction of knowledge. This chapter sets out to contribute to such awareness by reflecting further upon seven key areas of difference between project management and organisational change and learning processes, drawing extensively upon recently published research across a range of project-based environments.

In emphasising the effects of different types of project task and context, the chapter also moves towards a framework for understanding in greater empirical depth the relationship between project management processes, on the one hand, and organisational change and learning processes, on the other. Several key factors have been identified throughout the course of the discussion that are likely to moderate the relationship between project management and organisational change/learning processes. These are formulated as five sets of factors, whose differential impact upon project management and organisational change/learning processes is summarised in Table 4.1. The identification of such differences enables comparisons and contrasts to be drawn between diverse project settings based upon the particular constellation of circumstances that occur. For example, one would expect that projects with more relaxed deadlines and greater continuity in team relationships would be more conducive to the embedding of new management knowledge and learning since they provide, amongst other things, greater opportunity for socialisation and trust to develop. The implication for future research, and indeed for practice, is therefore not only that there is a need to be aware of the potential contradictions between project management and change management processes. There is also a need to be sensitive to variation in project conditions and thus to the contingent effects of project context on the introduction of new management initiatives and on the wider diffusion of organisational knowledge and learning in project environments.

References

Adler, P.S. and Kwon, S.-W. (2002) 'Social Capital: Prospects for a New Concept', *Academy of Management Review*, 27(1): 17–40.

Argyris, C. (1999) *On Organisational Learning*, 2nd edn. Oxford: Blackwell.

Argyris, C. and Schon, D.A. (1978) *Organisational Learning: A Theory of Action Perspective*. Reading, MA: Addison-Wesley.

Ayas, K. (1996) 'Professional Project Management: A Shift Towards Learning and a Knowledge Creating Structure', *International Journal of Project Management*, 14(3): 131–36.

Bergen, S.A. (1986) *Project Management*. Oxford: Blackwell.

Bijker, W.E., Hughes, T. and Pinch, T.J. (eds) (1987) *The Social Construction of Technological Systems*. London: MIT Press.

Blackler, F. (1995) 'Knowledge, Knowledge Work and Organisations: An Overview and Interpretation', *Organization Studies*, 16(6): 1021–46.

Boddy, D. and Buchanan, D. (1992) *Take the Lead: Interpersonal Skills for Project Managers*. London: Prentice-Hall.

Bouty, I. (2000) 'Interpersonal and Interaction Influences on Informal Resource Exchanges Between R&D Researchers Across Organizational Boundaries', *Academy of Management Journal*, 43(1): 50–66.

Bresnen, M. (1988) 'Insights on Site: Research into Construction Project Organisations', in A. Bryman (ed.), *Doing Research in Organisations*. London: Routledge, 34–52.

Bresnen, M. (1990) *Organizing Construction: Project Organization and Matrix Management*. London: Routledge.

Bresnen, M. (1996a) 'An Organisational Perspective on Changing Buyer–Supplier Relations: A Critical Review of the Evidence', *Organization*, 3(1): 121–46.

Bresnen, M. (1996b) 'Traditional and Emergent Professions in the Construction Industry', in I. Glover and M. Hughes (eds) *The Professional-Managerial Class*. Aldershot: Avebury, 245–68.

Bresnen, M. and Marshall, N. (2000) 'Building Partnerships: Case Studies of Client–Contractor Collaboration in the UK Construction Industry', *Construction Management and Economics*, 18(7): 819–32.

Bresnen, M. and Marshall, N. (2001) 'Understanding the Diffusion and Application of New Management Ideas in Construction', *Engineering Construction and Architectural Management*, 8(6): 335–45.

Bresnen, M. and Marshall, N. (2002) 'The Engineering or Evolution of Co-operation? A Tale of Two Partnering Projects', *International Journal of Project Management*, 20(7): 497–505.

Bresnen, M. and Swan, J. (2002) 'Organisational Politics and the Implementation of New Management Initiatives in Project-based Organisations', paper presented at 18th EGOS Colloquium, Barcelona, Spain, 4–6 July 2002.

Bresnen, M., Edelman, L., Newell, S., Scarborough, H. and Swan, J. (2003) 'Social Practices and the Management of Knowledge in Project Environments', *International Journal of Project Management*, 21(3): 157–66.

Bresnen, M., Edelman, L., Newell, S., Scarborough, H. and Swan, J. (2004) 'The Impact of Social Capital on Project-based Learning', in M. Huysman and V. Wolf (eds), *Social Capital and Information Technology*. Cambridge, MA: MIT Press, 231–58.

Briner, W., Hastings, C. and Geddes, M. (1996) *Project leadership*, 2nd edn. London: Gower.

Brown, J.S. and Duguid, P. (1991) 'Organizational Learning and Communities of Practice: Towards a Unified View of Working, Learning and Innovation', *Organization Science*, 2(1): 40–57.

Brown, J.S. and Duguid, P. (2001) 'Knowledge and Organization: A Social Practice Perspective', *Organization Science*, 12: 198–213.

Brown, S.L. and Eisenhardt, K.M. (1997) 'The Art of Continuous Change: Linking Complexity Theory and Time-Paced Evolution in Relentlessly Shifting Organisations', *Administrative Science Quarterly*, 42: 1–34.

Bryman, A., Bresnen, M., Beardsworth, A., Ford, J. and Keil, E. (1987) 'The Concept of the Temporary System: The Case of the Construction Project', in S. Bacharach (ed.), *Research in the Sociology of Organisations*, Vol. 5. London: JAI Press, 253–84.

Busby, J. (1999) 'An Assessment of Post Project Reviews', *Project Management Journal*, 30(3): 23–29.

Cammack, I. (2000) 'Project Management: A Right Brain Career for a Left Brain Century', paper presented at 15th IPMA World Congress, London, May 2000.

Cherns, A.B. and Bryant, D.T. (1984) 'Studying the Client's Role in Construction Management', *Construction Management and Economics*, 2: 177–84.

Clark, P. and Staunton, N. (1989) *Innovation in Technology and Organisation*. London: Routledge.

Cleland, D.I. and King, W.R. (1975) *Systems Analysis and Project Management*, 2nd edn. New York: McGraw-Hill.

Cohen, M.D. and Sproull, L.S. (eds) (1996) *Organisational Learning*. Thousand Oaks, CA: Sage.

Collins, D. (1998) *Organisational Change: Sociological Perspectives*. London: Routledge.

Cook, S.D.N. and Brown, J.S. (1999) 'Bridging Epistemologies: The Generative Dance Between Organisational Knowledge and Organisational Knowing', *Organization Science*, 10(4): 381–400.

Dawson, P. (2003) *Reshaping Change: A Processual Perspective*. London: Routledge.

DeFillippi, R.J. (2001) 'Project-Based Learning, Reflective Practices and Learning Outcomes', *Management Learning*, 32(1): 5–10.

DeFillippi, R. and Arthur, M. (1998) 'Paradox in Project-Based Enterprises: The Case of Filmmaking', *California Management Review*, 40(2): 125–40.

Dosi, G., Nelson, R.R. and Winter, S.G. (eds) (2000) *The Nature and Dynamics of Organisational Capabilities*. Oxford: Oxford University Press.

Drucker, P. (1993) *Post-Capitalist Society*. Oxford: Butterworth-Heinemann.

Dubois, A. and Gadde, L.-E. (2002) 'The Construction Industry as a Loosely Coupled System: Implications for Productivity and Innovation', *Construction Management and Economics*, 20(7): 621–31.

Dunphy, D.C. and Stace, D.A. (1988) 'Transformational and Coercive Strategies for Planned Organisational Change', *Organization Studies*, 9(3): 317–34.

Ekstedt, E., Lundin, R.A., Söderholm, A. and Wirdenius, H. (1999) *Neo-institutional Organising: Renewal by Action and Knowledge in a Project-Intensive Economy*. London: Routledge.

Elg, U. and Johannson, U. (1997) 'Decision-Making in Inter-firm Networks: Antecedents, Mechanisms and Forms', *Organization Studies*, 16(2): 183–214.

Faulkner, R.R. and Anderson, A.B. (1987) 'Short Term Projects and Emergent Careers: Evidence from Hollywood', *American Journal of Sociology*, 4: 879–909.

Galbraith, J.R. (1973) *Designing Complex Organisations*. Reading, MA: Addison-Wesley.

Gann, D.M. (1996) 'Construction as a Manufacturing Process', *Construction Management and Economics*, 14: 437–50.

Gann, D.M. (2000) *Building Innovation: Complex Constructs in a Changing World*. London: Thomas Telford.

Gann, D.M. (2001) 'Putting Academic Ideas into Practice: Technological Progress and the Absorptive Capacity of Construction Organisations', *Construction Management and Economics*, 19(3): 321–30.

Gann, D.M. and Salter, A. (2000) 'Innovation in Project-Based, Service-Enhanced Firms: The Construction of Complex Products and Systems', *Research Policy*, 29: 955–72.

Gargiulo, M. and Benassi, M. (2000) 'Trapped in Your Own Net? Network Cohesion, Structural Holes and the Adaptation of Social Capital', *Organization Science*, 11(2): 183–96.

Gibbons, M., Limoges, C., Nowotny, H., Schwartzman, S., Scott, P. and Trow, M. (1994) *The New Production of Knowledge: The Dynamics of Science and Research in Contemporary Societies*. London: Sage.

Goodman, R.A. and Goodman, L.P. (1976) 'Some Management Issues in Temporary Systems: A Study of Professional Development and Manpower – the Theatre Case', *Administrative Science Quarterly*, 21: 494–501.

Grabher, G. (2002a) 'Cool Projects, Boring Institutions: Temporary Collaboration in Social Context', *Regional Studies*, 36(3): 205–14.

Grabher, G. (2002b) 'The Project Ecology of Advertising: Tasks, Talents and Teams', *Regional Studies*, 36(3): 245–62.

Granovetter, M. (1973) 'The Strength of Weak Ties', *American Journal of Sociology*, 78: 1360–80.

Hansen, M.T. (1999) 'The Search Transfer Problem: The Role of Weak Ties in Sharing Knowledge Across Organizational Sub-units', *Administrative Science Quarterly*, 44: 82–111.

Hansen, M.T. (2002) 'Knowledge Networks: Explaining Effective Knowledge Sharing in Multiunit Companies', *Organization Science*, 13(3): 232–48.

Hansen, M.T., Nohria, N. and Tierney, T. (1999) 'What's Your Strategy for Managing Knowledge?', *Harvard Business Review*, 77: 106–17.

Hislop, D., Newell, S., Swan, J. and Scarbrough, H. (1997) 'Innovation and Networks: Linking Diffusion and Implementation', *International Journal of Innovation Management*, 1(4): 427–48.

Hobday, M. (2000) 'The Project-Based Organisation: An Ideal for Managing Complex Products and Systems?', *Research Policy*, 29: 871–93.

Hodgson, D. (2002) 'Disciplining the Professional: The Case of Project Management', *Journal of Management Studies*, 39(6): 803–21.

Hodgson, D. (2004) 'Project Work: The Legacy of Bureaucratic Control in the Post-bureaucratic Organisation', *Organization*, 11(1): 81–100.

Katz, R. and Allen, T.J. (1982) 'Investigating the Not Invented Here (NIH) Syndrome: A Look at the Performance, Tenure, and Communication Patterns of 50 R&D Project Groups', *R&D Management*, 12(1): 7–19.

Knorr-Cetina, K. (1999) *Epistemic Cultures: How the Sciences Make Knowledge*. Cambridge, MA: Harvard University Press.

Kotnour, T. (1999) 'A Learning Framework for Project Management', *Project Management Journal*, 2: 32–8.

Kotter, J.P. and Schlesinger, L.A. (1979) 'Choosing Strategies for Change', *Harvard Business Review*, 57 March–April: 106–14.

Lave, J. and Wenger, E. (1991) *Situated Learning: Legitimate Peripheral Participation*. Cambridge: Cambridge University Press.

Levinthal, D.A. and March, J.G. (1993) 'The Myopia of Learning', *Strategic Management Journal*, 14: 95–112.

Levitt, B. and March, J.G. (1988) 'Organizational Learning', *Annual Review of Sociology*, 14: 319–40.

Lindkvist, L., Söderlund, J. and Tell, F. (1998) 'Managing Product Development Projects: On the Significance of Fountains and Deadlines', *Organization Studies*, 19(6): 931–51.

Lock, D. (2000) *Project Management*, 7th edn. Aldershot: Gower.

Love, S.F. (1989) *Achieving Problem-Free Project Management*. New York: Wiley.

Lundin, R.A. and Hartman, F. (2000) *Projects as Business Constituents and Guiding Motives*. London: Kluwer Academic.

Lundin, R.A. and Midler, C. (1998) *Projects as Arenas for Renewal and Learning Processes*. London: Kluwer Academic.

Maylor, H. (2002) *Project Management*, 3rd edn. London: Prentice-Hall.

McPherson, J.M. and Smith-Lovin, L. (1987) 'Homophily in Voluntary Organizations', *American Journal of Sociology*, 52: 370–9.

Meredith, J.R. and Mantel, S.J. (2000) *Project Management: A Managerial Approach*, 4th edn. New York: Wiley.

Meyerson, D., Weick, K.E. and Kramer, R.M. (1996) 'Swift Trust and Temporary Groups', in R.M. Kramer and T.R. Tyler (eds), *Trust in Organisations: Frontiers of Theory and Research*. Thousand Oaks, CA: Sage, 166–95.

Morley, E. and Silver, A. (1977) 'A Film Director's Approach to Managing Creativity', *Harvard Business Review*, 55: 59–70.

Morris, P.W.G. (1973) 'An Organisational Analysis of Project Management in the Building Industry', *Building International*, 6: 595–615.

Morris, P.W.G. (1994) *The Management of Projects*. London: Thomas Telford.

Murray, F. (2002) 'Innovation as Co-evolution of Scientific and Technological Networks: Exploring Tissue Engineering', *Research Policy*, 31: 1389–1403.

Nahapiet, J. and Ghoshal, S. (1998) 'Social Capital, Intellectual Capital and the Organizational Advantage', *Academy of Management Review*, 23(2): 242–66.

Newell, S., Edelman, L., Scarbrough, H., Swan, J. and Bresnen, M. (2003) ' "Best Practice" Development and Transfer in the NHS: The Importance of Process As Well As Product Knowledge', *Health Services Management Research*, 16: 1–12.

O'Dell, C. and Grayson, J. (1998) 'If Only We Knew What We Know: Identification and Transfer of International Best Practices', *California Management Review*, 40(3): 154–74.

Oliver, A.L. and Liebeskind, J.P. (1998) 'Three Levels of Networking for Sourcing Intellectual Capital in Biotechnology: Implications for Studying Inter-organizational Networks', *International Studies of Management and Organization*, 27(4): 76–103.

Orlikowski, W. (2002) 'Knowing in Practice: Enacting a Collective Capability in Distributed Organizing', *Organization Science*, 13(3): 249–73.

Pavitt, K. (1984) 'Sectoral Patterns of Technical Change: Towards a Taxonomy and a Theory', *Research Policy*, 13(6): 343–73.

Pettigrew, A. (1985) *The Awakening Giant: Continuity and Change in ICI*. Oxford: Basil Blackwell.

Pettigrew, A. and Whipp, R. (1991) *Managing Change for Competitive Success*. Oxford: Blackwell.

Portes, A. (1998) 'Social Capital: Its Origins and Applications in Modern Sociology', *Annual Review of Sociology*, 23: 1–24.

Powell, W.W. and DiMaggio, P.J. (1991) *The New Institutionalism in Organisational Analysis*. Chicago: University of Chicago Press.

Powell, W.W., Koput, K.W. and Smith-Doerr, L. (1996) 'Interorganisational Collaboration and the Locus of Innovation: Networks of Learning in Biotechnology', *Administrative Science Quarterly*, 41: 116–45.

Powell, W.W., Koput, K.W., Bowie, J.I. and Smith-Doerr, L. (2002) 'The Spatial Clustering of Science and Capital: Accounting for Biotech Firm–Venture Capital Relationships', *Regional Studies*, 36(3): 291–305.

Prencipe, A. and Tell, F. (2001) 'Inter-project Learning: Processes and Outcomes of Knowledge Codification in Project-Based Firms', *Research Policy*, 30: 1373–94.

Ring, P.S. (1997) 'Processes Facilitating Reliance on Trust in Inter-organisational Networks', in M. Ebers (ed.), *The Formation of Inter-organisational Networks*, Oxford: Oxford University Press, 113–45.

Ring, P.S. and Van de Ven, A.H. (1994) 'Developmental Processes of Cooperative Interorganizational Relationships', *Academy of Management Review*, 19: 90–118.

Røvik, K.A. (1998) 'The Translation of Popular Management Ideas: Towards a Theory', paper presented at the 14th EGOS Colloquium, University of Maastricht, The Netherlands, 9–11 July 1998.

Sayles, L.R. and Chandler, M.K. (1971) *Managing Large Systems*. New York: Harper & Row.

Seymour, D. and Rooke, J. (1995) 'The Culture of the Industry and the Culture of Research', *Construction Management and Economics*, 13(6): 511–23.

Spender, J.C. (1989) *Industry Recipes*. Oxford: Blackwell.

Staw, B.M. (1981) 'Escalation of Commitment to a Course of Action', *Academy of Management Review*, 6(4) October, 577–87.

Swan, J. and Clark, P. (1992) 'Organisational Decision-Making in the Appropriation of Technological Innovation: Cognitive and Political Dimensions', *European Work and Organisational Psychologist*, 2(2): 254–85.

Sydow, J. and Staber, U. (2002) 'The Institutional Embeddedness of Project Networks: The Case of Content Production in German Television', *Regional Studies*, 36(3): 215–28.

Teece, D.J., Pisano, G. and Shuen, A. (1997) 'Dynamic Capabilities and Strategic Management', *Strategic Management Journal*, 18: 509–33.

Tidd, J. (1995) 'Development of Novel Products Through Intra- and Inter-organisational Networks: The Case of Home Automation', *Journal of Product Innovation Management*, 22(11): 307–23.

Uzzi, B. (1997) 'Social Structure and Competition in Interfirm Networks: The Paradox of Embeddedness', *Administrative Science Quarterly*, 42: 35–67.

Wearne, S. (1993) *Principles of Engineering Organisation*. London: Thomas Telford.

Weick, K. (1995) *Sensemaking in Organizations*. Thousand Oaks, CA: Sage.

Wenger, E. (2000) 'Communities of Practice and Social Learning Systems', *Organization*, 7(2): 225–46.

Winch, G.M. (1996) 'Thirty Years of Project Management. What Have We Learned?', paper presented to British Academy of Management Annual Conference, Aston University, 1996.

Winch, G.M. (1998) 'Zephyrs of Creative Destruction: Understanding the Management of Innovation in Construction', *Building Research and Information*, 26(5): 268–79.

Windeler, A. and Sydow, J. (2001) 'Project Networks and Changing Industry Practices – Collaborative Content Production in the German Television Industry', *Organization Studies*, 22(6): 1035–60.

Zollo, M. and Winter, S.G. (2002) 'Deliberate Learning and the Evolution of Dynamic Capabilities', *Organization Science*, 13: 339–51.

5

Problematising project management*

Janice Thomas

Introduction

The fundamental existence and nature of project management (PM) are largely taken for granted today. Literature on project management focuses on the prescriptive (how to manage projects) or the descriptive (war stories about what happens on projects) (Thomas, 2000). The function of project management is taken to be the accomplishment of some finite piece of work in a specified period of time, to a specified cost and so on. Project management is presented in a typically modern management fashion as 'a series of carefully delineated steps, executed in sequential order: optimal decisions are made by careful planning and rational logic' (Townley, 2002: 564). Context-independent project management 'best practices' proliferate as a result of the activities of 'experts' and 'professional' associations. These individuals and organisations exist to tell practitioners 'what they should do rather than to take action themselves in a world of second guessers and advisers with little action responsibility' (Meyer, 1994: 54).

However, accepting and applying this orthodoxy does not allow us to avoid project failures. Business press and consulting research (reports by the Standish Group and *CIO Magazine* to name a few) are replete with examples of the 'failure' of projects to achieve their objectives. A number of authors (Dyer and Paulson, 1976; Knight, 1976; Bryman *et al.*, 1988; Ford and Randolph, 1992; Shenhar, 1998) have called for more research and theoretical development around projects and temporary organisations. Another set of authors (Packendorff, 1995; Buchanan and Badham, 1999) have raised questions about the underlying functionalist bias inherent in most project management research. This chapter seeks to further this discussion by critically examining common project management practices utilising a Foucauldian (1972, 1977) analytical

---

*This paper was originally prepared for the International Research Network on Managing by Projects in Calgary in 1998.

approach based in critical management research as advanced by Townley (2002), Alvesson and Deetz (2000) and Flyvbjerg (2001).

I begin by providing a brief genealogy of the project management construct which provides an introduction to its historical construction. In the next section, I outline a similarly brief archaeological analysis (early spadework) of project management practices. Finally, I examine the contradictions inherent in the practice arising out of the dominant discourse of project management. In this way, I hope to illustrate the implications of studying project management practices as a discourse and technology of power rather than as a simple functional tool. I conclude by suggesting that a more critical analysis of project management based on detailed examination of practices may help us get beyond the prescription/failure conundrum.

Beginnings of a project management genealogy

A genealogical analysis (Foucault, 1977) examines 'the diverse set of conditions that make it possible, though not inevitable, that a particular discourse is constituted and developed' (Knights and Morgan, 1991: 270). The main contribution of this form of analysis is the development of an understanding of the historical constitution of the discourse. It is an attempt to show the processes through which discourses change into a qualitatively different set of practices over time. However, there is no assumption of a necessarily linear progression. In fact, recognition of the multiplicity of events impacting the changes is important to a genealogical analysis.

Foucault (1972) associated the term discourse with 'ways of doing things'. From this perspective, a discourse is a set of ideas and practices which condition what is 'seeable and sayable' (Townley, 1994). It is important to understand how certain practices came to be accepted as natural, self-evident and indispensable at certain historical periods, as it is this that allows a discourse to produce its own truth effects. Once a discourse is found to be 'true', problems are defined that the discourse can 'solve'.

The following analysis is not a full-blown Foucauldian genealogical analysis. It simply provides an illustration of how such an analysis would proceed and some guideposts to the type of insights it provides. I undertake two tasks in this section of the chapter. I first explore the definitions and description of projects and project management to provide a foundation for the rest of the analysis. Next I provide a preliminary genealogy of the project management discourse to illustrate the insights such an analysis could produce.

Projects and project management

What is a project? The traditional answer is that a project is any activity that results in a deliverable or a product (for example, Rakos, 1990). A slightly more refined answer would be that projects: involve teams, are temporary in nature, focus on a specific task and are scheduled to be completed within some defined time, cost and performance standards (for example, Ford and Randolph, 1992). These traditional definitions typically focus on a definable activity to be completed within certain constraints.

Over time, the definition of project has evolved. The Project Management Institute definition (PMI, 1996: 4) states that 'a project is a temporary endeavour undertaken to create a unique product or service'. However the next PMI definition (PMI, 2000) of a project evolved to the point that it now includes room for progressive elaboration of the undertaking. Progressive elaboration recognises that the ultimate characteristics of a project are worked out in detail in stages over the life of the project. This relatively recent elaboration of the definition attempts to recognise some of the flexibility needed in managing projects under ambiguous circumstances. However, this addition to the definition appears to be almost an afterthought that does not appear to influence the rest of the material in the PMBOK guide (see Buckle and Thomas, 2003 for a complete exploration of the assumptions embedded in the PMBOK).

Within traditional, hierarchical organisations, projects often function as special-situation structural devices used where a separate, self-sufficient sub-unit is created to oversee the completion of a special activity (setting up a new technological process, bringing out a new product, starting up a new venture, consummating a merger, seeing through the completion of a contract, supervising the construction of a new plant). The project approach is a relatively popular means of handling 'one of a kind' situations having a finite life expectancy and where the normal organisation is deemed unable or ill-equipped to achieve the same results in addition to regular duties (Hardy, 1994). In knowledge-intensive firms, projects tend to be the primary mode of organisation because of the ambiguity and 'one-of-a-kind' nature of the work. In general then, what gets defined as a project is that which is 'not normal' to the operation of the organisation.

The process of managing a project entails planning work in small measurable tasks and tracking effort against outcomes. It is associated with a belief in linear progress, absolute truths, the rational planning of ideal social orders, and the commodification of knowledge and production (Harvey, 1990). The application of project management to uncertain tasks is a way of imposing a scientific, rational approach, thereby increasing the predictability of the outcomes. In other words, it is a means of making 'non-normal' work more 'normal' and understandable.

Project management is defined as the process of planning, organising, directing and controlling professional staff for a relatively short-term objective that has been established to complete specific goals and objectives (Kerzner, 1979, 1992, 2001). Planning includes the preparation of plans and the operation of the tracking system. The organising systems ensure that the appropriate activities are tracked against plans and that deviations are reported to management. Project control provides for control and projection of the critical elements of the project and its process (change control mechanisms) (Humphrey, 1990). The directing or leadership activity addresses the critical human factors of motivation, team spirit and delegation. Note the similarity to standard management practices. The difference between the two seems to lie in the prescribed nature of the time frame and the explicitly defined work objectives. In other words, project management appears to be a more stringent application of management practices on a smaller scale.

Historical development of project management

While projects as an organised activity have been around probably as long as the human race itself, formal project management arose in the late 1950s to manage highly uncertain and typically large-scale projects. This highlights an interesting question. If projects are so central to human, let alone organisational, existence, how did we survive so long without the concept? I think Foucault would suggest that this is an example of the discourse creating the problems for which it claims to be the solution.

The genesis of PM techniques is attributed to the efforts expended by the United States in its race with Russia to built Intercontinental Ballistic Missile Systems (Killian, 1971). The military developed the Atlas missile system in five years. At the time, they estimated that it would have taken twelve years to complete under ordinary management practices. Much of the credit for this accomplishment was attributed to the project management techniques that evolved on an ad hoc basis as a means of dealing with the technological and organisational uncertainties of the project (Dyer and Paulson, 1976). Interestingly, the entire management activity involved in this project evolved in a form of trial and error and learning throughout the project. It was only upon completion of the project that the various tools and techniques developed and retained throughout the project were labelled 'project management'. The tools and techniques that were tried and discarded, and the process of trial and error and learning, were downplayed and eventually largely forgotten.

Subsequently, the Department of Defense forced its major contractors to use these new 'project management' techniques. NASA also adopted these practices in the 1960s space race. Project management became a well-publicised approach. For example, a 1970 *Business Week* article suggested that

> As project teams and task forces become more common in tackling problems, there will be more of what some people call temporary management systems as project management systems where the men [sic] who are needed to contribute to the solution meet, make their contribution, and perhaps never become a permanent member of any fixed or permanent management group. (Quoted in Kerzner, 1992: 31)

There can be no doubt that this publicity hastened the widespread application of the project management concept in such diverse areas as research and development, building construction, education and consulting (Dyer and Paulson, 1976). By the 1990s, project management played a central role in most organisations (Kerzner, 1992; Hardy, 1994; Weick, 1995).

The development of precedence network diagramming techniques for the Polaris submarine project in the early 1960s marks the origin of the academic study of project management (Fondahl, 1987). The primary purpose of this new area of research was to increase the efficiency of organisational operations (such as operations research areas). Much of this literature comes out of technical areas such as aeronautical engineering, construction, information systems and operations management. Early project management techniques focused on understanding the work involved in projects. The 'problem' was defined as how to efficiently coordinate and control the efforts of many workers to meet strict time, cost and results criteria. Research focused on the measurable aspects of project management (specifying the work, estimating the effort, coordinating and planning the work). These early efforts produced sophisticated tools and techniques such as the program evaluation and review technique (PERT) and the critical path method (CPM) that are still in use today.

However, researchers found that these sophisticated techniques alone could not guarantee project success. Researchers began to include the human dimension of projects by looking at the need for developing teamwork and leadership in projects. In the 1960s, studies tended to concentrate on single functional aspects of projects. Topics in this stream of research include assessing project success, questions of human resource management and the management of professionals, communication patterns across projects, and issues of group and team performance. The importance of leadership, motivation and teamwork came to the forefront in the late 1970s (DeMarco and Lister, 1977). While these studies expanded the scope of project management, they tended to do so in an *ad hoc* and singular fashion. Dyer and Paulson (1976) criticised this body of research for its largely prescriptive and descriptive nature. They suggested that empirical work was necessary.

Researchers responded by trying to empirically identify critical success factors for project implementation (Cooper and Kleinschmidt, 1987; Pinto and Slevin, 1988). Included in such universal lists of critical success factors are project mission, project planning and control, top management support, customer involvement and so on. Identifying these critical factors provided a basis for an assumed understanding of how to manage successful projects. That is, there now exists a foundation for a very prescriptive set of 'how to' literature that is acontextual and ahistorical in nature. For every project you must meet every requirement to succeed.

However, project management continued to prove itself fallible (Kharbanda and Stallworthy, 1983; Morris and Hough, 1987; Brunsson, 1993). Project failure is most often attributed to a lack of adherence to project management tools and techniques or poor application of the methods. Many practitioners and researchers indicate that more stringent application of project management tools or development of better techniques will result in more successful projects (Kerzner, 1992; Frame, 1995). At the same time, there is a growing recognition that not all projects are alike and suggestions that one should resist the tendency to characterise all projects as fundamentally similar (Pinto and Covin, 1989). This resulted in a move to identify critical contingencies and project characteristics to better apply appropriate project management tools and techniques in context (see in particular Shenhar, 1998).

In summary, the brief genealogical analysis of the project management concept suggests the following important forces at work in its constitution:

- Project management arose in a highly disciplined environment undertaking tasks that, while highly uncertain in total, were composed of relatively known tasks.
- It originated as a set of *ad hoc* practices developed and used on an as-needed basis over the course of a relatively large and long-duration project. Only after the successful completion of this project were these PM practices reified and made the basis of prescriptions. Practices that started out as emergent and flexible came to be presented as 'the way' to manage projects and the PM discourse took off.
- The publicity and prescriptive literature generated by the successful Atlas and NASA projects led to a widespread adoption of PM practices. In other words, identification of the discourse created the need for its application in more general situations.
- Application of PM practices in less similar circumstances to those in which it originated led to dissatisfaction with the practices and reports of project failures. Because the existing technical tools could not accommodate more complex, less-disciplined organisations or projects, the human factor became important. PM practices extended to include human relations and management needs. Thus, the PM discourse incorporated new and quite substantially different practices (leadership as opposed to CPM).
- Empirical analysis of PM practices in use led to 'truths' about the necessary components of 'successful' project implementation. The discourse created the practice that now supports the continued existence of the discourse. This elaboration and continuation of the PM discourse also led to the development of specialist practitioners and academics who elaborate and extend the discourse.

The whole study and practice of project management tend to support an approach to mastering the arts and teachings (or *techne* in Aristotelian terms) of the field. Largely missing from this area of endeavour is the intellectual grasp of the theory underlying the practice (the *episteme*) or the wisdom needed to use these techniques to deal with real-life problems in concrete cases (the *phronesis*). (See Flyvbjerg, 2001, for an exploration of these knowledge types and their impact on social sciences.) There is a recognition of the need for an understanding of the episteme evidenced in the increase in research and support of research in the field. However, the need for a localised rationality embedded in the specific circumstances of projects and organisations is largely ignored in the search for universalisable, disembodied knowledge and 'formal principles for transcending the contingent (historical) circumstances and particularities that are the foundation of a formal rationality' (Townley, 2002: 556). In this way, project management remains rooted and firmly embedded in the number one priority of modernity – the attempt to eliminate unpredictability (Townley, 2002).

This brief review of the historical constitution of PM as an important discourse in management provides the framework for a similarly brief examination of some of the key practices underlying the PM approach.

Preliminary archaeological spadework

This section aims to disrupt self-evidences of PM and explores how project management practices create order and knowledge that allow power to be exercised. Informed by research which undertakes this task in human resources management (for example, Townley, 1994), accounting (for example, Hoskin and Macve, 1986; Miller and O'Leary, 1987) and strategy (for example, Knights and Morgan, 1991), the theoretical basis for this work is Foucault's (1977) elaboration of the concepts of power–knowledge and governmentality. This is a preliminary presentation of the potential insights of such an analysis based on a small set of representative orthodox authorities, not a detailed and comprehensive analysis of all facets from a Foucauldian perspective.

Representative orthodox authorities

For the purposes of the remainder of this chapter, I illustrate the orthodox approach to PM using two key authors and six texts (Frame, 1994, 1995, 1999; Kerzner, 1979, 1992, 2001). These texts are not chosen as exemplars so much as representative of the dominant discourse over the period. J. Davidson Frame and Harold Kerzner are influential academics and practitioners in the project management field. All of Frame's texts are still in print and Kerzner's text is a well-recognised part of most project managers' and academics' libraries. Kerzner's text is commonly held to be the most comprehensive and academic volume on project management existing today. I use the comparison between the first edition (1979, 478 pages) and the seventh edition (2001, 1,203 pages) of this text to illustrate how project management discourse has changed over the period. Note that the bibliography has not changed dramatically over the period. That is, it is the same size and mostly relies on literature that is at least twenty years old. This supports Jessen's (1991) analysis that project management literature tends to follow organisational theory by about twenty years. An interesting genealogical project may be to show the evolution of Kerzner's *Project Management* text in the context of the organisational and societal changes going on at the same time. The 2001 text is longer at 1,200-plus pages but continues to refer only to those articles that have 'become classics'.

Frame is the founder and director of the International Centre for Project Management Excellence and a senior member of the Project Management Institute. The first two books, *Managing Projects in Organizations* (1995) and the *New Project Management* (1994), attempt to update project management practices with 'special emphasis on avoiding pitfalls and making things happen' (Frame, 1995: back cover). They were written in an attempt to make project management successful in the changing organisational environment. The third text, *Building Project Management Competence* (1999), addresses the same issues from the perspective of the need for increasing the competence of individuals, teams and organisations to manage projects.

Given the increasing evidence (Morris and Hough, 1987; Standish Group, 1994, 2001; Ewusi-Mensah and Przasnyski, 1997, to name a few) of the inability of project management to meet the goals it sets out for itself, both authors recognise some of the inadequacies of project management. However, Frame and Kerzner continue to focus on the benefits of PM and to see the primary function of the technique as the accomplishment of a task in a specified period of time for a specified cost. In many ways this approach seems to be of the 'head in the sand' variety. Knowing that projects do not often (ever?) behave as PM literature would suggest, we continue to study an idealised concept of project at the expense of the lived experience of projects (maybe similar to the study of reproduction versus sex). The implication is that it is not PM practice that is the problem but the faulty implementation of such in organisations. The concept of project management is never problematised or its practices critically explored in these texts.

Power-shaping practice

Foucault explored the 'how' of power rather than the question of 'who' holds power or 'where' it resides. That is, his interest lay in the practices, techniques and procedures that give power effect (Townley, 1994). Power, in this view, is a relational construct. It 'is exercised by the virtue of things being known and people being seen' (Foucault, 1980: 154). Power is also both creative and repressive in this view. Foucault recognises that power can aid in getting things done at the same time as it restricts others' activities. Knowledge formation is not a neutral process but a 'discipline' as simultaneously a body of knowledge and a system of control. Knowledge, acting through discipline, is the operation of power. Power defines what gets to count as knowledge. Foucault's concept of governmentality identifies processes through which objects are rendered amenable to intervention and regulation, being formulated in a particular way through regulatory systems, processes and methods (Townley, 1994).

By dividing work into small tasks and monitoring activity through the subdivision of time and the temporal elaboration of activities, project management can be viewed as a nexus of disciplinary practices aimed at making work predictable, calculable and manageable (Foucault, 1977; Townley, 1995). I will attempt to show that the project management approach increases control not only over work but also over workers. This is in contrast to the common understanding of the project approach which presents workers as relatively autonomous knowledge workers.

Using an approach based on the work of Townley (1994), I first examine how project management techniques identify the project and the team as separable and knowable entities through practices of enclosure, partitioning and ranking. Then I look at how these entities are further elaborated by inscribing the nature of the work and aligning it with time to control effort through implementation of the timetable and control practices. Finally, I discuss the various project management practices that help constitute individuals in particular ways and that allow them to be known and therefore manageable through processes of examination and confession. These concepts are drawn from Townley's use of Foucault to examine personnel practices. For a fuller explanation see Townley (1993, 1994).

Exploring the discipline of project management

Project planning occurs throughout the life cycle of a project. However, the initial phase of any project is usually termed 'project definition' and is the largest planning exercise. The output of this phase is a statement of work (SOW) which specifies the goals and objectives of the project. The SOW must provide all the necessary information so that all participants fully understand all of the work to be performed (Kerzner, 1979, 1992, 2001). This document forms the basis for determining what is considered to be in or out of scope as the project progresses.

In Foucauldian terms, this document serves to identify what is known and knowable with respect to the project and the dimensions of it. This SOW results in the conceptual separation of the project work from the ongoing work of the organisation. It constitutes/defines/creates a project, which then allows certain things to happen. The project is enclosed or 'place[d] heterogeneous to all others and closed in upon itself' (Foucault, 1977: 141). This process of enclosure serves to differentiate the project from the outside organisation. A second form of enclosure results from the spatial separation of the project team from other organisational members. Although introduced to generate cohesion and motivation in team members and to focus activity, physically separating the project team from the organisation increases the visibility of both the work and the team members. Time spent away from the project offices can be noted and commented on.

Once the project task is clearly defined, the work is further organised through the creation of a work breakdown structure (WBS). The WBS 'defines all of the effort to be expended, assigns responsibility to a specially identified organizational element, and establishes schedules and budgets for the accomplishment of the work' (Kerzner, 1992: 543). In Kerzner's (1992: 544) terms:

> The WBS is the single most important element because it provides a common framework from which:
>
> - The total program can be described as a summation of subdivided elements.
> - Planning can be performed.
> - Costs and budgets can be established.
> - Time, cost and performance can be tracked.
> - Objectives can be linked to company resources in a logical manner.
> - Schedules and status reporting procedures can be established.
> - Network construction and control planning can be initiated.
> - The responsibility assignments for each element can be established.

In other words, it provides a conceptual grid that allows the tasks to be known, analysed and managed. This partitioning serves to differentiate the internal workings of the project.

The first task in creating a WBS is to break the project into activities and then into smaller and smaller units. Once each task has been subdivided into work packages (non-subdividable tasks, uniquely identifiable), effort estimates are created. These estimates are often based on 'rules of thumb' for activities of similar nature under-taken in the past (if project management techniques were used in the past these might be based on actual time for similar tasks completed). When the nature of, and effort required, for each task is fully estimated, staffing requirements based on required skills can be drawn up, and individuals can be made accountable for specific tasks. Thus the WBS provides the basis for the vertical and horizontal partitioning of both the work and the individuals on the project. Through a process of ranking the work and individuals with regard to the skills needed, this process further increases the visi-bility of both the work to be done and the individual responsible for accomplishing it.

From this detailed definition of work and responsibility, it is possible to schedule the project and thereby define milestones and critical paths through the project. Not only must achievement of activity be precisely specified, activity must also be con-trolled and coordinated through time. PERT and CPM techniques, network diagrams and other tools are used in this process. In Foucauldian terms, this results in creation of the 'timetable'.

Once there is a clear definition of project scope and initial planning documents created, the next major function of project management is to control the implemen-tation of the plan. The primary way of doing this is through the institution of a pro-ject management or time-reporting system. This system allows for the systematic collection of information on the effort expended and planned effort remaining on all tasks of the project. It produces continual reminders to the project team of desired accomplishments and levels of effort. Activity of individuals thus becomes reported and controlled.

The above practice illustrates how the activity of individuals becomes known and controlled but says nothing about the individual themselves. The time-reporting sys-tem is crucial to the coordination of control on a project. It involves collecting reports of time and resources expended on tasks and estimates of time required to complete the task and applying this against the time scheduled for the task. In this way, the pro-ject team is subjected to a continual examination of effort. Such examination renders individuals and their effort visible and therefore manageable. This disciplinary mech-anism provides the basis of aggregate data through which efficiency and effectiveness can be measured and assessed.

Two points should be noted here. First, the time-reporting system acts to increase the visibility of the individual on a regular schedule. While it appears to reflect a lack of trust (Roberts, 1991), it also acts as a tool to enrol workers in a self-disciplinary examination of their work. One of the few references to anyone other than the project manager in Kerzner's earliest edition (1979) comes in the chapter on schedule and control. He suggests that providing a detailed report to 'doers' on resources expended versus budget and projected resources to finish the task allows the doer to become involved in contingency planning and recognising major deviations. This is an example of creating the state of being liable to answer for one's conduct, 'an extended state of constant liability' (Hoskin and Macve, 1986) on projects.

The second is that the time-reporting and projection task itself represents confession on the part of the worker as to effort expended and whether or not the task will be completed on time. This mechanical, calculative technology allows the individual and the project manager to figure out where they are and where they should be individually and collectively. As such, it is a rather early and rudimentary attempt at confession based on an assumption that workers are capable of, and willing to, accurately estimate remaining effort on tasks. Problems in this area often result in the '90% hold-up' (Frame, 1994) where only 75 per cent (or less) of the tasks are completed but 90 per cent (and holding) of the resources have been used up. More advanced methods of using confessional forms of evaluation will be discussed below.

As stated above, early project management techniques focused on developing knowledge of the activity or work to be performed and time lines. These practices taken together serve to objectify the nature of the work and make it visible. Until relatively recently, these practices formed the core of the project management approach. However, increasing evidence suggested that these practices were not sufficient to guarantee project success. This led to the introduction of a human relations component in project management practices (for example, *The Human Side of Project Management* (House, 1988)). Recent practices stress the importance of the human side of project management. For example, Kerzner's preeminent book on PM grew from 478 pages in 1979 to over 1,200 in 1992 largely through the addition of 'softer' people issues. In this way the original concern with enclosure and distribution of work expanded to incorporate techniques aimed at enlisting more of the team members' labour. Not only must the manager be aware of the objective components of work and individuals, he or she must also gain the cooperation of the worker or enrol the worker such that self-identity is impacted.

While knowledge of an individual's contribution is essential to increasing performance and productivity (Braverman, 1974; Burawoy, 1982), engaging the subjectivity of the worker is also a necessary component to increasing productivity (Knights and Willmott, 1985). This requires making the human element, the behaviour and thoughts of the individual, visible. Thus the discipline of project management expanded to incorporate activities involved in directing and staffing the project. The project manager evolved from strict disciplinarian to coach/mentor and the confessional became more consciously applied in the management of projects.

The confessional operates to gain an understanding of the individual's inner thoughts and to influence beliefs. The first role of the confessional is to access individuals' deeply held knowledge of themselves. Early PM attempts to gain access to individuals' deeply held knowledge focused almost solely on 'objective' measures. The first attempt involved requiring individuals to continually report effort and re-forecast completion dates through the time-reporting systems addressed earlier. As stated earlier, these efforts had a tendency to fail for a number of reasons: the human tendency to try to hide bad news, inability to accurately forecast remaining efforts and so on. To resolve this issue, PM evolved to include techniques aimed at improving estimating skills and to standardise effort. A second attempt to gain access to individuals' thoughts was the introduction of the 'structured walk-through' (Kerzner, 1992; Frame, 1994) evaluation process. In a structured walk-through individuals explain to project managers what they have accomplished and hope to accomplish in the next period. Decisions and variances from the plan must be explicitly justified. As Frame (1994: 277) puts it, such 'evaluation serves an additional function, beyond providing feedback information to keep the project on track: it is an instrument to heighten accountability'.

Other PM techniques were introduced in an effort to change individuals' behaviour (the second role of the confessional) in a way that is more productive for the project as a whole. These practices included emphasising the importance of 'raising the flag' (trying to destigmatise asking for help by reinterpreting it as recognising a need early) and the use of team meetings to keep the entire team informed of progress and their place in the overall plan. This in turn introduced peer pressure as a motivator to meet targets. Finally, PM tools and techniques evolved to encourage individuals to actively engage in, and belong to, the project. Studies of how to increase motivation, encourage team spirit and reduce conflict became prevalent. Each of these techniques involved the individual reconstituting themselves as team members first and foremost. Frame (1994, 1995) suggests three categories of team-building 'tricks' that illustrate these practices. The first of these is to make the team as tangible as possible by holding meetings on a regular basis, creating a team space and team signs, and publicising team efforts. A second technique is to develop rewards for good behaviour. Finally, Frame suggests that project managers must develop an effective personal touch (that is, positive one-on-one relationships with team members). Each of these activities is designed to increase association and membership with the team, so as to build commitment to the team. In other words, these are attempts to reconstitute individuals' identity in terms of their membership on the team. The expectation is that this will influence team members to put team goals and requirements ahead of competing requirements.

The foregoing has been a very brief examination of some of the main PM practices with an eye to exploring what it is that they facilitate and how they shape what is known and knowable, in other words an examination of how PM operates and the power relations it establishes, rather than what it is. I next examine explanations for PM (implementation) failure and some contradictions inherent in the application of the current discourse.

Contradictions inherent in practice

In this section of the chapter, I make two points about the difference between what PM advocates seek to accomplish and what the practices that make up PM are likely to produce. First, I look at the advantages and disadvantages claimed for the PM approach in light of the underlying power relations established. Next I explore how project management practices tend to be more closely aligned with rationalisation and increasing control than with managing uncertainty and ambiguity flexibly.

Advantages of project management

PM advocates suggest that the primary advantage of project work is increased flexibility and autonomy. Most of the advantages of project management forms derive from the creation of horizontal communication linkages and the information-processing problems this solves. Creating dual or multiple overlays of authority and influence results in improved communication flows and flexibility. Enhanced quality of work life and technical excellence of solutions are expected to result from this increased communication (Ford and Randolph, 1992). However, the analysis above indicates how project management practices work to enclose and partition the project and make it separate from other aspects of the organisation. The techniques of enclosure, partitioning and ranking create separable and knowable project entities. Information on these entities is manufactured in abundance, which in some ways must improve communications. At the same time, these processes direct attention internally to the project. By determining what is seeable and doable, these techniques also limit communication to the monitored phenomenon deemed of interest to this project. Interfaces and relationships are underplayed, under-understood and under-explored.

This paradox of increased information and communication, but only on the pre-specified topics of interest, results in the primary disadvantages of the project approach. Given that individuals may be also involved in different projects, the enhanced focus which is the advantage of project management can lead to distinct disadvantages as well. These disadvantages include increased ambiguity, conflict, and individual and organisational costs (Ford and Randolph, 1992).

Both the advantages and disadvantages of a project management approach are caused by the increased visibility that such an approach entails. Through increased visibility, a power–knowledge relation is created. Power acts simultaneously to create and repress (Foucault, 1977). The paradox of PM is that it both simplifies and increases control, and creates rigidities and blinders. Much of this paradox arises from the relationship of PM practice to the institutionalisation of instrumental rational action as discussed below.

Project management as a process of rationalisation

Weber defined rationalisation as the institutionalisation of instrumental or purposive rational action (Weber, 1962). This process of rationalisation encompasses several activities: refinement of techniques of calculation; an enhancement of specialised knowledge; an extension of technically rational control over natural and social processes; and the depersonalisation of social relationships (Brubaker, 1984). The rationality which is respected tends to be a technical, formal rationality based in universalisation of experience and rendering problems measurable or accountable and finding the most effective way of stating and solving problems through a process of generalisation (MacIntyre, 1984). Management becomes the relentless war against ambivalence espoused by Bauman (1991).

Application of the project management approach embedded in the dominant discourse illustrates the process of rationalisation identified by Weber above. One of the primary functions of project management is the ever more detailed refinement of the components of work and calculation of effort required for each work package. This relates to Weber's refinement of techniques of control. In pursuing this approach to management, a new form of specialised knowledge arises, based on the need for planning, estimating and controlling expertise. Associations such as the Project Management Institute now exist, and the *Guide to the Project Management Body of Knowledge* (PMBOK) has been developed, to define the knowledge needed by project managers. Frame (1995) comments on the growth in demand for qualified project managers and their value in business. Ultimately, as with any rationalisation process, the function of project management is to clarify a means–ends relationship and, through this, increase predictability, calculability, control and efficiency. Through these mechanisms, project management is a prototypical example of the rationalisation and technocratisation of management.

Weber saw processes of rationalisation as a key component of the ideal-type bureaucratic organisation. Ironically, projects and project management are currently touted as a means to avoid the problems of large-scale bureaucratic organisations (rigidity, rule boundedness and so on, as identified by Selznick (1949) and others). For example, Frame (1995: 2) states that 'Flexibility is the watch word of the new order and project management is a key to this flexibility' and Kerzner (1992: 8) proclaims PM 'an extremely flexible and highly effective approach to multi-disciplinary program management'. Yet the practice of project management directly results in the objectification and strict (rigid, some would say) control of work. It seems ironic that prototypical rationalisation of work is hailed as a resolution to the problems of organisation. Rather than moving away from rigid hierarchical controls by adopting project structures, we move towards loose agglomerations of a Weberian ideal-type organisation. PM does not resolve the issues surrounding the dysfunctional aspects of bureaucracies; it merely changes the scale of operation.

The results of this characteristic of project management are largely ignored for very good and human reasons. Townley (2002: 565) states that 'abstract management offers an epistemic and ontological security. It is this that perpetuates these systems and faith in the refinement of techniques'. These abstract management concepts and standards based in linear, rational, controlled systems provide a certainty which eliminates ambiguity and makes us comfortable. This desire to be 'comfortable' leads us away from the uncertain, uncomfortable, double-loop learning processes that allow us to deal with complex adaptive systems operating on the edge of chaos. Today's 'standards' establish a behavioural norm which in turn leads to self-reinforcing structures embedded with self-propagating logic.

From the above, it is evident that project management is an attempt to normalise the non-normal in organisations. It is because it is non-normal that it requires project management. However, project management itself is a bureaucratic procedure based on techniques of calculability.

Conclusions

PM attempts to normalise or rationalise that which is non-normal. It seeks to accomplish this through the use of practices which enclose, partition, rank, examine, control and incorporate confessionals. All these practices act to increase the calculability and visibility of both work and individuals. In this way, PM acts to reduce, rather than manage, the ambiguity of organisational work. By attempting to reduce or eliminate the ambiguity, PM advocates lose sight of the true nature of project work. The over-rationalisation and documentation of 'one right way' to manage projects actually limits the likelihood that project management will be successful.

The common response to the question of project failure now appears to be that projects fail because project management techniques are not appropriately applied. This in itself appears to be both self-serving, in that failure means you need to reapply yourself to the lessons of the wise ones, and scapegoating, in that if your project is not entirely successful it is obviously due to your inadequate project management techniques. The practical solution to this conundrum has been a significant focus on the need to increase the project management competencies within organisations and through professionalisation efforts for the occupation. The increasing commodification of project management seems to have contradictory implications for this initiative.

Project management has, for too long, been studied as a technical tool for enhancing the accomplishment of time- and resource-constrained tasks. I believe that what needs to be done is quite different. The practices underlying the project management process need to be critically examined. Two distinct forms of theoretical understanding are sorely missing. The first is the critical examination of the underlying functions of common practices. The second is exploratory theory grounded in the experience of 'normally competent persons in ordinary situations' (Bittner, 1965: 186).

This chapter exists as a preliminary attempt to open a dialogue about project management practices that explores their fundamental operation in the realm of power/knowledge. By examining how PM operates to influence what is knowable and therefore doable, I attempt to shed light on some of the fundamental contradictions evident in the operation of project management. Viewing PM as a process of rationalisation in Weberian terms also has implications for prescriptions based on a belief in the underlying flexibility and autonomy of project work. Problematising conventional views requires uncovering contradictions between project management predictions and outcomes and making them apparent for practical discussion. Forcing practitioners to face the dilemmas caused by these contradictions may force creativity and innovation with respect to these conventions that may lead to discursive change (Fairclough, 1992). Problematising the concept is a starting point for developing a different fundamental understanding of the function of projects in organisations. The primary contribution of this chapter is that it provides a critical review of PM practices which uncovers signposts to the implications and insights a more detailed analysis could provide.

Another necessary step is to try to learn from people instead of about them. What are needed are detailed and explicitly critical studies of project management practices. Such studies would look at the material, concrete practices that depend on and generate power relations and describe their linkages with knowledge. These studies must examine how project management methodologies constitute and sustain these practices and how they affect their change. Explicitly, these studies would explore the realm of practical embedded knowledge Aristotle called phronesis. Future research exploring the common-sense understanding of project management, the functions project managers identify for its use and how they make sense of the discrepancy between project management techniques and failure will provide a foundation from which to elaborate the study of projects in a meaningful real-world sense. Understanding how project managers make sense of the discrepancy between prescribed and experienced organisational activity should help to reduce the gap between abstract prescriptions and concrete practices. The ultimate goal of this research programme is to diminish the gap between abstract prescriptions and concrete practices.

In conclusion, I think it is past time to rethink project management taking a critical view of its underlying assumptions. Problematising the concept is a starting point for developing a different fundamental understanding of the function of projects in organisations. I see this chapter as an opening salvo in the dialogue that needs to be engaged in by practitioners and academics. I expect that it will raise many questions in the minds of both types of readers. I am happy to engage in discussion of these questions. You can reach me at: JaniceT@Athabascau.ca

References

Alvesson, M. and Deetz, S. (2000) *Doing Critical Management Research*. London: Sage Publications.

Avots, I. (1969) 'Why Does Project Management Fail?', *California Management Review*, 12(1): 77–82.

Bauman, Z. (1991) *Modernity and Ambivalence*. Cambridge: Polity Press.

Bittner, E. (1965) 'The Concept of Organizations', *Social Problems*, 32: 172–86, 239–58.

Braverman, H. (1974) *Labour and Monopoly Capital*. New York: Monthly Review Press.

Brubaker, R. (1984) *The Limits of Rationality. An Essay on the Social and Moral Thought of Max Weber*. London: Allen & Unwin.

Brunsson, N. (1993) *The Reforming Organization*. New York: Wiley.

Bryman, A., Bresnen, B., Beardsworth, A. and Kerl, T. (1988) 'Qualitative Research and the Study of Leadership', *Human Relations*, 41: 13–29.

Buchanan, D. and Badham, R. (1999) 'Politics and Organizational Change: The Lived Experience', *Human Relations*, 52(5): 609–29.

Buckle, P. and Thomas, J. (2003) 'Deconstructing Project Management: A Gender Analysis of Project Management Guidelines', *International Journal of Project Management*, 21(6): 433–41.

Burawoy, M. (1982) *Manufacturing Consent*. Chicago: University of Chicago Press.

Cooper, R.G. and Kleinschmidt, E.J. (1987) 'New Products: What separates winners from losers?', *Journal of Product Innovation Management*, 4(3): 169–84.

DeMarco, T. and Lister, T. (1977) *Peopleware: Productive Projects and Teams*. New York: Dorset House.

Dyer, L. and Paulson, G.D. (1976) *Project Management: An Annotated Bibliography*. New York: New York School of Industrial and Labour Relations.

Ewusi-Mensah, K. and Przasnyski, Z.H. (1997) 'Learning from Abandoned Information Systems Development Projects', *Journal of Information Technology*, 10: 3–14.

Fairclough, N. (1992) *Discourse and Social Change*. Cambridge: Polity Press.

Flyvbjerg, B. (2001) *Making Social Science Matter*. Cambridge: Cambridge University Press.

Fondahl, J.W. (1987) 'The History of Modern Project Management', *Project Management Journal*, 28(2): 33–6.

Ford, R.C. and Randolph, W.A. (1992) 'Cross-functional Structures: A Review and Integration of Matrix Organization and Project Management', *Journal of Management*, 18(2): 267–94.

Foucault, M. (1972) *The Order of Things*. London: Tavistock.

Foucault, M. (1977) *Discipline and Punish*. London: Allen Lane.

Foucault, M. (1980) *Power/Knowledge*. Hemel Hempstead: Harvester Wheatsheaf.

Frame, J.D. (1994) *The New Project Management*. San Francisco, CA: Jossey-Bass.

Frame, J.D. (1995) *Managing Projects in Organizations: How to Make the Best Use of Time, Techniques and People*, 2nd edn. San Francisco, CA: Jossey-Bass.

Frame, J.D. (1999) *Project Management Competence: Building Key Skills for Individuals, Teams and Organisations*, 3rd edn. San Francisco, CA: Jossey-Bass.

Hardy, C. (1994) *Managing Strategic Action: Mobilizing Change*. London: Sage.

Harvey, D. (1990) *The Condition of Postmodernity*. Oxford: Blackwell.

Hoskin, K. and Macve, R. (1986) 'The Genesis of Accountability: The West Point Connections', *Accounting, Organizations and Society*, 13(2): 37–73.

House, R.S. (1988) *The Human Side of Project Management*. New York: Addison-Wesley.

Humphrey, W.S. (1990) *Managing the Software Process*. New York: Addison-Wesley.

Jessen, S.A. (1991) *The Nature of Project Leadership*. Oslo: Universitetsforlaget.

Kerzner, H. (1979) *Project Management – A Systems Approach to Planning, Scheduling and Controlling*, 1st edn. New York: Van Nostrand Reinhold.

Kerzner, H. (1992) *Project Management – A Systems Approach to Planning, Scheduling and Controlling*, 4th edn. New York: Van Nostrand Reinhold.

Kerzner, H. (2001) *Project Management: A Systems Approach to Planning, Scheduling and Controlling*, 7th edn. New York: Wiley.

Kharbanda, O.P. and Stallworthy, E.A. (1983) *How to Learn from Project Disasters: True Life Stories with a Moral for Management*. London: Gower.

Killian, W.P. (1971) 'Project Management: Future Organizational Concepts', *Marquette Business Review*, 15(2): 90–107.

Knight, K. (1976) 'Matrix Organizations: A Review', *Journal of Management Studies*, 17(2): 111–30.

Knights, D. and Morgan, G. (1991) 'Corporate Strategy, Organizations and Subjectivity: A Critique', *Organizational Studies*, 12(2): 252–73.

Knights, D. and Willmott, H. (1985) 'Power and Identity in Theory and Practice', *Sociological Review*, 33: 22–46.

MacIntyre, A. (1984) *After Virtue*. Notre Dame, IN: University of Notre Dame Press.

Meyer, J. (1994) 'Rationalized Environments', in W. Scott and J. Meyer (eds), *Institutional Environments and Organizations*. Thousand Oaks, CA: Sage, 28–54.

Miller, P. and O'Leary, T. (1987) 'Accounting and the Construction of the Governable Person', *Accounting, Organizations and Society*, 12(3): 235–65.

Morris, P.W.G. and Hough, G.H. (1987) *The Anatomy of Major Projects – A Study of the Reality of Project Management*. Chichester: Wiley.

Packendorff, J. (1995) 'Inquiring into the Temporary Organisation: New Directions for Project Management Research', *Scandinavian Journal of Management*, 11(4): 319–33.

Peters, T. (2000) 'The New Wired World of Work: A More Transparent Workplace Will Mean More White-Collar Accountability and Less Tolerance for Hangers-On', *Business Week*, 28 August: 172.

PMI (1996) *A Guide to the Project Management Body of Knowledge*. Newtown Square, PA: PMI.

PMI (2000) *A Guide to the Project Management Body of Knowledge*. Newtown Square, PA: PMI.

Pinto, J.K. and Slevin, D.P. (1988) 'Project Success: Definitions and Measurement Techniques', *Project Management Journal*, 19(1): 67–72.

Pinto, J.K. and Covin, J.G. (1989) 'Critical Factors in Project Implementation: A Comparison of Construction and R&D Projects', *Technovation*, 9(1): 49–62.

Pinto, J.K. and Slevin, D.P. (1987) 'Critical Factors in Successful Implementation', *IEEE Transactions on Engineering Management*, 34(1): 22–7.

Rakos, J.K. (1990) *Software Project Management for Small to Medium Sized Projects*. Upper Saddle River, NJ: Prentice-Hall.

Roberts, J. (1991) 'The Possibilities of Accountability', *Accounting, Organizations and Society*, 16(4): 355–68.

Selznick, P. (1949) *TVA and the Grassroots*. Chicago: University of Chicago Press.

Shenhar, A.J. (1998) 'From Theory to Practice: Toward a Typology of Project Management Styles', *IEEE Transactions on Engineering Management*, 45(1): 33–48.

Standish Group (1994) The Chaos Report. Published on the web at http://www.standishgroup.com/sample_research/chaos_1994_1.php

Standish Group (1996) *The CHAOS Report: Unfinished Voyages*. Available at http://standishgroup.com/visitor/chaos.htm

Standish Group (2001) The Extreme Chaos Report. Published on the web at www.standishgroup.com/sample_research/PDFpages/extreme_chaos.pdf

Thomas, J. (2000) 'Making Sense of Project Management', in R.A. Lundin and F. Hartman (eds), *Projects as Business Constituents and Guiding Motives*. Boston, MA: Kluwer Academic Press, 25–44.

Townley, B. (1993) 'Foucault, Power/Knowledge, and its Relevance for Human Resource Management', *Academy of Management Review*, 18(3): 518–45.

Townley, B. (1994) *Reframing Human Resource Management: Power Ethics and the Subject at Work*. London: Sage.

Townley, B. (1995) 'Managing by Numbers: Accounting, Personnel Management and the Creation of a Mathesis', *Critical Perspectives on Accounting*, 6: 555–75.

Townley, B. (2002) 'Managing with Modernity', *Organization*, 9(4): 549–73.

Weber, M. (1962) *Basic Concepts in Sociology*. New York: Citadel.

Weick, K. (1995) *Sensemaking in Organizations*. London: Sage.

Wilemon, D.L. and Cicero, J.P. (1970) 'The Project Manager: Anomalies and Ambiguities', *Academy of Management Journal*, 13(3): 269–82.

part 2

Projects within organisations

6

Projects and prisons

Monica Lindgren and Johann Packendorff

Introduction

Project work is an increasingly widespread phenomenon, but the consequences of project work for people and society have rarely been the subject of critical scientific enquiry (Lindgren and Packendorff, 2006). While the mainstream theoretical foundation of project work has been heavily criticised for being an overly rationalist and surprisingly ineffective construct in industry (Morris and Hough, 1987; Packendorff, 1995; Söderlund, 2004), much work still remains in determining its consequences for people and society in practice. Project work is sometimes described as a non-bureaucratic way of unleashing the individual (Kidder, 1981/2000; Christensen and Kreiner, 1997; Gill, 2002); it is also clear that routines, ideologies and power structures on organisational and societal levels are inscribed into project practices in a way that deeply affects work life for modern people (Hodgson, 2002; Buckle and Thomas, 2003). It is therefore the aim of this chapter to critically analyse project work practices and discuss the implications of these practices for people involved in project-based work.

The chapter starts by relating project management research and established project practices, discussing the shortcomings of current knowledge on project work from a critical theory perspective. Then, the critical perspective of this chapter (based on Foucault's analysis of prisons) is discussed in detail, emphasising the importance of deconstruction as a way of exhibiting the inherent contradictions, disciplinary effects and time regulations in project work practices. Our criticism is thus based in a post-structuralist notion that work organisation can be seen as a set of disciplinary practices through which individuals are controlled and monitored for the sake of organisational efficiency and effectiveness. This framework is then used to analyse stories from two different project teams, one in the IT company Compute, one in the Baltic Opera House. We then discuss the project practices from a critical perspective where we view projects as a mental prison. The chapter is concluded by some thoughts concerning the consequences of project management discourse for life in contemporary society.

111

Towards critical perspectives on project management research and practice

From having been a rational methodology in construction and defence industries, the project concept and the project form of organising have diffused into almost all sectors of society, to both small and large tasks, to external contract-based projects as well as internal change efforts (Packendorff, 1995). The basic reason for this diffusion seems to be that the project – viewed as a task-specific and time-limited form of working – is perceived as a way of avoiding all the classic problems of bureaucracy that most 'normal' organisations struggle with (Stinchcombe and Heimer, 1985; Pinto, 1996; Scotto, 1998). In that sense, project-based work is usually seen as a part of the wave of adhocratic 'new organisational forms' that entered most industries during the 1980s and 1990s (see Kerfoot and Knights, 1998; Gill, 2002; Clegg and Courpasson, 2004; Hodgson, 2004).

In many industries and companies, the project is now the normal work form. This is obvious not only in cultural life, advertising, consulting, R&D, IT and so on, but also in several large industrial corporations which execute numerous projects on a daily basis. Given this trend, one might assess that work life for many people is becoming increasingly 'projectified', that is, that substantial parts of people's work life are spent in projects and similar temporary forms of organising (Packendorff, 2002). This is especially visible when it comes to work in 'project-based firms', that is, firms where almost all operations take place in projects and where the permanent structure serves merely to provide administrative support.

The basis of the existence of the project management discipline is an institutionalised agreement about the definition of 'a project'. The project is commonly defined as a unique, complex task with a foreseeable date of delivery, subject to goal formulations in terms of time, cost and quality (see Packendorff, 1995; Söderlund, 2004). Given this definition, one might also separate project operations from other types of operations and construct methods for managing the project as effectively as possible in order to achieve stated goals. The origins of project management can be traced back to the US defence industry in the 1950s (see Engwall, 1995) where the time factor was the most important one in the arms races of the Cold War. In time, projects became taken for granted even in commercial operations, and then cost and quality became important factors. Together, these three factors form the so-called 'project goal triangle', which tells us that a realistic project goal must be a well-balanced combination of them all (Meredith and Mantel, 2000). Since the cost factor is usually the most explicit limitation, practical project management is mostly concerned with balancing time against quality within a non-disputable cost budget (Stinchcombe and Heimer, 1985).

In the many comparisons made between project work and 'ordinary' work, project work is usually depicted as an opposite, an opposite positively described as challenging, creative and controversial (Pinto, 1996: 25; Gill, 2002). In a sense, project managers are often described in the same way as entrepreneurs, that is, as strong, controversial, creative and active men, successfully bringing their ideas into the market (Lindgren and Packendorff, 2003). The message is that project management is something objective and distinctive that could bring about real change and more effective work procedures. Compared to her colleagues in the corporate chain of command, the project manager is an individual who dares to put her head on the table, taking risks, building dedicated teams, coming up with creative solutions to deliver something unique within the limits of time, cost and quality (Christensen and Kreiner, 1997). Projects are not supposed to be chaotic, however; the project manager should also be able to make detailed plans for her project despite the inherent insecurity of unique endeavours (Stinchcombe and Heimer, 1985).

As the project form is becoming increasingly common, it is also clear that it is not always as rational and stimulating as intended. Even the most professional project-based organisations show high failure rates, often in terms of both delays and budget overruns (Morris and Hough, 1987). Like 'ordinary' firms, project-based organisations are also hurt by conflicts and internal politics, and in the relation between the project and its environment lie several problems (Buchanan, 1991; Lundin and Söderholm, 1995; Kreiner, 1995; Pinto, 1996). In several sectors of society (such as cultural life, European Union programmes, research and so on) the project is the only work form available, which means a severe risk that the division into different temporary projects makes it impossible to implement long-term strategies. The projects thus run the risk of just being isolated sequences of action lacking any meaningful links to both the context and the future.

Viewed from the perspective of the project worker, projects are often stimulating, but also sources of stress, loneliness, disrupted family lives and superficial workplace relations (Gill, 2002; Packendorff, 2002; Lindgren and Packendorff, 2006). One might even say that projects are a way of disciplining the individual in a way that organisations in general cannot do any more (Hodgson, 2002), and that the work form reinforces traditional masculine attitudes to work and life (Buckle and Thomas, 2003; Lindgren and Packendorff, 2006).

To sum this up, it appears that the established notion of what project management is about suffers from several taken-for-granted assumptions. In order to question project management theories, methods and practices, these assumptions must be made explicit and subjected to critical analysis. It is, for example, often said that one of the main advantages with projects is that they are created to reach concrete, specific goals – as opposed to the ambiguous, multi-constituency tactics governing most permanent organisations (Pinto, 1996; Ekstedt et al., 1999). Following this view of projects as efficient activity systems, it is not surprising to find that most theories, methods and practices of project management are aimed at projects as single entities (for exceptions, see Söderlund, 2004; Engwall and Jerbrant, 2003). Given an exogenous goal, it is the internal operations in the project that are interesting to all involved, and the relations to individuals, other projects and organisational and societal contexts are often overlooked. Moreover, as a discipline stemming from a need for efficient handling of temporary tasks, project management is most clearly a managerialist field. Almost all theories, methods and practices aim at improving the ways in which project tasks are managed, and perspectives focusing on anything else are rarely considered as legitimate (Packendorff, 1995). Unlike contemporary organisation theory, in which it is almost never assumed that all people in an organisation share the same goals and interests, project management thus departs from an ideal in which the project goal is the *raison d'être* for all involved. Given the preoccupation with efficiency, single projects and leadership, it is not surprising to find that traditional project management theories, methods and practices are mainly normative constructs. Often explicitly referred to as 'tools', the models and checklists of which all project management literature is full convey an image of project management as a way of achieving perfection (Packendorff, 1995).

From our point of view, it is important to view projects as a discursive practice in society, implying that project management is something people in organisations construct and reconstruct through daily action. What is interesting is how people act in projects and how it affects their lives – and thus our society – in general, and what hidden assumptions they express in making sense of these actions. In the words of Hodgson and Cicmil (this volume, Chapter 2, p. 26), we critically ask ourselves 'what do we do when we call something a project?' We will therefore go on to discuss how such a critical analysis can be performed.

Deconstructing project management theories and practices: a Foucauldian approach

One method of critical analysis of contemporary managerial practices is deconstruction, where Derrida's work on philosophical texts have inspired many management researchers during the last decades (Culler, 1983; Cooper, 1989; Martin, 1990; Calás and Smircich, 1991, 1992; Mumby and Putnam, 1992; Knights, 1997).

Derrida focuses on human interaction as production of texts, and states that there is nothing outside the text (Derrida, 1976). The text implicates hierarchical structures expressed in terms of binary dichotomies (such as male and female, black and white), a discourse that can be critically analysed. Derrida (1973) uses the term *différance* instead of 'difference' in order to emphasise that concepts are processual and non-static constructs, situated in time and space. *Différance* is the combination of differing and deferring, implying possibilities of going beyond hierarchical structures, thereby attacking the idea of identities resting on simple forms. Cooper (1989), drawing on Derrida, states that dichotomies consist of binary opposites that in themselves imply that one concept is privileged over the other (he provides two examples: good–bad, male–female). Cooper also highlights that in early historical eras opposites such as strong–weak and large–small were expressed through the same concept. From this position, he gradually develops a perspective where he suggests dichotomous concepts as being complementary to each other rather than being opposites. This should also be the case of other dichotomies such as the separation between work and private life and between project work and other work. This reasoning also implies that our focus can be lifted from the concepts as such, and that interaction processes should instead become central, that is, connections and co-construction are stressed. Interaction processes are also emphasised by Janssens and Steyaert (2002) where their 'third way' is characterised by pluralistic multi-voice thinking.

Deconstructions of different sorts of texts are viable given certain purposes, such as to open our eyes to patterns taken for granted or assumptions behind theories. This is not least important when it comes to thoughts or theories that are seen as elegant and compelling and therefore widely accepted – such as popular management models or new organisational forms. Kilduff (1993) has deconstructed the March and Simon classic *Organizations* (1958) and interprets the text as machine-oriented and based on an ideology of programming individuals and collectives. In the same way, Mintzberg's classical study *The Nature of Managerial Work* (1980) has been deconstructed by Calás and Smircich (1991) from a power/gender perspective, highlighting hierarchical influ-ence and masculinity as assumptions behind the seemingly critical original text. Linstead (1993) argues that research of organisational culture should be done from a deconstruction perspective that views culture as a paradox, as otherness, as seduction and as discourses, in opposition to the predominating harmony-based and unitary notions of corporate symbolism. The theory of project management can be decon-structed in the same way (see Hodgson, 2002; Buckle and Thomas, 2003). Texts to be deconstructed are not solely public printed ones – we can analyse empirical interviews, stories and so on in the same way, since every story can be interpreted in different ways.

In this chapter, we have chosen to use Foucault's (1977) notion of the modern prison system as a metaphor for the deconstruction of project work and its conse-quences in society. Foucault's view of the historical development of punishment is that it is an ever-increasing path towards total disciplining of people. The power thoughts are central in his texts, but the power concept is different as compared to Marx's: power is structured in and related to positions, not to capitalist society. He is also more interested in how people are exposed to power than who has the power. In the modern prison, people are (1) confined and separated within a secluded area, (2) subject to an agenda strictly governing both thoughts and actions, and (3) incessantly supervised and evaluated. In general terms, one might say that prisons operate out of the principles of disciplining space, disciplining time and disciplining the mind. Metaphorically, these principles also apply to modern organisations, and can be used in critical analysis of phenomena such as management accounting (Macintosh, 1994).

Disciplining space means that prisoners are confined in a secluded and self-supporting area, and they are able to live their entire lives there. Within the prison, space is further divided into cells, which implies that people are always to be found at identifiable places and that they – eventually – will start to identify themselves with these places. In organisations, this would mean that employees will have their needs fulfilled within the organisation, and through the structuring of operations into separate organisational units, spatial control and identification are achieved.

Where disciplining time is concerned, it rests upon an authoritative agenda for all tasks regulating with what all people should be occupied at every point in time. This agenda can be even refined through prescribed bodily movements (for example, military exercise) or clothing (for example, uniforms), through which the degrees of bodily freedom are further circumscribed. In organisations, time is heavily regulated in this manner through rule systems and agendas (Hassard, 1999), and there are also examples of explicit and implicit regulation of movements, conversational manners and clothes.

Disciplining the mind, finally, rests upon the principle of *panopticon*, that is, that it is possible to see, monitor and evaluate all prisoners. In prison, this is organised through hierarchies, which means that guards are ordered to monitor limited sets of prisoners, and that supervisors are assigned to monitor limited sets of guards. Through a widespread chain of command, the prison manager can thus constantly monitor each prisoner; the prisoners, on the other hand, are not able to monitor their surveillors. Hierarchic surveillance is further inscribed using sanctions when rules are broken, and through individual evaluation and comparison of the prisoners' individual performance. These principles of course also apply to organisations; in fact, these are the principles upon which Weber, Taylor and others built the ever-present notion of what modern organisations are about.

From this perspective, project work can be seen as an explicit expression of the disciplinary principles upon which all modern organising is built. Project work rose from an alleged inability of bureaucracies to handle exceptional, time-limited tasks, and it has thus been ascribed all the 'good' (that is, 'effective') properties that bureaucracies are not considered to have (Ekstedt *et al.*, 1999; Clegg and Courpasson, 2004; Hodgson, 2004). While successfully deviating from bureaucratic norms, project work has of course developed a set of strictly governing norms. One could even say that most project management theory stems from the ambition to formulate even more disciplining forms for controlling individual behaviour than those that had been developed for ongoing operations. Paradoxically, this has been presented as a liberation of people. Project work has been presented as a flexible work form, not only for organisations as units, but also for people working in these forms. Working in projects has a masculine image of being exciting and performance-oriented (Lindgren and Packendorff, 2001; Gill, 2002) and will also give people who have been normalised into these kind of cultures the opportunity to work in more and more 'exciting', 'creative' and 'risky' projects (these expressions intended to further entice people into project work).

Foucault (1977) described people in society as prisoners, drawing from the history of punishment in which there was a development from brutal violence to 'humane confinement'. He also applied this way of thinking to schools and other institutions. In this case, we use the project work form as another way of controlling and disciplining people for the sake of growth and profitability – through disciplining time, space and mind. In the following section, we will give some examples of how an empirical study can be interpreted in these terms.

Empirical analyses: the Baltic Opera House and Compute Software

We have used empirical stories from two different kinds of projects, one theatre project implemented in the Baltic Opera House (BOH) and one IT consultancy project implemented by the software company Compute. In each case, a number of team members working in the same project were interviewed: that is, they told us their uninterrupted stories about the specific project and project work in general (see Table 6.1). In this way, rich accounts of the project workers' experiences were generated. In light of Foucault's prison metaphor, statements on power and power relations were sought in the transcripts, and formulated in terms of discourses on disciplining time, space and mind: as 'intersubjectively produced texts that embody a dialogue between their experience and our research interests' (Clegg and Courpasson, 2004: 530).

What is interesting from a critical point of view is the discourses that are used. According to Asplund (1979), critical enquiry on societal phenomena involves three levels: figures of thought, discourses and practices. In a narrative, there are both systematic and erroneous narrative elements, and in the relations between these elements and the figures of thought, we find discourses. Figures of thought are the basic, often taken-for-granted, ideas that we cannot depart from without severe consequences for how we perceive life and society. Asplund provides the example of 'childhood' in order to explain the importance of figures of thought. Without 'childhood' as a specific figure of thought, the organisation of, for example, housing and recreation in society would look very different. By attending to the special needs of children, we (in interaction) produce/reproduce discourses on how to live with children: children need free space, children need time, children should be out in nature, and so on.

Table 6.1 Summary of the two case studies

	Compute Software Inc.	Baltic Opera House (BOH)
Project	Designing, installing and testing an executive information system at a customer company	Setting up an opera play, including rehearsal, stage design and marketing
Project results (according to team)	New customer that must be kept. System successfully installed, significant delay and cost overrun. Customer satisfied	Well-known Italian opera for a large audience. Performed at the first night as planned. Well-received by audience
Interviewed team members (fictitious name, age, role)	• James, 35, consulting manager • Eric, 34, project leader, acting consulting manager • Carl, 28, programmer • Matthew, 26, programmer • Eve, 38, adviser	• Rosalind, 45, producer, planning manager • Barbara, 41, costume manager • Roger, 48, stage design manager • Tom, 41, stage coordinator • Mary, 33, orchestra violinist

It is also important to understand that the difference and similarities between discourses cannot be analysed on the discursive level; it is the figures of thought that guide any such differences and similarities. Discourses can be analysed as expressions of values, while figures of thought are complex, implicit textures of such values. It is not always possible to relate a discourse to one or several figures of thought in a straight-forward manner, and figures of thought are not always found in the practices of individuals; each analytical level has a certain independence. What is interesting in narratives is thus how people talk about themselves in relation to contextual circum-stances, how they describe their values, what is important to them and what is not important. For example, life form practices where hard work is combined with ambi-tious child-raising are often expressions of self-fulfilment, economic needs, parental responsibilities and so on, building on discourses concerning modern enlightened people. Figures of thought can then be described as (for example) gender relations, growth and efficiency. What is interesting in discourses is of course how they can be related to underlying figures of thought, where we might find a high degree of incon-sistency and a tendency to emphasise economic success over human relations.

At BOH, the project studied through the individuals' stories was a regular opera pro-duction. The project started when a director for the play had been recruited, after which the producer at BOH constructed a rehearsal schedule for the actors and the orchestra. Parallel to rehearsals, a mobile stage setting was designed and constructed, and costumes for the actors sewn. All these complex parallel processes converged into the final rehearsals according to a strict time schedule. At BOH, it had never happened that a pro-ject deadline (the opening night) had not been met, and it did not happen this time either.

The Compute project was described as a typical one for them – neither big nor small, neither a brilliant success nor a disastrous failure. The project was ordered by the large car retailer Trucks with the intention to end information problems in their spare parts operations. It started when Compute received the order for the business system, and a project team was appointed. After going through a design phase, con-struction and implementation of the system followed. Because of technical problems and inadequate monitoring, the project was severely delayed, and was closed to every-one's satisfaction half a year too late and almost twice as expensive as initially offered.

Disciplining time: coordination, work time extensions and deadlines

The time schedule in the theatre project is characterised by interviewees as routinised in the sense that they have fixed hours when they must be there to rehearse and perform, but in practice they are in place from 1.00 p.m. to late in the evening, often until midnight:

> My formal work hours are 8 a.m. through 5 p.m., but then we have our deadlines where everything shall be delivered. Then there is no choice other than to work overtime, and then

there are rehearsals and performances in the evenings that you must attend. A lot of irregular work hours, indeed. (Barbara)

At the core of the project process are rehearsals, which cannot happen unless all required actors and musicians are present. Coordinating all these people into the same place at the same time is the task of the producer, implying issuing strict orders to everybody on where and when to be at work:

An orchestra is a strict hierarchy, from the conductor downwards. This fall, we had a concert and some days before, the conductor replaced one of the songs. He thought that we should have played the new one before, but we had not and it was also technically complicated. When these things happen, we eat take-away food the whole week and skip the laundry. (Mary)

While maintaining an image of the theatre culture as liberal and creative, the way of governing rehearsals is through enforced coordination and synchronisation. Meetings and discussions also take place during rehearsal time and often project participants are forced to work during weekends. All involved are usually free on Mondays, but they also perform for other audiences, or stay at home rehearsing their own songs and other performances:

My work hours vary a lot. Sometimes, I work weekends too. We almost exclusively work evenings and nights, and when we are on tour we can be away for weeks. (Tom)

However, they do not complain because they think they are privileged to be able to earn their living through culture (this is a common way of justifying long work hours and intense commitment). Few of them count how many hours they work per week, and those who do say that they usually work about 50 per cent more hours than they are paid for by BOH.

At Compute, most of the work hours in the project consisted of individual tasks, and all consultants worked full-time on the project (except for the project manager, who coordinated several parallel projects from Compute's headquarters). The different programming and testing tasks could be performed by individual consultants (given that they possessed certain skills), which meant that team members did not have to coordinate themselves according to a given time schedule. In practice, the consultants still tried to work together all the time, not least because there was a need for knowledge transfer from senior to junior consultants. What happened when the project was eventually delayed was that the project team realised there was a need for extraordinary effort:

My practical problems in the projects can always be traced back to bad communication between Sales and Consulting. Sales always tell the customers that their problems will be fixed through a fast installation of our software, but in practice, we always have to make far-reaching modifications. And those modifications mean delays. When the project schedule cracks down, we just have to sit there with our extra hours. In almost all projects I have been working it has been like that. (Carl)

The customer had accepted extra costs in the contract, so team members were kindly asked if they could put some extra hours into resolving the situation (after all, they were at least partly responsible for the delay). While the individual consultants had different opportunities for doing so – they had other different tasks in Compute and different family situations – they all accepted to work overtime:

> Well, you really got frustrated when it did not work, a bit stressed. Always the same thing, the memory problem. Should we change the code or replace the hardware? Quite heavy responsibility, I had written most of that code. I was held responsible for what I had done, yes, so I just had to take responsibility for fixing it. (Matthew)

In practice, those that had the most freedom to work extra hours (that is, young men living alone) set the informal time schedule, and all the others adjusted to that out of loyalty to colleagues, Compute and the customer:

> They worked very hard throughout May. Once – and this is something they will tell you about – they actually worked until early in the morning. Then they drove around trying to find a hotel in the vicinity, but since all hotels were fully booked, they returned to Trucks and continued their work. It was insane! It is OK to work like that for a single week, but in the long run it is harmful for everybody involved. (Eric)

Since they had all been assigned to various new projects from the planned end of the current one, the delay meant simultaneous work on two projects for all involved. The new projects had other project leaders, and no managerial coordination took place. From having a situation where an average workload of seven hours per day could be freely planned, they now had to plan for double work by themselves so that the requirements of all project leaders could be fulfilled:

> Well, you don't actually plan for that kind of work peaks. When you make a time schedule, you estimate the duration of each work package and then add some slack so that you get a reasonable project duration and workload in the end. You don't calculate on any bigger problems. No projects go exactly as planned and you don't know everything from start. But if you were to investigate and estimate everything beforehand, you would never come to the implementation phase. (Eric)

Disciplining space: place and bodily control

The main restriction concerning bodily movement at BOH is the coordinated and synchronised rehearsals. For some leading actors, musicians and backstage managers, all rehearsals are mandatory; if one or some of them are absent, the rehearsal must be postponed within an already narrow time schedule:

> An orchestra is like a construction team. The hall and the equipment is there generating costs all the time, and then you force everybody to come there at the same time. I certainly don't want to be the one who cause delays and extra rehearsals, so I must be well prepared. Of course this is stressful, and it is a stress that you must learn to live with here at the opera. (Mary)

And since opening nights cannot be postponed, all extra rehearsal time needed must be found through working extra hours – all of them also requiring full coordination and synchronisation. Compared to ordinary office work for backstage personnel and regular performances for actors and musicians, the rehearsal period is thus an episode of extreme control of the body:

> People are always worried, and some can get quite nasty when they are nervous. We rehearse during eight weeks, and when there are three weeks left to the first night, nobody thinks there will ever be a performance. It's just chaos. Then you must know that it is always like that, that is how it is supposed to be. If you had no deadlines, you could go on forever, which would be quite unsatisfying. Knowing that you will be ready and knowing that everybody is working in the same direction, that is a fantastic feeling. (Rosalind)

Moreover, all actors must keep their bodies free from all sorts of illness, which means a high level of self-control also out of work.

While there is no enforced synchronisation of work at Compute, there are still obvious spatial regulations concerning where to work:

> Those who work in projects, should be at the customers' offices. They are not to be here. At the customers' offices you have the important people, the information we need, and it is also there where the customer can see that they get value for money. You must also follow normal working hours at the customer's office, you should be there when they are there. I don't accept anything else. If you are a customer and you pass by a room where you expect to find consultants, never see anyone there and then receive a huge invoice every month … Then you will start questioning if you get value for money. (Eric)

All consulting hours must be spent at the customer's office, partly due to practical reasons (that is, the physical location of the server into which the software will be installed), partly because Compute want their customers to be able to see and monitor the progress of the project:

> We intended this project to be a quick fix. Trucks had major administrative problems and their 'list of presents' that was immense, so it was not easy to decide where to start … Anyway, we always want to deliver something within 3–6 months or so; we want to show some fast results to the customers. So in this case, we started with the inventory system. (Eric)

This also means that Compute consultants must adjust their behaviour to the organisation in which their current project is located, while being constantly reminded of them being there as high-priced outsiders:

> If you have a deadline, you have a deadline. It shows a lack of respect to the project and all the people in the project if you go away. A lack of respect to the customer, the project manager, the team members, you put them all in a bad situation. (Eric)

When the Trucks project was delayed, the Compute consultants seldom left their temporary office, seldom took coffee breaks during chargeable time, and they even hoped not to meet their contact persons in the corridors:

> It was really throwing away one month on the job. Despite all that work, we couldn't finish the project anyway, so I went on vacation as planned in June. After summer, I was scheduled for a new project at CellCom, so I could only be at Trucks in evenings and weekends. And our contact persons in their IT department never worked evenings and weekends, so our communication deteriorated. Sometimes, I was actually afraid to meet them in the corridors; I knew that they had been complaining to Eric. (Matthew)

Since Trucks was located in another town, all consultants spent long hours travelling every day, and even sometimes spent nights at hotels in the vicinity. Again, most of this was not the result of explicit orders from the project leader or other managers at Compute; the consultants were not monitored by anyone, so they just conformed to their own sense of loyalty, responsibility and (in some cases) greed:

> It is my responsibility as project manager to deliver the right thing at the right time to the right cost. I took it quite hard, I must say, despite the satisfied customer. I should have seen the problems coming. I am a very good project manager when I am able to devote all my time to the project. I'm really good, if I may say so. (Eric)

Disciplining the mind: self-responsibility, individualisation and careers

At BOH, there are differences between different categories of team members where individual evaluation and comparison are concerned. Despite a general discursive image of equality and collectivity, several team members are judged and punished/rewarded individually. Actors, musicians and backstage managers all participate as individual specialists, who are exposed to national and international career opportunities (if they are successful). Individual performances can be viewed as excellent even if the opera as a whole is not received well by the audience, and several team members were aware that they were individually evaluated:

> Our salaries are lousy, and it is hard for us to maintain our own house despite that we have both been working for ten years now. On the other hand, I learn new things all the time, and

there are always new challenges. It is an amazing feeling to be able to learn things that I had never been able to do before. Sometimes, I really feel privileged to get a salary for just playing the violin. But the extra work needed to be able to compete for higher posts in the orchestra, I won't take it. (Mary)

For backstage personnel, a successful career was the same thing as successfully taking on increasingly large responsibilities on sub-project, project and organisational levels. The musicians and the actors were able to compete for leading roles and solo performances, and could be recruited by bigger opera houses, orchestras and broadcasting companies. Those who had done so in the past were remembered with pride in BOH. This is also an elitist industry in the sense that there are few people with a reputation and high salary; the vast majority of people are not well-paid, 'superior' and well-known. Most interviewees said that they perceived their career opportunities as limited and that they were happy to have gone this far. The myth of a cultural-oriented occupation as free, creative and intellectual is still alive among people, not only those working within this sector. If they want to reproduce their identity as representatives for higher cultural values in society, other people outside (relatives, friends, the media and so on) must also confirm these values.

All interviewed team members were ambiguous concerning their own importance to the project. On the one hand, they said that they could always be substituted by somebody else, but, on the other hand, they usually felt indispensable. Driven both by the fear of not being able to cling on to their jobs and by a feeling of nobody else being capable of performing their tasks, they mentally assumed personal responsibility for the project, often beyond their personal tasks:

Of course I am replaceable, and I don't want to feel indispensable. But in some situations I am, and I don't like that. If I should die on the spot, the project would go one anyway, but often I just have to go down to the opera to ensure that work continues. You feel indispensable during quite long periods, especially when you are working against a deadline. (Roger)

Sometimes I can feel that something is not really a part of my job, and that it is not a part of someone else's either. Then I might of course go to my producer and complain, but that means handing over the problem to a colleague, and they have just as much to do as I have. (Tom)

As a producer, you are never at the centre of anything, you are never visible. But you are supposed to be everywhere, and that feels a bit unrewarding and lonely sometimes. Everybody assumes that everything will work, and if it doesn't, everybody come down on the producer. (Rosalind)

In the case of Compute, everybody (except for low-paid administrative clerks) was a potential future CEO of the company. They all had university degrees in business or computer science, they had all been recruited because of their skills, and they were all paid well over the average of the industry in order to deliver superior systems solutions to their clients. Despite an ambitious effort to create a career system that implied personal challenges and competence development for the consultants, most of the engineers felt that a large career step would be to leave implementation work in projects and to take on sales or managerial work (not necessarily managerial positions, though):

> I have been a project manager for eight years, and I find it damned boring. I don't want to do this full-time anymore, and I have old my bosses that I want to take on strategic development instead. (Eve)

Each project manager measured individual performance, and since all working hours were registered to be charged to the customer, there were always hard data available on each consultant:

> You try to keep track on their performance through time reports. If someone works ten hours a day you can let them do that for a month or two, but then you must tell them to slow down a bit. People are young, thirsty for money and could not care less about their health, so you must try to keep that down. It is quite usual to work a lot when a project approaches deadline, and we also pay people well then, but if they work a lot all the time they are probably ineffective. (James)

For most Compute employees, money was a main motivator, and they often compared their salaries and work contracts in order to negotiate an internal hierarchy. Unlike the cultural sector, the IT sector does not represent any higher values, which also means that the employees in Compute must legitimise and have other rewards/punishment than BOH. All the overtime required for finishing the Compute project paid off in this sense: they were all regarded as loyal and ambitious employees, and received huge additional salaries for their extra hours.

The people in these project work situations consider themselves as privileged by having an exciting job and they thus accept the circumstances. This means that being away from family during weekends and evenings does not upset them, and they adjust their life to non-flexible work settings. Even if there are people who seem to have problems with their childcare, they somehow manage to work it out. The normalising effect is obvious in that they do not question their way of dealing with this; personal problems are never transformed into problems for the organisation. Established institutional patterns in the cultural sector and the IT sector are viewed as not changeable, and they are also taken for granted in the internal organisational culture. It follows that it is up to individuals to solve problems with these settings and patterns on their own.

Project prisons: unresisted disciplining

The project is in many ways the extreme form of present organisational practices. The traditional bureaucratic way of organising work was not very effective for controlling people and resulted in a massive critique against bureaucracy in organisations. Project organising offered a solution for this and is now a frequently used work form. The advantage of the project form – as mentioned above – is that time and space can be controlled and the tasks kept in focus; time schedules and internalised commitment to the project goal become important control mechanisms.

In practice, this becomes even more a prison than the Taylorist scientific management theory of organising, because the assumptions leading people to see the advantages of project work are invisible to most of them. In both the case studies (Compute and BOH) people experience glory and career possibilities when being chosen for 'exciting and stimulating' projects. They seemed not to be able to reflect and resist this, however, and they hardly analysed projects as a way to control people, to get commitment and time from them and even to get them to work harder than they usually would. In that sense we can say that projects form an unresisted mental prison for people, in the worst case a prison much harder to envision and escape from than those of traditional bureaucratic structures.

The people interviewed all have 'convincing arguments' to continue to work within projects. It appears that people in different industries (in this case the IT industry and opera) legitimise their work forms in different ways, however. Even though there of course are individual differences, people working at the same workplace seem to construct a set of shared beliefs on why and how they work, beliefs that are used to convince both themselves and each other (Alvesson, 1991). We will therefore look closer into the two cases to analyse what figures of thought are used to underpin the current discursive practices as they are expressed above.

In Compute, there is a basic understanding of work as a way of creating economic effectiveness and wealth. Customers place orders for Compute's business systems in order to enhance their own profitability, and the profitability of Compute rests upon their ability to deliver expensive software with a minimum of effort. All Compute consultants are aware that projects often become more expensive to the customer than initially stated, but they think that the value they create in their work is still worth more. They strive for high salaries and even higher overtime payment, but they still envy the few colleagues who resigned and stayed with the customers as free lance consultants in order to make even more money. As compared to most people of their own age, they have got a much better start in their working lives (in economic terms), but they are just as eager as anyone else to improve their standard of living, achieve increased status in society and, in the end, become wealthy and happy. In order to fulfil these dreams, they subject themselves to imprisonment in a work situation that often is much different from the life for which they strive. If they just work hard, Compute and all future employers in the IT industry will deliver the good life to them. They are thus not only imprisoned in projects, they are imprisoned in the taken-for-granted dream of economic growth and technological development upon which all Western societies are founded (von Wright, 1993). Even though they might want to be promoted away from project-based work, they will never leave the industry.

In BOH, the basic notion of work is somewhat different. Many of the BOH employees know that they could have been better off, given that most of them are well-educated and active professionals, and they do want a high standard of living just like anybody else. On the other hand, they consider themselves fortunate – they are actually being paid for devoting their days to create acclaimed performances at a prestigious opera house. Unlike the Compute consultants, many of them have spent substantial parts of their lives and their economic resources on education, preparation and rehearsals in order to become what they are today.

Values like responsibility, competence, commitment, motivation and creativity are embraced in BOH. Individuals primarily seek interesting, intellectual and exciting projects. The overall aim is to develop themselves as well as other people in society (the audience). People and societies must be educated and developed through culture, music, theatre, literature and other cultural expressions, even though they may sometimes express reluctance towards such education. Within the culture sector there is also a clear difference between so-called high culture and culture that many people want to consume (often regarded as popular culture). In the high-culture sector, we can also see the same expression of modern society of a longing for growth in society (but in cultural-based terms). Therefore, we cannot dichotomise our cases in that sense. Both are expressions of society, and their ways of legitimising work in projects are different but at the same time expressions of growth (in an economic or cultural sense). Moreover, most people want to have both cultural and economic outcomes of their jobs.

As we can see in these cases people are imprisoned without thinking explicitly in such terms; they work hard, accept rules, punishment, supervision – the whole concept of effective and rational project management. Both project examples here have to an extent the same construction and therefore to an extent the same impact on people: time schedules with tightly held plans, unique/unusual exciting tasks, and other attractive dimensions that engage people to commitment – in other words typical project characteristics. The project work form is perceived as legitimate in itself, assumed to be the best way to achieve personal and organisational goals, notwithstanding what those goals are. While contemporary organisations are required to provide a balance between task orientation and relationship orientation in order to be viewed as attractive to people, projects need not be balanced – or should not be.

Another form of structure in both these cases is the gender-related assumption that different individuals handle the notion of project work in different ways. Our working life in society is constructed from gender relations, and we can also analyse that from project-based work (Lindgren and Packendorff, 2006). There is an ongoing masculinisation of project work (for example, working time, need for achievement, goal orientation, rationality and the separation of work and private life). By this we do not mean that women cannot be committed to these kinds of values; on the contrary there are women who argue in line with masculine structures (Lindgren and Packendorff, 2006). A dichotomous relationship between private life and work life often implies problems for people with children and other responsibilities and values (Holmquist and Lindgren, 2002). These responsibilities become a problem they have to resolve by themselves and not something that should affect companies and projects.

Project work as a societal discourse: some thoughts

When the first prophecies on an increased 'projecticisation' of society were presented in the 1960s, the general idea was that bureaucracies had failed and would be replaced by other, more effective organisational forms (Bennis and Slater, 1968). A common denominator of these forms was that they would be 'temporary', that is, time-limited, goal-focused sequences of action (Miles, 1964). While there were worries about the social consequences of this, such as fragmentation of life and identity and a lack of long-term relations at the workplace (Miller and Rice, 1967; Palisi, 1970), this trend was still seen as attractive since it was expected to liberate people from their bureaucratic iron cages.

Now that projecticised society – at least partially – is in place, we can say that the expectations were relevant in many ways (Sennett, 1998). However, we can also see new and different consequences of projecticisation, consequences that are related to changed values in society. When we now make project work subject to critical enquiry, we do it from the values and perspectives of today, which means that we see other things. Yes, many individuals have more stimulating and self-controlled work situations than forty years ago, and yes, they sometimes pay for that by having – on the surface – a more fragmented life. On the other hand, changing work contexts and decreased dependence upon single organisations are today seen as a virtue rather than a drawback; in that sense, people have changed their values in interaction with changing conditions for work (Arthur et al., 1999).

What we have highlighted in this chapter is that people can still be regarded as the 'obedient victims' of their work situations, but in other, and subtler, ways. On the surface, the project work form can be seen as providing freedom, a sense of doing something important and stimulating. Beneath this surface, we understand people to be even more (self-)controlled in time, in space and in their mindsets. To put it starkly: bureaucracies failed, not because they controlled people too much, but because they could not control them enough. Where bureaucracies failed in this respect, projects have succeeded, at least to a point.

Expressed in terms of Foucault's prison, project work implies disciplining people in space, in time and in their souls. In the traditional bureaucracies, this disciplining was open, formal and general, implying that it was a mandatory part of organisational membership, supported by written rules and structures, and 'fair' in the sense that everybody was subject to the same rule system. In modern project work, there are fewer such open, formal and general forms of disciplining people, since many of the traditional management responsibilities have been transferred to individuals themselves (see also Hodgson, 2004). Instead, the sources of discipline have become subtle, informal and individualised.

Space, that is, the dimension of bodily movement and control, is not formally regulated neither in Compute or in BOH. What happens is that people themselves regulate where to be and how to behave given the institutionalised habits of their organisations. It is hard for single consultants to question the tradition of working at the customer's office at Compute, just as it is hard for single actors to question the rehearsal procedures at BOH. The individual can be seen as formally free to choose, but on the other hand institutionalised habits/values seem hard to resist – reproduction rather than resistance.

A similar way of disciplining can be seen where time regulations are concerned. Compute formally requires a certain number of charged hours for each consultant each year, and BOH employees are supposed to work full-time (that is, 40 hours per week). In practice, though, work time is guided not by these regulations, but by project goals. Compute consultants are expected to work until projects are finished according to specifications, and BOH employees are expected to work until the successful deliverance on the opening night can be secured. Sometimes, this can be done within normal work hours, sometimes not. The point is that responsibility for goal accomplishment rests with the individual, and that the individual thus will personally have to take all consequences in terms of work hours.

Self-disciplining in space and time presupposes a self-disciplined mind, a mind accepting immediate, self-inflicted confinement in project routines in exchange for long-term rewards, be they money, prestige, societal responsibility or personal development. Those people that subject themselves to such self-disciplining are not just a certain category in the labour market, whose work-life specifics can be juxtaposed to other categories and where advantages and drawbacks can be found just as anywhere. They can also be seen as the elite of the labour market, holding the most attractive and/or well-paid positions in the most attractive and/or affluent organisations. Elites have always – for better and for worse – been extremely influential in constructing institutionalised beliefs on how life should be lived in society, and in that way also shaped the norms by which the population at large would live in the future.

Disciplining discourses (in this case projects) construct a context that includes and excludes different kinds of people, different kinds of values and different kinds of lifestyles. In general terms there are some groups of people that will be preferred over others. Project settings tend to be dominated by men, leaving other minorities outside. This is clearly the case in the Compute project. However, we can see similarities between the two sectors in how they have built their work settings for 'free' people without any main responsibility for anyone else but themselves. Since these individuals set the level of what is considered as 'good performance', the result is that many people with childcare responsibilities are seen as 'second-class employees'; in both these cases, women were in the minority and experienced problems with working schedules.

If we look at the acceptance for other minorities (like psychologically unstable people) we will find it more likely that the cultural sector will attract more of these people; the history of theatre, music, painting and so on is full of examples of 'different' people. This sector has an image of people being special in their way of living in society – a stereotypical image, which positions 'outsiders' to mainstream society as 'insiders' within cultural industries.

As researchers, we both enquire into projects and work by project, often multiple; we are the living examples of projectified working life. If we take a step aside and look at ourselves, we can see the same consequences for us as people as we have seen for our cases. However, we can be expected to have some self-reflection upon our own lives; sometimes we have crises that force us to reflect on our way of living (Lindgren and Wåhlin, 2001). Nevertheless, in our daily practice we reproduce the project society and project work. The life of a contemporary researcher is one of temporary positions, time-limited research grants, scholarships, courses – all intended to keep us at the competitive edge in the quest for new knowledge. Many management researchers of today are torn between the respective discourses of the Compute and BOH employees; we do think that we have something important to contribute, and from time to time we consider ourselves fortunate and privileged. Nevertheless, we also sometimes compare salaries with our old friends from undergraduate business and economics courses, and when companies call for some extra help, we look forward to the invoicing stage. When we ask ourselves what could be done to improve the working and living conditions for Compute and BOH employees, we agree that reflection, questioning and emancipation are the natural way to go. However, what we need to reflect upon, question and emancipate ourselves from is not only organisational practices, it is the general ideological foundations upon which our society is built. In the same way, our own emancipation as researchers is closely intertwined with the foundations of the university system. The present powerful institutional prison of projects can be as good as any new one – we know what we have, but we do not know what we will get.

References

Alvesson, M. (1991) 'Organizational Symbolism and Ideology', *Journal of Management Studies*, 28(3): 207–25.

Arthur, M.B., Inkson, K. and Pringle, J.K. (1999) *The New Careers: Individual Action and Economic Change*. London: Sage.

Asplund, J. (1979) *Teorier om framtiden*. Stockholm: Liber.

Bennis, W.G. and Slater, P.E. (1968) *The Temporary Society*. New York: Harper & Row.

Buchanan, D.A. (1991) 'Vulnerability and Agenda: Context and Process in Project Management', *British Journal of Management*, 2(3): 121–32.

Buckle, P. and Thomas, J. (2003) 'Deconstructing Project Management: A Gender Analysis of Project Management Guidelines', *International Journal of Project Management*, 21; 433–41.

Calás, M. and Smircich, L. (1991) 'Voicing Seduction to Silence Leadership', *Organization Studies*, 12(4): 567–602.

Calás, M. and Smircich, L. (1992) 'Re-writing Gender into Organizational Theorizing: Directions from Feminist Perspectives', in M. Reed and M. Hughes (eds), *Re-thinking Organization: New Directions in Organizational Theory and Analysis*. London: Sage.

Christensen, S. and Kreiner, K. (1997) *Projektledning: Att leda och lära i en ofullkomlig värld*. Lund: Academia Adacta.

Clegg, S. and Courpasson, D. (2004) 'Political Hybrids: Tocquevillean Views on Project Organizations', *Journal of Management Studies*, 41(4): 525–47.

Cooper, R. (1989) 'Modernism, Post Modernism and Organizational Analysis 3: The Contribution of Jacques Derrida', *Organization Studies*, 10(4): 479–502.

Culler, J. (1983) *On Deconstruction*. London: Routledge & Kegan Paul.

Derrida, J. (1973) *Speech and Phenomena*. Evanston, IL: Northwestern University Press.

Derrida, J. (1976) *Of Grammatology*. Baltimore, MD: The Johns Hopkins University Press.

Ekstedt, E., Lundin, R.A., Söderholm, A. and Wirdenius, H. (1999) *Neo-Industrial Organizing: Action, Knowledge Formation and Renewal in a Project-Intensive Economy*. London: Routledge.

Engwall, M. (1995) *Jakten på det Effektiva Projektet*. Stockholm: Nerenius & Santérus.

Engwall, M. and Jerbrant, A. (2003) 'The Resource Allocation Syndrome: The Prime Challenge of Multi-project Management', *International Journal of Project Management*, 21(6): 403–9.

Foucault, M. (1977) *Discipline and Punish: The Birth of the Prison*. London: Allen Lane.

Gill, R. (2002) 'Cool, Creative and Egalitarian? Exploring Gender in Project-Based New Media Work in Europe', *Information, Communication & Society*, 5(1): 70–89.

Hassard, J. (1999) 'Images of Time in Work and Organization', in S.R. Clegg and C. Hardy (eds) *Studying Organization: Theory and Method*. London: Sage.

Hodgson, D.E. (2002) 'Disciplining the Professional: The Case of Project Management', *Journal of Management Studies*, 39(6): 803–21.

Hodgson, D.E. (2004) 'Project Work: The Legacy of Bureaucratic Control in the Post-Bureaucratic Organization', *Organization*, 11(1): 81–100.

Holmquist, C. and Lindgren, M. (2002) 'Why Opposites Attract – On the Problems of Dichotomisation in Research', paper for the Academy of Management annual meeting, 11–14 August 2002, Denver, Colorado, USA.

Janssens, M. and Steyaert, C. (2002) 'Qualifying Otherness', in S. Leijon, R. Lillhannus and G. Widell (eds) *Reflecting Diversity*. Gothenburg: BAS Publishers.

Kerfoot, D. and Knights, D. (1998) 'Managing Masculinity in Contemporary Organizational Life: A "Managerial Project"', *Organization*, 5(1): 7–26.

Kidder, T. (1981/2000) *The Soul of a New Machine*. Boston, MA: Little, Brown.

Kilduff, M. (1993) 'Deconstructing Organizations', *Academy of Management Review*, 18(1): 1–13.

Knights, D. (1997) 'Organization Theory in the Age of Deconstruction: Dualism, Gender and Postmodernism Revisited', *Organization Studies*, 18(1): 1–19.

Kreiner, K. (1995) 'In Search of Relevance: Project Management in Drifting Environments', *Scandinavian Journal of Management*, 11(4): 335–46.

Lindgren, M. and Packendorff, J. (2003) 'A Project-Based View of Entrepreneurship: Towards Action-Orientation, Seriality and Collectivity', in D. Hjorth and C. Steyaert (eds), *Entrepreneurship: New Movements*. Cheltenham: Edward Elgar.

Lindgren, M. and Packendorff, J. (2006) 'What's New in New Organisational Forms? On the Construction of Gender in Project-based Work', *Journal of Management Studies* (forthcoming).

Lindgren, M. and Wåhlin, N. (2001) 'Identity Construction among Boundary-Crossing Individuals', *Scandinavian Journal of Management*, 17(3): 357–77.

Linstead, S. (1993) 'Deconstruction in the Study of Organizations', in J. Hassard and M. Parker (eds), *Postmodernism and Organizations*. London: Sage.

Lundin, R.A. and Söderholm, A. (1995) 'A Theory of the Temporary Organization', *Scandinavian Journal of Management*, 11(4): 437–55.

Macintosh, N.B. (1994) *Management Accounting and Control Systems: An Organizational and Behavioral Approach*. Chichester: Wiley.

March, J.G. and Simon, H.A. (1958) *Organizations*. New York: John Wiley & Sons.

Martin, J. (1990) 'Deconstructing Organizational Taboos: The Suppression of Gender Conflict in Organizations', *Organization Science*, 1: 339–59.

Meredith, J.R. and Mantel, S.J. Jr (2000) *Project Management: A Managerial Approach*. New York: Wiley.

Mintzberg, H. (1980) *The Nature of Managerial Work*. Englewood Cliffs, NJ: Prentice-Hall.

Miles, M.B. (1964) 'On Temporary Systems', in M.B. Miles (ed.), *Innovation in Education*. New York: Teachers College Press.

Miller, E.J. and Rice, A.K. (1967) *Systems of Organization: The Control of Task and Sentient Boundaries*. London: Tavistock.

Morris, P.W.G. and Hough, G.H. (1987) *The Anatomy of Major Projects: A Study of the Reality of Project Management*. Oxford: Wiley.

Mumby, D.K. and Putnam, L.L. (1992) 'The Politics of Emotion: A Feminist Reading of Bounded Rationality', *Academy of Management Review*, 17(3): 465–86.

Packendorff, J. (1995) 'Inquiring into the Temporary Organization: New Directions for Project Management Research', *Scandinavian Journal of Management*, 11(4): 319–33.

Packendorff, J. (2002) 'The Temporary Society and Its Enemies: Projects from an Individual Perspective', in K. Sahlin-Andersson and A. Söderholm (eds), *Beyond Project Management: New Perspectives on the Temporary-Permanent Dilemma*. Malmö: Liber/Copenhagen University Press.

Palisi, B.J. (1970) 'Some Suggestions about the Transitory–Permanence Dimension of Organizations', *British Journal of Sociology*, 21: 200–6.

Pinto, J.K. (1996) *Power & Politics in Project Management*. Sylva, NC: Project Management Institute.

Scotto, M. (1998) 'Project Resource Planning', in J.K. Pinto (ed.), *Project Management Handbook*. San Francisco, CA: Jossey-Bass.

Sennett, R. (1998) *The Corrosion of Character: The Personal Consequences of Work in the New Capitalism*. New York: W. W. Norton.

Söderlund, J. (2004) 'Building Theories of Project Management: Past Research, Questions for the Future', *International Journal of Project Management*, 22: 183–91.

Stinchcombe, A.L. and Heimer, C.A. (1985) *Organization Theory and Project Management*. Oslo: Norwegian University Press.

von Wright, G.H. (1993) *Myten om framsteget*. Stockholm: Bonniers.

7

The contested object: on projects as emergent space

Manuela Nocker

Introduction

'Objects are back in strength in contemporary social theory ... a new world of materialities and objectivities has emerged with an urgency which has turned them into new sites of perplexity and controversy' (Pels *et al.*, 2002: 1). In line with the authors, in this chapter I argue that the mainstream idea of 'project' and related project management methodology can be seen as such new objectivities. Against the background of an increasing 'projectification of the firm' (Midler, 1995), the role of projects takes on multiple meanings that suggest the importance of looking more closely at the implications of the mainstream idea of 'the project-as-object'. In Europe, project-based organising ranks high among the strategic issues for addressing change in companies (Whittington *et al.*, 1999) and there is a constant augmentation of discourses with the purpose of extending its role. For instance, projects are seen to be enabling or facilitating global change (PMI, 2000). From such a vantage point, an explicit effort is made to ascribe agency to projects as artefacts. Projects have thus 'been promoted as a universal promise of solutions' (Cicmil, 2003: 6).

Hence, researchers and practitioners *encounter* the project as objective reality 'out there' that can be managed through the use of specialist knowledge, prescriptive tools and standards of professional practice.

However, despite the effort to codify ever more knowledge by the most authoritative professional bodies in the field, projects continue also to fail. Failures are not only frequent (Kharbanda and Pinto, 1996; Ciborra, 2002); they take on different forms, including the lack of commitment of practitioners towards project management methods (Forsberg *et al.*, 1996) as well as slow rates of renewal of associated methodologies (Morris, 1994). Sources of potential and actual failure are therefore not integrated in specific literature while there is only scant evidence that the application of formalised knowledge actually brings about better project outcomes (Morris, 2003). The call for a 'paradigmatic transformation of the discipline' is tied to the urgent need to analyse the theoretical underpinnings that paradoxically contribute to bring about problems in project management (Koskela and Howell, 2002: 12). The shortcomings are around the dynamics of project organisation, which 'are often overlooked, and so are the project's relations to its environment' (Söderholm, 2001: 1). 'We consider the "mainstream" Project Management approach, as it is expressed in textbooks and PMI's PMBOK, to be highly advanced in prescribing *how projects should be organised*' (Söderholm, 2001: 1, emphasis in original). Hence, the traditional focus on project management on issues of planning and control has several limitations. In order to offer an alternative reading, in this chapter I suggest viewing the project as an emergent space with multiple ontologies. These shape what I will henceforth call the 'project horizon' – the crystallisation of possibilities and expectations that define the project definition by stakeholders.

The chapter is organised as follows. The first section explores the necessary background to conceptualise space creation and introduces the theory of Lefebvre, used here to make distinctions regarding the specific nature of social space. In the second section I approach the notion of the project horizon as emerging from a multiple narrative space constituted and shaped through every day's performance of the social practice of project work. The third section of the chapter describes the qualitative methodology used to identify the complex nature of the project horizon in the case under study. I then narrate three different stories to account for the generation and transformation of action spaces by the project team and other stakeholders. The stories are crucial in order to show the substitutions, extensions or restrictions of the different kind of spaces discussed. In the concluding section, the narratives will be discussed in terms of the 'project' as a multiple and differential space of performance.

The creation of social space

The concept of space takes on many meanings. 'Space is a particularly popular trope. We are bombarded with mental/cognitive space, discursive space, knowledge space, social space, architectural space, object space, Euclidean/Cartesian space, dwelling space, body space, haptic space, optical space, acoustic space, personal space, existential space, network space, communications space, travelling space, narrative space, memory space, sacred space, geographic space, cartographic space, space-time, cosmological space, abstract space, mathematical space …' (Turnbull, 2002: 135). Thus, identifying differences of assumptions in the usage of the term is important as it provides the ground for conceptualisations and also for action, including political action and struggle (Massey, 1994). It is not my intention to focus on how the space metaphor has been used to specifically convey an understanding of power or emancipation – for this I invite the reader to refer back to relevant literature (for example, Arendt, 1951;

Foucault, 1977). At the same time, the narratives in this chapter fully incorporate a view that space is not politically neutral nor is it devoid of power effects. The case under study will show that space is often constructed as tension between different expectations. Hence, I try to offer an exploration of some of the multiple spaces of action and experience that can be created by focusing on project work. I suggest that the 'project' is constituted by heterogeneous spaces that interweave to create different kinds of experience and agency over time. Therefore, we need a starting point to understand the kind of space that I try to make sense of here – 'social space' – and how it is generated. From all possible starting points, I chose the work of Henri Lefebvre (1991) because of his profound analysis on the production of space based on spatial relations and the 'social space' of lived action. He conceptualised space as performed through the interaction of bodies, objects and environments (1991: 33–38). The various productions of space therefore result from both the actual and the possible material and social relations engendered.

Lefebvre (1991) was one of the first authors to stress that social space is an emergent process. According to the author, space is not simply there or a 'thing in itself' (1991: 90). The space of experience is more than a concept or a container to be filled. If space is materially produced, it is not separated from its creation process. The traditional view of organisation and organisations is to think in terms of space as an 'inside/outside', an entity *in* a context and, in the case of projects, as a project *in* a context. It is less common to examine how those actions or processes become themselves boundaries which produce other spaces (Hernes, 2004). This is here seen as a departure to start understanding the conceptualisation of the project as emergent space. Further, Lefebvre pointed out that space includes or excludes and takes on an active quality. 'Every social space is the outcome of a process with many aspects and many contributing currents, signifying and non-signifying, perceived and directly experienced, practical and theoretical' (1991: 110). This allows for actors to be viewed as active in the space construction and able to 'manipulate it' – a much neglected aspect in mainstream project management approaches.

Lefebvre's different currents point to the many aspects that construct space, including history and theories in vogue in a certain epoch. This is useful in order to conceptualise a multiple space – the project – as constituted through collective experience and social practice. Lefebvre speaks of a 'generative past' that inscribes 'upon the writing-tablet, so to speak, of space' (1991: 110). His work is rich and elaborated and my rendering takes only some of his insights. Lefebvre distinguished between three main ways to understand the use of space: *spatial practice, representational space* and *representations of space* (1991: 16–18). 'A critical point is how the different notions of space can be brought down to the world of organisation' (Hernes, 2004: 70). In an effort to translate Lefebvre's work for the organisational realm, Hernes (2004: 72–3) describes *spatial practice* as referring to the 'perceived spaces' of our everyday action such as meetings that both produce interactions and constitute a particular space. *Representational spaces* are the 'lived spaces that evolve from our historical past'. They refer to codes and signs about forms or shapes we imagine and give to space. *Representations of space* are the 'conceived spaces' that are those of 'imageries that are created by people in power'. These are, for instance, representations of organisational structure or rules. Lefebvre specified his original distinction regarding the main use of space in those three ways further as *mental, social, and physical space*. Trying to simplify the more sophisticated conceptualisation, Lefebvre's *mental space* refers to theory and concepts, philosophy and epistemology; the *social space* is a site of social relations and (re)production; the *physical space* refers to the materiality of locations such as urban spaces and territories. Lefebvre's two main sets of distinctions are not quite overlapping; what counts here is his aim to explain how those different spaces relate to each other to produce a space that is inherently social. The second set of distinctions can fruitfully be introduced here as a 'lens' to interpret the generation of what I call the project horizon – a multiple space of performance and jointly created meanings about 'what the project is about'. In this sense, Lefebvre's work helps to better distinguish the nature of spaces that were being generated and transformed.

Performing the object

This chapter takes the view that the object under consideration – the project – is *performed* in many ways, recursively creating boundaries for other performative spaces. In spatial terms, a performative view introduces another vantage point to look at project ontology. The performative nature of object construction has been theorised by Law (2002). He posits that objects are not 'things' but networks of relations and performances. According to Law, objectification depends on those relations and networks that, relatively speaking, become stable. The object construction depends on strategies that bind together relations that gain a spatial character. This space enables or constrains a certain continuity of the object. This is an important contribution to support the perspective taken in this chapter of the project that is not an entity or a mere architecture of positions and forms. In Law's view, space is not 'geographical' and takes on other forms like networks and fluids. The approach allows to think of space differently: the object is not defined any more by fixed boundaries. Law suggests giving voice to those fluid processes that are 'missed out' when focusing on the much used network metaphor and stresses the political dimension in the process of objectification. In the case study described in this chapter, for instance, the inherent political dimension of project work is explicitly rendered also in team members' accounts.

Social order is constituted mainly in discursive action (Harré, 2002). A material object becomes a 'social object' as a product of different narratives. Accordingly, objects are always constructed through stories by human beings who attribute a passive or active stance to those objects. For Harré, the object's identity changes with changing narratives and the effects of objects are always an interpretative issue. It is the construction of negotiated meanings that counts for the attribution of an overall meaning to the object, and this does not rule out how humans give meaning to material artefacts. The narratives which embed the object define what is considered 'real'. This resonates with the approach taken in this chapter to account for the construction of the 'project' through different enacted narratives of a team and other stakeholders. They are dynamically constructed through performances that invoke specific ways of ordering social relationships and materialities over time, opening up or restricting the project space.

If spaces can take on various forms while the meanings and identities of objects are negotiated in narratives, a performative reading of projects invites making a further step. The object is not just entangled in different relations and performances, and expressing different meanings; it also constrains or enables people's *movements*. Performances are *embodied* in movements. More recently, this has been stressed by Turnbull (2002), who focuses on landscape archaeology to see how space and knowledge 'come together' in readings of ancient monuments. In this view, monuments like megaliths can be approached as 'theatres of knowledge' (Turnbull, 2002: 127) that objectify spatial narratives of human action. Turnbull moves away from the mere listing of shapes, position, context and functions in the reading of monuments. Accordingly, a monument reflects different practices that changed over time that, in turn, reflect a particular society and epoch. In the view of Turnbull, rather than performing objects through an architectural plan, people move 'through and around' buildings. For the author, objects also 'perform people' in the sense that they constrain or enable our movements. Therefore, spaces influence the way individuals and groups move in space. Following this suggestions, projects would not be 'peopled' by passive spectators or defined (subject) positions. Boundaries are continuously formed; they shift and change the constellation of relationships and activity. This perspective challenges, for instance, a traditional idea of project participants' roles. In project management, roles are defined in advance and generally interpreted as functionally fixed. This can cause considerable problems in managing the actual situation for project actors. Instead, roles are tied to situated practice and experience that need to be taken into account being redefined in the situation (Nocker and Garcia-Lorenzo, 2003). Similarly to Turnbull, in anthropology Ingold (2000: 155) reminds us of 'feeling your way' when 'moving around' in spaces. In project management methodology, these aspects are marginalised or totally neglected: for instance, differences of experience and emotions are generally considered 'counterproductive' in order to 'streamline' the project structure in the pursuit of the 'common goal'. Hence the object inscribed in the mainstream perspective is one devoid of a view of performing that actively constructs the spaces of action and experience of participants (and non-participants). In this sense, seeking to understand the project as an emergent space means to 'keep fluid the many fixtures that performances, mediations, and techniques necessarily engender' (Pels *et al.*, 2002: 18).

This chapter seeks to 'keep fluid' those fixtures by exploring how social spaces are constituted and transformed through the enactment of shared but not univocal narratives that define the project horizon for the team and other stakeholders. As such, the space created allows or hinders the possibilities of 'becoming' (Tsoukas and Chia,

2002) and defines the transformations of the emergent project space. The chapter describes the shifts between mental, social and physical spaces in Lefebvre's terms that dynamically co-created each other and 'gained momentum' in the project team's story. What will be explored are the transformations in the way of ordering and enacting the ongoing project horizon. Unlike the abundant project management literature, this chapter offers a performative view of a *multiple project space* that is not already known from the outset and where *movement* is at the heart of 'coming to know' the project by the team and other stakeholders. In the next section I describe the research methods used to gather and analyse the data to reconstruct the team's narratives. I will subsequently present the case context for this research.

The empirical study: methodology

This section first describes the research methods used to gather the data for the longitudinal analysis of the project team's experience and activity that underlie the composition of the narratives that will be discussed in terms of space generation and transformation. The research strategy involved a case study research and a qualitative methodology that allowed the exploration of the dynamic nature of social practice, action and experience with the project team as focal actor of the narratives presented.

This study was inspired by ethnography in organisations and the observation of weekly team meetings became the main social setting and the method to gather data. I observed the team for three months, from the formal project start-up to its ending, after which I continued to gather data via interviewing and documents for another two months. The weekly team meetings were held at the client's headquarters, which also was the official project site. Several other *ad hoc* meetings were observed too, involving particular team members and other stakeholders. The observation of meetings was accompanied by 23 ongoing interviews (13 in-depth and face to face, five over the phone and five via email) with all team members and other participants in the project. Other data collected were field notes and team documentation such as memos, agendas, project risk and issue logs and presentations to the team's client. The use of different methods enabled the inclusion of different viewpoints to refine our understanding of the phenomena under study (Flick, 1992). The data so collected were analysed taking into account a 'grounded theory' approach (Glaser and Strauss, 1967) that produced a 'thick description' (Geertz, 1973) of team processes and events over time and formed the basis for the reconstruction of team narratives.

The longitudinal analysis was accomplished in two different steps. The first step sought to identify the activities, experience and processes of the team while they were engaged in the design of the front office system. It consisted of multiple readings of the meeting and interview transcripts, field notes and team documentation for the identification of everyday activities, experience and events. These were initially coded according to three main areas: the context and conditions of the project, the main team activities and processes, and the network of relationships between team members and other stakeholders. The coding was achieved with the aid of Atlas-ti, a qualitative research software system for data analysis and management (Murh, 1997). The second step involved the analysis of the specific ways of collective knowing that emerged from the situated activities and experiences of the team. Hence, knowing is viewed as constituted through interaction and communication (Tsoukas, 1996), generated by a group (Cook and Brown, 1999) and practice-based (Nicolini *et al.*, 2003). The present analysis focuses on the actual processes underlying the production of spaces that define the emerging project. The transformations reflect the workings of particular boundary spaces in three different narratives. Following this, I describe the background to this research in terms of the project team studied and aim of the project, the main actors involved and the conditions for project inception.

The case context

The study focuses on a front office information system design project carried out by an ICT inter-organisational project team. The team was initially composed of eight consultants from a Big 5 management consulting firm in the UK – Blooming Consulting – and a client representative engaged on a full-time basis. Blooming Consulting is a global management consulting firm with around 150 offices throughout the world with an extensive information technology consulting business. The project work was carried out at the headquarters of Blooming's actual client – Dill UK – one of the UK's leading recruitment agencies. Established in the 1980s, at the time of this research Dill UK had expanded into more than 50 branches across the country, employing up to 500 people. It supplies temporary and permanent secretarial staff to UK business companies. Dill UK was a subsidiary of Giant US, one of the world's major global temporary and permanent recruitment corporations. Within the UK, Giant US was branded autonomously as Dill UK. As will be shown, a larger recruitment corporation – Ride US – took over the business from Giant US during the project under study which forced it to a halt within a short period thereafter.

The reason for the project set-up was Dill UK's operating procedures. These were not standardised between company branches and there was no electronic network in place. Data on clients and applicants for temporary and permanent jobs were kept on paper files and processed manually and a great deal of business was done through informal communication between recruiters and applicants. Giant US's headquarters had previously conducted a study which examined the corporate European approaches to implementing recruitment software applications. Giant US concluded that the UK subsidiary – Dill UK – needed to implement a new front office system and its related infrastructure, in order to reduce the branch operating costs and improve communication between head office and branches, as well as reducing administrative efforts. The aim was also to improve staff morale and customer service, providing customers with direct email access to branches as well as increasing competitiveness, particularly in the corporate market. After six months of negotiations and preparations, the sponsor Giant US and Blooming Consulting in London jointly decided to start the project in Giant's subsidiary Dill UK. The initial business case provided the scope for the design, prototyping and development of a front office system and the roll-out of networked computers to Dill's recruitment branches. It was planned that design and prototyping would extend over six months, after which the system should be implemented (coinciding with the start of a new project/phase).

For initiating the project, the project team had to consider the potential modification and implementation of 'O2K', a software application already being used by Giant US's recruitment business. Blooming Consultants believed that the application was a reasonable functional fit with Dill's business requirements, though they still needed to confirm its feasibility and make the necessary changes to the source code to meet Dill's requirements. If that was not possible, alternatives would have to be found. The team also tried to ensure Giant US involvement during this phase so as to leverage the US team's expertise and knowledge during the project. That is, the team needed to access already existing knowledge regarding the O2K software application as well as to develop new knowledge identifying the requirements that branches of Dill UK would need. They also needed to 'get organised' as a team: set up the actual project organisation, plan the action, address the main issues and take the first steps in terms of specific team activity. The next section reconstructs the narratives on the creation and transformation of the social, physical and mental spaces in the construction of the ongoing project horizon.

Reconstructing the project horizon as multiple narrative space

The aim of this section is to present the project team's story in order to show the heterogeneous nature of 'the project' through the particular transformations of the ongoing project horizon that emphasises the collective experience of participants. In organisational research, stories have been seen as 'a poetic elaboration on actual events' (Gabriel, 2000: 152) – a position stressing the need to distinguish the story from a 'fact' but maintaining that the latter is nevertheless reconstructed. Also, narratives offer a space for sense-making and interpretation where the ordinary and the exceptional can coexist (Bruner, 1990) and are particularly useful to present a dynamic view of the multiple space construction in this research. The narratives highlight different kinds of spaces of experience and social practice enacted by the team together with other stakeholders which, in turn, created new boundary spaces for collective action and experience. I have built the framework presented in Table 7.1 upon two main dimensions. The vertical dimension allows a reconstruction of the narratives by identifying the scenario, main participants and the main action, adapting Burke's *pentad* in dramatism (1945). The horizontal dimension reflects the temporal positioning of the narratives

Table 7.1 Complete narrative framework with vertical dimensions (story elements) and horizontal dimensions (boundary spaces and ongoing transformations of the project horizon)

Narratives/evolution of project horizon	The options	Synchronising	The drift
Story elements			
Scene and purpose (where and why)	Gathering technical requirements	Identifying viable solutions	Redefining the project
Actors (who)	The team and the *resisting* US consultants	The team and the *eschewing* client	The team and the US *virtual* stakeholders
Act/action (what and how)	Developing alternatives	Formalising activity	Improvising goals
Space/boundary created (Lefebvre, 1991)	'Social space'	'Physical space'	'Mental space'
Project horizon	Identification	Viability	Reframing

and also highlights the nature of the ongoing space construction *focused* by the project team according to the earlier framework for interpretation inspired by Lefebvre on the mental, social and physical space construction. As such, the first narrative exposes the project team's extension and intensification of sociality, the second looks at project inscription through a shift to the physical space and the last narrative stresses the project horizon as a (mental) space of possibilities.

I now present the three stories, 'The options', 'Synchronising' and 'The drift'. These emphasise the enactment of particular social practices, the experience and the meanings generated by the team and other stakeholders in this project. Each narrative highlights the collective performance of different ways of knowing which generate and shape the movement of spaces and boundaries of the emerging project horizon.

'The options'

This story relates to the start of the project and the identification of the technical and functional requirements for the design and prototyping of a front office system for Dill UK. The narrative tells about 'capturing requirements' that were not already available but had to be accessed through a software source code (O2K) that could only be obtained via the collaboration of US consultants at the client's headquarters in the USA. The story accounts for how the team was trying to find a way to establish an action space under considerable resistance from other stakeholders. The issue of 'knowledge accessibility' was present throughout the duration of the project but was prominent in this narrative. The story demonstrates the problem of thinking of knowledge that can be 'transferred'. Indeed, the team could not just 'capture' the technical requirements of the software application for the client because the competitors were not ready to 'give away' knowledge easily. This forced the team to develop the social space in an effort to learn and develop micro-strategic action (Johnson *et al.*, 2003) in order to convince other stakeholders who were openly opposing some initiatives by the team. In project management mainstream approaches, this kind of situated social practice is not taken into account and for mainstream information systems methodology requirement analysis is mainly considered a functional process although empirical research in the field suggests otherwise (for example, Walsham and Han, 1993; Myers, 1995; Brown, 1998). The story shows not only how goals are not 'transparent' and need to be negotiated but also the importance of setting learning goals in the process of accomplishing objectives and different steps in the project.

Gathering technical requirements

The team was working on three different strands of activities to identify and later document the requirements for the front office information system at Dill UK. They needed to understand the business processes in the recruitment agency's branches to gather the functional requirement of the system and the infrastructure needed in terms of hardware for all branches. The most urgent priority was the technical requirements of the software application for the recruitment business. Specifically, the team wanted to know if the software application O2K used at the client's headquarters in the USA was offering a reasonable technical and functional fit also for its subsidiary Dill UK. 'Capturing requirements' was therefore not just a matter of individual effort or collecting documentation, which was not readily available; it entailed acquiring relevant knowledge via communication to other participants in the process. In the first instance these were some prospective users, the hardware and network suppliers, and the main stakeholders in this period: the consultants at the client headquarters of Giant US. The main team story begins with the question for the project team of whether the O2K software application could be modified and implemented in the UK, as put by the business developer in the project team:

> Basically, there is going to be a certain amount of technical input into the direction of the project whether we take the existing US application or we don't take it ... If we do go for the O2K application, then we need to either interface with the US team – they're gonna be responsible for that redevelopment phase – or we gonna need to run that re-development ourselves. So it's a case of learning how the O2K application works internally and making the changes.

But the idea to adopt the software application O2K for Dill UK caused the team to worry about the technical functionality of the software application for the UK:

> I don't think it's a good idea to use O2K, to use the American application, I don't think that's a good idea ... There are technical flaws in O2K that I'm not happy about leaving Dill UK with because they essentially run the risk of investing a lot of money in an obsolete product.

With this background, the project team planned a visit to the client's headquarters in the USA with the goal of 'getting access' to the software source code of the application via the US consultants and executives. The aim was to know the actual application's requirements better, which would allow the team to make recommendations about its adoption for Dill UK.

The team and the resisting US consultants

The level of collaboration at Giant's headquarters turned out to be unsatisfactory. Gathering technical requirements was tied to unexpected corporate politics which forced the team to review its action strategy. The main challenge became how to face the US consultants' resistance to 'give away' their knowledge about the software source code O2K and its procedures. The reasons for the resistance was that the US consultants had already implemented an office system at headquarters which was based on that source code. The project history thus impinged on current relationships to a degree that cooperation was severely obstructed. The US consultants felt they 'owned' the project and saw the UK team as competitors:

> Behind that: The thing is there's a lot of ... these guys have been working on this project for a long time in the US. They have a very strong ownership of this software, a very strong ownership of the project. Also the project hasn't run, it's been a success overall, but it hasn't run as smoothly as they hoped and then ... a lot of defence over their project, so they didn't just want to kind of show their cards at once, they didn't want us to see ... they were very helpful but they were trying to make us realise that 'we have the procedure' ... So, at that point they'd gave us a lot of warnings that things may not be as easy as we thought.

Further, the project supervisor was backed in his preferences for Blooming Consultants by another top executive at Giant US (here called Robert), which seemed to irritate the US consultants even more. In the project manager's account, the team's action strategy was therefore to be attentive and convince US consultants of their expertise for the project but they were not really able to defuse the competitive stance:

> It wasn't a good start. I think we addressed that during the week by being present and efficient and convincing them of our capabilities but nevertheless they have a concern that Arthur [project supervisor] is using Blooming because they used Blooming a lot more. It's Robert's idea and these guys don't like it much. So that was an issue.

Gathering requirements could therefore not be pursued in a 'straightforward' way on the basis of technical information considerations; it became only possible through a sounder understanding of the complex corporate relationships at Giant US's headquarters.

Developing alternatives

In this situation, the team decided to adopt a cautious communication strategy towards key stakeholders. Without it any attempt to 'capture the requirements' would fail. The goal became satisfying the stakeholders' expectations and to temporarily suspend definitive answers regarding the choice of the software to implement for the client Dill UK:

> If there were no political dimensions, I think even now we would have concerns with O2K, a weak candidate, *we'll keep the option open but we're thinking of ditching it*. If it wasn't for the politics we'll be saying that now but because of the politics we won't say quite that now; what we will say is 'We have got some reservations; we need to search for other alternatives and make a final decision in about a month so'. We are giving them a watered-down-message. (Italics added)

Careful communication to maintain relationships becomes paramount for the team and the only way to 'manage' the knowledge exchanges between the different stakeholders. In this context, the team started to consider various options simultaneously and came to the decision to pursue certain activities in parallel. They wanted to evaluate the situation and generate alternatives for action. Alternatives were not given; they needed to be generated and supported through targeted action:

> So what we've decided to do is, over the next week, we've gonna summarise the findings from the process, technical and infrastructure, and then *suggest some steps in parallel*, so that may involve package selection. The other answer is to take the current software development as we'd originally planned. A third option is to wait and to build the infrastructure ... So there are the main options. In terms of what we will recommend, we are not sure yet. (Italics added)

The team felt it did not have enough knowledge yet to actually decide on a particular type of alternative nor was it allowed to do so freely. Hence, they shifted perspective and instead of focusing on O2K they accelerated the requirements-gathering via users – crucial for justifying the team's choices. The generation of alternatives was therefore based on the creation of various options that postponed the final decision on the choice of the software application.

'The Options' tells about the transformation of a rather 'physical' interpretation of the team's own action space – epitomised by an artefact (software application) – into an explicit extension of social space construction. The boundaries of this space are defined by what can be called 'the allowable' (Hernes, 2004: 72). In the initial assumption of the team, identifying technical and functional requirements of the system was a 'straightforward' matter; they needed 'to have a look at the source code – to see what is inside'. The concentration was on the manipulation of procedures and technical feasibilities – a process that was not problematised by the team. Pels (2002) calls this the 'Münchhausen effect', a practical everyday reification of socially constructed objects. These create fixed ways in maintaining social relationships. According to Pels, any produced 'facts' can be accepted or rejected without actors being aware about the degree to which they themselves contribute to the performance of those facts. Also, those processes are not a 'one-off' moment of objectification but are continuously built and changed. Within project management practice, this is exemplified in many routine practices like the design of a business process. In the situation, changing assumptions and actions turned out to be a difficult endeavour. It required the team to first transform its perception of the action space, which was tied to 'getting access' to the necessary knowledge via the US consultants. In order to accomplish the goal (to know the 'technical fit' of the software), the team needed to engage with stakeholders more intensively to support cooperation, attending to relationships and corporate politics. The team also had to quickly incorporate in its habitual practice a view of the political dimension of project work in order to proceed and not to jeopardise the project.

'Synchronising'

The team was now entangled in European corporate management issues but continued to be heavily affected by the project sponsor Giant US. The team also temporarily 'lost' its objectives and the story is about the difficulties in 'getting on route' again, albeit not on the previous one of designing and prototyping the front office system. 'Synchronising' is about coordinating the actions within the team and with other stakeholders in order to carry on the project. In this narrative what really is at stake is ownership and legitimacy. The case narrates serious ambiguities in this realm within the team and from other stakeholders. The team tried to extend its own influence in this project and was constantly 'testing' the boundaries of what can be called 'the permissible' (Hernes, 2004: 72). In order to extend the space of influence, the team – almost paradoxically – needed to 'tighten' the boundaries. Indeed, inclusion and exclusion are relevant processes and the story 'Synchronising' particularly tells how those processes are related to the coordination of team action. In order to influence other stakeholders, the team accelerated and intensified coordination activities and communication by searching for alliances. The narrative shows the effort to formalise, thus to 'materialise' (physical space), an inherent social space. This story also illustrates how this was not taken on board lightly by some team members (for example, the client representative as joint project manager) and was a matter of different understandings about project management practice.

Identifying viable solutions
The US consultants continued to refuse to take on board the UK project team's reservations about O2K. The team searched for another way to satisfy the client's front office system requirements better than the contested application O2K. The 'way out' was to seek alliances that could support the team's strategy in the European corporate management in Paris:

> Well, the European management are meeting in Paris … we've got to communicate the findings … is part of our communication strategy for getting this information to the United States … and may help us to get some stuff done so this way we go to Paul Ardenne right on the top and any another route, it would stop on a level under the top.

Rather than implementing O2K, the team would now set up the process for software package selection. This decision would further be validated by the users in the recruitment agency through some workshops. The project scope was no longer as originally laid out. Therefore the team had to both adopt a cautious behaviour regarding the US team and become proactive by searching support and alliances with the European management to be able to implement an alternative front office solution for Dill UK. The process of package selection had to be planned on a very solid ground for negotiations in the USA and marked a fundamental change of perspective in the project. Overall, this was seen as a positive step by the team but still needed to be 'internalised' by all team members as noted by the project manager:

> Listen, I think it's a quite fundamental shift of the project, which was all around design, all around O2K ... so we can manage our own idea. (Team meeting)

The team and the eschewing client

Seeking alliances for rendering solutions viable was not just a matter of 'knocking on doors' of the European corporate management. The strategy involved attending to problems with the main referents for the team: the project supervisor and the company's CEO. Up to this moment the team had followed the supervisor's preferences regarding project actions but now the relationship started to change as a result of a number of issues. For instance, there were concerns in Dill UK regarding the software post-implementation user support. These concerns were never addressed by the project supervisor. As a result, the team found itself in an ambiguous position regarding its actual role. The team decided to draw boundaries: reciprocal expectations should be made clear at this point. Also, for the team it was time to clarify the project scope with Dill UK. This was tied to membership issues too: some Dill managers felt 'entitled' to join the team on their meetings whereas the project team was reluctant to grant them membership. The first boundary to draw was thus reminding top management of the original project scope since they were finding signs that the CEO of Dill UK was expecting the team to intervene in organisational issues:

> Charles: 'Let's be clear, we are not kind of reengineering Dill UK ... let's keep the boundaries tight!'
> Julie: 'Bill needs to be made aware of that and because as far as he is concerned he's putting in that.'
> Charles: 'We can't ... I mean, if we redesign the whole business would be a lovely job to do but it's not in the scope, you know.' (Team meeting)

For the team, managing boundaries meant starting to push the client and taking on responsibilities in this project. Negotiations with hardware and network suppliers demanded a decision from the project supervisor that the latter was not yet prepared to make. This directly influenced the work of the network expert dealing with suppliers, who was starting to suffer from the supervisor's lack of decision-making.

Charles: 'OK, that's fair, I wouldn't want to recommend cause we are not sure if he wants this.'
Phil: 'Is exactly what I was gonna say, I do not feel qualified to write a letter of intent.'
Charles: 'So, Steve has to write it himself …'
Phil: 'Yeah.'

In this sense, drawing boundaries involved taking stock of the current situation regarding decision-making and the state of relationships in this project. The solution envisaged was to start being more proactive and clarify roles and responsibilities between team and client.

Coordinating and formalising activities

The team was working to become more influential regarding its own proposals on the front office solution for Dill UK. The adoption of the software O2K could not be excluded but the team proceeded with different actions in parallel. The goal was to eventually select a software package and not the final solution yet. In order to prevent backlashes from the USA, the team accelerated some steps and this required a higher degree of coordination from the team and stakeholders. It became necessary to introduce certain procedures and common rules for documenting and speeding up joint activities:

Review of risks and issue log: At the moment there is no info sharing between branches, but CR insisted that we shouldn't mimic processes as they are but should enable future functional requirements. Central info management might be required in the future, for billing for example … CR *insisted on need to accelerate process* of identifying functionalities in order to select package in order for PS to clarify infrastructure requirements. *To be formalised in R&I log.* (Document, italics added)

It also meant revising the project plan and centralising communication in this project:

The project manager: '… just to *make sure that the plan is showing progress* for each activity.'
A junior consultant: 'I need *emails to track communication!*'

Formalising was also tied to a general reinforcing of teamwork procedures. This was not taken on board by all team members in the same way. In particular the joint project manager as client representative in the team was ambivalent over the use of common procedures:

Charles: 'Anything else to talk about?'
Julie: 'Actually, can we sort out to know where people are, whether people are in, when the people are around, whether people are having meetings or meetings somewhere else? You guys work projects, I'm learning as I'm going along but it is difficult to know where people go, when they're in, when they're out. You all guys can quite easily work from home or … but it's just so that we know when people are in this place, people are not working full time.'
Charles: '*How about a white board* and we put the name on for each day of the week?'
Julie: 'No, the problem is that it would never be updated!'

The subsequent introduction of the so-called 'location map' for tracking presence and absence of team members in the project office was not really enough to dissipate this kind of frustration. In fact, the expressions of the client representative (also joint project manager) had much deeper roots in her perceived 'knowledge gap' when comparing herself with Blooming Consultants' experience of project management:

> Is it possible, OK, to walk through all the stages, when I should be reading, when I shouldn't be reading? ... like documents and stuff like that ... or email, sensitive. I need to sit down and have a walk through something! You guys are going off to meetings! I feel I have to try and catch up all the time for knowing what to chase up. I mean, if there's something I should be doing. I do not actually know where you're focussing on. You guys know the processes and what you're supposed to do ... It makes me become very frustrated!' (Team meeting)

The narrative presented is about the construction of *actual viability* of the previously identified action alternatives. In order to increase efficiency of coordination, the team accelerated processes but could not do so without finally addressing the counterproductive state of top management relationships. These restricted considerably the action space of the team. Also, the 'knowledge gap' experienced by some participants regarding habitual professional practice was widened due to the 'tightening effect' of formalisation. The story highlights the material ordering of sociality through coordination of joint activity and emphasises the space of organising by 'regulation and binding' (Hernes, 2004: 82). William Pietz (2002) discusses social relationships that become objectified on the base of formal contracts. These are representative of how moral obligations are not enough in themselves to stabilise the social contract between people. The latter must become a 'tangible' fact in order to have effects. In this sense the materiality of (legal) objects becomes a condition of social relationships. 'Synchronising' shows the move of the project team towards a higher degree of materialisation of relationships. The coordination activities simultaneously point at the extension of the social space. The team was proactively building alliances in an effort to integrate knowledge and validate solutions and the chosen action strategy. In Haraway's sense (1991), synchronising activities become mediators of social and cultural orders as well as of political relations. The narrative therefore tells about boundary spanning but also about the particular way this was achieved (through the physical space of formalisation) and the conspicuous individual differences in sharing the experience.

'The drift'

The last story in this chapter tells how the project team was taken by surprise by the announcement of the project sponsor's takeover. Giant US was soon to be to be owned by a larger corporation in the USA called Ride US. This first posed a serious thread to the project in the UK and subsequently brought it to a halt. In 'The drift' the mode of ordering is based upon the mental space of 'stretching' the project horizon through scenario planning and sense-making about the immediate situation. In these circumstances, a bounded view of the already complex situation of the client organisation was no longer enough to understand the implications of the takeover for the project. Hence, the team shifted to a predominantly mental space construction of the project horizon. The team also learnt to improvise when focusing on immediate priorities in the absence of direction. This was the only way to develop goals even if they were transient. Questions about the future project's identity and the team's role under the new 'virtual' owners were emerging while potential relationships with key stakeholders and first referents were played out only in an 'imagined world'.

Redefining the project

The 'hard won' team strategy to pursue an alternative route to implementing the contested software application O2K for the client Dill UK could not be further pursued. Once again the team had to 'figure out' their own role and the expectations of new stakeholders. The first task was to redefine the project's scope following some high-priority goals from top management (project supervisor and Dill's CEO) without much information regarding the impact of the American takeover. Goals and working strategies shifted: to select a software package was no longer a priority; however to gather all requirements for the hardware and network infrastructure was urgent now. The takeover as a completely unforeseen major event felt to the team as if someone was 'playing dice' with the project. The uncertainty experienced by the team about the future existence of the project also increased:

> Julie: 'We don't know if we have a project, not really!'
> Charles: 'We have, we've definitely got an infrastructure project and we've definitely got a front office project. The front office project I think could have a gap while we resolve the extend of Ride's influence on the options ... and then it's go again!'
> Julie: 'Do you think it will just slow down and stop to delay for a while?'
> Charles: 'I could imagine that happening. No one is suggesting actually kind of formally delaying it and stop.'
> Julie: 'So we ... there won't be any more packages at the moment?'
> Charles: 'I think that's being appropriate because the one clear message from Ride US at the moment, rightly or wrongly, is we shouldn't proceed on that.' (Team meeting)

In this context, the team tried to 'work out a route forward' through the completion and documentation of the 'requirement capture'. What was at stake for the team now was not just a particular software solution but the project itself since a new powerful stakeholder had entered the scene and the team needed to take that into account.

The team and the virtual US stakeholders

The project's complexity increased since Ride US's recruitment corporation seemed to have a completely different solution from those explored by the team already implemented:

> Charles: 'But then there's the interesting question of where the Ride want to go … And also, they had a quick look at O2K and think it's tremendous! Which is interesting … So at the moment, they're taking the view, it's not clear whether Ride will adopt MAX, OLE or migrate to O2K. All is clear, is they don't want to go down a package route in Europe because they had a look at it a year ago …'
> Phil: 'Hang on, sorry! Ride is for O2K in the US?'
> Charles: 'Well, yeah …' (Team meeting)

So it seemed that O2K – the contested software application – was 'back again'. Furthermore there was no clear indication who the 'other' stakeholders or competitors would be either:

> Phil: 'How does our relationship go with Ride US?'
> Charles: 'Again, there's lack of clarity. It is not sure if it's Reach or Hack Consulting. It's not sure if they're just advising all the bid or if they're dealing ongoing IT stuff. We don't know basically.' (Team meeting)

The team engaged in a form of stakeholder analysis for identifying referents, trying to find out the kind of relationships between new stakeholders, the client and potential competitors. This sense-making strategy was enacted in the absence of any 'real' relationship dealing with the project's 'virtual' stakeholders:

> Then somehow we need to get into Ride US and work out who is in charge of IT Europe and say 'Here are our requirements. We'd had a look at O2K, off-the-shelf packages, and O2K didn't work. We thought off-the-shelf packages did. In your view, what options should we now be considering?' And try and work out a direction. We don't know at the moment who is in charge of direction. (Team meeting)

The team's effort to improvise a tentative strategy after the US takeover was intended to reframe the project scope in the light of ongoing activities and also to imagine scenarios involving sense-making, speculations and attempts at identifying stakeholders and potential competitors as critical referents.

Improvising a route forward

The lack of knowledge about the impact of the takeover and the new stakeholders, though, prompted the team to act on what they knew from before and impinged on goal achievement. In order not just to 'wait for direction' the team was aware that some decisions could have been taken already but were systematically postponed by the client.

The priority to complete the document about infrastructure requirements, for instance, pointed to the need to address top management's behaviour, particularly regarding the state of relationships between the project supervisor and the company's CEO. The idea was to bring them to agree at least on policies affecting users at Dill UK:

Julie: '*I don't think we have any resolution* on the whole training issue.'
Charles: 'To continuing that training thread, to confirm the training arrangements we need to have the policy around email and get that. We got some decision we've got to get made basically, OK? What do we need to do to get those decisions made, have we progressed that?'
Phil: 'We need to get to meet Arthur and Bill. So far we never managed to have Bill and Arthur in the same room! ... *We cannot just go bouncing backwards and forwards, try it!*'
(Team meeting)

Hence, the state of relationships between the main referents in this projects now directly influenced team actions:

Julie, I think, if you could push Arthur and Bill to *make sure we get to understand what our options are* and get the chance to look at those options at an early point, cause that seems to be where we are running into a wall. *We don't know what our options are and we can't look at them*, you know. (Team meeting)

Therefore, knowing how to facilitate decisions was based on setting criteria in the process. For the team it was paramount to 'unfreeze' decision-making in order not to 'get stuck' around possible progress in the project. The team experienced this as highly relevant now because it was aware about possible repercussions on users. The team planned that the set-up of a viable training strategy around the email system could be a viable goal to pursue – the only one left that seemed not to be changing because of the takeover:

Charles: 'We still got the email, so *I think that's the strongest thread* that we're definitely go ahead without delay as far as I'm concerned.' (Team meeting)

The project was soon to be brought to a definitive halt by the new American owner Ride US which would not further finance the project in the UK; any hope of the team to resume work was vanishing. Other narratives in this research tell about the considerable frustration and reflections of 'living in drifting environments' but this would make it necessary to add yet another story.

In these circumstances, a bounded view of the already complex situation of the client organisation was no longer enough to understand the implications of the takeover for the project. The narrative shows how the team had to 'drop' the hard-won strategy to pursue software package selection because of the takeover of Giant US. The project team was now engaged in sense-making and improvising a route forward. It engaged mainly in hypothesising about potential expectations of virtual stakeholders and scenario-planning regarding possible goals in the immediate context. These were mere conjecture and the team tried to identify potential referents in the yet unknown authority structure. The physical and social space were not characterising the project horizon anymore and 'The drift' was experienced particularly in thoughts and emotions rather than in the actions of team members. Through a mainly mental space construction – reframing – the team actively worked for the survival of the project in the hope that it would be carried on in another form.

The project as emergent space

This chapter started out with the aim of exploring the possibility of expanding our view on the nature of projects and thus to question the ontological roots of projects. This seems particularly important to aid our understanding about the 'naturalisation' of practices that currently make up the bulk of knowledge in project management (Hodgson and Cicmil, 2004: 7). Through the narratives in this chapter, I have invited the reader to focus on the construction of the 'project horizon' of a team in relation to other stakeholders. The project horizon was 'crystallising' the ongoing definition of the project and shaped the way to approach it. Following Henri Lefebvre's suggestions of the fundamentally social nature of space, I ventured on the journey of trying to look at the kind of spaces (mental, social, physical) that were being generated by a project team and were shaping the experiential, ideational and material dimensions of the project. The character of the space considered here is no longes a geometry or Euclidian space as put forward by mainstream project management methodology. I have tried to challenge the idea that there are fixed points, bounded regions, defined centres or margins. Indeed, the narratives encourage viewing the emerging project as a space which is 'always *heterogeneous* and *becoming*' (Chia, 2002: 866, emphasis in original).

Thus, space was concurrently enabled and constrained by participants and other stakeholders. At times, it was a site of struggle and resistance but the narratives refer also to the subtlety of processes, and describe the ambiguities in actors' practice. Looking at space as an *ongoing performance* has meant not interpreting those tensions 'just' as an issue of power. The latter has been a main concern in spatial readings. In this chapter, the materiality of practice, negotiations of interpretation and the imagined as the space of possibility (Lefebvre, 1991; Soja, 1996) all 'gain citizenship' in the construction of the project space and no singular space plays the protagonist. In mainstream project management methodology, the social and the lived seem often to be 'erased'. The status and roots of certain experiences in projects are not questioned. The performative character of space fundamentally reminds us that projects are not just about 'doing' (project activities) or discourse, and that social practice is always also about identities or better, certain forms of identification. Project team members in this story were having difficulties in incorporating such a perspective in their work, being often 'caught up' in and enacting a functional view of process.

The narratives are also about issues of inclusion and exclusion. At times, this was tied to the project team's narrow notion of 'project-making' – partly, though not exclusively, because of respective habitual professional practice. In this sense, viewing the project as an emergent space and ongoing performance means refining our understanding of social practice and paying attention to difference. The differential character of space is not however a property or characteristic of project participants; on the contrary, it is one enacted in practice and arising out of all the potential ambivalence of relationships and context. Therefore, important differences can 'go unnoticed' or be 'rejected' in traditional understandings of project management that forge a one-sided representation of practice and maintain the idea of difference as the intrinsic property of individuals or the situation.

The narrative approach used in this chapter has proved to be useful for *exposing* the complexity of organising and the uniqueness, chaos and surprise of lived experience (Tsoukas and Hatch, 2001; Bruner, 2002). What becomes 'central' to the efforts and attention of project participants is not necessarily placed centrally in spatial terms. A multiple space is space that allows the exploration of liminality. The three narratives explore spaces that themselves are boundary spaces and are made more complex through the restrictions, substitutions and extensions of space also due to peculiar rhythms of space dynamics. For instance, seeking to 'belong' (to the experts), one of the team members – the joint project manager – was herself an example of liminal space. She dwelled in a liminal space, not just in a the sense of taking on different project roles; it was about the constant crossing of the boundaries of identity, her different speed of learning, and her minority position in the team. This liminality was performed in related representations, emotions and actions. Hybrid spaces and the movements 'inbetween' are not attended to in current project management approaches and tend to be downplayed, and this was partly the case in the enactments of team members too.

Therefore, project spaces constantly *move* and transform over time. Space 'is in a sense actuated by the ensemble of movements deployed within it' (de Certeau, 1984: 115). The team 'came to know' the project by engaging in the creation and transformation of their own project horizon. Taking this perspective means to 'let go' of a structured idea of project and a project management methodology that can be prescribed. Hence, the project and its management become an ongoing accomplishment that enacts different interweaving 'fields of spaces' (Hernes, 2004: 75). In this perspective, the project can no longer be considered as a separate entity and begs questions beyond the identification and formalisation of tools, standards and technologies to meet requirements. Indeed, in this case the focus on prescriptions and routines in project management would not have allowed sense-making about the often surprising emergence of spaces that constantly 'moved the stakes' of what the project was meant to be and the particular space construction over time. However, the narratives presented can only be partial and incomplete. What is accounted for are the main narratives on the jointly experienced project space with the project team as focal actor. Indeed, other stories could be told about the many facets and embedded narratives of this shared experience. Still, the narratives offer a view of the multiple nature, and I hope a more comprehensive understanding of the project as emergent space. As such, project horizons are not set and could also be 'constructed differently'.

References

Arendt, H. (1951) *Origins of Totalitarianism*. New York: Harcourt Brace Jovanovich.
Brown, A.D. (1998) 'Narrative, Politics and Legitimacy in an IT Implementation', *Journal of Management Studies*, 35(1): 35–58.
Bruner, J. (1990) *Acts of Meaning*. Cambridge, MA: Harvard University Press.
Bruner, J. (2002) *Making Stories: Law, Literature, Life*. New York: Farrar, Strauss & Giroux.
Burke, K. (1945) *A Grammar of Motives*. New York: Prentice-Hall.
Chia, R. (2002) 'Essai: Time, Duration, and Simultaneity: Rethinking Process and Change in Organizational Analysis', *Organization Studies*, 23(6): 863–8.
Ciborra, C. (2002) *The Labyrinths of Information. Challenging the Wisdom of Systems*. New York: Oxford University Press.
Cicmil, S. (2003) 'Knowledge, Interaction and Project Work: A Complex Responsive Process Perspective', presentation to subtheme 'Project Organisations, Embeddedness, and Repositories of Knowledge', EGOS Colloquium, July 2003, Organization Analysis Informing Social and Global Development, Copenhagen.
Cook, S.D.N. and Brown, J.S. (1999) 'Bridging Epistemologies: The Generative Dance Between Organisational Knowledge and Organisational Knowing', *Organizational Science*, 10(4): 381–400.
de Certeau, M. (1984) *The Practice of Everyday Life*. Berkeley, CA: University of California Press.
Flick, U. (1992) 'Triangulation Revisited-Strategy for Alternative to Validation of Qualitative Data', *Journal for the Theory of Social Behaviour* 22(2): 175–97.
Forsberg, K., Mooz, H. and Cotterman, H. (1996) *Visualizing Project Management*. New York: John Wiley & Sons.
Foucault, M. (1977) *Discipline and Punish*. Harmondsworth: Penguin.
Gabriel, Y. (2000) *Storytelling in Organisations. Facts, Fictions, and Fantasies*. Oxford: Oxford University Press.
Geertz, C. (1973) 'Thick Description: Toward an Interpretative Theory of Culture', in *The Interpretation of Cultures*. New York: Basic Books, 3–30.
Glaser, B. and Strauss, A. (1967) *The Discovery of Grounded Theory*. Chicago: Aldine.
Haraway, D. (1991) 'A Cyborg Manifesto: Science, Technology, and Socialist-Feminism in the Late Twentieth Century', in Donna Haraway (ed.), *Simians, Cyborgs and Women*. London: Free Association Books, 149–82.
Harré, R. (2002) 'Material Objects in Social Worlds', *Theory, Culture & Society*, 19(5/6): 23–33.
Hernes, T. (2004) 'The Spatial Construction of Organization', manuscript prepared for the series Advances in Organization Studies, edited by Steward Clegg and Alfred Kieser. Amsterdam: John Benjamins.
Hodgson, D. and Cicmil, S. (2004) 'Are Projects Real? Reconstructing the Foundations of Project Governance', paper presented at EURAM, University of St Andrews, 'Specialist Track: The Governance of Projects'.
Ingold, T. (2000) *The Perception of the Environment: Essays on Livelihood, Dwelling and Skill*. London: Routledge.
Johnson, G., Melina, L. and Whittington, R. (2003) 'Micro-Strategy and Strategising: Towards an Activity-Based View', *Journal of Management Studies*, 40(1): 3–22.
Kharbanda, O.P. and Pinto, J.K. (1996) *What Made Gertie Gallop: Learning from Project Failures?* New York: Van Nostrand Reinhold.
Koskela, L. and Howell, G. (2002) 'The Underlying Theory of Project Management is Obsolete', *Proceedings of the PMI Research Conference*, ed. D. Slevin, D. Cleland and J. Pinto: 293–302.
Law, J. (2002) 'Objects and Spaces'. *Theory, Culture & Society*, 19(5/6): 91–105.
Lefebvre, H. (1991) *The Production of Space*. Oxford: Blackwell.
Massey, D. (1994) *Space, Place, and Gender*. Minneapolis: University of Minnesota Press.
Midler, C. (1995) '"Projectification" of the Firm: The Renault Case', *Scandinavian Journal of Management*, 11(4): 363–75.
Morris, P. (1994) *The Management of Projects*. London: Thomas Telford.
Morris, P. (2003) 'Science, Objective Knowledge, and Theory in Project Management', ICE James Forrest Lecture. Downloaded from personal page at Bartlett College, UCL, London. 19 March 2003.
Myers, M.D. (1995) 'A Disaster for Everyone to See: An Interpretative Analysis of a Failed IS Project', in C. Dunlop and R. Kling (eds), *Computerization and Controversy*. San Diego CA: Academic Press.
Murh, T. (1997) *Atlas-ti: The Knowledge Workbench. User's Manual*. Berlin: Scientific Software Development.

Nicolini, D., Gherardi, S. and Yanow, D. (eds) (2003) *Knowing in Organizations. A Practice-Based Approach.* Armonk, NY: M. E. Sharpe.

Nocker, M.O. and Garcia-Lorenzo, L. (2003) 'Teaming In Action: Stories of Knowledge Creation and Sharing in Project Teams', *International Journal of Knowledge, Culture and Change Management*, 3: 208–35.

Pels, D. (2002) 'Everyday Essentialism. Social Inertia and the "Muenchhausen Effect", *Theory, Culture & Society*, 19(5/6), 69–89.

Pels, D., Hetherington, K. and Vandenberghe, F. (2002) 'The Status of the Object: Performances, Mediations, and Techniques', *Theory, Culture & Society*, 19(5/6): 1–21.

Pietz, W. (2002) 'Material Considerations. On the Historical Forensics of Contract', *Theory, Culture & Society*, 19(5/6): 35–50.

PMI (2000) *A Guide to the Project Management Body of Knowledge.* Pennsylvania, PA: PMI.

Söderholm, A. (2001) Presentation page 'Research on Temporary Organisations and Project Management'. Downloaded at: www.usbe.umn.se/project/

Soja, E. (1996) *Thirdspace: Journeys to Los Angeles and Other Real-and-Imagined Places.* Cambridge, MA: Blackwell.

Tsoukas, H. (1996) 'The Firm as a Distributed Knowledge System: A Constructionist Approach', *Strategic Management Journal*, 17(Winter Special Issue): 11–25.

Tsoukas, H. and Chia, R. (2002) 'On Organisational Becoming: Rethinking Organisational Change', *Organization Science*, 13(5): 567–82.

Tsoukas, H. and Hatch, M.J. (2001) 'Complex Thinking, Complex Practice: The Case for a Narrative Approach to Organizational Complexity', *Human Relations*, 58(8): 979–1013.

Turnbull, D. (2002) 'Performance and Narrative, Bodies and Movement in the Construction of Places and Objects, Spaces and Knowledges', *Theory, Culture & Society*, 19(5/6): 125–43.

Walsham, G. and Han, C.K. (1993) 'Information Systems Strategy Formation and Implementation: The Case of a Central Government Agency', *Accounting Management and Information Technology*, 3(3): 191–200.

Whittington, R., Pettigrew, A., Peck, S., Fenton, E. and Conyon, M. (1999) 'Change and Complementarities in the New Competitive Landscape: A European Panel Study, 1992–1996', *Organization Science*, 10(5): 583–600.

8

An Actor Network Theory perspective on IT projects

Anneli Linde and Henrik C.J. Linderoth*

Introduction

IT projects aimed at changes in organisational structures and work processes have often ended up in gross miscalculations regarding intended goals, timelines and budgets (see, for example, Lucas, 1975; Lyytinen and Hirschheim, 1987; Holmström and Stadler, 2001). The project management literature, as well as streams in IS research, has tended to blame failures on the lack of clearly defined goals, or a poor implementation plan (for example, Maylor, 1996; Thompson and Ang, 2001). However, other researchers argue against setting goals and detailed implementation plans, especially in the early stages of a project process, because of an inability to create clarity and accuracy about the coming project process (Kreiner, 1995). Because of the interpretative flexibility of technology (Orlikowski, 1992: 403), and knowledge development in the project process (Rosenberg, 1982; Rice and Rogers, 1980), usage and interpretation of IS technology tend to drift from the designers' and managers' predefined objectives and goals (Ciborra, 1996: 8). Bearing these uncertainties in mind, how do we as researchers and practitioners analyse these IT-related projects? *What does the project process look like? If a traditional project approach is not the most effective what could an alternative be? And, what does an alternative view imply for management of such projects?*

In the traditional project management literature, interpretative flexibility of technology and tendencies to drift are seldom taken into account. The IT system tends to fade away or to be taken for granted, or is assumed to be unproblematic when it has once been designed and installed (Orlikowski and Iaccono, 2001). The focus in the IT project

* We want to thank Associated Professor Christine Räisänen for her valuable contribution to an earlier draft of a paper that formed the starting point for this chapter. Furthermore we want to thank Professor Barbara Cornelius for useful comments on the structure and the language of this chapter.

is either a technical implementation *or* an organisational change project, that is, the focus is either on the technical dimension or the social dimension. Thus, we will therefore follow Monteiro and Hanseth's (1995) recommendation and take the technology into consideration, although still focusing on the social aspects of implementation.

Since the 1980s Actor Network Theory (ANT) (for example, Callon, 1986; Law, 1986; Latour, 1987, 1999) has evolved as a promising approach for a closer scrutiny of technology-related change processes. ANT is grounded in a fairly simple observation which the social sciences and humanities had ignored until the 1970s – that is, how science actually is done and the way technological artefacts actually are designed and deployed, rather than how science normatively is supposed to be carried out, and how textbooks in engineering instruct us to design and deploy technological artefacts (Monteiro, 2000). ANT builds on the assumption that society is an interwoven socio-technical seamless web, consisting of heterogeneous actors (human and non-human), changing formations of actor networks, inscriptions, work practices and institutional and organisational arrangements (Hanseth and Monteiro, 1997: 185). As shown in this chapter, the specific alternative approach, Actor Network Theory, can be applied to the analysis of a project process and can expand project management theory. This approach has some useful implications for practitioners, the project managers of specific technology-related projects.

Implementation as translation

Today, processes of change and renewal in organisations are mostly carried out as projects (Lundin and Söderholm, 1995), which invariably include IT implementation (Boddy and Buchanan, 1992; Henfridsson, 1999). The traditional representation of a project is a standardised stage-gate model (for example, Duncan, 1996; Gunnarson *et al.*, 2000) with a rational and straightforward life cycle divided into predefined phases: pre-study, feasibility, execution and conclusion. These sources advocate a formal specification of goals, time/cost frames and predetermined implementation plans for the entire project already in the feasibility phase. This traditional project management approach has been described as a normative framework focused on a project's content and the development of generic project management techniques (Engwall *et al.*, 2003). For example, phases in projects and activities in these phases are standardised to a stage that could be described as institutionalised (Blomquist and Söderholm, 2002). Professional organisations like the American PMI (Project Management Institute) and the European IPMA (International Project Management Association) are the main carriers of such institutionalised perspectives.

However, as argued, a predetermined, formalised approach to project management may be counterproductive for diverse IT-mediated change projects. Instead, to understand these types of projects, we need to view the deployment of activities against the background of a network consisting of heterogeneous actors shaping a socio-technical network. In view of the special nature of IT-mediated projects, with their expected inherent interpretative flexibility and drift tendencies, we argue that the project process should be analysed as a translation process. In this process goals are formulated as visions to be reassessed, modified and revised through the interaction between actors such as the management of the organisation, the users and the project group. As Latour (1986: 267) points out, the destiny of an idea (for example, the vision of a project) is in the hands of its potential 'users', who have the power to appropriate, ignore, modify or betray the idea. Therefore, if actors are to realise an idea, for example ensuring that their implementation project results in the expected organisational change and use of IT, a forum for ongoing translations of the project vision incorporating the actors' interaction needs to be established. Callon (1986: 203 ff.) has shown that imposing this vision on others and thus expanding the forum requires a successful translation strategy deployed over time and space and consisting of four interwoven stages: problematisation, interessement, enrolment and mobilisation of allies.

At the *problematisation* stage, the vision is, implicitly or explicitly, defined as a question-raising issue by a group of actors, for example, why start this IT-mediated change project at all? Dealing with this issue requires the identification and involvement of a number of actors whose roles and relationships configure an initial problem-solving network. However, these actors may have different objectives for participating in the network. Thus, it is crucial to formulate a question whose answer will be of common interest for the identified actors despite their different agendas and goals. This formulation is called an obligatory passage point (OPP), which allows the actors to recognise that they will reap benefits from their involvement (Callon, 1986: 205 ff.). This implies that the vision of the IT-mediated project has to be broad enough to be translated by a diversity of actors as the solution to a range of problems (see Christensen and Kreiner (1997) for similar views on project goals). Thus, the actor group initiating the project try to make themselves into spokespersons for the technology, arguing that the only way ahead is via use of the technology that the project would implement.

When a problem has been defined and new actors and their tentative roles are identified, the network has to be stabilised. Callon (1986: 207 ff.) calls this step *intéressement*:

> The group of actions in which an entity attempts to impose and stabilize the identity of the other actors it defines through its problematization.

In a project process analysed from a traditional project management perspective identities and roles are rather clearly defined. But the role of technology and especially how it imposes and shapes the roles of other actors is neglected. The technology is designed with certain assumptions and some actions are delegated to technology, while others are delegated to the human actors (Latour, 1992). This is what in ANT is labelled as inscriptions (Akrich, 1992), meaning that technology designers inscribe programmes of actions into technology and these are translated and realised in an intended manner when the technology is ready for use in the setting where it is implemented. It is important to emphasise that the actors' formulations of their vision and their mutual roles develop during ongoing action. At this stage the new actors' links with the network need to be strengthened. Through interessement the developing network creates sufficient incentives both to lock actors into fixed places – so that they participate in the project – and to weaken the influence of other entities that may jeopardise the developing network.

In the third stage (enrolment), roles in the network are delineated and coordinated through 'multilateral negotiations, trials of strength and tricks that accompany the interessements and enable them [actors] to succeed' (Callon, 1986: 211). In this crucial step, the set of interrelated roles are defined and attributed to actors, which means that the problem/issue formulated as the OPP has to be translated into a series of clear and convincing statements. In this step the vision of the project must be divided into more specific sub-goals, which must be accepted by and discharged by the actors in order to create the intended organisational change and use of the IT.

In the fourth stage, mobilisation, a network is generally represented by spokespersons who have been authorised to speak legitimately for the rest of the actors that they represent. A critical point in the destiny of a project vision, therefore, is to 'silence' actors in whose names the spokesperson speaks in order to get a successful translation and establish a network. If the process of translation of a vision has succeeded, a contained network of relationships will have been built and room for individual manoeuvre will have been limited for the entities concerned (Callon, 1986: 214 ff.). This network of tightly linked relationships could reach a point of stability, most accurately described as a black box. A situation is reached where many elements are brought together and act as one (Latour, 1987: 131), or where things put in the black box no longer have to be questioned and tested (Callon and Latour, 1981). For example, when a specific IT system becomes so prevalent in an organisation that it becomes difficult to question and/or change, or has become transparent, we can say that it has been black-boxed.

Given this background to the translation process and the main characteristics of mainstream project management models, it can be claimed that ANT can help researchers and practitioners to gain a deeper insight into human/technology interaction in the project process. The mainstream PM models predefine roles and functions in a project process and ascribe certain features to the actors who should fit into the structure (Borum and Christiansen, 1993). But the PM models do not deal in depth with the complex interactions that occur during the process. ANT, by contrast, gives an opportunity to highlight the interactions between actors in the project process, thereby increasing the understanding about how roles and relations are shaped. By using an ANT perspective for the analysis of the project process, there is an opportunity to study interactions not only between humans but between humans and technology. ANT includes the technological system in the analysis as in the case of IT projects, contributing to an understanding of how technology shapes the project process.

Data collection and case descriptions

The empirical base is from two apparently quite dissimilar IT implementation projects. The first case concerns the implementation of a project management model at Swedish customs, and the other case concerns the implementation of telemedicine (video conferencing systems) in a Swedish healthcare organisation. Even though the projects were dissimilar, they were chosen in order to demonstrate general problems that IT-mediated change projects can run into, and how using concepts from ANT as an analytical tool can increase our understanding of the project process.

The management-model implementation project

One of the consequences of today's projectified society (Lundin and Söderholm, 1995) is a trend towards a standardisation of project activities by means of formalised, generic project management models (PMMs) (Gunnarson *et al.*, 2000). The rationale behind this development seems to be a quest for a common conceptual platform and work method for all projects. Typical of such models is that the project work flow is subdivided into a predetermined set of sequential phases (stages), with stipulated formal managerial decisions as boundaries. This 'stage-gate' or 'toll-gate' metaphor is the core of a PMM (Cooper, 1991).

One of today's well-known commercially available IT-based PMMs, PROPS, was originally developed by the telecom company Ericsson and applied in Ericsson subsidiaries worldwide. The model is comprehensive, covering the single-project perspective as well as the organisation's business interests, including leadership and organisational long-term strategies, that is, a multi-project perspective. PROPS is not only intended as a guide for the project manager; it is also a monitoring and control tool for managers at different levels in the organisation (Räisänen and Linde, 2001, 2004). PROPS describes what to do and when to do it, but not how to do it. This means that the model has to be adapted to new settings: for example, documents, tools and best practice have to be tailored for the needs of specific organisations.

The goal of the management-change project studied here was the redesign and implementation of PROPS at the Swedish Customs Authority between 1999 and early 2002. The case study has focused on the project group, the model and some major local settings and large projects. Twenty semi-structured interviews, as well as numerous informal discussions and email conversations with top management, members of the project office, project managers and members of the project group have been carried out. Project-specific documentation and the PMM were analysed. In addition, on-site observations at the project office and four local offices and five project group meetings were carried out.

In 1999 a decision was made to 'projectify' the Swedish Customs Authority, that is, to create an effective multi-project organisation. To fulfil this goal, a project group, consisting of representatives from head office, local offices and the IT department, was formed. The project manager was a top manager from the development department.

The vision of this group was that the PROPS model would function as the intermediary through which the organisation would govern all its projects, support its project managers and increase knowledge about handling project portfolios. As one of the initiators put it: PROPS would 'bring order to their project organisation'. Thus the initial goal of the project was to implement PROPS within the organisation.

Already in the early stage of the project, during the planning stage, the goal and task shifted focus from a straightforward implementation of the model and change of the organisation to a redesign of the PMM. The new vision resulted in wide-ranging changes to the model enacted through multiple negotiations and realignments of spokespersons for and against it. To gain support for the PMM project and increase project management knowledge, specific PROPS courses were offered to relevant actors at all levels of the organisation.

As one step in the process of changing the organisation and also to facilitate the implementation phase in the project a new organisational unit was created: the project office. As advocated by the PMM, their task was in the long term to function as a support unit for the projects in the organisation and in the short term to support the transformation process towards effective multi-project management. Members of the project office became an essential part of the project group.

Despite painstaking efforts to prepare for organisational change and to adapt the model to its new context, the actual implementation of the PMM generated many problems and caused enormous delays. At the beginning of 2002 a tentative model was finally launched on the intranet. However, a major part of the 'user test' of the model and the implementation of organisational change was still incomplete. In 2004 the new multi-project management approach could finally be described as implemented even though there were still ongoing activities related to adaptation and change. In all major development projects and IT projects at the Swedish Customs Authority the PMM is used. The PMM project is now seen and described as a success by the organisation. The effect on the organisation of the implementation of this model and of the creation of a multi-project organisation is substantial and can be found at all levels in the organisation.

Telemedicine projects in the Swedish healthcare sector

Telemedicine consists of IT applications supporting healthcare services via electronic transmission of information or expertise in order to improve the effectiveness of resource utilisation and allocation (Bashshur, 1995). Generally telemedicine is based on different video conferencing systems to which optical medical equipment can be connected in order to transmit live or still pictures. The general interest in telemedicine technology increased slowly in the early 1990s. In the mid-1990s a boom could be witnessed regarding the number of telemedicine projects in the Swedish healthcare sector.

The methods used for studying the project were semi-structured interviews and participant observation between 1994 and 1999. Sixty-three interviews with medical specialists, general practitioners, hospital managers and politicians were carried out within one county in Sweden. From 1994 through 1999 on-site observations were conducted at 18 meetings of the project group. Ten of the observations were done before the installation of the systems. After accomplishing the main study, in 1999, contacts were maintained with key informants. In 2002 a small follow-up study was conducted concerning the status of telemedicine use in the county.

The studied county was an early adopter of telemedicine and in 1994 concrete general goals were identified for such projects. The general goals were: increase value for patients through access to medical specialists irrespective of location; support the development of competence in the organisation; decrease the costs of the county council; and investigate the long-term effects telemedicine may have on the structure of health care in the county. A project group was formed consisting of physicians and personnel from the department of medical technology. Their main task was to find adequate equipment and to plan for the introduction of the technology, for example to determine the physical location and the need for education. In August 1996 the telemedicine equipment was purchased and installed.

During the pre-study phase two projects crystallised: general telemedicine (GTE) and tele-pathology (PAT). In both projects, the technical platform was a video conferencing system that could be connected to medical equipment. The GTE project concerned communication between general practitioners at health centres and specialists at the county or university hospitals. The specialities involved were dermatology, orthopaedics and otolaryngology. Most specialists were located at the university hospital; the orthopaedists were located at both the university and county hospitals. By connecting optical equipment to the video conferencing system it was possible for general practitioners to examine the ear or the skin, for example, of a patient and transmit pictures, live or still, to the specialists. The specialists could then advise the general practitioners about further treatment of the patient, and whether the patient should be hospitalised.

The PAT project concerned communication between medical specialists, that is, gynaecologists and surgeons at a county hospital could communicate with pathologists and cytologists at the university hospital. In this case there were two major applications: first, remote examination of frozen sections and of cytological sections. A microscope placed at the county hospital could be manoeuvred by the pathologists and cytologists at the university hospital. The microscope, connected to a video system, was used to examine the sections. The standard question from county hospital physicians was whether a section was malignant. The second application was to pathology conferences aimed at gathering further information concerning the section samples sent from the county hospital for expert consultation. When additional information was required, the pathologist at the university hospital could mobilise appropriate specialists and set up a video conference.

The use of telemedicine in Swedish hospitals is still in its early stages of development and can vary significantly from setting to setting. However, the extent to which the technology has become a part of local practice among certain hospital networks has largely depended on the efforts of a few key actors, who have influenced and enthused colleagues and staff to develop and use the resources offered by the technology. The important role played by these fiery spirits can clearly be seen among the dermatologists and gynaecologists in these cases.

IT projects in an ANT perspective

In the projects studied, the change initiative inaugurating the project came from a few actors in the respective organisations. To gather support to accomplish their visions, these actors needed to mobilise strong networks of influential actors and decision-makers within their organisations. They had to translate their visions and select their allies in order to create interessement for key actors in the organisation. To enrol decision-makers in support of their ideas, these actors appointed themselves as spokespersons of the collective. In the telemedicine case, the physicians took on the role of spokespersons for colleagues and patients. In the PMM project, a top manager in the development department of Swedish customs spoke for colleagues and customers (the public). Some of these self-appointed spokespersons had high visibility and authority in their organisations, which gave them the legitimacy to speak in the name of their fellow actors. Not surprisingly these spokespersons made the technology visible and most of all made the ideas inherent in the technology visible. However, the technology had not yet materialised in the network, being still represented as an idea of something that could mediate a change.

In the projects feasibility phase, when the technology materialised in the network, visions and goals in project plans and discourses in project groups changed from an overall focus to technology-related issues. The intended execution phase of the project, the actual implementation, which should have mobilised a large and comprehensive network representing use of the new technology and organisational change, did not happen as expected in either case. In the PMM project the main focus shifted from a straightforward implementation of the model with consequent change of the organisation to a redesign of the model mobilising a small group of redesigners, focusing on details in the text, technical issues and some legal issues concerning the PMM. In the telemedicine project, representatives from the health centres and the medical specialities involved should have identified in which situations and for what kind of medical diagnosis the technology could be used. During the feasibility phase this idea changed into a 'wait, see and try' strategy. The focus, during the early stages, came to be on technical issues such as costs of bandwidth, compensation for consultations and who should have equipment. Despite this, one actor repeated the need to think in terms of how telemedicine should be used in the future, but at the time the other actors were concerned with more practical issues.

If using the terminology of ANT, the project process in the execution phase will be focused on a translation of the technology into the interests of enrolled actors. The success of the project will be seen in an expanded network of actors using the new IT and demonstrating the reach of organisational transformation, and actors as a 'support system' for the technology use and organisational change. However, the projects studied were implemented in different geographical settings and organisational units. In both cases, networks needed to expand in time and space with the translation of project goals and the project process evolving within only limited control of project managers. Given this situation programmes of action and key actors came to have a crucial influence on the project trajectory in the execution phase.

Translating technology

Programmes of action inscribed in technology are derived from technology designers' assumptions about the networks in which the technology would be used and their assumptions about the roles and relations between actors (Akrich, 1992). Programmes of action can in turn be delegated to human and non-human actors (Latour, 1992). The technology implicitly puts demands on how activities would be organised in the setting where the technology is implemented, if it were possible to mobilise the indispensable actors. This fact emphasises the importance of analysing programmes of action inscribed in the technology, its impact on actors and their ability to perform actions needed for a desired change. Nevertheless, as the technology is open in character, it will never be possible to wholly analyse the fit between actors' prevailing programmes of action, how things are done and interpreted in the organisation at the time, and those actions inscribed in the technology imposing the intended change. What is known is that prevailing programmes of action, reinforced by local or institutional sources, in a local setting can conflict with or support the programmes of actions inscribed in the technology (Linde and Linderoth, 2000; Linderoth, 2002). A programme of action reinforced by a local source can reflect local variations in developing solutions to tasks similar to those utilised by similar organisations. Those programmes reinforced by institutional sources reflect deeply embedded stocks of knowledge, norms and rules guiding practical applications, logics and the division of labour.

In the projects studied, the meetings between programmes of action inscribed in the technology and programmes of action influenced by local and institutional sources resulted in both hard clashes and unproblematic acceptance during both the project feasibility and execution phases. At first glance, the PMM project seemed to be the project where technology was a complex bundle of inscribed programmes of action, since the aim of the model was to create a new behaviour in the organisation implementing the model. The model contains more than 800 pages of textual inscriptions. This can be contrasted to the telemedicine system, which consisted of just a few instructions on which buttons to press when a video conference was to be organised. However, despite its apparent simplicity, the inscribed programme of action in the telemedicine system came to cause as many clashes between inscribed programmes of action and prevailing programmes of action as did the more complex PMM project.

In the PMM project, visible clashes between programmes of action had already occurred in an early stage of the project process (during the redesign phase). Central concepts in the model, such as 'project', 'sponsor' and 'customer', triggered conflicting translations in the project group. Questions like 'who is a sponsor in an IT project, is it a manager at the IT department, or a manager at the development department at the head office?' and 'do we have a customer, and who is the customer?' were raised. It took a long time to merge these into a common definition and find agreement between actors, in some cases several years. The different translations of the central concept 'project' created an ongoing conflict that resulted in one actor group excluding themselves from the network. They concluded that they did not work with projects but that they worked with pre-studies. Representatives from the IT department, however, had little problem in accepting definitions given in the model. This was probably due to the fact that the IT department already used the project form for organising their activities. In this sense, their prevailing mode of organising activities came to function as a supporting programme of action where programmes of action inscribed in the model could be accepted.

The ambitious redesign of the model not only caused conflicting translations among actor groups; the model itself also was a much more powerful actor than the project group had imagined at the outset. When the project focus was changed to the redesign of the model, the intention was to adapt the model to the organisation as far as possible. This modification was given up by the project group because of the complexity of the model. For example, the changing definitions of concepts done on one web page could not necessarily be transposed to other pages as it was impossible to know in how many other pages changes were required and it was hard to grasp what the effect of change in one concept would be on other concepts inscribed in the model. The complex task of redesigning the model ended in the management of the organisation redefining the goals for the project. When the redesign phase was finished the management chose to terminate the part of the project concerning the redesign. However, the project was immediately restarted after being transferred to a new project group, the newly established project office, for implementation. The new group was to manage the change efforts, a function prescribed by the model that demonstrated its influence on the organisation.

In the telemedicine project clashes between inscribed programmes of action and prevailing programmes of action developed when the system was implemented and tested in daily operations. The inscription causing the main challenges for the project and for the technology's integration into daily practice was the need for actors' mutual presence whenever a conference or a consultation was conducted. After only a few months of technology usage, the project manager for the GTE project was frustrated over the low frequency of consultations. He could only influence routines in his own department, where management of ad hoc consultations was supported by a prevailing programme of action for managing urgent incoming telephone calls. However, over the routines at health centres he had little influence. He found it difficult to get other actors to adapt to the new technology. At the health centres general practitioners were always in doubt whether the medical specialists could be mobilised when an ad hoc consultation was to be conducted. The ad hoc consultations were thought to be the majority of consultations. But the lack of supporting programmes of action created difficulties in mobilizing the indispensable actors. When medical specialists were concerned, they could temporarily be unavailable, since they were engaged in another network, or they were unable to handle the equipment properly. Thus, every attempt to organise an ad hoc consultation opened up potential clashes between programmes of action.

In the PAT project activities were both planned and *ad hoc*, but the situations in which ad hoc consultations could occur were well-defined. This gave the project manager better control over the project process and opportunities to reflect over programmes of action needed in order to enrol actors into the network. One of the first indispensable actors to be enrolled into the network, by the project manager, was the technology. A central ingredient of ANT is that each actor influences the roles and relations of the others. For example, in the PAT project, the technology put a demand on human actors that they should be present simultaneously. They, in turn, demanded that the technology should be able to deliver pictures of a satisfactory quality. To ensure the quality of delivered pictures, the project manager organised a validation test of the equipment. This validation removed any objections about the quality of the pictures, which otherwise could have been a primary argument for not using the technology. Since the validation, or the scientific study, is an institutionalised programme of action in healthcare organisations, it should support the future use of the technology. Despite validation, only one of the major applications became successful in terms of usage. The remote examination of frozen sections and of cytological sections was less successful during the test period, because of the dependency on surgeons who needed to initiate the mobilisation of the network. In this case no supporting programmes of action were developed at the department of surgery at the county hospital and no actor took the role of spokesperson for the project in the local setting. On the other hand, pathology conferences between gynaecologists at the county hospital and pathologists at the university hospital were perceived as successful by the actors involved. There were three reasons for this: (1) these kinds of conferrals are already an institutionalised programme of action in healthcare organisations and actors know beforehand the roles and relations to be performed; (2) local programmes of action were set up in order to support the organising of conferences, and procedures were developed to hold conferences on a particular topic on a certain day in the week, and always at the same time; (3) the head of the department at the county hospital spoke actively for the project among his employees.

To translate a vision and realise changes in organisational structures and work processes, new networks need to be mobilised, stabilised and expanded throughout an organisation. For the project process to work, it is crucial that programmes of action inscribed in technology are implemented based upon an understanding of existing programmes of action. In the projects described, these processes turned out to be complex and frustrating: far from the straightforward implementation/project processes anticipated and expected by respective managements. This was a complicated situation from a management perspective. As indicated in the previous discussion it is impossible for a single project manager to realise all needs, match all demands on the technology and manage all settings where the project should be implemented. Instead, there is a need for key actors to speak and act for the project in the different local settings.

Key actors creating networks and change

In both the PMM and the telemedicine case the role of key actors who were committed to the projects provides an explanation for the outcomes of the project process. During the first years, the presence of key actors in local contexts had a large influence on the frequency of use of the IT and change in behaviour and work structures. Networks representing different interpretations of the new IT could be found in different projects, departments and groups crossing organisational boundaries. Most of these networks were represented by enthusiastic actors, holding high positions in the organisational hierarchy. Their power positions provided them with the legitimacy needed to experiment with and develop the technology as well as to prescribe routines that supported the new systems. They could also grant similar privileges to their colleagues. Such a key actor was one of the top managers in the Customs Authority's IT department, who was also an occasional member of the initial project group. He saw to it that the IT department started to develop work procedures and a support system for the new PMM even before the IT department was given full access to the model. The influence that this key actor and the network he mobilised had on the project outcome was immense. There were several ideas about how to use the model at the IT department which has influenced the adoption of the technology by the entire organisation.

Another example of a successful key actor for the organisation was a project manager in a local setting who started to use and adapt the PMM for his own purpose in one of his projects. From there he developed an interpretation of the PMM that was transferred to later projects and created a network of users. However, in none of the networks that existed in parallel in the organisation were interpretation of the IT and/or the context of use totally similar to the organisation's official interpretation represented by the project department office and there were also dissimilarities of different ranking between the networks in local settings – for example, different interpretation of the power of a project manager, the role of a sponsor, or sub-project versus project, just to mention some differences in use of the PMM.

The same pattern of a broad range of key actors and networks with similar or dissimilar interpretations could be found in the telemedicine case. For instance, a majority of consultations were done from a health centre where two general practitioners were strongly committed to the project. One of them stated that you must always take into consideration whether a consultation can be done, in order to find out when the technology can be used.

However, a network is never totally constant; it is always changing and often not totally in the control of the project manager. In a setting with actors highly committed to a project, interest can fade away as time goes by, and, conversely, in setting of low commitment, interest in a project can suddenly increase. This is the kind of development that occurred in the telemedicine case. The top management of the county seemed to have accepted the technology. An expression for this is the support centre for telemedicine that was established after the first two years of test use of the technology. However, at the operational level the results of the project were more mixed. The original project process continued simultaneously in different directions, to new settings where new projects were initiated and booming. In the settings engaged from the outset, technology use either became a part of the routines (as in the case with pathology conferences), or tended to fade away. At the health centre where two general practitioners had been committed to the project, the frequency of usage started to decrease and the network weakened. One of the physicians moved and the other, who had been one of the strongest advocates for the project, stated that it was very hard work to convince colleagues in specialist departments to start to develop consultation services that could be offered to the health centres. Now this key actor sporadically uses the technology for consultations, and he has been involved in other work and projects that need his attention. Another physician interviewed stated that the key actors involved from the outset just have energy to promote the project for a couple of years. Furthermore she stated that *ad hoc* consultations, which at the outset were he seen as the main application for the technology, turned out to be hard to implement, and that it would be mentally hard for actors involved from the outset to do a restart.

However, even if there are tendencies for a project to fade away, key actors can come into the process in the later stages and turn around attitudes in a department or a part of the organisation by identifying the right tasks to be solved by the technology. That is, they develop a new translation of the technology or the context in which it can be used, finding a new match and with that mobilising a new network. At a specialist department with a highly sceptical attitude to the technology, attitudes were changed when the department got a new manager who was committed to the technology and saw new opportunities for problem-solving. The department had the responsibility for staffing a county hospital 140 kilometres away from the university hospital. The old solution had been for four to five physicians to follow a rotating schedule, commuting by bus to the remote hospital two to three times per week – an activity they did not appreciate. The new head of the department saw a possibility for using the telemedicine consultations instead of sending physicians by bus. A new project was initiated where a few physicians were trained in using the equipment and a nurse was trained at the remote hospital to take pictures, operate the equipment and 'direct' patients during the consultations. The project was very successful in that the department now is mainly doing video consultations rather than sending physicians by bus. The big difference compared to earlier consultations with health centres was that the whole process was under control of the specialist department. Additionally, medical specialists translated the technology use into something that could release them from a burden, instead of creating a burden.

The PMM project also struggled with difficulties at the outset, but at the end the project could be described as a success. As described earlier the PMM was in the end implemented and a broad range of changes were established. The implementation process was managed by several project managers but most of the time it was developed in collaboration with and negotiation between key actors in the organisation. The different translation of the inscribed and prevalent programmes of action creating separate networks and even competing networks forced the project managers, and the project office, through the entire project process, to take the role of negotiators among these key actors representing competing networks. They had to create programmes of action that were accepted by the networks and in line with the organisations' goal of implementation and intended organisational change.

Concluding remarks: the management of networks, key actors and programmes of action

In this chapter we have given some examples of how concepts from Actor Network Theory can add to the theory of temporary organising and project management practice. The focus has been on a specific category of projects: IT-related projects aiming at organisational changes in work practices and organisational behaviour. We have argued that ANT is a fruitful perspective to use in analysing, describing and even to some extent in managing such projects. It is especially suited to translation processes where the technology as well as human actors have to be taken into consideration. The results show that several features of these 'fuzzy' projects differ from traditional PM.

First the project goals cannot (and should not!) be identified in the planning stage; they are to be viewed as a vision with considerable interpretative flexibility connected to both the IT and the organisational context. This means that the specific goals have to be developed during the project process in a complex interaction between a large number of actors, both human and non-human, over a considerable time in order to ensure a well-adapted technology and an accepted and legitimised organisational change.

Second, the entire project process and the final project result is a chain of translation along the project trajectory, in which a number of networks are created around key actors developing and translating both the project goals as well as contextual features.

Third, the role of the project manager is 'power-drained'. This means that management situations will occur where the project managers' ability to control and foresee the process in relation to a formal project plan is delimited.

The consequences of these findings from a management perspective are several and can be summarised as: *project management of IT-related fuzzy projects is the management of networks, key actors and programmes of action.*

Project managers need not only to reveal the programmes of action that are inherent in the technology, that is, a technology focus, they also need to explore possible issues that may block the interessement that they are trying to create throughout the project process, that is, an organisational and human-related focus. They need to reflect over ways in which to counter these blocks so that they do not give rise to contending programmes of action in the organisation. The success of the IT-related change project seems to be tightly connected to how well intended programmes of action can be matched to prevailing programmes of action. In that process the project manager needs to ensure that they understand and can monitor the potential chains of translation that arise along the project trajectory. However, probably the most important management task is to support and manage the emergence of key actors, a process in which project managers have to be open to compromises with powerful key opponents.

We strongly believe that ANT can be used as a strategic project management approach. Adding ANT to project management theory and practice will provide better insight into the complexities of both human and non-human behaviour, taking both technical and social features into consideration in these common but problematic 'fuzzy' projects.

References

Akrich, M. (1992) 'The De-scription of Technical Objects', in W.E. Bijker and J. Law (eds), *Shaping Technology/Building Society*. Cambridge, MA: MIT Press, 205–24.

Bashshur, R.L. (1995) 'On the Definition and Evaluation of Telemedicine', *Telemedicine Journal*, 2(1): 19–30.

Blomquist, T. and Söderholm, A. (2002) 'How Project Management Got Carried Away', in K. Sahlin-Anderson and A. Söderholm (eds), *Beyond Project Management: New Perspectives on the Temporary – Permanent Dilemma*. Malmö: Liber, 25–38.

Boddy, D. and Buchanan, D. (1992) *The Expertise of the Change Agent*. London: Prentice-Hall.

Borum, F. and Christiansen, J.K. (1993) 'Actors and Structures in IS Projects: What Makes Implementation Happen', *Scandinavian Journal of Management*, 9(1): 5–28.

Callon, M. (1986) 'Some Elements of a Sociology of Translation: Domestication of the Scallops and the Fisherman of St Brieuc Bay', in J. Law (ed.), *Power, Action and Belief. A New Sociology of Knowledge?* London: Routledge.

Callon, M. and Latour, B. (1981) 'Unscrewing the Big Leviathan, or How Actors Macro-structure Reality and How Sociologists Help Them to Do So', in K. Knorr-Cetina and A. Cicourel (eds), *Advances in Social Theory and Methodology: Toward an Integration of Micro and Macro Sociologies*. London: Routledge & Kegan Paul, 277–303.

Christensen, S. and Kreiner, K. (1997) *Projektledning- Att leda och lära i en ofullkomlig värld*. Lund: Academia Adacta AB.

Ciborra, C.U. (1996) 'Introduction: What Does Groupware Mean for the Organizations Hosting It?', in C.U. Ciborra (ed.), *Groupware and Teamwork*. Chichester: John Wiley & Sons, 1–19.

Cooper, B. (1991) 'New Product Processes at Leading Industrial Firms', *Industrial Marketing Management*, 2: 137–47.

Cooper, R. (1991) 'Stage-Gate Systems: A New Tool for Managing New Products', *IEEE Engineering Management Review*, Fall, 5–12.

Duncan, W.R. (1996) *A Guide to Project Management Body of Knowledge PMI Standards Committee*. Upper Darby, PA: Project Management Institute.

Engwall, M., Steinthóesson, R.S. and Söderholm, A. (2003) 'Temporary Organizing – A Viking Approach to Project Management Research', in B. Czarniawska and G. Sevón (eds), *The Northern Lights – Organization Theory in Scandinavia*. Malmö: Liber, 111–30.

Gunnarson, S., Linde, A. and Loid, D. (2000) 'Is Standardization Applicable to Project Managers of Multi-Project Companies?', in *Paradoxes of Project Collaboration in the Global Economy: Interdependence, Complexity and Ambiguity. IRNOP IV*. Sydney: University of Technology, 136–46.

Hanseth, O. and Monteiro, E. (1997) 'Inscribing Behavior in Information Infrastructure Standards', *Accounting, Management & Information Technology*, 7(4): 183–211.

Henfridsson, O. (1999) 'Inventing New Meaning for Technology in Organizations,' unpublished doctoral thesis, Umea: Department of Informatics, Umea University.

Holmström, J. and Stadler, F. (2001) 'Drifting Technologies and Multi-Purpose Networks: The Case of the Swedish Cash Card', *Information and Organization*, 11(3): 187–206.

Kreiner, K. (1995) 'In Search of Relevance: Project Management in Drifting Environments,' *Scandinavian Journal of Management*, 11(4): 335–46.

Latour, B. (1986) 'The Powers of Association', in J. Law (ed.), *Power, Action and Belief: A New Sociology of Knowledge*. London: Routledge.

Latour, B. (1987) *Science in Action*. Cambridge, MA. Harvard University Press.

Latour, B. (1992) 'Where Are the Missing Masses? The Sociology of a Few Mundane Artefacts', in W.E. Bijker and J. Law (eds), *Shaping Technology/Building Society*. Cambridge, MA: MIT Press, 225–58.

Latour, B. (1999) *Pandora's Hope*. Cambridge, MA: Harvard University Press.

Law, J. (1986) 'On Methods of Long Distance Control: Vessels, Navigation and the Portuguese Route to India', in J. Law (ed.), *Power, Action and Belief. A New Sociology of Knowledge?* London: Routledge, 196–233.

Linde, A. and Linderoth, H. (2000) 'Remove the Blinkers and Discover the Conflicting Programs of Action: A Dynamic Perspective on Management of "Fuzzy" Projects', in D.P. Slevin, D.I. Cleland and J.K. Pinto (eds), *Project Management Research at the Turn of the Millennium – Proceedings of PMI Research Conference 2000*, Newtown Square, PA: Project Management Institute, 357–68.

Linderoth, H.C.J. (2002) 'Fiery Spirits and Supporting Programs of Action – The Keys to Exploration and Exploitation of Open Technologies', *International Journal of Healthcare Technology and Management*, 4(3/4): 319–32.

Lucas, H.C. Jr (1975) *Why Information Systems Fail*. New York: Columbia University Press.

Lundin, R.A. and Söderholm, A. (1995) 'A Theory of the Temporary Organization', *Scandinavian Journal of Management*, 11(4): 437–55.

Lyytinen, K. and Hirschheim, R. (1987) *Information Systems Failure – A Survey and Classification of the Empirical Literature*. Oxford: Oxford University Press.

Maylor, H. (1996) *Project Management*. London: Pitman.

Monteiro, E. (2000) 'Actor-Network Theory and Information Infrastructure', in C. Ciborra (ed.), *From Control to Drift: The Dynamics of Corporate Information Infrastructure*. Oxford: Oxford University Press, 71–84.

Monteiro, E. and Hanseth, O. (1995) 'Social Shaping of Information Infrastructure: On Being Specific about the Technology', W. Orlikowski, G. Walsham, M.R. Jones. and J.I. DeGross (eds), *Information Technology and Changes in Organizational Work*. London: Chapman & Hall, 325–43.

Orlikowski, W.J. (1992) 'The Duality of Technology: Rethinking the Concept of Technology in Organizations', *Organization Science*, 3(3): 398–427.

Orlikowski, W. and Iacono, C.S. (2000). 'The Truth Is Not Out There: An Enacted View of the Digital Economy', in E. Brynjolfsson and B. Kahin (eds), *Understanding the Digital Economy: Data, Tools, and Research*. Cambridge, MA: MIT Press, 352–80.

Räisänen, C. and Linde, A. (2001) 'The Social Construction of Project Management: A Critical Analysis Perspective on Project Management Models', paper presented at 17th EGOS Colloquium 'The Odyssey of Organizing', Lyon, France, 5–7 July 2001.

Räisänen, C. and Linde, A. (2004) 'Technologizing Discourse to Standardize Projects in Multi-Project Organizations', *Organization* 11(1): 101–21.

Rice, R.E. and Rogers, E.M. (1980) 'Reinvention in the Innovation Process', *Knowledge*, 1(4): 488–514.

Rosenberg, N. (1982) *Inside the Black Box. Technology and Economics*. Cambridge: Cambridge University Press.

Thompson, S.H.T. and Ang, J.S.K. (2001) 'An Examination of Major IS Planning Problems', *International Journal of Information Management*, 21: 457–70.

9

Reorganisation projects and five uncertainties

Eamonn Molloy and Richard Whittington

Introduction

Both in theory and in practice, the stability once attributed to *organisations* is increasingly dissolving into the ceaseless uncertainties of *organising*. From theory, Hatch (1999) captures this sense of restless change with the jazz notion of structural improvisation, while Tsoukas and Chia (2002) propose a conceptual shift from 'organisations' to 'organisational becoming'. The same appreciation of organisational instability is reflected in contemporary managerial writings, with its appeals for organisational 'flexibility' (Volberda, 1996) or the responsiveness implied by organisational 'patching' (Eisenhardt and Brown, 1999). Empirically too, the pace of organisational change is high and increasing. During the 1990s, the rate at which the top 50 UK firms engaged in major organisational restructuring increased from about once every four years to once every three years (Whittington and Mayer, 2000). In a recent survey, human resource professionals reported experiencing on average seven reorganisations over the past three years (Mayer *et al.*, 2004). These kinds of reorganisations are just the more prominent episodes in the continuous organising efforts required to sustain organisation.

Organising and reorganising are therefore endemic features of contemporary organisations. From this perspective, organisation is a skilful but precarious practice, rather than a stable and unambiguous state of affairs (Whittington, 2002). In this chapter, we shall be drawing upon a wider research programme on organising praxis and practices to focus specifically on reorganisation projects.[1] These reorganisation projects, or 'temporary organisations' (Lundin and Söderholm, 1995; Packendorff, 1995; Linderoth, 2002) are centrally involved in how managers cope with the chronic uncertainties of organisation and organising. We shall show that the uncertainties encountered by reorganisation practitioners in these projects correspond closely to the five uncertainties identified by Bruno Latour (Latour, 2002) within the social sciences generally. Briefly, these five uncertainties are:

1 uncertainty about group formation
2 uncertainty about agency
3 uncertainty about objects
4 uncertainty about matters of fact versus states of affairs
5 uncertainty about epistemology.

In this chapter we suggest that many common reorganisation practices are directed at addressing and, at least temporarily, reconciling the uncertainties mentioned above. It is argued that the skill to recognise, accept and manage uncertainty about groups, agency, objects, matters of fact and epistemological assumptions is a key feature of reorganisation practice. The picture is complicated by the attendant difficulties of establishing what exactly it is about the organisation that needs to change and why, and what the organisation needs to become and why, and connecting these causally to ideas about how this can be achieved. In other words, reorganisation practitioners are involved in simultaneously constructing, stabilising and problematising multiple definitions of what counts as the organisation and assembling these into a linear, rational sequence of events.

In light of the above observations, we wish to avoid a position where we invoke 'the organisation' as an explanation or 'context' for reorganisation practices and to avoid imposing rigid definitions upon the objects of study, in this case 'reorganisation projects'. By definition, what counts as the organisation is changing and more often than not the definition of a reorganisation project is far from settled. Instead we broadly interpret 'project' following Lundin and Söderholm's (1995) definition of 'temporary organisation' and build upon Latour's 'sociology of association'[2] to deploy a multiplicity of frames of reference, originating with the reorganisation practitioners, to understand what they are doing. We are interested in understanding reorganisation activity as constitutive of the reorganisation, not using reified notions of reorganisation projects to explain reorganisation.

The following section presents Latour's five uncertainties in more detail and explains why they matter for social scientists and their relevance for studying reorganisation projects and the practices of which they are constituted. This section is followed by a brief introduction to our case study reorganisations in order to convey some idea of what is meant by reorganisation projects and reorganisation activities. Next, we illustrate the relevance of the five uncertainties to reorganisation practice using a sample of extracts from interviews with reorganisation practitioners in two of the case studies. The extracts have been selected to present an illustrative range of examples at this relatively early stage of the research project at the time of writing. The chapter concludes with a summary.

Sociology of association

Bruno Latour is a social scientist associated with the field of science and technology studies (STS). STS is a diverse interdisciplinary community that includes anthropologists, sociologists, philosophers, engineers and natural scientists. What this community shares is an interest in relationships between science, technology and society. Perhaps Latour's enduring contribution to the field emerges from his early ethnographic work with scientists in laboratories (Latour, 1986, 1987; Latour and Woolgar, 1986). This work was principally focused on the question of how scientific knowledge is produced and how a scientific fact is established. One of the outcomes of this and later work on the establishment of technological systems with Michel Callon was the 'sociology of association' (Callon, 1986a, 1986b; Latour, 1987, 2002). Latour observed that science and engineering work as well as other forms of activity was about building society – social construction – and as a result talking about society as if it existed prior to or independent of this activity was a nonsequitur. Tsoukas and Chia (2002) make a similar point when they argue for an 'ontological reversal' where change is understood as ontologically prior to organisation, a condition of possibility of organisation, not a property of organisation.

Latour argues that 'the social' is not a discrete, objectively identifiable domain of reality that can be mobilised to explain society itself or to clear up what cannot be explained by other disciplines, professions or communities with reference to their own particular conceptual resources. For example, from the tautological sociology of the social perspective, 'social factors' such as racism, sexism, homophobia or class bias could explain why the legal system appears to be prejudiced in relation to particular groups of people. Similarly, 'social factors' such as poverty, oppression and the existence of autocratic regimes might function as 'social explanations' for the popularity of religion in any given time or place. In this view, 'social explanations' are the preserve of the sociologist whose job it is to point out to other disciplines, professions and communities how 'social factors' impact upon their knowledge and practices. In contrast, Latour insists that the 'social', or by extension social 'factors' or 'forces', cannot be used to explain or account for institutions, organisations, disciplines, professions or communities because it is 'the social' that needs to be explained and accounted for. For Latour, what counts as the social is always composed of and constituted by heterogeneous connections and it is these connections that social theorists should be concerned with. Other actors, not just social theorists, build society through active construction and maintenance of connections between humans and non-humans. Furthermore, and this is a crucial point for this chapter, actors (in this case reorganisation practitioners) appear to be less wedded to 'pure' ontological and epistemological categories such as 'structure' than the change literature would suggest (Orlikowski, 1996; Weick, 1998). Reorganisation practitioners in connection with 'regular' members of organisations build organisations through (de)construction and maintenance of heterogeneous identities and connections. The challenge for social theory then, according to Latour (1987, 2002), is to uncover how actors construct society and to avoid theorising their activity with uncritical reference to categories such as the social. This challenge is what lies at the heart of the sociology of association. In order to meet this challenge, Latour suggests the social theorists must confront five 'uncertainties' that are papered over by the 'sociology of the social'. In the following we describe these five uncertainties for social science and in doing so set out a framework for understanding reorganisation projects.

Uncertainty 1: group formation

'Sociology of the social' works with ostensive definitions of groups, for example, government, firms, organisations or environmental activists, many of which are naturalised ontological categories such as nation states or races. Yet, groups and their boundaries are constantly changing, forming and re-forming. Sociology of association requires examination of how groups perform their own and other definitions, actively producing what might be called 'the social' in doing so. The implications for studying reorganisation – an activity that is to a large extent concerned with group formation – are that the identities of the organisation (pre-, during and post-reorganising) and the numerous groups, regions, departments, teams, cultures, committees, systems and clusters within 'it' are understood as an effect of continuous and contingent processes of negotiation, maintenance and construction. The examples drawn from our research show that group definition is a major activity in reorganisation projects. This includes among many other things redefining geographical and functional business units, office allocations, software suites, pay scales, branding and redundancies. Group definition can be a difficult task for reorganisation practitioners and often one to be handled with diplomacy and tact. People in organisations can become attached to their colleagues, identity, tools, spaces and hours, and reconfiguring these relationships to form new groupings can require convincing justification. Nevertheless, from an organisational theory perspective, the point to note is that reorganisation practitioners regard these relationships as more or less malleable. Indeed, the widespread consensus about the ever-increasing pace of change suggests these are increasingly uncertain.

Uncertainty 2: agency

As mentioned previously, 'the social' ('social forces', 'social conditions', 'social factors', 'society') is often invoked in order to explain individual and collective behaviour, beliefs, action and activities. The theory of action that underpins appeals to the explanatory potential of an unexplored category of the social is, in its extreme form, one in which everything individuals do is determined by forces over which they have no control. The extreme opposite of this position is a theory of action that assumes 'mastery' – individuals are in total control of their own actions. In this latter view action and behaviour are reduced to individual rational choice preferences and are not in any way influenced by or connected to prior decisions taken by other actors. Lundin and Söderholm (1995) illustrate the inadequacy of this dualism when they argue for 'action', in contrast to 'decision', as a central component of a theory of temporary organisation. However, while both understandings of agency are premised upon the intuition that one action necessarily leads to another, claiming that the agency involved in further action is 'the social' is not sufficient. Reorganisation practitioners construct, attribute and assign agency in multiple ways to a diverse range of entities including projects, project management techniques, software (including PowerPoint), leaders and leadership teams, individual co-workers and events such as away days and workshops. However, this agency appears not to be an essential property of the entity in question as perspectives on the nature and extent of agency vary between actors and across time with the ontological status that is accorded to them. Connecting agency with human and non-human actors is a key aspect of reorganisation practice, and particularly so in objectification practices. Objectification does not necessarily delete agency, it may be the prerequisite for its operation.

Uncertainty 3: objects

For analytical purposes at least, the social sciences have traditionally distinguished between humans and non-humans as actors, the assumption being that to under-stand agency one needed to look no further than humans. However, when studying reorganisation projects and practices it soon becomes clear that many non-human agencies may be at work in any given setting. Methodologically, as mentioned above, this implies not deciding in advance what kind of agency is doing the action. If objects can make a difference to a state of affairs – for example, telephones influence the way we communicate – then it follows that they can act and that they may be considered as actors. Our research so far indicates that this is an important point. Reorganisation practitioners draw upon a wide range of physical artefacts as well as non-physical technologies in their day-to-day practice. These often apparently mundane objects are attributed with considerable agency in quite sophisticated and subtle ways, sup-ported by years of 'hands-on' experience. For example, it is a familiar practice for reorganisation practitioners to 'capture' output from meetings, away days or work-shops on Post-it notes or flip charts and then condense these into small, often card-board pyramids or cubes that are subsequently circulated around the organisation. A number of such 'change objects' are shown in Figure 9.1. In the foreground, in front of the laptop computer – omnipresent in all our reorganisation case studies along with the cellular phone – is a seven-sided cube, six conical 'hats', brochures, VHS videos, DVDs, CDs, project management charts, whiteboard, marker pens, desktop calendars and desks. All of these objects are credited with multiple ontological status and agencies such as tools, techniques, technologies, methods, communication devices, processes, symbols and so on. Attempting to adequately and fairly represent the practices of reorganisation practitioners without reference to the repertoire of devices that help them in their task and that litter the offices and workshops of organ-isations undergoing change – 'the missing masses' (Latour, 1987) – would be a seriously partial account.

Figure 9.1   A selection of change objects

Uncertainty 4: matters of fact versus states of affairs

Studies in the sociology of scientific knowledge (SSK) show that what counts as a matter of fact (uncontroversial, black-boxed), a 'state of affairs' (contested, open, debated) or indeed 'scientific' was the product of negotiated connections between arrays of human and non-humans, mediators and intermediaries (Mannheim, 1952; Merton, 1957, 1970; Hessen, 1971; Fleck, 1979; Knorr-Cetina, 1981; Barnes, 1982; Knorr-Cetina and Mulkay, 1983). This realisation led to the reflexive insight that what counts as 'social' or what could count as a 'social explanation' was also the product of negotiated connections between humans and non-humans. How these naturalised categories are arrived at is what is interesting. In a similar fashion, in this research we are interested in how controversy about what an organisation is – particularly one that is being changed – is settled. Reorganisation practitioners routinely deal with shifting certainties in relation to the knowledge they have about progress of the reorganisation project – timelines, budgets, scope – reliable sources of data and information, the status of decisions about courses of action and what they regard as still the subject of negotiation.

Uncertainty 5: accountability and responsibility

For the social sciences, this uncertainty refers to their implication in producing and disseminating the idea that 'the social' exists as an object that can be invoked to account for particular configurations of social relations without itself being an object that can be empirically investigated. Perhaps the most heavily debated example of this is evidenced in how the social sciences alternate between two impossible sites, the macro and the micro. Interaction must be understood in context, but when the context is examined there are only local interactions so the analyst is sent back and forth between these two sites. At the heart of Latour's sociology of association is a commitment to exploring where and how context is being assembled. However, Latour emphasises that he is not interested in trying to link, synthesise or reconcile the macro and micro – the two impossible sites – as this would be to 'add another useless artefact to two other gigantic and useless artefacts' (Latour, 2002). Instead, the recommendation is to ignore the categories completely and to look at how 'macro' rhetoric, technologies, logics and pressures come to be incorporated as agencies in everyday practice.

There are two implications of this uncertainty for understanding reorganisation projects. First, just like social scientists, reorganisation practitioners draw upon macro and micro rhetorics, as well as other ontologically uncertain categories, and struggle to reconcile these. Second, again like social scientists, reorganisation practitioners are implicated in and responsible for reproducing, creating and circulating ontologically unstable categories. This is particularly evident within very large organisational change projects such as those that we introduce in the following section. Individual practitioners may be working to connect and configure a handful of entities while trying to bear in mind thousands of others that may be affected by them. Under these circumstances, notions such as the micro/macro and local/global become very convenient constructions.

Before moving on to demonstrate how this framework can help to improve our understanding of reorganisation activity with examples from our case studies, we outline our research methodology and describe in more detail what is meant by reorganisation projects in this research.

Methodology

Reorganisation projects are being explored through ten case studies over a period of three years. Each case study focuses on at least one major reorganisation project (while recognising that these are often composed of and constituted by a series of subprojects or initiatives). We aim to have ten case studies over the three years of the project of which 8 are discussed here (see Table 9.1). We have chosen to cover a wide range of organisations and reorganisations in order to identify the extent of common organising practices across specific sectoral and organisational contexts. At the same time, in order to capture organising in action, we aim to follow reorganisation projects as they unfold, though our actual point of entry varies from case to case.

Each case study consists of ten to fifteen semi-structured one-hour interviews with a range of people involved in the reorganisations, including senior managers, project managers and workers, external consultants and those on the receiving end, the 'consumers' of the reorganisation. Interviews are generally about one hour long, and almost all have

Table 9.1 Summary of case studies

	Type of organisation	Type of reorganisation	Phase of reorganisation
Case study 1 (Multi)	Multinational manufacturer and distributor	Global SAP implementation and 'culture change'	30 months into 60-month programme
Case study 2 (WaterGen)	Utility company	Merger followed by 'culture change'	Merger complete. 18 months into 24-month culture change
Case study 3	Qualifications accreditation network	From network of volunteers to private company	Board recently approved the plan
Case study 4	Qualifications accreditation charity	From charitable sole provider to competitive marketplace provider	24-month programme of work. Went 'live' in April
Case study 5	Home and personal care manufacturer and MSO	Merger followed by 'culture change'	Ongoing 'continuous change' programme
Case study 6	Geographical information provider	Public sector body to private sector organisation	20 months into 36-month programme (keeps changing)
Case study 7	NHS	'Modernisation'	About to start project design
Case study 8	High street food and clothing retailer	Moving headquarters	Launched May 2003 – 24-month project

been tape-recorded and transcribed verbatim. Where possible, we also sit in on relevant project meetings and make observations of other events and conversations including taking photographs of sites. We ask reorganisation practitioners about their education, training and skills and the tools, techniques and methods that they find helpful and unhelpful in their jobs. While physical technological artefacts are interesting, we also include other forms of management tools such as Microsoft Project, PowerPoint, Office, Excel, Pyramid models, 'Five Forces', 'Seven Ss', project management software and programmatic initiatives in our definition of management technologies. It is probably fair to say that this latter kind of management technology – the 'conceptual' tools – have been overlooked in academic literature overall (Molloy, 1999, 2002), although the idea that they can be regarded as such is relatively commonplace within organisation studies, science and technology studies and critical studies of accounting and sociology. An important methodological implication of this observation is that there is always an exercise of choice, if not construction, in the way that the character of the technology in question is represented. As we hope to show later, the sociology of association approach does not overcome this difficulty, though it does allow the actors to define what counts as the technology, its boundaries and the various entities that constitute it too (Molloy, 1999).

We also ask practitioners about their role in the reorganisation, how they came to occupy that role and for details about the project as a whole – timescales, resources, planning and administration. In addition, documentation including minutes of meetings, flow charts, project plans and so on is collected and analysed. However, we are aware that accounts of activities – in other words, discourses – may shift across registers. For example, the meaning and interpretation of spoken versus written discourse, emails versus project plans may often provide different versions of what ostensibly ought to be the same event (Mulkay et al., 1983). This is an important point as it raises interesting questions about the variability of practitioners' accounts, the mechanisms by which common understandings are facilitated across and between different actors and the way that work is coordinated and aligned in accordance with shared concepts. In this chapter we present only data from interviews although we have collected a variety of other documents, artefacts and photographs that will be analysed at a future date. Sociology of association (Latour, 1986, 1987, 1991, 1997; Callon, 1986a, 1986b) is particularly helpful in thinking through these issues as well as a range of other theoretical resources from the sociology of science and technology (STS) such as social worlds/arenas theory, 'boundary objects' and 'standardised packages' (Star and Griesemer, 1989; Fujimura, 1992). For example, from the critical project management literature, Sahlin-Andersson (2002) and Linderoth (2002) show how it may be useful to think about how an array of practices becomes bundled and objectified (black-boxed) to take the form of a project that is then mobilised to coordinate, align, mediate and negotiate other activities (boundary object).

In the following section, case study 1, Multi and Project EXPLORE, and case study two, WaterGen and Project DRAKE, are briefly introduced. Examples of ways in which the five uncertainties were encountered in each of these projects are then provided.

Five uncertainties in practice

Case study 1: Multi and EXPLORE

Multi is one of the largest international beverage and confectionery companies in the world with a market capitalisation of £7.2 billion (end December 2002). Established for over 200 years, Multi currently employs over 55,000 people and sells its products in over 200 countries worldwide. The business has been through a number of significant mergers over the last thirty years or so and continues to expand its business through a programme of acquisition-led growth. Multi's recent strategy has been to strengthen its brand portfolio through almost fifty acquisitions.

Project EXPLORE was initiated in September 2000, following recommendations from Phase Zero, a feasibility study. During the course of this feasibility study, potential for commonality in processes across the Multi group was identified. The adoption of 'common processes' across the groups, 'better process design' and 'better technology' could, it was believed, deliver a benefit of up to £398 million over five years. At its 'launch' the CEO of Multi introduced EXPLORE as follows:

> EXPLORE plays a crucial role in enabling Multi to meet its value creation goals. EXPLORE seeks to radically increase our operating efficiencies and enable the achievement of our agendas for top line growth. At the heart of EXPLORE is the need to reengineer our business processes to reflect world-class best practice and commonality. EXPLORE will be based on a global system.

EXPLORE had a budget allocation of £158 million pounds, is scheduled to run for five years (now at the beginning of year four) and has a full-time dedicated workforce of approximately 300 people, almost half of whom are external consultants. Standardisation of business processes across the regional business units is a key objective of the project and this is expected to be realised by implementation of an SAP system and corresponding changes in working practices.

Case study 2: WaterGen and DRAKE

The idea of Project DRAKE was established in November 1999 to address aligning the asset and operation businesses within Water Co. (a domestic and industrial water utility company) and Generator Distribution (a gas and electricity utility company). A key driver of the project was the requirement of the combined businesses to meet a £400 million reduction in operating costs to satisfy their licence-to-operate conditions with their regulator. In effect, DRAKE was to address merging the two companies in order to realise financial benefits from closer working practices between the two organisations and come up with an appropriate organisational structure for the combined business. Following a number of reiterations with the two companies' boards, the chief executive of the parent company announced his intention to merge the two companies to the City and launched Project DRAKE in July 2000. A project team of 40 full-time individuals was assembled from within the two companies and given three months to design the structures for the new multi-utility company. Crucial considerations included issues of employee motivation, selection, trade union consultation and communication within the two businesses, each of which was regarded as having deeply entrenched and distinct organisational cultures.

The following sections provide a selection of extracts of interviews with key individuals in these two reorganisation projects illustrating instances where they encountered each of the five uncertainties. The quotes refer to various stages of the reorganisation project and are intended simply to highlight the variety of ways in which the different uncertainties are manifest.

Uncertainty 1: group formation

Among other things, the ways in which groups are defined as global, regional, organisational, local or individual can have implications for establishing consensus about whether or not reorganisation is necessary or appropriate. Thus one of the fundamental uncertainties to be negotiated is who or what should be included within the reorganisation project scope. Despite the definition of EXPLORE as a 'global system' the scope of the project has been continually challenged. As a process director of EXPLORE commented:

> So, when we start the dialogue in Europe, for example, we immediately hit, from EXPLORE's view point, significant issues that say, you know, every business unit says, 'not for us, not right,' without even getting to the stage of evaluating the benefits or the options. So that is a good example where now actually, if you look at the EXPLORE benefit case based on shared regional services, we have delivered that in Australia, but there are very clear question marks in Europe.

Individuals' preferred definition of groups and the relationships implied by those may not always be commensurate with those of 'head office'. A senior manager at Multi charged with implementing EXPLORE identified the following moment at which group definition became of critical importance:

> There is that resistance to, who is this head office people telling me this, I am the director here and I am going to make my name.

At WaterGen 'competency' functioned as a rationale for defining groups. The designer of Project DRAKE observed:

> I started having a look around the group and recognised that there were probably elements of operations businesses that could be brought together on a competency footing.

Though 'competency' was to define groups in one sense, other group formations were identified during implementation of DRAKE. For example, the Human Resource Director at WaterGen realised the implications of the recognition that the workforce was not homogeneous in its levels of literacy:

> It was interesting how it kind of, through DRAKE, the knowledge of our employees increased quite significantly. We found out that a significant proportion of them couldn't read or write. We basically employed people over the years to dig ditches and do manual work and they didn't need written skills or literacy skills. And so the kind of blind notion that you could communicate in traditional ways to those people just got blown out of the water when we realised that.

The definition of groups, in turn points to questions of agency. Who, or what, will be the critical actors in determining the evaluation of success or failure of a reorganisation project?

Uncertainty 2: agency

In contrast to the suggestions implicit in abstract representations of reorganisation projects in flow charts, Gantt charts and project management work task sheets, reorganisation projects are not isolated, disconnected processes that will occur of their own independent volition. If EXPLORE or DRAKE, for example, has any agency, that is, realises organisational change, then this agency must be produced through the mobilisation of resources in such a way that can be collectively recognised as corresponding to a defined process. Projects such as EXPLORE or DRAKE have at least a double identity as both a process to be implemented and the methods for its implementation. As a process it is attributed with considerable agency – 'this will add value to our business' – yet it requires the coordinated agencies of people, hardware, software, data and systems in order to realise this. The following interview extracts highlight some of the uncertainty around the different agencies involved. The point to note is the heterogeneity of agencies suggested in the examples.

In this first quote, a process director at Multi identifies limited agency as an issue in persuading an organisation to change:

> in each project, even in Multi, you would have more or less influence in those areas, depending on what it is you are trying to do. The problem isn't what we have to do or doing it, it's this huge attitude and 'Oh my God' so that is a massive piece. And probably more and more of the project is going to have to focus in around here, about how one gets the organisation to go through what they are going to have to do.

The same director articulates some of the tensions between imposing new working practices and trying to persuade people to accept those consensually:

> It's more about control and sharing control. And it's also about having to and it's also about trust. Here at EXPLORE among other things a huge amount of things we do are around changing how we work and a lot of what's changing how we work, is that we are going to work one way, rather than your way, or my way.

Questions of agency were an issue at the design stage of Project DRAKE at WaterGen. As the project manager put it:

> You can't give this job to a first line manager, however experienced they might be because they just don't have the organisational clout.

The project manager also had a clear view of his own particular agency early on in the project:

> On the bad cop routine, my view was, particularly at that time was just the persistent ability to get things delivered. And get answers out of people and get answers that they would either agree, or they would agree. So there was that whole side of it. And that was good, because that was like, you know, your typical Anderson storm-trooper type stuff. Slapping in and just getting things done.

Non-humans are also attributed with agency in reorganisation projects. For example, the IT manager on project EXPLORE regards systems and structures as key actors in EXPLORE.

EXPLORE is a transformation project, but at its centre is reengineering processes and systems. And organisational structures are changing to support the processes. The hierarchy, from my end is processes and then systems and organisational structures to support those processes. So the driver is process reengineering, and the benefits come from consistent best practice processes across the globe and a sort of simplified systems infrastructure which enables you to run your systems at lower cost and upgrade then at a lower cost.

Even 'projects themselves' are attributed with agencies that extend beyond their instrumental deployment. As one of the workers on the DRAKE project team remarked:

I think DRAKE did a lot. Like I said, you know, DRAKE did a lot for me politically.

What is interesting about these quotes is the diversity of agencies involved: humans, systems, technologies, even 'the projects themselves'. The implication here is that to understand agency in reorganisation projects, we need to pay attention, as practitioners do, to the classification of and attribution of agency to the objects that populate and circulate through reorganisation projects.

Uncertainty 3: objects

Perhaps the most obvious 'object' attributed with agency in these cases is the reorganisation programmes, evidenced in statements along the lines of 'DRAKE did a lot' or 'EXPLORE will play a crucial role'. Many different kinds of objects – and non-objects objectified – feature in the day-to-day practice of reorganisation practitioners but their status as objects is often ambiguous. Consider the following extracts from interviews with two different process directors on the EXPLORE project:

those business processes, and all the definition behind that, which is all the organisational sort of building blocks, like job definitions, performance measures, all of that resides in something called Ascendant. And that's where all the project documentation is driven from. So when you get into building the model, we actually get into a systems design on things like function specs and change requests, and all issues get logged in Ascendant. So that is the prime EXPLORE toolkit. I tend to use the team for access to that. And they have expertise in different areas so they tend to be not necessarily process specialists, more and more, the team's a system. I use Lotus Notes, I use PowerPoint and I use a secretary, that tends to be how I operate really. I use a diary. Yes, I use my phone quite a lot!

Take that model and create a people organisation process, which says, where is your highest value stake in the business, what is the business going to do to close the gap, and what are the social implications of that, what do you have to change to get there, and then what's the cost of that change, what's the length of time and so on. We expect each business to have a road map after business strategy. That is a key technology, which we developed two years ago independently.

The systems described above, hybrids of people and technology in objectified forms, can have drawbacks and benefits:

> you have now got a system and that system can restrain the sort of things you want to do organisationally. Once you get into some processes, like demand management, demand planning it is quite difficult to actually specifically design the local roles without understanding how the thing works.

Project management techniques and 'home built' tools also played a significant role in DRAKE. The thing to notice here is also the agency attributed to the objects:

> There was Microsoft Suite. But the important thing was to use separate tools that I had developed over a certain period of time. For planning and estimating. A planning and estimating tool that I had built. And basically we just ran through all the numbers on them. Number of interviews, number of training sessions to be done. Quite detailed. That translates into several medium complex which have standard number of days that I normally associate with. So a simple training scheme, might be three hours. If I have to do 30 of these for 18 process controllers that translated into x number of days. And then we basically just add that together on a Gantt chart, and up popped the plan.

> It is all very well having the vision and the underpinning model, but if you don't document and project manage and organise yourself the whole thing just runs into the sand.

More fundamentally perhaps, the objects which the companies were principally concerned with as products had an obduracy that amplified the uncertainties about objects, agency and groups. The DRAKE project manager expressed this well:

> There is a fundamental difference in the asset between an electricity network and a water network. Electricity network is a passive network, you don't touch it unless it's broken, you don't maintain it, you don't operate it. Oh, you do maintain it, but you don't operate it unless its broken, you don't go anywhere near it. Same with gas. Water network is completely different. You have to actually go out and physically operate the network. And the characteristics come all the way through, the whole way up and down the chain. Two very different sort of characteristics in terms of organising work and the structures around organising that work.

If the status of objects is uncertain, either as agential actors or as authoritative sources of information, then further uncertainty about what can be treated as an objective and reliable definition of what the organisation is, how the reorganisation is progressing and allocation of resources is inevitable.

Uncertainty 4: matters of fact versus state of affairs

Establishing whether a situation is a matter of fact – robust, unproblematic, black-boxed, non-negotiable – or a state of affairs – contestable, debatable, open-ended – is another key uncertainty for reorganisation practitioners. Senior managers at Multi recognise the importance of this uncertainty:

> What these guys are sceptical about is the way that they have to go through the process. They have to start from zero. You cannot drop in at point eight and think you are going to get to point ten. I think that was one of the biggest learnings with the group I deal with, because they are factual people, they want to see evidence before they do anything.

> ... the agonies come when you decide which process you are going to codify. Is it any one of the ones you use today, or is it something new and different, and what organisation assumptions, what business assumptions are you putting behind those choices?

Devices such as flow charts, spreadsheets and project management techniques are key resources in presenting data in such a way that they appear objective, neutral and as a matter of fact although the users of the devices are reflexive about the contingencies involved. A Multi manager:

> The business case is based on numbers for say 2000, but you already have got changes in the cost base. You've already got business units implementing initiatives that could potentially overlap with some of the EXPLORE initiatives, so you've already got that happening.

The Human Resource Director at WaterGen:

> People will say I know the organisation so well I can redesign it. I have heard some of the most senior people say why do I need project management because I know what needs to be done. It is only when you work out the things that you need to do to get from the current position to the desired position that you realise that doing all those requires organisation. It maybe that some people can visualise what the new organisation should be, but they sure as hell cannot hold all the balls in the air to get them there, and that is where project management comes in, to make sure nothing slips between the chairs and everything gets done in a timely way to deliver the outcome.

Uncertainty 5: political epistemology

Taken together, the examples of uncertainties provided above illustrate that reorganisation practitioners are constantly engaged in defining and deciding upon groups, agencies, objects and matters of fact/states of affairs. The implications for theory are that imposing *a priori* predetermined social science analytical categories upon reorganisation practice runs the risk of failing to capture the ways in which these categories are continually performed, negotiated and contested. Such categories might include definitions of professional and non-professional groups, technology, assumptions about human/non-human agency and the status of quantitative and qualitative data. Of course, reorganisation practitioners too have inherited analytical categories and assumptions that are held onto with more or less conviction in any given situation. Many of these categories may have been inherited from the social sciences through education and training but they may also have been developed, tried and tested through long experience. What is interesting here is the ways in which reorganisation practitioners are reflexively able to reconcile – not necessarily overcome – the multiple and competing uncertainties in their day-to-day work. As one senior manager at Multi put it:

> You get on with the job. People don't thank you for being slow. Which is interesting, because if you think about it, living in ambiguity is potentially what we are all likely to do. And therefore, people close down ambiguity pretty quickly because actually human beings are not meant to live in an ambiguous world. Not happy in that environment, so change that goes from one certainty to another quickly, is actually physiologically a lot more easier to do than change that doesn't know where it is going or change that has no, that's actually a lot more difficult.

The following extracts illustrate some reflections on the key skills, methods, tools, techniques and strategies that reorganisation practitioners have for dealing with this uncertainty and ambiguity. From a senior manager at Multi and WaterGen respectively:

> [We are looking for people] who have to be at a high degree of what I would call significant facilitation skills. And they have to be able to make connections and to think strategically.

> Have a clear view of where you intend to be. Plan and project manage to get there. Make sure that you deal with the soft issues as well as the hard issues on the way because surviving the organisation and managing your business afterwards is the objective. Not concentrating on the re-organisation. And as soon as you have got to where you think you need to be just close down all the machinery because otherwise it just perpetuates. Close all the offices take out the special coms, dismantle the machinery of re-organisation otherwise people still think it is going on. And effectively say we are in the new organisation now let's get on with business. Re-organisation is a means to an end not an end in itself.

It's worth noting that traces of the uncertainties about groups, agency, objects and matters of fact/states of affairs are still present in these responses. What they have in common, however, is the emphasis on connection and disconnection, interaction and relational communication. Further, connection is not only between people, but also between people and things, each of which has varying amounts of agency. Reorganisation practitioners know that uncertainties are not overcome once and for all and finally settled. What they can do is recruit people who are particularly skilled at living in ambiguity, as at Multi, and then, periodically, imposing a self-consciously arbitrary sense of closure on reorganisation, as at WaterGen.

Conclusion

Organising is now recognised as an endemic feature of organisations. Reorganisation projects are both a response strategy to the uncertainties implied by change and a method for generating and implementing change. In other words, change is recognised, identified, constructed, known, realised and experienced as and in relation to reorganisation projects. What then have we learnt so far about reorganisation practices? First of all, Latour's sociology of association has been a useful theoretical resource for throwing light on reorganisation practices. By focusing on how practitioners negotiate paths across the sacred analytical boundaries of social science – individual/group, active/passive, human/non-human, fact/fiction, micro/macro – reorganisation activity comes into view as the sophisticated recognition, construction, connection and association of diverse entities. Further, reorganisation practitioners appear as savvy engineers of these connections – building and dismantling simultaneously – with a wide repertoire of skills, tools, techniques and methodologies at their disposal.

The framework of five uncertainties has enabled us to interpret reorganisation practices in a way that seems to resonate with the articulations of the experiences of reorganisation practitioners derived from our interviews. Reorganisation projects impose, discover, challenge, establish and redefine groups, and this can involve some complex politics and questions of agency. Establishing who or what has agency in relation to whom or what groups, objects, individuals at any given time is another uncertainty expressed by reorganisation practitioners. Project management techniques and a range of other devices function as a resource in settling the uncertainty in this respect. Recognising the role and agency of hardware, software, and other kinds of technologies, artefacts and objects, and practitioners' relationships with them, is something that reorganisation practitioners are involved with and implicated in all the time. Establishing matters of fact or states of affairs is another key area of uncertainty in practice that the case studies illustrate. Reorganisation practitioners are simultaneously constructing and dismantling organisations and often face chronic uncertainty in this respect. The fifth uncertainty – political epistemology – reminds us that like social theorists, reorganisation practitioners work with and sometimes struggle to reconcile and connect abstract categories and classifications inherited from authoritative sources.

The implications for theory are that imposing predetermined analytical units upon organising activity runs the risk of missing the creative ways in which organisations are assembled. Of course, our approach has theoretical and methodological limitations too. For example, we are interviewing a relatively small selection of individuals in very large projects. We are not 'following the actors' in the strict ethnographic sense urged by Latour (1987), only accessing activity through interviews and brief episodes of observation. Further, well-established critiques of the sociology of association could also apply to our work. Who has been excluded from the accounts (Star, 1991)? Where do we stand in relation to the connections being studied (Singleton and Michael, 1993; Molloy, 1999)? In the final analysis, it is up to us to conjure out of the empirical materials the connections that we wish to emphasise. This latter point is of particular relevance in this chapter. For example, it is easy to imagine how the examples we provided to illustrate uncertainty about agency could be reinterpreted as uncertainty about objects. Equally, uncertainty about political epistemology – whose knowledge gets to count – could be reinterpreted as an uncertainty about group formation, or agency, or objects and so on.

In response, we argue that the value of the framework of uncertainties lies in its ability to reveal how diverse entities and their agencies are constructed and configured in multiple ways. How, why and when some configurations occur and not others – in theory or in practice – is precisely what is interesting as it enables the question of how things could be otherwise to be asked. The implications of this recognition for organ-isation theory are that putative analytical categories may be inadequate at capturing the creative association of organisational elements that takes place in practice. Further, there may be a case for calling for new propositions to describe the myriad connec-tions and relationships within organisational matrices. In practice, the implications are that reflexive encounters with uncertainty can be regarded as creative opportunities.

Notes

1. 'Organising for Success' is a three-year research programme commissioned by the Chartered Institute for Personnel and Development (CIPD) to investigate the practices and capabilities involved in con-temporary reorganisations.
2. In contrast to Linderoth (2002) we refrain from using the acronym ANT to denote the sociology of association as we are concerned that the term reifies a particular analytical vocabulary whose applica-tion tends to favour description rather than analysis.

References

Barnes, B. (1982) 'The Science-Technology Relationship: A Model and a Query', *Social Studies of Science*, 12: 166–72.

Callon, M. (1986a) 'The Sociology of an Actor-Network: The Case of the Electric Vehicle', in M. Callon, J. Law and A. Rip (eds), *Mapping the Dynamics of Science and Technology*. London: Macmillan, 19–34.

Callon, M. (1986b) 'Some Elements of a Sociology of Translation: Domestication of the Scallops and Fishermen of St Brieuc Bay', in J. Law (ed.), *Power, Action and Belief: A New Sociology of Knowledge?*, Sociological Review Monographs No. 32. London: Routledge.

Eisenhardt, K.M. and Brown, S. (1999) 'Patching: Restitching the Business Portfolio', *Harvard Business Review*, May–June: 72–80.

Fleck, L. (1979) *Genesis and Development of a Scientific Fact*. Chicago: University of Chicago Press.

Fujimura, J. (1992) 'Crafting Science: Standardised Packages, Boundary Objects and Translation', in Pickering, A. (ed.), *Science as Practice and Culture*. Chicago: University of Chicago Press.

Hatch, M.J. (1999) 'Using Improvisational Jazz to Redescribe Organisational Structure', *Organization Studies*, 20(1): 75–100.

Hessen, B. (1971) *The Social and Economic Roots of Newton's Principia*. New York: Howard Fertig.

Knorr-Cetina, K. (1981) *The Manufacture of Knowledge*. New York: Pergamon.

Knorr-Cetina, K. and Mulkay, M. (1983) 'Introduction: Emerging Principles in Social Studies of Science', in Knorr-Cetina and Mulkay (eds), *Science Observed*. Beverley Hills, CA: Sage.

Latour, B. (1986) 'The Powers of Association', in J. Law (ed.), *Power, Action and Belief: A New Sociology of Knowledge?*, Sociological Review Monographs. No. 32. London: Routledge.

Latour, B. (1987) *Science in Action: How to Follow Scientists and Engineers Through Society*. Cambridge, MA: Harvard University Press.

Latour, B. (1991) 'Technology Is Society Made Durable', in J. Law (ed.), *Power, Action and Belief: A New Sociology of Knowledge?*, Sociological Review Monographs No. 32. London: Routledge.

Latour, B. (1997) 'On Actor Network Theory: A Few Clarifications', unpublished Working Paper, Centre for Social Theory and Technology, Keele University, Keele.

Latour, B. (2002) The Clarendon Lectures in Management Studies, Saïd Business School, University of Oxford, October 2002.

Latour, B. and Woolgar, S. (1986) *Laboratory Life: The Social Construction of Scientific Facts.* Princeton, NJ: Princeton University Press.

Linderoth, H. (2002) 'Bridging the Gap Between Temporality and Permanency', in K. Sahlin-Andersson and A. Söderholm (eds), *Beyond Project Management: New Perspectives on the Temporary–Permanent Dilemma.* Copenhagen: Liber.

Lundin, R.A. and Söderholm, A. (1995) 'A Theory of the Temporary Organization', *Scandinavian Journal of Management,* 11(4): 437–55.

Mannheim, K. (1952) *Essays on the Sociology of Knowledge.* Oxford: Oxford University Press.

Mayer M., Smith A. and Whittington R. (2004) *Reorganising for Success: A Survey of HR's Role in Change.* London: Chartered Institute for Personnel and Development.

Merton, R. (1957) 'Priorities in Scientific Discovery: A Chapter in the Sociology of Science', *American Sociological Review,* 22(6): 635–59.

Merton, R. (1970) *Science, Technology and Society in Seventeenth-Century England.* New York: Howard Fertig.

Molloy, E. (1999) *Management Technologies: Ideas, Practices and Processes,* unpublished PhD thesis. Lancaster University.

Molloy, E. (2002) 'When is a Spade Not (Only) A Spade? When it's an Environmental Management Tool', in Markandya, A., (ed.), *Towards a New Environmental Research Agenda.* Basingstoke: Palgrave Macmillan.

Mulkay, M., Potter, J. and Yearley, S. (1983) 'Why an Analysis of Scientific Discourse is Needed', in Knorr-Cetina and Mulkay (eds), *Science Observed.* Beverly Hills: Sage.

Orlikowski, W. (1996) 'Improvising Organisational Transformation Over Time: A Situated Change Perspective', *Information Systems Research,* 7: 63–92.

Packendorff, J. (1995) 'Inquiring into the Temporary Organization: New Directions for Project Management Research', *Scandinavian Journal of Management,* 11(4): 319–33.

Sahlin-Andersson, K. (2002) 'Project Management as Boundary Work: Dilemmas of Defining and Delimiting', in K. Sahlin-Andersson and A. Söderholm (eds), *Beyond Project Management: New Perspectives on the Temporary–Permanent Dilemma.* Copenhagen: Liber.

Singleton, V. and Michael, M. (1993) 'Actor Networks and Ambivalence: General Practitioners in the UK Cervical Screening Programme', *Social Studies of Science,* 23: 227–54.

Star, S.L. (1991) 'Power, Technologies and the Phenomenology of Conventions: On Being Allergic to Onions', in J. Law (ed.), *A Sociology of Monsters: Essays on Power, Technology and Domination.* London: Routledge, 26–56.

Star, S.L. and Griesemer, J.R. (1989) 'Institutional Ecology, Translations and Boundary Objects: Amateurs and Professionals in Berkeley's Museum of Vertebrate Zoology, 1907–39,' *Social Studies of Science,* 19: 387–420.

Tsoukas, H. and Chia, R. (2002) 'On Organisational Becoming: Rethinking Organisational Change', *Organization Science,* 13(5): 567–82.

Volberda, H.W. (1996) 'Toward the Flexible Form: How to Remain Vital in Hypercompetitive Markets', *Organization Science,* 7(4): 359–74.

Weick, K. (1998) 'Improvisation as a Mind-set for Organizational Analysis', *Organization Science,* 9(5): 543–55.

Whittington, R. (2002) 'Corporate Structure: From Policy to Practice', in *Handbook of Strategy and Management.* London: Sage.

Whittington, R. and Mayer, M. (2000) *The European Corporation: Strategy, Structure and Social Science.* Oxford: Oxford University Press.

10

A tale of an evolving project: failed science or serial reinterpretation?

Charles Smith

Introduction

My purpose in this chapter is to discuss the science of project management, within the context of the events of a particular project. The project was completed in an office of around 130 staff providing a financial service, and concerned the introduction of new IT systems, reengineering of the administration processes and a significant reduction in the number of staff. The project took place over a period of two years. The office was a part of a major UK corporation, which I shall call BigCo. While the financial services office itself had little experience of formalised projects, the wider BigCo had a strong culture of project management. The author of this chapter was injected into the financial services office as project manager.

The chapter presents the story from the project manager's point of view; it has not been discussed or negotiated with other parties. It has been compiled from memory, supplemented by notes of decisions and explanations, recorded during evenings and weekends at the time of the relevant events. I will track the main events of the project, and also discuss the unfolding interpretations of the nature and characteristics of the project as understood by the various involved parties. My presentation of this project is recognised as being entirely personal – a particular version of the 'truth' about its completion, told from position of a particular interested party. In taking this approach, I have no intention of claiming this as the only possible description of events or their interpretation: I do not exclude other possibilities. My intention is only to take this particular version, and to use it as a basis for discussion about the science of project management: to ask what this particular story can tell us about the nature of projects and their performance.

In discussing project management, a particular issue I wish to consider is that concerning the application and limitations of conventional management thinking, and whether social constructionist thinking can be of help to those working on projects. To address this question, I have chosen to highlight two specific topics. The first concerns the nature of success and failure. While conventional thinking treats a project as a planned set of actions, either completed to plan ("success") or not ("failure"), a constructionist approach will recognise that these concepts themselves, and their use on this project, are social constructions – emerging from the live activity of the project. The second highlighted topic concerns the potential for new forms of thinking, and specifically a social constructionist approach, to inform those engaged in managing projects, and assist their performance.

While this chapter is about project management, I have discussed, elsewhere, other matters concerning this project and its context: the multifarious forms of authority in operation (Smith, 2000a), and the enactment of the isolated and defensive culture of the office (Smith, 2000b).

The science of project management

There are various possibilities for defining the composition of project management science. For the purposes of this chapter I have defined three levels relevant to the discussion:

Level 1 – the deterministic model. A set of tasks is defined to achieve a specified end point. The project manager arranges for tasks to be listed, planned and completed. The process is wholly deterministic. This model is defined by wider society, and comprises the essential elements of the socially constructed identity of project manager: a minimum set of acts that must be performed for an individual to be eligible for that title.

Level 2 – the Project Book. The science includes level 1, but extends it to a wider regime of knowledge and management practice: understanding of the market, stakeholders and requirements, control of changes in scope, resource planning, design, procurement, handling of risks, handover to the client, and external review and phased life-cycle sanctioning of the project. This model, for the example discussed in this study, is developed and owned by the expert project management community within the wider company of BigCo. It defines the expectations of how projects are to be managed within BigCo, and the behaviours, artefacts and props expected of its practitioners. Membership of this community, together with the ownership of its artefacts, confers, in turn, legitimacy on the individual project manager, enabling him or her to act with authority on project matters in the local organisation. Despite these extensions, this version remains a machine model. It defines an ideal set of actions that will take the project through a defined process to a defined conclusion.

Level 3 – social construction of reality. Different people, groups of people and communities of practice have different understandings of the project reality. The involvement and interests of the parties vary throughout the project life. The project and its attributes are thus socially constructed and dynamic. A science applied at this level will recognise the diverse views of the project, its mutations though its life and its interactions with its political context. This version of the science will advance us beyond the machine model to incorporate paradigms of organism (responding to the environment), learning, sense-making and political systems.

Failed science or serial re-interpretation?

The professional skill and science of project management is embodied at level 2. BigCo and most project-orientated organisations have adopted, or are adopting, similar standard practices. The expected capabilities of individuals operating at this level have also been set out in detail within various professional Standards, for example Bodies of Knowledge or the National Occupational Standards for Project Management of the Engineering Construction Industry Training Board (ECITB). The profession of project management is defined by these standard practices, and this forms the basis on which individual performance will be judged.

I have considered two contrasting approaches to discussing the issue of success and failure in the application of project management. We may choose:

(a) to define 'failure' at level 2 – that the science of project management, embodied in the Project Manager and the Project Book, was applied or mis-applied, to the attainment of planned end points (delivery, time, cost) that were then not delivered; this constitutes 'failure', and the aims of analysis are to identify the root causes and consequences of this failure, and to plan remedial actions; or

(b) to step beyond this to level 3, outside the dichotomy of success and failure, and see the science and its associated concepts of success and failure as discursive tools, legitimising decisions, developing individual identity and roles, explaining actions and outcomes, and providing resources for the various parties to position themselves, associating or dissociating themselves from the project.

Performance of individuals

If project managers are to progress their thinking beyond the mechanistic, then the science at level 3 should give some indication of the skills that will be of specific value to project players. While I have not examined in any detail the performative actions of the individuals taking part in my tale, it is of value to consider the conclusions we may reach about the nature of project management to see whether they can cast light on the sorts of matters a skilled performer might deal with in a project setting.

Methodology

My general methodological approach is to record and analyse decisions and the explanations that accompany them, seeking to expose and explain the forms of 'reality' that frame the thinking and practice prevailing in the organisation. My analytical framework is based on the work of Foucault (1972) concerning the nature of knowledge and its organisation: the construction of objects and their attributes and functions, the concepts and procedures that are employed to control them, and the importance of groups who deploy specialist disciplines (sciences), having power and authority to act in particular ways within these structures. This basic philosophical position is expounded in the organisational context by Weick (1995), who discusses the mechanisms through which common understandings are created, justified and enacted – the creation of sense and explanations, and their embodiment in the decisions, practices and artefacts of the organisation.

For the analysis presented in this chapter, my approach has been to consider the project as a socially constructed entity, scanning the decisions and explanations that surrounded its production and continuing evolution, extracting those that determined its nature, and noting the ownership and purpose of the different versions of truth that emerged.

Names and details have been amended to protect the anonymity of the organisation and its people.

The organisation and the project

The background of the project is set out here in sufficient detail to provide a context for the project mapping and discussion that follows.

Within the administration office, prior to the project, there were a number of existing zones of expert practice: sciences, practised within their recognised expert communities, and referenced in decisions and sense-making. The main zones were:

- Administration: delivery of a complex financial service, applying rules to scheme members – characterised by low-pay entry, low mobility and an extended hierarchical promotion ladder, based on knowledge of the extensive and complex rules to be applied
- Finance: determination of the rules applying to the service and their interpretation, actuarial assessment, protection of corporate finance – characterised by professional high-pay entry, high mobility and immediate responsibility
- Data control: applying controls to data, and to the activities of administration staff, granting permissions for use of the IT system – characterised by specialist capabilities in IT systems, practised by high-mobility professionals.

The office as a whole was perceived, from within and without, as excessively bureaucratic, rule-bound and subject to hierarchical authority. Individual status within it emanated primarily from knowledge of, and control of, the complexity of its financial products and processes.

The IT systems and work processes had been developing incrementally for some 25 years and were considered obsolete. Previous attempts to update these systems, led by the data control community, had not delivered any significant change. There was therefore a communal feeling of failure, and a fear that further failure would be very damaging to reputation and could well lead to corporate BigCo closing the office and outsourcing its function. As a consequence of this perception of an unknown but threatening headquarters agenda, the possibility and consequences of 'failure' became an ever-present narrative in day-to-day decision-making, and encouraged an inward-looking and defensive culture, which was to be a key influence on the unfolding rhetoric surrounding the project (Smith, 2000b).

A new project, to implement radically different administration processes and IT systems, was outlined, and a number of existing staff were assigned to a new project team, which was established as both organisationally and physically separate.

Project management as a science was not a primary zone of expertise in this local office. The headquarters demanded, as a condition for financial sanction for the project, the injection of a project manager from outside the office. He was expected to act as a member of the wider BigCo community of expert project management practice, bringing this science into the local office and situating the new project within that wider community. Along with that science, he brought its power base and its edifices: his own ratified position as a 'Project Manager', the 'Project Book' (a manual setting out the practices to be followed), and the identification of a 'Project Director' to oversee the proper application of these practices, remote, but powerful as a member of the BigCo corporate executive.

The primary content of the project, which remained stable throughout its life, comprised the procurement and configuration of IT systems to establish the administration processes, and a significant reduction in staff numbers (levels perceived to be three times the norm for this type of administration). Other agenda emerged and retreated as discussed below. A go-live date for the new systems (and downsized organisation) had been declared to corporate headquarters and to staff.

Mapping the project

Table 10.1 and the paragraphs below summarise the project at a number of stages, reflecting major step changes in the positions of the various parties during the course of the project.

Table 10.1 summarises the main strands of thinking. The project under consideration concerns a major internal change. Those who work on it are therefore not dealing with some impersonal object, but with the future of their own working lives. I have therefore noted, in the table, the thinking that frames the project itself, and also that concerning its expected impact on the jobs of those involved.

Three parties are presented, being those with key roles and showing significant shifts in their thinking. They are: (1) the project team – the identified group responsible, for

Table 10.1 Changing perspectives on the project

Stage and timing (months)	Project team perspective	Administration team perspective	Executive perspective
Stage 1: planning (1–4)	*Aims*: commitment to meet expectations of admin. team and go-live date *Project*: full authority, trusted to complete; replicating complexity; create full plan and do it, or lose credibility and betray trust *Impact on jobs*: part of project, but not our remit	*Aims*: as good as current *Project*: no faith in project team; not our responsibility; we are the client, with power of rejection *Impact on jobs*: demand to know terms of new jobs/departures	*Aims*: staff reductions by due date; destruction of power groups (hierarchy, data control, record office) *Project*: naive team + complexity = high risk to programme and cost; not compatible with needs of outside clients *Impact on jobs*: give warning of job losses; we will look after them
Stage 2: commit and design (5–18)	*Aims*: minimum complexity to operate new system *Project*: plan to achieve minimum; continuous negotiation of scope; less comprehensive than intended, and lost ownership (to admin. team, outside clients, suppliers), lost morale *Impact on jobs*: part of project, but not our remit	*Aims*: prefer as good as current; forced into unwanted negotiation *Project*: little faith in project team, but we will help them; we lead organisation and practice design; we are the client, but pressurised into accepting less than we want *Impact on jobs*: applying for new jobs; departure terms look OK, but we don't really trust them – wait and see	*Aims*: hold a feasible line; maximise supplier's role; meet programme; avoid complexity and additions; corporate finance agenda *Project*: closely control strategy to minimise risk to programme and cost; not enough drive to completion *Impact on jobs*: generous leaving terms but dependent on performance; vulnerable to early departures; interviews and appointments to new positions
Stage 3: dash to the finish (19)	*Aims*: go live on any terms, as defence against interference *Project*: transfer data; do the rest later; not professional; poor management; diverted resources *Impact on jobs*: who cares; I've got my new job/I'm getting out of here as soon as I can have the money	*Aims*: imperative to go live on committed date – just give us the data – claim success or our enemies will gloat *Project*: main project has failed; run our own project; punish the guilty *Impact on jobs*: 'I've got my new job?'/'I'm leaving'	*Aims*: must hand over to outside parties; admin. can go live – will have data; work manually until rest is complete *Project*: work all hours to transfer the data, the rest can wait *Impact on jobs*: new teams identified; support to leavers

(Continued)

Table 10.1 Continued

Stage and timing (months)	Project team perspective	Administration team perspective	Executive perspective
Stage 4: handover (20–21)	*Aims*: operational system; identify serious deficiencies for later rectification *Project*: planned and orderly completion and handover; managed, audited *Impact on jobs*: looking forward to new job	*Aims*: give us something we can use; get operational *Project*: dropped on us despite objections and deficiencies; will have to make do *Impact on jobs*: new job; leavers departing; end of an era	*Aims*: we've made it, so don't panic; orderly transition; can transfer to external parties *Project*: managed, authorised handover *Impact on jobs*: get rid of troublemakers; why pay the performance bonuses?
Stage 5: new operations (22–24)	*Aims*: operational system; deficiencies scheduled for later rectification *Project*: tidy up as service to administration team *Impact on jobs*: let me out	*Aims*: operational; sort the deficiencies *Project*: our project was a success; was there a project team? *Impact on jobs*: leavers' stories sound good; they did better than me	*Aims*: let's settle down; targets met, so bonus payment can be paid *Project*: brilliant success; just clearing up *Impact on jobs*: target reductions achieved; painless thanks to bonuses and buoyant job market; must be our good HR management

most of the duration, for delivery of the project; (2) the administration team – who deliver the financial service to outside customers and will be the users of the new system; and (3) the executive team – sponsors of the project, holding responsibility for its overall strategy, but also, individually, managers of teams and other functions (legal, accounts, communications, office services and so on) within the office.

These three groups are organisationally defined, and are not directly equivalent to the zones of expert practice. For example, the project team included experts in both administration and data control, each expected to apply their specialist knowledge within the team. Some individuals had multiple memberships of these groups, or transferred during the course of the project.

There were a number of other parties with an interest in the project: the BigCo headquarters, who set a primary agenda of finance and staff reduction; the data control department; external clients – other companies to whom sections of the service would be transferred (under a continuing programme of divestments of parts of BigCo); the main supplier of the new IT system, under-resourced and seeking to minimise commitments; and the outside customers of the service.

These parties had overt interests. Their positions were also progressively constructed and reconstructed, by the main project parties, throughout the course of the project. For example, the BigCo headquarters was, as already noted, constructed, by the local executive team, as hostile. The data control department was assigned the blame for past failures and was to be closed down as part of the new drive to success. The outside customers of the service were habitually constructed as ignorant and unscrupulous, thereby justifying their exclusion from any meaningful interaction with the project.

The summary below briefly presents the arguments and explanations holding sway within the main parties through the stages of the project. Important dissensions are also noted and discussed.

Stage 1: planning

Detailed commitments had been given, before the arrival of the project manager, that the new system would be comprehensive and efficient ("better than the old system"), and would be operational by the declared completion date. The project team claimed full responsibility for delivery, denying the validity of any external viewpoint, and generated detailed plans. The leaders of the project saw full competence and full delivery as being necessary to claim their legitimacy and protect them against failure. "We have been trusted to do this, and if we fail we will have betrayed that trust." The executive team (and the project manager) were not convinced that the promises were credible, nor necessary to meet their own more limited aims of new IT systems and staff reductions. Thus the project defined at this stage was owned by the project team, but not by the executive. The administration team were happy to adopt the comfortable but disengaged role of a sceptical and demanding client ("We won't accept it if it isn't good enough").

Positions shifted to stage 2 at the moment of financial commitment (placing the order with the external supplier of the IT system). In accordance with the Project Book, the project manager could argue that this stage was pre-project, in that there was no committed plan or funding. However, the shift to stage 2 caused much distress to project team members, undermining promises they had made to their colleagues in the administration team. It diminished their new status as managers of the project. In their own eyes they had already failed before the project manager considered that the project had begun.

Stage 2: commitment and design

This extended stage covered detailed specification of the software, organisation design and development of the software. There was tight control of the strategy by a steering group, who operated to minimise complexity. This need was emphasised by the recognition of outside clients who were admitted to the project at a strategic level. Commitments, other than the minimum necessary to do the job, had to be avoided for fear that they might not be met. This could potentially be construed as 'failure' in the eyes of the outside clients and, through them, the critical headquarters of BigCo. The members of the project team were pressurised into delivering less than they would wish and were seen by their administration peers to be delivering a poor system. The managers of the administration team were compelled to buy in, and sign off decisions on administrative practice. There was thus an increasing atmosphere that the new system was "not good enough, but management are forcing it through". In the latter part of this stage, technical complexities, problems and faults emerged. These were expected risks (such as data transfer problems and software deficiencies) but they were exacerbated by the preference of the project and administration teams to play out their narrative of "not good enough", and reject minor deficiencies. During the latter part of this stage the new administration team was appointed, so that it was known who was staying and who was leaving.

There was a growing realisation that the declared completion date would not be achieved. When this was admitted publicly, the administration team as a group broke ranks in an attempt to dissociate themselves from the 'failure' of the main project, and to set up their own version.

Stage 3: dash to the finish

For a period of four weeks, the project was split. The administration team made their own arrangements to operate on a minimum new system (transfer the data and administer the service manually), as soon as possible (that is, within the declared programme). They stated that the main project was late and flawed, and had thus failed, but that through their own efforts they were rescuing the reputation of the office.

Their plans addressed the issue of going live on the due date, their immediate concern. However, their work diverted resources from the main project, jeopardising achievement of the executive's aims, promised to headquarters, of staff reductions and associated cost cuts. A move was concocted by the director of the office and the project manager. They issued a new formal organisation chart, transferring responsibility for completion and acceptance of the new system to the office managers (not the project team). This had a dramatic effect, since these managers now found themselves nominally responsible for a project they had declared to have failed. There were objections and heated disagreements about responsibilities.

At the moment when the administration team could take the system live on their minimal plan, the risks were too great. In the fear that the cost cuts might not be achieved on time, the executive put off the decision to go live, and transferred their allegiances and resources back to the main project.

Stage 4: handover

The project approached the moment when the new systems would go into live operation. It became essential to demonstrate order so that external criticism could be discounted. Systemised practices (from the Project Book) were put in place so that the extensive and continuing deficiencies could be shown to be under management control. The organisation as a whole was reconnected to the main project. The primary narrative shifted abruptly to one of order and control, and of expected 'success'.

There were dissenters, who continued to talk of the deficiencies of the project and the dubiousness of its impending implementation, but this view threatened the narrative of the majority, who were intent on pursuing their needs to claim success. The dissenters were pressurised, by managers and peers alike, into acceptance of the new era, or to an early assisted departure.

Stage 5: new operations

The system went live, two months behind the declared programme but within the timescale promised to headquarters. The departing staff left the company at the same time, with minimal ceremony.

The omissions, deficiencies and errors were extensive. However, they were systemised and categorised into a fault schedule for "ongoing operational improvement plans", and hence brought in line with the narrative of project 'success'. The project team was run down, and the administration team now owned the new practices. All parties claimed success. This claim was directed at the critical outside parties, but also served to support the identity development of the individuals. They had achieved the status of proficient project personnel. They had taken part in a challenging project, delivered a new administration system and reduced staff numbers to the target level. The idealised picture was completed by the widespread circulation of optimistic stories about the experiences of the departed staff.

Observations: the life of the project

I have presented this tale as being primarily about a project, and the application of project science within it. However, the rational–scientific model of project management was only one of many paradigms operating during the course of the project. Other 'sciences' with significant impact included:

- corporate financial security, including reduction in head count, control of financial risk and transfer of liabilities to external parties: this agenda provided political drive, framed decisions and dominated other agenda when critical
- the defence of the organisation against its external customers (the users of the service), and skills employed to prevent them from having any voice, both before, during and after the completion of the project
- territorial defence by the organisation against its critical outsiders: the management skills and practices that defend personal and organisational survival.

Project management science as such did not lead the agenda. It existed, initially, outside the office, and was then summoned in and put into action, as a secondary field of activity, to fulfil the purposes of the other agenda. Actions were therefore framed by a wide range of forms of authority, which I have discussed in Smith (2000a), and were not dictated by a unitary project management science.

The simple rational (level 1) model of project management was an essential resource to claim ownership, to resist external interference and to claim competence. "I can do it, and I have a plan, and therefore I am entitled to act." The ownership of project management science at level 2, invoking its expert community within BigCo, legitimised managerial action, bestowed identity and status, and gave authority to speak about the project.

Concepts of success and failure were regularly employed to describe both the project and the project manager. They were used extensively to assign and segment responsibilities, to claim achievement of a plan or partial plan, and to assign to others the blame for non-completion of plans. These concepts are key discourses in the world of organisational politics.

The project under study experienced a series of mutations: substantial step-shifts in its definition and primary attributes. These were driven by:

- the demand for 'projectification', the forces that determined that a particular set of corporate aims (and excluding others) would be transformed into a defined 'project', sanctioned by BigCo headquarters
- the needs of those initially assigned to the project team to claim legitimacy for their new status and roles, and to design a project that served the agenda of their peers in the administration team
- the dominant agenda of corporate finance, and the efforts of the different parties to reposition themselves, and the project, to comply with the demands of that agenda
- the different strategies adopted through the project life to control external interested parties – initial exclusion, then controlled inclusion and finally a highly systemised handover; these strategies served to defend the organisation boundaries from external attack
- the recognition and interpretation of complexities and problems that emerged into the light of day as the project progressed

- the strategies of the various internal parties (for example, individual managers and non-project departments such as the administration team) to associate themselves with, or dissociate themselves from, the project, defining and redefining 'success' and 'failure' to suit their ends
- the endgame politics surrounding the transfer of responsibility from the (temporary) project team to the (permanent) administration team – intentions to reject the project, attempts to divide the successful from the unsuccessful (and associate oneself with the former), the switch from discourses of failure to those of success, and the creation of edifices of project order to underpin that success.

The mutations in the project were assisted by the creation of a number of tangible objects: the definition of the project itself, its substance and its boundaries, the Project Book, the external client agenda, the deadline and its significance to the office reputation, the formal organisation chart, supplier and resource shortages, the agenda of BigCo headquarters (as constructed and interpreted by the executive), and finally the documented evidence of the 'successful' project and the credit (and financial bonuses) emanating from membership of a successful project organisation.

A number of groups and individuals did not accept the versions of reality created and defended by the mainstream organisational groups. When this dissent was widespread (for example, on simplification of the project scope in stage 2), it was manifested in a grudging acceptance of the corporate agenda. On the other hand, in later stages, when the narrative of success was generally preferred, and staunchly defended, dissenting individuals were compelled to change their position or be excluded.

Discussion

Project management failings

A conventional management interpretation of the events I have described would be in terms of project management failings. The science of project management and its associated artefacts were brought in to the office I have described, carrying promises of the delivery of objectives. The possession of this science gave the team well-established techniques to plan actions, and the authority to implement and control them. The science was therefore well established at the level 2 described earlier, implementing a wide range of corporately sanctioned practices.

We could, if we wished, consider this as a legitimate management science, and assess the performance of the project under observation against the standards of this science. Were we to do so, we could then, with ease, identify numerous 'failures' – instances where explicit intentions were set out, incorporated into plans, and then subsequently not delivered.

Under conventional management thinking, we would then proceed to analyse these failings. This we could do from any of a number of standpoints: as external custodians of project management science, to ask whether the techniques had been expertly applied; as one of the various stakeholders in this project, to ask whether our objectives had been adequately delivered; or as experts in wider management science, to ask whether the management of the project had, in this instance, been effective management practice.

A root-cause analysis of such failures could enable distinctions to be made between omissions in the systems and procedures adopted and failures by the project manager and others to apply their skills in an appropriate manner. Conventional management practice would then seek to apply remedial measures: procedural changes, increased management supervision and audits, training in new practices, or the reassignment of deficient individuals to lesser duties.

However, it is apparent from the project described in this chapter that there were wider influences, arising from the dynamics of the organisation and its environment, that had enormous impact on the out-turn of the project, but are not accounted for in this conventional management approach.

These wider influences, and the disruption they cause, can usually be handled by the astute and agile project manager, who will be proficient at segmenting responsibilities and deflecting blame when shifts of direction take place. If general competence has been exercised within the defined science, then success can be claimed, and any diversions from the plan can be ascribed to causes beyond the project manager's remit. This cycle is a common feature of projects: commitment is made to a set of objectives, the objectives are not achieved, explanations are generated and blame assigned. "The project management was a success, but we did not deliver what was expected because the client failed." As Machiavelli infamously observed, almost 500 years ago, in *The Prince*, "no prince ever yet lacked legitimate reasons with which to colour his want of good faith".

The cynical may describe this picture of project management as 'realistic', but we should perhaps at least consider whether a more constructive interpretation might be found. Rather than accept the step-shifts in the project definition as normal 'failures', to be explained away or located somewhere outside our zone of influence, can the science be extended to incorporate these wider matters?

Serial reinterpretation

An alternative analysis is to consider the shifts in project definition as legitimate serial re-interpretation. The science of project management, as conventionally defined, is only a partial description of the life of a project within an organisation. There are many influences beyond its implied machine model: local construction of 'reality', ignorance and learning, politics and personal alliances, overlapping and conflicting zones of expert power and knowledge, and the impact of fluctuating institutional agenda, which assault a project from beyond its boundaries.

The project does not exist *a priori* as an objective entity. It arises from an act of 'projectification', bringing the project into existence, and setting its aims, frontiers and primary attributes. The creation of the project is context-dependent, a response to the higher-order agenda of the day, and to political moves and alliances, both inside and outside the organisation. In a complex organisation, different parties can and will claim different coexisting versions of the project. As the project progresses, this context, and with it the ascendancy of particular versions, will almost certainly change, and the project will consequently undergo a series of mutations.

For the project described in this chapter a number of factors led to its repeated reinterpretation. While these factors have been identified from this specific example, it is considered that they can be broadly generalised, in that any complex project is likely to be subject to similar influences. The main factors can be summarised as:

- the unfolding and increasing dominance of the higher-level agenda (corporate finance), to which the project, and its science, were inevitably subservient
- the generation of over-ambitious, over-confident plans (to claim project ownership) that proved to be unstable
- the defence of the boundaries of the organisation against outside parties, to define and limit their influence on the project
- the revelation of hidden complexities and problems as the project progressed
- the forces arising from the changing positions of different parties during the establishment, progress and handover of the project.

Thus there are a number of iterative feedback loops in operation. The project is established and defined in response to the prevailing context, the project makes some degree of progress, the project team and other parties then reinterpret the project and revise their positions, and the context of the project is then reconstructed. It is not only the changing environment that drives the evolution of the project; it is also the multiple influences as the project and its context progressively interact. The diversion and reinterpretation of projects are not merely bad luck or bad management. They are an inevitable feature of organisational life.

In this iterative model of the project in its context, the concepts of 'success' and 'failure' can no longer be claimed as objective assessments of the project condition. They have become primary rhetorical resources employed by different parties, within this iterative process, to define the project and its status, and to associate themselves with, or dissociate themselves from, different aspects of the project.

Lessons for individual performance

This assessment, an evaluation of the dynamic life of a project, gives useful indications of the types of issue that must be handled by competent project players. Traditional forms of competence – the following of procedural rules, associated with the mechanistic process-driven view of projects – are not to be undervalued, but they must be framed within a wider set of capabilities and concepts. The ability to 'read' the forces and influences at work within the organisation can now be seen as a vital skill. If shifts in the definition and enactment of the project are inevitable, then an enhanced awareness of how these arise will enable managers to anticipate them, be prepared to switch direction at a moment's notice, deploy their more conventional procedural skills to greater effect, and hone their powers of politics and creative manipulation, so that they may realign the project, or include or exclude disparate factions to boost their chosen direction. Thus the repeated reinterpretation of the project will cease to be an unfortunate and regrettable diversion, and will become an essential part of the operating territory of an expert project manager.

Conclusions

The tale of an evolving project presented in this chapter, though personal and subjective, has provided useful material to inform an understanding of projects in general, and the forces that lead to their serial re-interpretation through the project life. While conventional management thinking may see the shifts and turns of a project in terms of successes and failures, a more useful understanding can be gained by taking a wider social constructionist view of the project, and the dynamics of its organisation and its context. The handling of these matters could be incorporated into a more complex and socially aware project management science, with practitioners who are able to read the forces and influences at work, and consequently able to take due account of these matters.

This is not to say that enhancement of management understanding and skills will change the basic structures that drive the construction and reconstruction of projects. Executives will undoubtedly continue to demand over-optimistic project strategies that respond to their agenda of the day, project teams will continue to make unwarranted claims of certainty in their plans, different internal and external parties will continue to pursue their own ends, exercising their power over the project and its interpretation, and client teams will continue to raise objections to acceptance. Furthermore, project managers will continue to commit themselves to undeliverable promises, positioning themselves and their projects favourably in the wider organisational context in which they operate, in the knowledge that these can be renegotiated and revised when the need arises. These behaviours are not abnormal, and nor are they specific to project management. They are inevitable facets of the transactions that take place within organisations.

It may be hoped, however, that a more overt recognition of the processes by which project reality is socially formed, shaped, interpreted and reinterpreted may greatly help individuals working on projects understand and be effective within the organisational world in which they operate.

References

Foucault, M. (1972) *The Archaeology of Knowledge.* London: Tavistock.
Smith, C.R. (2000a) 'An Organisation in Transition: Constructing New Realities', in J.M. Fisher and N. Cornelius (eds), *Challenging the Boundaries: PCP Perspectives for the New Millennium.* Farnborough: EPCA Publications.
Smith, C.R. (2000b) 'Organizational Culture in Practice', *Human Resource Development International*, 3(2): 153–8.
Weick, K.E. (1995) *Sensemaking in Organizations.* Thousand Oaks, CA: Sage.

part **3**

Inter-organisational projects

11

Understanding power in project settings

Nick Marshall

Introduction

> What would be proper to a relationship of power, then, is that it be a mode of action on actions. That is, power relations are rooted deep in the social nexus, not a supplementary structure over and above 'society' whose radical effacement one could perhaps dream of. To live in a society is, in any event, to live in such a way that some can act on the actions of others. A society without power relations can only be an abstraction.
>
> Foucault, 2002 [1982]: 343

The mainstream project management literature is largely silent on issues of organisational power. Where it is acknowledged, power appears either as an aberration, a negative and damaging phenomenon that needs to be eliminated for the rational progress of the project process to be restored, or as a resource to be controlled and managed as part of a toolkit of project management techniques. This chapter argues that the lack of an adequate conceptualisation of power leads to an impoverished understanding of organisational behaviour and social interaction in project settings. However, to suggest that this omission needs to be addressed is not to say that all aspects of project work can or should be reduced to questions about the manifestation, exercise or effects of power. What is understood by power can easily become so diffuse and all-embracing, relating to virtually every dimension of social life, that there are those who propose that it should be dropped altogether. The argument is that by attempting to explain everything it ends up explaining nothing (for example, Baudrillard, 1980; Dews, 1984). This is not the position adopted here. To argue that power, in all its various guises, is a prevalent feature of most social relations is not necessarily to adopt an unspecific and totalising view of power. However, in order to escape the problem of treating power as everywhere and thus nowhere, it is important to adopt a conceptual vocabulary that is capable of recognising the varieties of power, their expression within different social settings, and the implications of these varying modalities.

By drawing insights from the long-standing debates about power in social theory, this chapter considers how far different positions within this tradition are relevant to understanding the specific nature of organising within project settings. Of particular importance here is the tendency to draw a strong distinction between orthodox, prohibitive conceptions of power and those that treat it in more productive terms, as evident in, but not limited to, the work of Foucault. The difference has been summarised as that between 'power over' versus 'power to'. The former treats power as a matter of competing interests where individuals or groups draw on various resources to achieve their objectives at the expense of others. The latter regards power in more anonymous terms, not as something to be possessed and wielded solely as a tool of coercion, but more as a shifting arrangement of materials, relations, dispositions and techniques that are simultaneously the medium and effects of power, and which enable and constrain particular patterns of action. It is tempting to see power-over and power-to as incompatible viewpoints, the acceptance of one implying the rejection of the other. At its most extreme, this results in a caricature consisting, on the one hand, of a social world in which power is about the goal-directed, strategic and intentional actions of fully formed subjects and, on the other, one where even the constitution of subjectivities is an effect of power and there appears to be little room for any intentionality. Yet, as Law (1991: 170) has argued, 'so long as we understand that there is no necessity about these relations then there is no reason why we should not treat power as a condition, a capacity, something that may be stored, as well as an effect or a product'. This offers the possibility of effecting a reconciliation between the agency-driven, strategic concerns of conventional analyses of power-over, and the decentred, largely anonymous, networks and arrangements of power-to.

These themes are especially relevant for project settings because it is difficult to avoid the conclusion that projects are the site of both strategically acting and interacting agents and places where multiple techniques, dispositions, norms and discourses intersect. On the one hand, the temporary nature of projects as discontinuous endeavours, often characterised by uncertainty and complexity, and drawing upon contributions and expertise from multiple functions, disciplines and organisations, makes them fertile ground for disputes and disagreements. They are negotiated engagements in which actions are interdependent and emergent and need to be coordinated in an ongoing fashion. In so doing, project participants constitute and set in motion a range of materials, techniques and strategies to negotiate their way through different encounters. This is very much the realm of personalised and overt power relations, corresponding to the episodic circuit of power proposed by Clegg (1989). In contrast with more permanent and routine forms of organising, projects are arguably more likely to be the setting for such episodic power since it is potentially more difficult for power relations to be normalised into customary patterns of practice and discourse.

On the other hand, this does not mean, as Meyerson *et al.* (1996) seem to suggest, that projects are largely lacking any normative, dispositional or institutional fabric

through which activities are articulated. As Engwall (2003) has argued, it is cruc
see projects not as isolated 'islands' of activity, but as being variously embedd
wider contexts of institutionalised norms, values and routines. While these may be
integrative, providing generative structures through which coordinated activities are
constituted and reproduced over time and across project settings, they may equally be
differentiating as varying project subgroups often tend to be embedded within alternative institutional fields. In short, some norms will be shared while others will not. A
key analytical question concerns how to connect the episodic domain of actions and
interaction with the domain of norms and dispositions. While perhaps appealing, it
is a mistake to draw too direct a relationship between the two domains. This would
be to suggest, for example, that actions flow directly from some preexisting normative
background or set of dispositions, with people simply acting out predetermined patterns of action or following clear rules of conduct. A possible link between these
domains can be found in the notions of enactment (Weick, 1995) or instantiation
(Giddens, 1984), which suggest a reciprocal and recursive relationship between structures and actions. Through action and interaction, different norms and dispositions
are constituted, reproduced, modified or destroyed in an ongoing and shifting interplay. Actions are never totally determined by the constitutive power of normalisation,
but equally neither are they about the free-floating and unconstrained play of overlapping and/or competing intentions. They take place within more or less open or
closed zones of manoeuvre which are themselves augmented through the unfolding
of concrete actions.

How the different modalities (or circuits) of power interact in practice is a largely
empirical question. Consequently, the chapter concludes with an illustration drawn
from recent research into a multi-organisational civil engineering team comprising
a client organisation, engineering consultant and contractor. This example indicates
how ostensibly overlapping norms of conduct, in this instance relating to a general
discourse of 'collaboration', are variably constituted through particular practices
that suggest quite different interpretations of what it means to collaborate. Although
well-established in the language of team members, the idea of collaboration is
not a fixed point of reference closely steering their actions, but rather a contested
resource that they employ in a variety of ways as they attempt to negotiate their way
through a series of potentially divisive issues. This suggests a dual character to power
relations in this setting. On the one hand, there is an idealised norm of collaboration
that (incompletely) guides expectations about acceptable behaviour within the team.
On the other hand, these same normative rules of conduct provide the material out
of which team members improvise novel discursive strategies in attempts to resolve
problematic issues in their favour (for example, concerning the allocation of risks
and rewards, timing of work and contractor involvement in the design process).
This implies a more intricate interplay between power-to and power-over than
tends to be acknowledged by accounts that regard these views of power as opposing
alternatives.

Alternative conceptions of power

Although power has long been recognised as an 'elemental concept' in social theory (Giddens, 1976), it is at the same time one which has proved particularly elusive, generating vigorous debate and a plethora of competing perspectives. This has prompted some commentators to doubt the explanatory value of power, seeing it as an overburdened or chaotic conception that needs to be tamed by more precise definition and parsimonious usage (Wrong, 1968; Bacharach and Lawler, 1980). Nevertheless, while hardly a focal concern of social theory, or organisation theory more specifically, the notion of power is something that has been periodically revisited, reflecting an unwillingness to dispense with the concept altogether in the belief that it still has something important to offer our understanding of social phenomena (for example, Perrow, 1970; Clegg, 1979, 1989; Kotter, 1979; Pfeffer, 1981, 1992; Mintzberg, 1983; Astley and Sachdeva, 1984; Barnes, 1988; Jermier et al., 1994). Unfortunately, for those who do not reject the concept outright, something of a schism has developed in how to approach the issue of power. This is reflected in a typically binary (or sometimes triadic) characterisation of perspectives which are usually depicted as absolutely opposing and incompatible. This has been particularly evident since the influential contributions of Foucault to the debate (for example, Foucault, 1977a, 1977b, 1980a, 1980b), although arguably Lukes (1974) played a similar role in differentiating existing theories along lines that have subsequently become solidified and impassable. Perhaps ironically in the case of Foucault, his efforts to disrupt what he saw as the dominant, sovereign conception of power, as personalised, intentional and prohibitive, were often based on a rhetorical strategy that displaced or erased this conception entirely, rather than supplementing it with, or relating it to, an alternative view of power as anonymous, capillary and constitutive. The aim of this section is to sketch some of the main positions within the literature on power and consider whether the differences are as insurmountable as sometimes appears.

Most orthodox approaches to power are influenced by the formulation offered by Weber (1958: 113) whereby it is portrayed as 'the chance of a man or of a number of men to realize their own will in a communal action even against the resistance of others who are participating in the action'. Dahl (1957: 202–3), for example, replicated this formula in suggesting that 'A has power over B to the extent that he can get B to do something B would otherwise not do'. In this sense, power is thought of in personalised terms as a property of individuals or groups. Moreover, it tends to be regarded as a zero-sum game to the extent that its possession by one individual or group is necessarily mirrored by its absence among those over whom this power is exerted. Power, then, 'is seen as a disputed commodity; increments of it pass back and forth across a "frontier of control" as a result of struggles between parties with particular locations of "interests"' (Bloomfield and Coombs, 1992: 466). Thus, the exercise of power is ↓separable from conflicts of sectional interest. Indeed, the analysis of ↓flict became the cornerstone of the so-called pluralist view of power

ing power in project settings

most closely associated with Dahl (1957, 1958, 1962). This was a critical response to the 'reputational' approach, which attempted to assess the power of city leaders through 'expert' rating of their reputation (Hunter, 1963 [1953]). The main criticisms of this related to the problems of third-party perceptual measures (Finkelstein, 1992), and to the abstract and undifferentiated characterisation of power that remained unrelated to specific spheres of decision-making activity. For the pluralists, this led to an emphasis on the outcome of concrete decision-making episodes where there are conflicting preferences between actors (for example, Polsby, 1980; Merelman, 1984). The assumption was that those individuals and groups who are most successful in achieving their preferred outcomes in particular spheres of activity are, by implication, more powerful than those who fail to do so.

The pluralist view did not remain unchallenged, but the alternatives offered still did not question the prohibitive, zero-sum conception of power. Instead, they focused on criticising the pluralist dependence on observable instances of overt conflict and the outcomes of concrete decision-making processes. Bachrach and Baratz (1963, 1970), for example, drawing on the notion of *mobilisation of bias* (Schattschneider, 1960), suggested that it is important to examine not only decision-making but also *non-decision-making*. In other words, power is not only manifest in active decision-making choices between clearly defined alternative courses of action. Individuals or groups also exercise power to the extent that they are able to influence which issues are considered within the decision-making agenda and which are excluded or suppressed. Despite this refinement to the understanding of power as involving both overt expressions of control and covert manipulations, it is still portrayed as a range of mechanisms and practices through which one person or group secures the compliance of others.

According to Lukes (1974), both the pluralist approach to power and the non-decision-making critique share an excessive behaviourist and individualist orientation. In each case, power is about observable behaviour, whether overt or covert, by individuals actively and consciously pursuing what are assumed to be clearly defined sets of interests. For Lukes, this ignores the collective and systemic nature of power. It runs the risk of voluntarism because all manifestations of power are reduced to conscious attempts by individuals to achieve their preferences. In contrast, there are many instances of collective activity where outcomes are not attributable to any particular individual's behaviour, but rather to the interaction of multiple decisions within the collectivity. Moreover, outcomes may be the consequence of system-level or organisational effects, socially structured and culturally patterned behaviour, which can not simply be treated as the sum of individual actions (see Lipps, 1991). Activity is not always driven by conscious, goal-directed behaviour and expressions of power may be the result of unintended consequences. In addition, according to Lukes, power relations are not only a matter of one person getting somebody else to do something they do not want to do. Power is also exercised where the very wants and desires of individuals are themselves shaped and influenced. In this sense, power slips below the surface because it appears that there is an ostensible identity of interests between the powerful and those who are dominated.

Unfortunately, it is only a short step from suggesting that preferences can be moulded and values shaped to arguing that such influences represent a distortion of individuals' 'true' interests. It is on this issue that Lukes's view on power has been most vigorously criticised. Knights and McCabe (1999: 202), for example, approve of Lukes's insight that 'power can operate to define reality so that consent gives the false appearance of the absence of any contest or alternative viewpoint', but then go on to argue as follows:

> The danger here is of collapsing into an essentialist view of interests, identity or subjectivity, as if they existed independently of power at one point only to be corrupted by it at another. Apart from the contradiction of being 'free' of power and yet controlled by it, the idea of 'real' interests or subjectivity is simply another version of the neo-Marxist thesis of 'false-consciousness'. (Knights and McCabe, 1999: 202)

Not unlike Rawls's 'original position' or Hobbes's 'state of nature', the problem of order is depicted as something superimposed over an underlying, more pristine and authentic state. It is therefore not surprising that power, in this formulation, is regarded wholly in negative terms as something that prohibits and distorts. Wandel (2001: 375) has usefully encapsulated the critique of the ideology/reality dualism as follows:

> The notion of power as a negative force – one that violates, censors, obstructs – suggests that the absence of that force would allow a natural order of things to flourish in its true, raw being. Negative power is trickery; an evil, spellbinding force that distorts and manipulates, casts dark shadows on a pure, innocent reality ... Stuck with ontic oppositions between appearance and reality, subject and object, the only strategy available against objective claims of a revelation of an absolute truth, hidden in the secret depths of consciousness or reality, is to counter it with new claims of having unmasked even deeper truths, truer, so to speak, than the truth posed by the object of the critique.

The negative view of power also derives from its continuing identification with attempts by one individual or group to achieve the compliance of others. Despite criticising the behaviourist and voluntarist assumptions of earlier approaches, Lukes still appears to be largely trapped within the traditional Weberian formula by claiming that 'A exercises power over B when A affects B in a manner contrary to B's interests' (Lukes, 1974: 34).

It is in opposition to such negative conceptions of power that arguments concerning its productive or constitutive nature, predominantly inspired by Foucault, have emerged. While traditional approaches tend to consider power as something possessed by individual actors to be used as a resource in guiding social relations, the Foucauldian perspective focuses less on the capacities of individuals and more on the webs of relations in which they are caught up.

For Foucault, it is important to focus not on properties but on detailed practices and relations through which power is constituted. Power should be 'conceived not as a property, but as a strategy, that its effects of domination are attributed not to "appropriation", but to dispositions, manoeuvres, tactics, techniques, functionings; that one should decipher in it a network of relations, constantly in tension, in activity, rather than a privilege that one might possess' (1977a: 26). Consequently, 'power has to be re-thought as a problem of connectivity and consistency rather than of posses- sion and organization, as a force of trans-relationality, crossing lines and opening borders rather than as a power of gathering resources and defining limits' (Beddoes, 1997: 34). It is here that the connection between the so-called *micro-physics* of power and the notion of power as productive intersect. If power is a property of relations, rather than a relation of properties as in the traditional view, then all those partici- pating in the network of relations are implicated in its production. This leads Foucault (1977a: 194) to issue the following call: 'We must cease once and for all to describe the effects of power in negative terms: it "excludes", it "represses", it "censors", it "abstracts", it "masks" it "conceals". In fact, power produces; it produces reality; it produces domains of objects and rituals of truth.'

While the Foucauldian view has helped to shed new light on the conceptualisation of power, it is not without its detractors. In part this is because Foucault's writing on power by no means presents a wholly coherent and unified theoretical programme. Instead, it is often contradictory and ambiguous. For Hardy and Clegg (1996), there is the concern that Foucauldian-inspired organisation theory is excessively distant from practical concerns. It does indeed appear that there is a tendency within this literature to remain at a high level of theoretical abstraction. However, this is perhaps more to do with how Foucault's ideas have been translated into the study of organisations. The difficulty of doing justice to the intricacy and interconnectedness of his thinking means that it is tempting to latch onto those individual concepts which are seemingly more amenable to application in organisational settings, the exemplary case being the notion of the panopticon (McKinlay and Starkey, 1998). Yet, in following the spirit of Foucault's concern with understanding the detailed practices and techniques of power/knowledge there arguably lies the basis for a situated investigation of how power, knowledge and action interpenetrate within given contexts. The difficulty, of course, is in generating conceptual lenses through which to make sense of actual prac- tices. Taylor (1984) criticises Foucault for never adequately explaining how dis- ciplinary power/knowledge practices actually operate.

Ironically, it is traditional conceptions of power, with their view of power as some- thing to be possessed or traded, that have been more concerned with identifying its spe- cific sources or bases. Typically this has taken the form of a list of attributes or capacities. The typology offered by French and Raven (1959) often forms the basis for such lists. In their view there are five primary bases of power: (1) coercive, based on punishment or negative reinforcement; (2) reward, based on being able to deliver something the receiver wants; (3) legitimate, based on hierarchical position; (4) expert, based on spe- cialist knowledge; and (5) referent, or influence based on acceptance and admiration for a leader by subordinates. Raven (1965) later added a sixth basis, informational

referring to the influence achieved by possessing and controlling access to rele-
nformation. Other similar typologies have been presented by Astley and
̱ ̱ ̱eva (1984), Finkelstein (1992) and Pfeffer (1981). Of course, the identification
of sources of power, as presented in these accounts, is wholly congruent with a static,
entity-based view which regards power as deriving from command over a range of
material and symbolic resources (Bacharach and Lawler, 1980). The idea that power
exists in the ability to command scarce and valued resources, such as money, information, or network relations, has been especially influential in the study of organisations
(for example, Hickson *et al.*, 1971; Salancik and Pfeffer, 1974; Pfeffer, 1981). These
approaches are broadly informed by the work of Emerson (1962) on power–dependency
relations where the power derived from control over resources is related to the latter's
perceived importance, scarcity and the availability of substitutes.

However, there is nothing necessary about the connection between an entity-based
view and the recognition of multiple sources or bases of power. It is equally possible
to view these forms as part of a relational view of power. This means ceasing to treat
such features as hierarchical authority, charisma or expertise as unproblematic or
immutable categories that can simply be ticked off on a checklist or balance sheet of
power. It also means moving away from seeing resources in decontextualised and
entitative terms as a series of ready-made materials waiting out there to be used by
those capable of accessing them (Hardy and Clegg, 1996). Instead, it is crucial to see
how capacities and resources are constructed, reproduced or undermined through a
variety of situated material and discursive practices. The recognition of multiple bases
or forms of power also helps to address some of the criticisms aimed at Foucault's
apparent *pancratism*, or the tendency to relate all aspects of social action to the exercise of an all-embracing and totalising disciplinary power (for example, Dews, 1984;
Merquior, 1991; Feldman, 1997). These criticisms have principally challenged the
Foucauldian analysis of power on two interrelated issues: first, for its treatment of
agency, and second, concerning the question of resistance.

Giddens (1995: 265), for example, goes so far as to accuse Foucault of promoting a
'subject-less history'. Similarly, McCarthy (1990, 1993) is concerned that Foucault
tends to exclude all questions about who exercises power, who benefits and who suffers, by focusing more on the 'how' than the 'who' of power. By reducing the individual
to 'an effect of power' (Foucault, 1980b: 98), which is, moreover, an anonymous and
impersonal power, McCarthy (1990: 449) questions how 'we can gain an adequate
understanding of most varieties of social interaction by treating agents simply as acting in compliance with pre-established and publicly sanctioned patterns – as what
Foucault calls "docile bodies" or Garfinkel calls "cultural dopes"'. For defenders of
Foucault this is all a big misunderstanding (for example, Knights and Vurdubakis,
1994). They point to a number of instances where Foucault recognises the potential for
resistance against the power of normalising discourses. For example, Foucault (1980b:
142) suggests that 'there are no relations of power without resistances; the latter are all
the more real and effective because they are formed right at the point where relations

of power are exercised'. However, one can not help but sympathise with Fairclough (1992: 57) who argued that 'the dominant impression is one of people being helplessly subjected to immovable systems of power'.

One way to approach this problem would be to give more attention to concrete instances of social action and interaction to show the variable ways that power and knowledge are constituted. However, the risk here is to move too far in the opposite direction towards voluntarism and particularism, where specific social exchanges appear disconnected from preestablished normative structures with no history or evolution. This is precisely the danger faced by earlier theories of power which tended to focus solely on specific episodes of interaction in which individuals and groups endowed with different power resources engaged in struggles for predominance (for example, Dahl, 1957, 1962; Bachrach and Baratz, 1963). The question arises whether it is possible to effect a reconciliation between the agency- and structure-driven traditions in theories of power. There are certainly dangers attendant on such attempts at synthesis, not least because the different approaches follow largely incompatible ontological and epistemological assumptions. It is for this reason that efforts to synthesise theories on power have often been less than persuasive (for example, Heiskala, 2001). Having said that, there are a number of approaches which offer the potential to combine the benefits of detailed analyses of specific interaction episodes with an appreciation of the guiding, but not determining, role of norms and rules for governing such interactions (for example, Clegg, 1989; Bourdieu, 1991; Fairclough, 1992, 2001; Bradshaw, 1998; Heracleous and Barrett, 2001). What is interesting is that, with a few minor points of difference, these accounts all tend to offer a rather similar resolution of the structure–agency problem.

In each case, it is not a question of structures producing agency, or agents producing structures, but a weaving together of the two in an ongoing and emergent chain whereby social regularities, of varying endurance and generality, are produced, reproduced, modified and/or destroyed. This means that agency, whether individual or collective, is not purely an effect of power/knowledge strategies which constrain through normalisation, but neither can it be characterised wholly in terms of unconstrained, knowledgeable and intentional action. However, this raises the question of precisely how to represent the domain of rules, norms, routines and regularities, on the one hand, and the domain of acting, interacting and negotiating agents, on the other. The response has been to move away from a conception of structures as immutable, invariable, determining social objects, to the structural properties or conditions of possibility which are variably instantiated or enacted through different social practices (Giddens, 1984; Weick, 1995).

This position is evident in the circuits of power framework developed by Clegg (1989) which traces the linkages between episodic, dispositional and facilitative forms of power. Episodic power refers to the day-to-day exercise and unfolding of power in concrete relationships between individuals and groups (Cobb, 1984). It takes place within a 'field of force' created by the other two modes of power. Dispositional power, which is linked to what Clegg terms the circuit of social integration, involves the establishment of 'rules of meaning and membership'. These are the norms, relations and resources which are drawn upon and instantiated in ongoing episodes of power. Facilitative power, associated with the circuit of system integration, concerns the techniques and mechanisms of discipline and production which have changing implications for processes of empowerment and disempowerment. It is by flowing through the different circuits that power is produced, reproduced and modified. 'Power, viewed episodically, may move through circuits in which rules, relations and resources that are constitutive of power are translated, fixed and reproduced/transformed' (Clegg, 1989: 211).

There are also parallels here with the sympathetic reworking of Giddens's structurationist approach offered by Mouzelis (1995), which considers the relation between the paradigmatic and the syntagmatic. The paradigmatic refers to general rules which can be applied in a variety of circumstances, whereas the syntagmatic concerns actual instances of social interaction which give expression to these rules and independent of which they have no existence. The paradigmatic is associated with the position–role and dispositional dimensions of social action, while the syntagmatic corresponds with the interactive–situational dimension identified by Mouzelis. The position–role dimension relates to normative expectations surrounding particular roles, the dispositional dimension concerns historically acquired schemes of perception, thought and action (broadly similar to Bourdieu's concept of habitus), and the interactive–situational dimension refers to the open-ended and contingent enactment of these dimensions through concrete practices of social action and interaction.

A key issue in each of the above approaches concerns the conditions under which the generative structures of power, knowledge and discourse are formed, reproduced or transformed. This is why an adequate conception of practice is so central. Fairclough (1992: 58) states the problematic as follows:

> if structures may be reproduced or transformed in practice, what is it that determines actual outcomes in different instances? More generally, what is it that determines the cumulative outcomes of practice in particular social domains or institutions, and differences between them in the reproductive as opposed to transformative tendencies of discourse? I would want to suggest that structures are reproduced or transformed depending [on] the state of relations, the 'balance of power', between those in struggle in a particular sustained domain of practice.

In other words, it is only through practice, through the concrete actions, interactions and communication of people, that norms, rules and regularities are instantiated. This unfolds in a contingent and provisional fashion depending on the precise conditions of particular domains of practice and the detailed flow of actions and interactions. It is through these practices, in turn, that social regularities are created, reproduced, modified and/or destroyed. The suggestion is that there are multiple and intersecting modalities of power, some of the various mappings of which include episodic, dispositional and facilitative (Clegg, 1989), interactive–situational, dispositional and position/role-based (Mouzelis, 1995), or manifest/surface, latent/deep, individual and collective (Bradshaw, 1998). However, while these conceptualisations offer a way out of the binary oppositions that have paralysed the theorisation of power, how they actually come together within different social settings is a largely empirical question. Consequently, after first providing a brief overview of the treatment of power in project organisations in the next section, the section after that offers an empirical illustration of project work in a civil engineering team to indicate some of the ways that these varying modalities of power interact. The key question to be addressed concerns the relationship between the multiple normative and dispositional features of projects and specific episodes of interaction in which power relations are manifest, in particular the extent to which interaction episodes are guided by established norms and dispositions and the conditions under which the latter are constituted, reproduced or transformed.

Project settings and power

It is fair to say that there has not been a great deal of explicit interest in the issue of power in project organisations. Where it has been considered, it is largely within the terms set by the orthodox understanding of power as a matter of drawing upon available resources to achieve intended outcomes. Thus, within mainstream project management texts, the use of power and associated ideas such as political behaviour, dispute resolution and conflict management are more or less presented as part of the portfolio of tools and techniques to be mastered by the successful project manager (for example, Pinto, 1996). This fairly well mirrors the minor shift in wider managerial commentaries away from seeing power and politics as dirty words, to absorbing them as just something else to be managed along with such equally troublesome phenomena as trust and culture (Kanter, 1983). Typically, the treatment of power is very much at a personal or interpersonal level, consistent with more orthodox approaches; it is about using individual capacities and skills to negotiate through the competing interests and perspectives that multifunctional and multi-organisational projects are often associated with. This is not an unreasonable position given the wealth of empirical examples, not to mention the day-to-day experiences of people involved in projects, that confirm the often fraught and political character of complex project work (for example, Sayles and Chandler, 1971; Sapolsky, 1972; Hall, 1980; Morris and Hough, 1987).

The depiction of projects as temporary and unstable endeavours outside the realms of 'normal' organisational activity is used to explain the likelihood of power struggles developing. For example, Newcombe (1996: 77), drawing inspiration from Cohen and Bradford (1990), has suggested that projects, especially those under traditional contractual conditions, are characterised by a deficit of legitimate authority: 'the traditional approach sets up a system of weak formal legitimate power which is supplemented by a crucial and sophisticated exchange and reciprocity system in which recognised "currencies" are "traded" between the parties involved in a construction project'. In the absence of clear authority, so the argument goes, project participants need to draw on alternative bases of power, such as expert or referent power, as they bargain over disputed goals. The reference to the resource-dependency approach to power is clear, with the same limitations, namely the tendency to focus purely on surface-level interpersonal exchanges without considering how different resources are constituted, valued and deployed under different contexts.

Meyerson *et al.* (1996: 167) have also contributed to the impression of projects as highly interactional settings because of their temporary character, which 'seem to lack the normative structures and institutional safeguards that minimize the likelihood of things going wrong'. However, in considering the problem of order in temporary groups, they begin to suggest more persistent social and cognitive features on which activities can be built. In an argument redolent of Mead's distinction between generic and specific subjectivity (Mead, 1934), it is suggested that participants in temporary groups rely more heavily on generalised role- and category-based attributions rather than personalised attributions (Krauss and Fussell, 1990), although reputational expectations are also important in close-knit professional communities. This indicates the importance of moving away from seeing projects purely as isolated islands of activity and interaction to understanding how they are embedded in wider contexts of social relations and institutionalised norms, values and routines (DeFillippi and Arthur, 1998; Grabher, 2002; Sydow and Staber, 2002; Engwall, 2003). However, there have been few attempts to explore the implications of this shift in relation to the issue of power and how the normative/dispositional and interactional dimensions intersect. Two important exceptions are Hodgson (2002) and Clegg *et al.* (2002).

Hodgson (2002), for example, working from a Foucauldian perspective, has argued that disciplinary power in project settings has a dual character. On the one hand, project management as an ideal and abstract form of knowledge with its own specific language and rules of conduct is inscribed in the subjectivities of project participants such that they conform to appropriate patterns of behaviour. This is a form of self-discipline, yet it is not wholly internalised, but rather enforced and reproduced through ongoing performances and collective rituals and judgements of appropriateness. Power, in this interpretation, is largely subterranean and normalised, obscured by appeals to objectivity and technical neutrality in project management discourses. On the other hand, projects are also the site of more overt techniques and practices of direct control and surveillance, where power relations are more manifest. However, the analysis stops short of fully exploring the relationship between these alternative forms of power. In addition, there is a sense in which the effectiveness of professional self-discipline is presented as overly secure and immune from transformational impulses. Certainly there are features of professional discourses that insulate them from criticism, but there are also likely to be points of resistance, as well as gradual or more radical transformations wrought through participation in ongoing and concrete practices of project work. These are perhaps underplayed, with the overwhelming image being one of project employees being fixed within an immovable web of self-discipline and overt control.

Clegg *et al.* (2002) also draw inspiration from Foucault, and particularly his concept of *governmentality* (Foucault, 2002 [1978]). Echoing the earlier observation of projects being characterised by a legitimation deficit, governmentality is depicted as follows:

> Governmentality poses an alternative to policing, litigation and arbitration, especially in situations where there are multiple actors and interests, through the design of a more collective and coherent practical consciousness within which to make sense. Literally, it seeks to make conflicting modes of rationality redundant by delivering economies in authoritative surveillance through building a collaborative commitment and transparency into the moral fibre of a project. (Clegg *et al.*, 2002: 325)

Again, the focus is on indirect and normalised forms of power and control inscribed and internalised as specific rules and principles of appropriate conduct constituted through the ongoing development of a common mode of rationality. In the case study explored by the authors, collaborative commitment and an 'alliance culture' are portrayed as important dimensions of attempts to build a common mode of rationality. As such, there are interesting parallels to be drawn here with the empirical illustration offered below, which is also concerned with how norms of collaborative conduct are constituted as a guiding rationality. However, while Clegg *et al.* (2002) acknowledge the limitations of governmentality, particularly in extending it to constituencies beyond the core project team, they are arguably too ready to accept the effectiveness of its guiding principles among key project participants. Again, points of resistance and potential transformational impulses in concrete activities and interactions are downplayed at the risk of overstating the guiding power of the normative domain. In attempting to address this danger, the next section considers an empirical illustration through the conceptual lenses of episodic and dispositional/normative power, and the incompleteness of relationships between them, that indicates a greater scope for improvisation and fluidity in how dispositions and norms are enacted.

Power, conflict, and collaboration in a civil engineering team

By way of illustration, the remainder of the chapter draws on a case example of a multi-organisational civil engineering team in the road transport sector.[1] The core team, which for convenience will be referred to as RoadsTeam, consists of representatives from a client organisation (RoadsOrg), a consulting engineering company (ConsultCo), and a civil engineering contractor (CivilsCo).[2] ConsultCo and CivilsCo each have a five-year contractual agreement with the client and together they are involved in two main streams of activity within an overall programme of work. First, they are responsible for the ongoing repair and maintenance of the network of major roads that falls within their geographical area of responsibility. This includes cyclical activities, such as cleaning signs, collecting litter and grass cutting; seasonal activities, such as gritting the roads during the winter months; and responsive activities, such as emergency repairs following accidents. These are all fairly standardised and repetitive activities for which there are established procedures. Second, they are involved in the identification, planning, design and implementation of repair and road improvement projects up to a threshold value. Projects that exceed this value are beyond the scope of the five-year agreements and, while design and project management services are still provided by ConsultCo in these cases, CivilsCo is not necessarily the contractor responsible for project implementation.

Formal discourses of collaboration play a similar role in the example of RoadsTeam to that of professional project management analysed by Hodgson (2002). That is to say, they offer an idealised vision of appropriate conduct that serves as a generalised set of regulative principles that project participants must aspire to if they are to be regarded by their peers and colleagues as suitably up to date in their attitudes and proficient members of their professional or business community. Enshrined in a series of key texts that are widely known and referred to in the construction sector (for example, CII, 1989; Latham, 1994; Bennett and Jayes, 1995, 1998; CIB, 1997; Egan, 1998), these principles promote the virtues of mutuality, respect, reasonableness, unified effort and the equitable sharing of risks and rewards. As suggested elsewhere (for example, Marshall and Bresnen, 1999; Bresnen and Marshall, 2000a), the promotion of these principles is discursively complex, drawing on a range of techniques and arguments that minimise the possibility of rejecting them. These include appeals to common sense, where the principles are presented in naturalised form as innate human values that have been blocked or distorted in the past by traditional contractual arrangements. They have been offered as the only rational way forward in what is depicted as an environment of increasing competition, again contrasting them with what are presented as outmoded and irrational types of behaviour such as adversarialism, mistrust and narrow self-interest. The point is that it is hard to disagree with these sentiments and to do so is to be stigmatised as behind the times, irrational and insensitive. However, the arguments for collaboration are not wholly based on appeals to reasonableness and virtuous conduct. There is also a strong pragmatic dimension in the argument that individual interests in project work are best served by achieving collective goals, that is, what is good for the project is also good for me and my organisation.

Within RoadsTeam, the guiding influence of collaborative principles, particularly those specified by the Egan Report, are clearly acknowledged. As one of ConsultCo's senior managers commented:

The general concept of the whole contract in the relationship between [ConsultCo] and [CivilsCo] is one of a partnering type arrangement which sort of goes along the theory of the new guidelines issued by central government for changes to construction ... There were a series of guidelines really reviewing how construction is done ... and really the gist of that was that partnering was better ... 'Rethinking Construction', that's it ... So that was one of the drivers, 'Rethinking Construction', whereby we're all sort of in partnership and less confrontational.

That RoadsTeam is supposed to be a collaborative or 'partnering' arrangement is something that staff at all levels are keenly aware of. In formal terms at least, it has been primarily a top-down initiative, with the message of collaboration being reinforced through a range of devices. A series of partnering workshops were held relatively soon after the team was formed, there is a partnering forum that meets on a bimonthly basis with a number of working groups involved in implementing improvements, and there are visible reminders posted around the joint office, such as the 'partnering charter' signed by team members that states the core values to be followed by the team. However, it would be a mistake to interpret the formal discursive construction of collaboration as entirely effective in establishing normalised codes of conduct or set meanings about the nature of project work in RoadsTeam. There is considerable scepticism, particularly, but not exclusively, among less senior staff members, about the extent to which partnering represents an accurate reflection of their experience of work, or indeed how far it is thought to be practical. Another common view is to deny that partnering differs in any significant respect from what used to happen on previous road maintenance contracts before the term was introduced. According to one of the works supervisors, a local authority employee subcontracted to ConsultCo:

Partnering, if you like, is a [ConsultCo] word. When we were [the local authority] and worked with [CivilsCo] under the ... term maintenance contract, we were doing ... we were partnering but we didn't call it partnering. We just called it getting on with our work ... So it's not a big new thing. It's just this buzz word that came in.

There is also resistance to partnering because it is perceived as an initiative imposed by senior management that is unduly abstract and removed from the day-to-day concerns of the team. CivilsCo's contract manager described the situation as follows:

There were some workshops last year where all three organisations were involved in the workshops and they were a disaster, basically. They were partnering workshops to get people to work better together and the view was that we do all this already. Why are you telling us this? This is being inflicted from on high. Imposed from on high. And if the chiefs sorted out what they were meant to be doing then we wouldn't have any problems delivering it on the ground.

It would be tempting to interpret this simply as a failure of implementation in the face of resistance, suggesting that changing established norms of conduct with the introduction of a newly ascendant dominant discourse is by no means a simple or uncontested process. This would be consistent with a straightforward ideology critique, contrasting the ideology of partnering against the reality of continuing conflict in project relationships. However, this would be to reify and hypostatise discourses of collaboration, treating them as a stable and coherent set of meanings that flow outwards from a centre of control, albeit unevenly and encountering varying acceptance or resistance. As has been suggested in studies of other popular management ideas and recipes (for example, Huczynski, 1993; Grint, 1994; Clark and Salaman, 1998; Røvik, 1998), this diffusionist argument fails to acknowledge the processes of translation and transformation through which different ideas are interpreted and reworked under varying local contexts. What is interesting in the case of RoadsTeam is not that the language of collaboration is widely employed, critically or otherwise, while the practices of the team exhibit such non-collaborative behaviours as commercial and contractual conflict, disputes over the timing and status of different types of work, or the failure to involve the contractor in any significant way in the design process. It is that the notion of collaboration itself is used as a discursive resource that participants construct in a variety of ways in their attempt to negotiate disputes in their favour.

In this sense, collaborative discourses operate at both normative/dispositional and episodic levels, with an important interplay between the two. On the one hand, they are a regulative ideal that, in the current illustration at least, come up against established normative and belief structures, such as those covering the respective role of designers and contractors, the temporality of work and the distribution of risks and rewards. As a result, they are incomplete and contested as a set of principles to guide expected conduct. On the other hand, the normalising character of collaborative discourses, and whether they are effective or not in becoming internalised as rules of self-discipline, are closely related to how they are constituted and enacted within particular settings of action and interaction. These may simply reproduce existing patterns of behaviour and attitudes, but equally they may generate gradual or more radical changes in the ongoing construction of what it means to collaborate. To provide some support for this argument, main areas of dispute in RoadsTeam concerning commercial considerations, control over the timing of work and contractor involvement in the design process will be outlined, along with the alternative strategies and tactics involved in their negotiation, to indicate how the episodic power of concrete interactions simultaneously constitutes, draws upon, reproduces and/or transforms alternative norms and dispositions.

An important area of recurrent dispute in RoadsTeam concerns the commercial and contractual elements of the relationship and how risks and rewards are allocated. Many attempts to implement partnering have focused on formal incentive mechanisms to motivate project participants to collaborate in the pursuit of mutual goals (Bresnen and Marshall, 2000b). These often take the form of some kind of risk/reward arrangement where all of the partners involved in a project share financial savings, or some of the burden of cost overruns, according to some agreed formula. The logic behind this is that if different participants have a common commercial stake in the project, then they will collectively orientate their activities to doing what is best for the project rather than trying to maximise their own gains at the expense of others. This is not the type of arrangement that RoadsTeam works under. Instead, the contractual framework is rather traditional in form. ConsultCo and CivilsCo each hold a separate contract with the client, the former on a conventional time-based consulting fee, and the latter on a lump sum basis for ongoing repairs and maintenance and works orders for carrying out small repair and improvement projects.

The contractually specified relations between the different parties are also fairly traditional. ConsultCo acts as the client's managing agent and is responsible for controlling the flow of financial resources to CivilsCo and ensuring that the latter meets agreed performance criteria. The contractual framework ostensibly establishes the formal authority of the managing agent in the relationship. This would appear to lend itself to a conventional analysis of power, with the contract providing ConsultCo with legitimate power based on its position, as well as giving it control over the activities of CivilsCo through the deployment of rewards (reward power) and penalties (coercive power). However, this is not a straightforward matter of drawing upon stable and distinct resources 'out there' that have unambiguous implications for the relationship between ConsultCo and CivilsCo, and which mean that the balance is invariably tipped in favour of the former. To become meaningful, relations, such as those based on authority, reward or punishment, have to be actively constituted through concrete practices. The contractual framework, as a codified set of rights and responsibilities, can never offer complete instructions for what should happen in every situation and there are crucial elements of interpretation and discretion. According to one of ConsultCo's supervisors, 'the contract is so grey. It doesn't seem to be anything in black and white ... you're forever trying to get other people's interpretation. Things where four people can read it and get four different ideas.'

Contracts will always support a greater or lesser degree of interpretative flexibility, and this becomes particularly relevant at times of commercial conflict when different parties attempt to lay claim to contractual legitimacy by presenting their interpretation as the 'true' meaning. In the construction sector, which has a notorious history of legal wrangling over contractual conditions, the attempt to move towards less adversarial relations has often been premised on the need to change attitudes towards the role of the contract. The argument is that the situation would be vastly improved if project participants did not constantly refer to the precise terms of construction contracts, disputing every last clause, but rather adopted an open and reasonable approach to reaching mutual agreement about the general direction needed to achieve project goals. It is about following the spirit rather than the letter of the contract. This is encapsulated in a common expression among project members: 'keeping the contract in the bottom drawer'. In the case of RoadsTeam, however, as CivilsCo's contract manager commented, 'There's still a bottom drawer ... And *here* there is a bottom drawer. We don't throw the contract out.' The potential to exploit ambiguities in the contract has proved too great an opportunity for CivilsCo to miss. According to ConsultCo's maintenance manager:

> We're putting that down really to the contractual side because the contract that [CivilsCo] have got is full of errors, inconsistencies, lacks clarity in certain areas, and ... there have been

some significant financial consequences as a result of some of the issues on there. There's a bit of tension. I think that that's filtering throughout because obviously [CivilsCo's] senior people are saying we've got to make money out of this so they're looking for every opportunity ... Putting it simplistically, they're trying to bob out of it and they're looking ... when it comes down to doing the job on the ground, [CivilsCo's] agents are sort of asking our supervisors to ... I don't know how to put it really ... they're coming up with unnecessary issues to try and generate variations stroke additional moneys. Whereas before you could just say, 'Can you go and do x, y, z, here's the order', they went off and did it. Now they're contesting bits and pieces. It's just sort of additional aggravation which never used to be there.

However, there are limitations to how far CivilsCo's managers can pursue their own short-term financial self-interest because they do not wish to jeopardise their chances of winning future work from the client. 'There's going to be other [five-year contracts] coming up, so again if there is some issue going on one wants to have the best picture of your own particular organisation so that you don't lose favour with the client' (senior manager, ConsultCo). In attempting to legitimise to the client their respective behaviour concerning commercial issues, managers from ConsultCo and CivilsCo have constructed alternative conceptions of collaboration as part of their strategies of argumentation. There is an interesting symmetry in the tactics employed in that both sides offer a variation of the same argument. This involves, first, spelling out what is considered appropriate and inappropriate for a partnering relationship, and then accusing the other side of failing to meet the expected standards. In short, the paradoxical claim is made that 'we're collaborating all right, it's them who are the problem'. In the words of ConsultCo's design manager:

> If you've really got to partner, you've got to partner, not just a sort of trendy phrase that doesn't really mean anything ... Some people think partnering means that I get what I want. We're partnering if you give me what I want. We're not partnering if you don't give me what I want. And of course partnering is meant to be that everybody gets a reasonable amount of what they want and accept that some of the things they won't get ... Sometimes when the partnering breaks down, it's money, because the driving forces are different.

The suggestion is that CivilsCo do not always meet the model of collaborative behaviour that ConsultCo managers have constructed, portraying the former as sometimes unreasonable with respect to the distribution of rewards. According to ConsultCo's maintenance manager: 'Shall we say the spirit of partnering is that we jointly resolve issues and all the rest of it. But at the end of the day [CivilsCo] have got a commercial dimension and are trying to make money out of the contract. And so, you know, that spirit goes out the window at times.' However, from the perspective of CivilsCo's managers, their actions are justifiable because ConsultCo also fails to accord with what the former define as the 'spirit' of partnering. This argument mainly focuses on the position that ConsultCo managers adopt with respect to the tripartite relationship between client, consultant and contractor, and on the implications this has for the openness and mutuality of decision-making. CivilsCo's contract manager presented the situation as follows:

> The best I've had is where the client says right I want this built, gets someone from the contractor, gets someone from the designer, gets someone from the overseeing organisation ... stick them all together as a project team and let them get on with it. That's the best. Where we are here is probably ... we've got the client and the designer deciding between themselves what we're going to build. We've then got the designer designing it, independently. We've then got the overseeing organisation and the contractor taking what they get from the designer and coming up with a solution to build what the client wanted. But there are still boxes. It goes from one box to the other and never goes back.

ConsultCo, as managing agent and designer, is depicted as assuming the traditional role of client's representative, seeing itself as the privileged mouthpiece through which the needs of the client are communicated in a linear and unidirectional fashion. This is portrayed by CivilsCo's managers as out of tune with the more horizontal and integrated team approach of the partnering ideal. As ConsultCo's design manager admitted, 'the [RoadsOrg] relationship is still very much the old, I'd call the old kind of nice consultant stroke client type relationship, like it was fifteen years ago'. This is arguably a comfortable position for the consulting engineers to be in, conferring status upon them which, from the perspective of CivilsCo's managers, they have been ready to display by exerting their control over the flow of information and resources and largely excluding the contractor from involvement in the planning and design process. As CivilsCo's works manager described it: 'Our contract is with [RoadsOrg], but very often we deal through [ConsultCo]. So they give us our instructions. They hold the purse strings and they spend the money.' The flow of design information is a particularly contentious point. The design team is perceived to be rather distant from, and unconcerned with, the day-to-day activities of the operations and implementation team, a view that is symbolised by the fact that the designers are located in a different office to the rest of RoadsTeam. According to CivilsCo's works manager:

> The designers tend to be a little bit blinkered because all they ... they're ensuring they're keeping their resources busy and they can deliver the amount of design they have to. And all they do is make sure their designers are kept busy. Whereas what they should be doing is, right, this is what needs to be constructed, this is when we would like it to be done, and therefore the designs come out when [CivilsCo] want to do it. So there is a slight conflict there ... Designs come out whenever [ConsultCo] want to deliver them.

The design team plans and programmes its work flow to optimise the use of its own people and resources. However, this is sometimes achieved to the detriment of CivilsCo's ability to allocate resources efficiently, leaving them with peaks and troughs of activity which mean that their operations staff are over-employed at some times, and under-employed at others. This also has an impact on CivilsCo's cash flow and, along with the incidence of rework and implementation difficulties associated with the linear and removed character of the design process, has been used by CivilsCo's managers to justify their financially self-interested behaviour. The disjuncture between design and implementation is reinforced by what are depicted as quite distinct normative orientations between the two parts of the team. As one of ConsultCo's managers involved on the implementation side acknowledged:

> Generally speaking the people down at the operational level, a lot of the supervisors and inspectors and people like that, they've tended to work up from the crews, to be promoted to this sort of level ... Whereas shall we say the design teams, they are totally academics or graduates, who never really got involved in that sort of side of it. So there is a culture difference between the two teams ... We're desperately trying to encourage some of the staff from [the design office] to become ... work closer and become more familiar with our guys, the supervisors, because our supervisors are looking after a defined number of roads day in, day out, year in, year out, so they know a lot, local history and things that go on and all the rest of it ... But there's reluctance. We still can't work out why. They seem to fear our people, but there's nothing to fear ... We're just trying to break down that barrier.

The image here is of two different lifeworlds that are kept relatively separate through defensive isolation and, consequently, it is unlikely that the normative beliefs characterising the differences between designers and implementation staff will be challenged and revised to any great extent. CivilsCo's managers have used the separation between design and implementation to argue that ConsultCo has not been conducting itself in a manner consistent with a collaborative relationship. After raising the issues of contractor involvement in design and the timing of work repeatedly at a series of high-level meetings, they have gradually made headway in persuading RoadsOrg's managers of the reasonableness of their position. However, there is still resistance from ConsultCo, who are portrayed as attempting to defend their privileged position with the client. As CivilsCo's contracts manager explained:

> [ConsultCo] are reluctant to release ... to get us involved in design. But they can see that [RoadsOrg] want us to be involved in it, so ... it's a matter of time. The writing's on the wall. But [ConsultCo's] not too keen to get there too quick. They haven't seen the benefits to it yet. They're suspicious about the real motive behind it.

Managers at RoadsOrg are ambivalent about the justifications being offered by the consulting engineer and contractor, seeing plausibility in both of their arguments. On the one hand, they are not approving of CivilsCo's attempts to extract additional money through variations, but, on the other, they also accept that ConsultCo need to be more open and integrated in their approach to design because it is likely to lead to more appropriate designs that are easier and cheaper to implement. The ongoing negotiation around the nature of RoadsTeam's work, drawing in different ways on alternative constructions of what it means to collaborate and identifying alleged departures from those ideals, finds expression in shifting alliances within the tripartite organisational relationship. One of ConsultCo's supervisors described the situation as follows: 'The contractor sees it one way. We see it as another. I think [RoadsOrg] see it another way. It's all grey. And we started off the contract seeing it [CivilsCo's] way. We've now gone over to [RoadsOrg's] way. We're in the middle still. And it causes tension.' In this sense, collaborative discourses, articulated in varying ways by the different participants, do not have clear and unambiguous implications in their regulative impact. They represent an incomplete and contested resource that mutates as they are enacted through particular episodes of power-laden interaction, sometimes bringing different groups into alignment and pushing them apart at others. Overall, however, it is difficult to ignore the paradox of a relationship where appeals to some notion of collaboration are being used as weapons in a decidedly conflictual contest over position. As a result, under these conditions of interaction, it is unlikely that collaborative discourses will have much transformational potential, leaving normative differences in terms of established roles, and the distribution of risks and rewards, largely undisturbed.

Conclusion

This chapter has argued that there is a general absence of any sustained consideration of power in the mainstream study of project organisations. With a few notable exceptions, where power has been considered in these settings, it has mainly been treated in conventional terms as a struggle for control between individuals and groups who draw upon available resources in their attempts to gain ascendancy. On the face of it, this is not an unreasonable position to adopt for understanding the character of project relationships. Since project settings typically involve multiple, yet interdependent, roles, functions and disciplines, often with their own perspectives and differing interests, they are frequently the site of intense bargaining and negotiation in which participants vie for strategic position and compete over potentially incompatible project goals. However, this image of strategically acting and interacting agents is incomplete because it overplays the voluntaristic and visible nature of power relations. This view has been decisively challenged within the wider literature on power in social theory. The personalised and prohibitive conceptualisation of power-over has been confronted by an alternative image of power-to as a constitutive network of relations, normalising social conduct through a range of largely anonymous techniques, dispositions and manoeuvres. However, there is the risk of moving too far in the opposite direction to portray social actors as immovably caught in webs of normalising relations where they appear to be acting simply in accordance with preexisting rules of conduct. In consequence, this chapter has attempted a modest reconciliation between the power-over and power-to perspectives. This has been informed by the claim 'that not only power over, but also power to, can be treated *relationally*. Like agency, power in all its forms, including power storage and power discretion, is about the way in which objects are constituted and linked together' (Law, 1991: 185, emphasis original). To try to gain some purchase on this conceptual endeavour, insights have been drawn from a variety of authors who share a concern with connecting up the domain of situated actions and interactions with that of normative and dispositional orientations. The aim has been to indicate some of the ways that the two domains are mutually constituted.

The example of a multi-organisational civil engineering team has been used to illustrate how varying modalities of power are relationally constituted. The particular focus is on how a generalised discourse of collaboration, widely referred to in the construction sector, is employed and augmented by team members in their ongoing negotiations over a range of contentious issues about commercial considerations, the timing of work and contractor involvement in the design process. This results in a paradoxical situation where 'collaboration' becomes the target of a struggle over meaning as the consulting engineer and contractor attempt to persuade the client of the validity of their respective positions with regard to key areas of dispute. As Moch and Huff (1983: 297) have argued, the negotiation of meaning is an inherently political process in which communicative acts help 'define reality and are particularly important when there is little consensus about the facts or when there are divergent perceptions; in short, when the cues are equivocal'. By negotiating what it means to collaborate, and pointing to authentic and inauthentic instances of collaboration, the different parties are fashioning a normative ideal through their episodes of interaction which is intended to regulate conduct. However, this is an incomplete and contested normalisation because there is little agreement about what these regulative principles should be. As such, they are constantly revisited and reworked through communicative interactions, rather than becoming stabilised, sedimented and internalised by members of the team. In this sense, the productive power of collaborative discourses, referring to their ability to constitute the subjectivity of project participants as 'good collaborators', is largely truncated and ineffective, failing to displace established norms of self-seeking behaviour. Indeed, the ultimate irony is that the power-to of collaboration is actually used as a discursive strategy in the power-over struggles between the project participants.

Notes

1. The empirical illustration is taken from a wider two-year study of twelve project teams across a range of sectors conducted as part of the 'Managing Knowledge Spaces' research project funded by the UK Engineering and Physical Sciences Research Council (grant reference GR/R54132/01). The research is based upon a combination of in-depth, semi-structured interviews with informants occupying different positions and roles within each project, of which 120 have been conducted to date, respondent-driven mapping of project relationships, non-participant observation of formal and informal interactions, and the analysis of documentary sources. In the case of RoadsTeam, thirteen interviews were conducted with staff representing the client, consultant and contractor organisations. Observations were also conducted within the team offices and at a two-day off-site 'collaboration workshop'.
2. The names of the organisations have been changed to preserve anonymity.

References

Astley, W.G. and Sachdeva, P.S. (1984) 'Structural Sources of Intraorganizational Power: A Theoretical Synthesis', *Academy of Management Review*, 9(1): 104–13.

Bacharach, S.B. and Lawler, E.L. (1980) *Power and Politics in Organizations*. San Francisco, CA: Jossey-Bass.

Bachrach, P. and Baratz, M.S. (1963) 'Decisions and Nondecisions: An Analytical Framework', *American Political Science Review*, 57: 632–42.

Bachrach, P. and Baratz, M.S. (1970) *Power and Poverty: Theory and Practice*. New York: Oxford University Press.

Barnes, B. (1988) *The Nature of Power*. Cambridge: Polity Press.

Baudrillard, J. (1980) 'Forgetting Foucault', *Humanities in Society*, 3(1): 87–111.

Beddoes, D. (1997) 'Deleuze, Kant and Indifference', in K.A. Pearson (ed.), *Deleuze and Philosophy: The Difference Engineer*. London: Routledge, 25–43.

Bennett, J. and Jayes, S. (1995) *Trusting the Team: The Best Practice Guide to Partnering in Construction*. Reading: Reading Construction Forum.

Bennett, J. and Jayes, S. (1998) *The Seven Pillars of Partnering*. London: Thomas Telford.

Bloomfield, B.P. and Coombs, R. (1992) 'Information Technology, Control and Power: The Centralization and Decentralization Debate Revisited', *Journal of Management Studies*, 29(4): 459–84.

Bourdieu, P. (1991) *Language and Symbolic Power*. Cambridge: Polity Press.

Bradshaw, P. (1998) 'Power as Dynamic Tension and Its Implications for Radical Organizational Change', *European Journal of Work and Organizational Psychology*, 7(2): 121–43.

Bresnen, M. and Marshall, N. (2000a) 'Partnering in Construction: A Critical Review of Issues, Problems and Dilemmas', *Construction Management and Economics*, 18: 229–37.

Bresnen, M. and Marshall, N. (2000b) 'Motivation, Commitment and the Use of Incentives in Partnerships and Alliances', *Construction Management and Economics*, 18: 587–98.

Clark, T. and Salaman, G. (1998) 'Telling Tales: Management Gurus' Narratives and the Construction of Managerial Identity', *Journal of Management Studies*, 35: 137–61.

Clegg, S.R. (1979) *The Theory of Power and Organization*. London: Routledge & Kegan Paul.

Clegg, S.R. (1989) *Frameworks of Power*. London: Sage.

Clegg, S.R., Pitsis, T.S., Rura-Polley, T. and Marosszeky, M. (2002) 'Governmentality Matters: Designing an Alliance Culture of Inter-organizational Collaboration for Managing Projects', *Organization Studies*, 23(3): 317–37.

Cobb, A.T. (1984) 'An Episodic Model of Power: Toward an Integration of Theory and Research', *Academy of Management Review*, 9: 482–93.

Cohen, A.R. and Bradford, D.L. (1990) *Influence without Authority*. New York: Wiley.

CIB (Construction Industry Board) (1997) *Partnering in the Team*. London: Thomas Telford.

CII (Construction Industry Institute) (1989) *Partnering: Meeting the Challenges of the Future*. Austin, TX: Construction Industry Institute.

Dahl, R.A. (1957) 'The Concept of Power', *Behavioral Science*, 2: 201–15.

Dahl, R.A. (1958) 'A critique of the Ruling Elite Model', *American Political Science Review*, 52: 463–9.

Dahl, R.A. (1962) *Who Governs?* New Haven, CT: Yale University Press.

DeFillippi, R.J. and Arthur, M.B. (1998) 'Paradox in Project-Based Enterprise: The Case of Film Making', *California Management Review*, 40(2): 125–38.

Dews, P. (1984) 'Power and Subjectivity in Foucault', *New Left Review*, 144: 72–95.

Egan, J. (1998) *Rethinking Construction*. London: DETR.

Emerson, R.M. (1962) 'Power–Dependence Relations', *American Sociological Review*, 27: 31–41.

Engwall, M. (2003) 'No Project is an Island: Linking Projects to History and Context', *Research Policy*, 32: 789–808.

Fairclough, N. (1992) *Discourse and Social Change*. Cambridge: Polity Press.

Fairclough, N. (2001) *Language and Power*. Harlow: Pearson Education.

Feldman, S.P. (1997) 'The Revolt Against Cultural Authority: Power/Knowledge as an Assumption in Organization Theory', *Human Relations*, 50(8): 937–55.

Finkelstein, S. (1992) 'Power in Top Management Teams: Dimensions, Measurement, and Validation', *Academy of Management Journal*, 35(3): 505–38.

Foucault, M. (1977a) *Discipline and Punish: The Birth of the Prison*. Harmondsworth: Penguin.

Foucault, M. (1977b) 'Intellectuals and Power', in D.B. Bouchard (ed.), *Language, Counter-Memory, Practice*. New York: Cornell University Press, 205–17.

Foucault, M. (1980a) *The History of Sexuality, Volume 1: An Introduction*. Harmondsworth: Penguin.

Foucault, M. (1980b) *Power/Knowledge: Selected Interviews and Other Writings by Michel Foucault 1972–1977*, edited by C. Gordon. New York: Pantheon.

Foucault, M. (2002 [1978]) 'Governmentality', in M. Foucault, *Power: Essential Works of Foucault 1954–1984*, Vol. 3, edited by J.D. Faubian. London: Penguin, 201–22.

Foucault, M. (2002 [1982]) 'The Subject and Power', in M. Foucault, *Power: Essential Works of Foucault 1954–1984*, Vol. 3, edited by J.D. Faubian. London: Penguin, 326–48.

French, J.R.P. and Raven, B.H. (1959) 'The Bases of Social Power', in D. Cartwright (ed.), *Studies in Social Power*. Ann Arbor, MI: University of Michigan Institute for Social Research, 150–67.

Giddens, A. (1976) *New Rules of Sociological Method*. London: Hutchinson.

Giddens, A. (1984) *The Constitution of Society: Outline of the Theory of Structuration*. Cambridge: Polity Press.

Giddens, A. (1995) *Politics, Sociology and Social Theory*. Cambridge: Polity Press.

Grabher, G. (2002) 'The Project Ecology of Advertising: Tasks, Talents and Teams', *Regional Studies*, 36(3): 245–62.

Grint, K. (1994) 'Re-engineering History: Social Resonances and Business Process Reengineering', *Organization*, 1: 179–201.

Hall, P. (1980) *Great Planning Disasters*. London: Weidenfeld & Nicolson.

Hardy, C. and Clegg, S.R. (1996) 'Some Dare Call It Power', in C. Hardy, S.R. Clegg, and W.R. Nord (eds), *Handbook of Organization Studies*. London: Sage, 622–41.

Heiskala, R. (2001) 'Theorizing Power: Weber, Parsons, Foucault and Neostructuralism', *Theory and Methods*, 40(2): 241–64.

Heracleous, L. and Barrett, M. (2001) 'Organizational Change as Discourse: Communicative Actions and Deep Structures in the Context of Information Technology Implementation', *Academy of Management Journal*, 44(4): 755–78.

Hickson, D.J., Hinings, C.R., Lee, C.A., Schneck, R.E. and Pennings, J.M. (1971) 'Strategic Contingencies: Theory of Intra-organizational Power', *Administrative Science Quarterly*, 16: 216–29.

Hodgson, D. (2002) 'Disciplining the Professional: The Case of Project Management', *Journal of Management Studies*, 39(6): 803–21.

Huczynski, A. (1993) 'Explaining the Succession of Management Fads', *International Journal of Human Resource Management*, 4: 443–63.

Hunter, F. (1963 [1953]) *Community Power Structure*. Garden City, NY: Anchor Books.

Jermier, J.M., Knights, D. and Nord, W. (eds) (1994) *Resistance and Power in Organizations*. London: Routledge.

Kanter, R.M. (1983) *The Change Masters*. New York: Simon & Schuster.

Knights, D. and McCabe, D. (1999) ' "Are There No Limits to Authority?" TQM and Organizational Power', *Organization Studies*, 20(2): 197–224.

Knights, D. and Vurdubakis, T. (1994) 'Foucault, Power, Resistance, and All That', in J. Jermier, D. Knights, and W. Nord (eds), *Resistance and Power in Organizations*. New York: Routledge, 167–98.

Kotter, J.B. (1979) *Power in Management*. New York: Amacom.

Krauss, R. and Fussell, S. (1990) 'Mutual Knowledge and Communicative Effectiveness', in J. Galegher, R. Kraut, and C. Egido (eds), *Intellectual Teamwork: Social and Technological Foundations of Cooperative Work*. Hillsdale, NJ: Lawrence Erlbaum, 111–46.

Latham, M. (1994) *Constructing the Team: Final Report of the Government/Industry Review of Procurement and Contractual Arrangements in the UK Construction Industry*. London: HMSO.

Law, J. (1991) 'Power, Discretion and Strategy', in J. Law (ed.), *A Sociology of Monsters: Essays on Power, Technology and Domination*. London: Routledge, 165–91.

Lipps, H.M. (1991) *Women, Men and Power*. Mountainview, CA: Mayfield.

Lukes, S. (1974) *Power: A Radical View*. London: Macmillan.

McCarthy, T. (1990) 'The Critique of Impure Reason', *Political Theory*, 18: 437–69.

McCarthy, T. (1993) *Ideals and Illusions*. Cambridge, MA: MIT Press.

McKinlay, A. and Starkey, K. (1998) 'Managing Foucault: Foucault, Management and Organization Theory', in A. McKinlay, and K. Starkey (eds), *Foucault, Management and Organization Theory*. London: Sage, 22–35.

Marshall, N. and Bresnen, M. (1999) 'The Evolution of a Fad: Partnering in the UK Construction Industry', paper presented to subtheme 5 'Management Fashions and Fads' of the 15th EGOS Colloquium 'Organizations in a Changing World: Theories, Practices and Societies', University of Warwick, Coventry, UK, 4–6 July 1999.

Mead, G.H. (1934) *Mind, Self and Society from the Standpoint of a Social Behaviorist*. Chicago, IL: University of Chicago Press.

Merelman, R. (1984) *Making Something of Ourselves: On Culture and Politics in the United States*. Berkeley, CA: University of California Press.

Merquior, J.G. (1991) *Foucault*. London: Fontana Press.

Meyerson, D., Weick, K.E. and Kramer, R.M. (1996) 'Swift Trust and Temporary Groups', in R.M. Kramer, and T.R. Tyler (eds), *Trust in Organizations: Frontiers of Theory and Research*. Thousand Oaks, CA: Sage, 166–95.

Mintzberg, H. (1983) *Power In and Around Organizations*. Englewood Cliffs, NJ: Prentice-Hall.

Moch, M.K. and Huff, A. (1983) 'The Enactment of Power Relationships through Language and Ritual', *Journal of Business Research*, 11: 293–316.

Morris, P.W.G. and Hough, G.H. (1987) *The Anatomy of Major Projects: A Study of the Reality of Project Management*. Chichester: Wiley.

Mouzelis, N. (1995) *Sociological Theory: What Went Wrong?* London: Routledge.

Newcombe, R. (1996) 'Empowering the Construction Project Team', *International Journal of Project Management*, 14(2): 75–80.

Perrow, C. (1970) 'Departmental Power and Perspectives in Industrial Firms', in M.N. Zald (ed.), *Power in Organizations*. Nashville, TN: Vanderbilt University Press, 59–89.

Pfeffer, J. (1981) *Power in Organizations*. Marshfield, MA: Pitman.

Pfeffer, J. (1992) *Managing with Power: Politics and Influence in Organizations*. Boston, MA: Harvard Business School Press.

Pinto, J.K. (1996) *Power and Politics in Project Management*. Newtown Square, PA: Project Management Institute.

Polsby, N.W. (1980) *Community Power and Political Theory*. New Haven, CT: Yale University Press.

Raven, B.H. (1965) 'Social Influence and Power', in I.D. Steiner, and M. Fishbein (eds), *Current Studies in Social Psychology*. New York: Holt, Rinehart & Winston, 371–81.

Røvik, K.A. (1998) 'The Translation of Popular Management Ideas: Towards a Theory', paper presented to subtheme 7 'The Creation and Diffusion of Management Practices' of the 14th EGOS Colloquium 'Stretching the Boundaries of Organizational Studies into the Next Millennium', University of Maastricht, Maastricht, The Netherlands, 9–11 July 1998.

Salancik, G.R. and Pfeffer, J. (1974) 'The Bases and Uses of Power in Organizational Decision Making: The Case of a University', *Administrative Science Quarterly*, 19: 453–73.

Sapolsky, H. (1972) *The Polaris System Development: Bureaucratic and Programmatic Success in Government*. Cambridge, MA: Harvard University Press.

Sayles, L.R. and Chandler, M.K. (1971) *Managing Large Systems: Organizations of the Future*. New York: Harper & Row.

Schattschneider, E.E. (1960) *The Semisovereign People*. New York: Holt, Rinehart & Winston.

Sydow, J. and Staber, U. (2002) 'The Institutional Embeddedness of Project Networks: The Case of Content Production in German Television', *Regional Studies*, 36(3): 215–27.

Taylor, C. (1984) 'Foucault on Freedom and Truth', *Political Theory*, 12: 152–83.

Wandel, T. (2001) 'The Power of Discourse: Michel Foucault and Critical Theory', *Cultural Values*, 5(3): 368–82.

Weber, M. (1958) *From Max Weber: Essays in Sociology*, edited by H.H. Gerth, and C.W. Mills. New York: Oxford University Press.

Weick, K.E. (1995) *Sensemaking in Organizations*. London: Sage.

Wrong, D.H. (1968) 'Some Problems in Defining Social Power', *American Journal of Sociology*, 73: 673–81.

12

The management of projects in the construction industry: context, discourse and self-identity

Stuart Green

Introduction

The UK construction industry has always been the epitome of a project-based industry. It abounds with project managers at every level. Contractors employ project managers, subcontractors employ project managers, consultants offer project management services and large repeat clients frequently retain their own project management expertise. The vast majority of construction projects are unique. Furthermore they are delivered by temporary multi-organisational coalitions specifically set up for the purpose of project delivery (Cherns and Bryant, 1984). The industry is further characterised by a multitude of procurement arrangements with different arrangements for the allocation of risk amongst the various parties. When viewed from the baseline of the UK construction industry, Lundin and Söderholm's (1998) optimistic vision of a new 'projectified' society of organisational projects seems somewhat ill-founded. Linkages between project-based organisation and notions of postmodernism also ring hollow to those in an industry who consistently see themselves as lagging behind other industry sectors. If the shift to project-based organisation is indeed indicative of postmodernism, then perhaps the construction sector provides a vision of the future for other business sectors. But project-based organisation is played out differently in different sectors. Context is important in shaping practice; and practice is important in shaping context.

The discipline of project management has never been far removed from the construction sector. Morris (1994) prefaces his book on *The Management of Projects* with the statement that he has read most of its literature and has a wide experience of its practice. In contrast, I would profess to being bored by most of the literature and unfulfilled by my limited experience of its practice. But then I am not at all clear on what 'it' is. The literature abounds with definitions and repeated attempts to codify the underlying 'body of knowledge' (for example, Pinto, 1998; APM, 2000; PMI, 2000). Morris (1994: 217) further comments that project management 'is in many respects still stuck in a 1960s time warp'. In an attempt to shrug off perceived obsessions with instrumental tools and techniques, Morris chooses instead to talk about the 'management of projects'. This subtle linguistic shuffle aims to liberate the debate from the constraints of the discipline to address various 'strategic' issues previously underemphasised. But the orientation remains undeniably managerial and uni-dimensional. There is no overtly critical perspective in the sense proposed by Fournier and Grey (2000). Perhaps most striking is the recurring insistence that project management can be understood in terms of its substantive content. In this sense, Morris (1994) is arguably stuck in the same time warp as those who remain obsessed with instrumental tools and techniques.

In contrast, this chapter focuses on the discourse of project management (or the management of projects) as applied to the construction sector. It is not concerned with the definition of project management, but with the interplay between discourse, human agency and industry structure. Whilst remaining cautious of meta-narratives, of particular interest is to explore how this interplay has shaped the self-identities of those who work in the industry and the experienced realities of their day-to-day existence.

Project management in construction

Notwithstanding the generic project management literature, there is an extensive sub-literature directed specifically (allegedly) at project management in the construction industry (for example, Barrie and Paulson, 1991; Pilcher, 1992; Woodward, 1997; Levy, 1999; Harris and McCaffer, 2001). In common with the generic literature, such sources tend to be dominated by tools and techniques such as the critical path method (CPM), program evaluation and review technique (PERT) and work breakdown structure (WBS). Several more recent sources have attempted to provide a more conceptual basis for understanding project management in the construction sector (for example, Moore, 2002; Walker, 2002; Winch, 2002). However, such sources are written for management, and their message is how to 'do' management better. Noticeably absent from the literature is any critical evaluation of how the discourse of project management shapes the lived realities of 'project management' for the construction industry's workforce. Winch (2002) follows Morris's lead in shrugging off any worries about the definition of 'project management' by preferring to talk about 'managing construction projects'. Winch's contribution is notable for the way he seeks to understand how the institutional context constrains project management and shapes project management practice (Winch, 2002). This is a significant shift in thinking away from the articulation of generic principles that are supposedly applicable universally. The generic project management literature too easily forgets that the vast majority of construction projects are embedded within localised contexts. However, Winch's approach would seem to lean towards the structural determinism of 'old' institutional theory (cf. Powell and DiMaggio, 1991). There is seemingly little recognition of the role of discourse in shaping the self-identities that lead to action, and how such streams of action combine over time to reshape context.

Theoretical foundations

The arguments developed in this chapter draw from a variety of theoretical ideas. The initial inspiration to examine construction project management from a critical perspective is drawn from the domain of critical management studies (CMS) (for example, Alvesson and Willmott, 1996; Alvesson and Deetz, 2000; Fournier and Grey, 2000; Burrell, 2001). Fournier and Grey (2000) are especially clear in arguing what it means to be critical, and also in demonstrating that CMS comprises a fragmented and contested domain that draws from a plurality of intellectual traditions. One of the biggest schisms within the field occurs between structural neo-Marxists on the one hand and post-modernists on the other. Personally, I feel uncomfortable with such starkly drawn dichotomies, preferring an analysis that emphasises the complex interplay between structure and agency as it unfolds over time. Although undoubtedly anathema to some, the ideas in this chapter are shaped by the work of Giddens (1984), Pettigrew (1985, 1997) and Weick (1979, 1995). At risk of oversimplifying a complex literature, it is necessary to provide a brief overview of their respective contributions. Weick (1979), drawing from social psychology, has long advocated that researchers should focus on dynamic organisational processes rather than static forms of organisation. Elsewhere, within the domain of organisation studies, the 1990s saw a rapid transformation in focus from stability to change (Ropo *et al.*, 1997). Pettigrew (1997) has been influential in promoting 'processual analysis' as a distinctive research approach. In seeking to understand processual research, it is important to be clear on the adopted definition of a process:

> ... a sequence of individual and collective events, actions, and activities unfolding over time in context. (Pettigrew, 1997: 338)

This chapter seeks a critical understanding of the management of projects as a 'process' in accordance with the above definition. History is rescued from the dustbin to create a grounded understanding of the context within which managers operate. The guiding supposition is that any enactment of project management is embedded in context and can only be studied as such. Project management in the construction industry cannot therefore be understood in isolation from the dynamics of sectoral change. Of central importance is the accumulative interplay between human action and the institutional context within which it occurs. The enactment of project management is part of human action; it is therefore inexorably *shaped* by context, but equally actions accumulate over time to be *shaping* context. Attempts to codify 'bodies of knowledge' comprising universally applicable axioms in isolation from the context at which they are aimed are therefore deeply flawed. The dynamics of context must be conceptualised as an active part of any understanding of project management. The point is not to conceptualise structure and context as barriers to project management, but as essentially involved in its production (see Pettigrew, 1985, 1997).

Any consideration of the interaction between action and context must be informed by an understanding of the structure–agency debate that has long characterised the broader domain of social theory (Walsh, 1998; Ritzer, 2000). Issues of consideration include the relationship between language and action, the way that human agency relates to structural aspects of society and the way that action is structured in everyday contexts. Whilst any attempted resolution of such issues will always be subject to criticism from alternative theoretical perspectives, an essential point of reference is provided by Giddens's (1984) *theory of structuration*. Although structuration theory is by no means uncontested ground, its underlying tenets have been increasingly appropriated within strategic management research (Pozzebon, 2004). Perhaps the most important contribution of structuration theory is the rejection of the view that structure necessarily has a fixed form:

> The structural properties of social systems are both the medium and the outcome of the practices that constitute those systems. (Giddens, 1984: 25)

Structuration theory further offers a reconceptualisation of 'agency'. For Giddens, agency is not limited to the intentions of individuals, but relates more to the flow of their collective actions. Both of these ideas are clearly reflected in Pettigrew's model of processual analysis, thereby strengthening the justification for a research perspective on project management that includes industry structure as an essential part of the analysis. It follows that the enactment of project management cannot be understood in isolation from the dynamics of industry change. Structure and context must be conceptualised as active components in the way that project management is interpreted and implemented. A critical orientation grounded in structuration theory mediates the schism between neo-Marxist positions and those who advocate a discursive understanding of power drawing from postmodernism. Even more importantly, a structuration perspective opens up space to consider the interactions between the enactment of project management in the micro-worlds populated by practising managers and the 'big picture' of structural change over time.

Micro-worlds of project management

The social systems of project management comprise a myriad of micro-worlds populated by actors who continuously engage in a process of sense-making. Practitioners strive to make sense of their experienced reality by constructing an interpretation of events and their implications (Weick, 1995). They then take action accordingly. Management seeks to have an influence on this process by the propagation of particular narratives in the form of 'vision statements' or 'culture change programmes' (Dunford and Jones, 2000). Such narratives undoubtedly play a role in shaping the self-identities of practising managers. Furthermore they provide the scripts against which the dramas of management are acted out. In this respect, narratives have a direct influence on the collective actions that shape practice and (at least according to Giddens) progressively shape the context within which practice takes place. Postmodernist scholars are of course fond of citing the 'linguistic turn', whereby language is involved in all processes of human communication and reality construction. Language in its narrative form therefore dictates the agenda. It frames the way that people understand and act. As McCloskey (1994: xvii) puts it in his study of the rhetoric of economics: 'figures of speech are not mere frills, they think for us'.

Management creates narratives to promote change, but such narratives invariably compete with alternative (subversive) narratives. Individuals are more likely to mobilise narratives for the purposes of sense-making if they resonate with their own experienced realities. The point here is that resources for sense-making are accumulated over time as a result of previous experience. Actions in the present are conditioned by the past. It follows that arguments about the social construction of reality need to be mediated by an intertemporal perspective. Rhetoric cannot easily overcome the accumulative structures of the past. History therefore stands as a perennial anecdote to the excesses of managerialist rhetoric. Employees are more likely to be cynical about management's latest improvement initiative if they directly experienced the failure of the last one, or if they consistently observe that senior managers' actions fail to live up to their rhetoric (see Ogbonna and Harris, 2002).

Insights from the dramaturgical metaphor

The concept of gaining insights into the meaning of managerial discourse through the use of metaphors is well-established (Grant and Oswick, 1996; Morgan, 1997). The traditional discourse of project management resounds with the machine metaphor (Green, 1998). The defining literature repeatedly characterises project organisations as goal-seeking machines that need to be subject to better control and command. From this perspective, the primary task of management is to ensure that the machine operates efficiently. Morris (1994) acknowledges the antecedents of project management in operational research and systems engineering, both of which are characterised by an overriding allegiance to the machine metaphor (Keys, 1991). The discourse of project management has undoubtedly expanded beyond these mechanistic roots since the 1980s. Narratives on 'strategic project management' draw from the organic metaphor by emphasising the need to interact with the wider environment (Walker, 2002;

Winch, 2002). Numerous sources draw from the teamwork metaphor to emphasise notions of project leadership (for example, Briner *et al.*, 1996). Others draw from the political metaphor to promote the need to build consensus amongst disparate stakeholders (for example, Pinto, 1998). However, to date there are very few who have invoked the dramaturgical metaphor to conceptualise project managers as actors in the ongoing drama that is 'project management'. Such a metaphor is especially useful within the context of micro-worlds.

Although the roots of the dramaturgical metaphor can be traced back as far as Goffman (1959), the notion that 'management' can usefully be perceived as a performing art owes much to Mangham (1990). Clark and Salaman (1996) have since examined management consultancy from a dramaturgical perspective. That is, they argue that insights can be gained by thinking in terms of the consultant's *performance* in front of a client. The way in which project management (at least in the construction industry) is increasingly seen as a consultancy service makes the dramaturgical metaphor especially powerful. The conceptualisation is that project managers attempt to create a reality for their audience (that is, other project participants) that captures their imagination and commitment. All participants are assigned roles that are acted out in accordance with a previously agreed script. The success of the project manager is primarily judged in terms of their *performance*.

The performance is initially commissioned by the client in accordance with the accepted scripts on how 'best practice' clients should behave. The decision to appoint a project manager is therefore the outcome of a previous 'act' in the drama of management. The appointee would then be required to act out the expected role of a project manager in accordance with the accepted scripts. Different scripts would be invoked at different stages of the project life cycle. Furthermore, different scripts would be mobilised at different levels of the project in accordance with their perceived relevance.

The determination of 'relevance' depends upon the usefulness of the proposed script for the purposes of sense-making. As previously argued, this clearly depends in part on previous experience, but it also depends upon the participant's domain of responsibility. Those with solely operational responsibilities are unlikely to be immediately interested in narratives arguing for a more strategic approach to the management of projects. This is the point that seems to evade mainstream authors. The vast majority of those involved in project management are engaged in operational tasks. They are concerned with time-and-cost control of particular work packages. The *performance* of these tasks is central to their self-identities as project managers. There are heavy expectations that these are the roles that they will perform. Their working lives comprise a series of acts that draw from the scripts of operational project management. The scripts of critical path analysis and cost control provide the language of their day-to-day action. They provide the basic lexicon of project management. Such scripts frame what project managers talk about and what they do. But in the construction sector, this is now much less true than it was in the mid-1970s. Over a thirty-year period the traditional scripts of operational project management have become progressively less relevant to practitioners in the construction sector. To understand why, it is necessary to address the dynamics of structural change that have characterised the sector over the same period. It is also necessary to understand how the discourse of project management is in competition with other scripts developed with the espoused aim of construction sector improvement. Different scripts continually compete for adoption as sense-making resources. These processes play out continuously over time and in a myriad of ways across the construction sector in all its diversity. The outcome of these processes is action, and individual actions progressively accumulate to reshape the structure of the sector.

Power games in the micro-worlds

Prior to addressing the 'big picture' of structural change it is appropriate to revisit the notion that management promotes particular narratives to promote change. Whilst this is undoubtedly true, it is necessary to think beyond a unitary conceptualisation of management. Political perspectives on organisation present 'management' not as a unitary entity, but rather as an arena where different interests compete for power and influence. Groups of individuals form temporary coalitions for the purposes of mutual self-interest. These groupings are always changing as new power groups emerge and individuals transfer allegiance from one group to another. Furthermore, the careers of individual managers will depend in part on their ability to absorb and reflect the narratives favoured by the currently dominant power group. Managers also need to be aware of which other narratives are in the ascendancy and judge the most appropriate time to switch their allegiance from one interest group to another (Shapiro, 1995). Management gurus play a crucial role in repeatedly providing fresh scripts that can be adopted (Jackson, 2001). Total Quality Management (TQM) is replaced by business process reengineering (BPR), which in turn is replaced by lean production. These are the scripts endorsed by the company CEOs who govern the career paths of project managers. An ability to resonate with scripts beyond the domain of project management therefore becomes necessary when dealing with the power brokers from head office. This is true even in a project-based industry such as construction.

Political power games are continually acted out throughout organisations. Narratives are mobilised as resources and gain legitimacy through reference to external agendas. To be seen to behave in a particular way is important not only internally, but also for the purposes of building relationships with clients. 'Empowerment' is strictly conditioned by those scripts deemed to be acceptable. Hence discursive practices become inseparable from power. Consciously or unconsciously, they are deployed to structure perceptions and reinforce existing power structures. There is of course an extensive sub-industry attempting to interpret Foucault's work on knowledge, discourse and power (see Burrell, 1988; Sewell and Wilkinson, 1992). For present purposes, it is sufficient to emphasise that the advocates of operational project management have lost the discourse/power game, and continue to lose it at every juncture. If individuals want to progress their career they must leave the tools and techniques of project management behind at a very early stage. There are more important games to be played, and more persuasive discourses to be mobilised. Furthermore, it would seem that the discourse of 'strategic project management' has similarly slipped out of fashion, although it did arguably play a role in shaping the self-identities of practising managers in the 1980s and early 1990s before being supplanted by the discourse of supply chain management.

The enterprise culture and the incentivisation of self-employment

A recurring theme of this chapter is the way that micro-worlds continuously reflect and reinforce the big picture. Guru recipes such as TQM, BPR and lean production gained legitimacy within organisations because they resonate with the rhetoric of the 'enterprise culture' that came to prominence during the Thatcher era. The prevailing political climate of the 1980s made strategies based on 'cutting out the fat' much more socially acceptable than would have been the case in previous decades. The espoused doctrine of the free market reduced the task of management to the achievement of 'customer responsiveness' (du Gay and Salaman, 1992). The social democratic consensus of the postwar era was shattered and replaced by the neo-liberal doctrine of trickle-down economics. A full-frontal assault was launched on trade unionism in the cause of labour market flexibility. Competitiveness in the global economy became the new mantra. It is of course easy to demonise Margaret Thatcher as the personalisation of neo-liberalism, but any reading of history demonstrates that broader forces were at work. The spread of globalisation owes much to time–space compression due to technological change, and cannot be explained solely as an ideological construct. During the 1970s the heavy hand of history undoubtedly hung over the structure of the UK economy. Many would argue that the changing role of Britain in the global economy required significant readjustment, not least because of the loss of the protected markets of empire. What cannot be disputed is that the 'sick man of Europe' received a harsh dose of ideological medicine.

The major industrial relations disputes of the 1960–70s placed construction at the forefront of the ideological battle. This was especially true in the City of London where unionisation and union power were at their strongest. But the project-based nature of construction demanded different tactics from those used in other sectors. From the mid-1970s, government and employers acted to encourage self-employment as a means of emasculating trade union power (Harvey, 2003). The discourse of the 'enterprise culture' legitimised a dramatic increase in self-employment in the cause of labour market flexibility. The period 1980–95 saw the extensive implementation of incentives for self-employment through the expansion of the 714 and SC60 system, which provided a progressive and deliberate relaxation of the criteria for registration as self-employed (Harvey, 2003). An ideologically inspired policy initiative combined with managerial preferences to cause a dramatic reduction in the direct labour employed by contractors (and subcontractors) in favour of outsourcing (ILO, 2001). Whilst subcontracting has always been prevalent in the construction sector, its dissolution into multilayered 'labour-only' contracting systems initiated an extensive casualisation of the construction sector workforce. In 1977, self-employed labour in the UK construction industry comprised under 30 per cent of the total workforce. By 1995 the figure had risen to a high point of over 60 per cent (ILO, 2001). While statistics relating to construction sector employment are notoriously unreliable (see Cannon, 1994), there is no denying the substantive shift towards outsourcing and self-employment. Subsequent attempts to tighten up the self-employment tax regime have only been partially successful in encouraging firms to revert to direct labour. The overall picture is one of government vicissitude. Prolonged periods of deregulation are punctuated by occasional half-hearted clampdowns.

By avoiding direct employment, it is estimated that contractors achieve a cost saving of between 20 and 30 per cent (Harvey, 2003). The avoidance of the responsibilities of supervision and the associated costs of employment legislation provides a direct commercial incentive to firms to extend their reliance on subcontractors. Small and transient labour-only subcontractors are much more able (and willing) to evade such costs (Winch, 1998). Firms also benefit by offloading the risks of inclement weather and poor organisation. Such risks are borne by a casualised workforce that lacks representation in the workplace. There is therefore an institutionally embedded 'industry recipe' (Spender, 1989) that provides little incentive for firms to invest in the skills of managing production for several decades. The growth of labour-only subcontracting has served to undermine the role of trade unions and the machinery of collective bargaining (Green and May, 2003). The deregulation of labour markets is of course a central tenet of the 'enterprise culture'. However, it is important to emphasise that the operatives have also been incentivised to adopt self-employed status as an entry ticket to the enterprise culture. 'Essex man' (*sic*) derived his self-identity from the political discourse of the time, and willingly swapped his trade union membership card for a 714 self-employment certificate (latterly a CIS card) and a mobile phone. He also exercised the 'right to buy' on his previously council-owned home, thereby further undermining stable employment regimes within publicly controlled property maintenance organisations.

Lean construction without the rhetoric

As a direct result of the above trends, the UK construction sector has become increasingly characterised by the 'hollowed-out' firm that retains only a small core of white-collar staff. Traditional contractors are progressively more removed from the physical work of construction, choosing to concentrate on management and coordination functions (ILO, 2001). Such trends have been exacerbated by the popularity of 'management' procurement routes, whereby a team of management consultants whose responsibilities are limited to coordination replaces the main contractor. To withdraw from an active involvement in construction and retreat into 'project management' became highly desirable for both firms and individuals. This was much preferable (and profitable) than actually employing people to build things. The legitimising narrative was provided in part by project management (cf. CIOB, 1982; CIC, 1996). But this is a particular form of project management that rests entirely on contract trading as administrated through articulated chains of subcontract.

Under the reconstituted model of project management, managers are not expected to take responsibility for the detailed planning or control of production. Responsibilities for the employment and training of craftsmen (and, very occasionally, craftswomen) are delegated to small firms. Several major contractors of the 1970s have since evolved into service companies. The government-sponsored discourses of partnering and supply chain management increasingly provide the scripts through which firms seek to extract value from the construction process without having to take on the responsibility for employing people. Coupled with the declining influence of the public sector, the result of this trend has been a massive casualisation of the construction workforce. Whilst self-employment undoubtedly has a legitimate role in the construction industry, there are continuing concerns regarding the way that firms avoid their responsibilities through *bogus* self-employment. Harvey (2001) drew from a range of sources to estimate that 361,000 workers are currently falsely self-employed in the UK construction industry. Harvey's evidence included a survey of the scale of self-employment on ten major construction sites. On average, 85 per cent of the workforce was found to be nominally self-employed. Even more strikingly, the vast majority of these were classified as bogusly self-employed. Whilst there is evidence that some workers have recently shifted back to direct employment as a result of the latest clampdown by the Inland Revenue, a return to the direct employment levels of the 1970s remains unthinkable. Any attempt to constrain the 'innovation' of the private sector is fervently resisted by those with a vested interest in the current system.

The outsourcing of construction labour through subcontractors is a well-established tendency in many countries (ILO, 2001). However, the corrosion of subcontracting into bogus self-employment is by no means inevitable. Many countries continue to resist the excesses of neo-liberalism and the global trend towards labour market deregulation. For example, in France and Germany self-employment is illegal, other than on a small-business basis (Winch, 1998). Subcontracting is undoubtedly the means by which firms achieve 'structural flexibility' in the face of an unpredictable workload due to the vagaries of tendering. However, if this were the only reason for subcontracting the current trend towards 'framework agreements' between clients and contractors would initiate more stable employment patterns. Unfortunately, there is little evidence to support such a connection. A more convincing explanation is the desire of contracting firms to avoid the responsibilities of supervision and the associated costs of employment legislation and welfare provision. The long-term casualisation of the construction workforce has had significant adverse implications for job security, training and health and safety. The basic level of employment rights in the UK construction industry increasingly equates to that in developing countries. The apprentice system is in terminal decline with no obvious means of ensuring the next generation of craft skills. Trends towards prefabrication are further deskilling local communities whilst the costs of transportation are subsidised by the taxpayer.

Within the UK context, the following diagnosis rings especially true:

> In many countries private clients are organised into groups and have used their enhanced power in recent years to force contractors to lower their costs and improve their delivery. Unfortunately, as we have seen, this has too often been at the expense of the workforce and of the investment in human capital required to ensure the long-term capacity to deliver high-quality construction. (ILO, 2001: 56)

The construction sector is not of course unique in its reliance on casualised labour and non-standard forms of employment. What is unique is the way that a relatively small number of powerful clients have shaped a discourse of improvement that is now accepted as 'common sense' (cf. DETR, 1998). Fairclough (1989) argues that when ideology becomes common sense, it apparently ceases to be ideology. He further argues that this in itself is an ideological effect. Recipes for industry improvement are therefore judged in terms of the 'common sense' accumulated over thirty years. The result is a hollowed-out industry that fails to provide a stable employment domain for its workforce. Lean construction has arrived and damaging side effects are there to be observed.

The management of construction projects: a view from below the waterline

The setting

What is so strikingly absent from the debate about project management in construction is any empirical research into the 'lived reality' of the above trends as experienced by the industry's workforce. The following case study is derived from a series of interviews with a group of joiners working on the construction of a major hotel complex in London's docklands. The project was a five-star hotel development for employees and business travellers working at Canary Wharf. The complex around the hotel included two tower blocks containing luxury residential apartments for corporate letting or for sale to private clients. Also included in the development was a custom-built gym and swimming pool for hotel guests and residents.

The main contractor for the development was a well-known national company which had been at the forefront of 'management contracting' (hereafter referred to as

'Natcon'). They were in effect project managers who took overall responsibility for project delivery whilst subcontracting the entire work content. Certainly they acted out the role of producing a 'work breakdown structure' whilst subdividing the project into discrete work packages. There was also an overall schedule that dictated the dates that the various trade contractors would start and finish their subcontracts. The internal fit-out of the hotel was subcontracted to one of Ireland's leading contractors (hereafter 'Greensub') who were at the time aggressively expanding their presence in the UK. They in turn subcontracted the fabrication and installation of the specialist joinery work to a subcontractor based in the Midlands ('Timfix'). It was at this level that the researchers gained access to on-site operatives to understand their interpretations of the enactment of project management as viewed from 'under the waterline'.

The ground floor of the hotel required extensive elaborate joinery work in an open-plan layout. The work on the first floor included an elaborately decorated ballroom requiring extensive specialist joinery. The second floor was intended for corporate events and included hospitality rooms for presentations and seminars. In total the Timfix contract was estimated to be worth approximately £3 million.

The cast

The account that follows focuses on the men (and they were all men) who worked for Timfix directly, or were hired to work through agencies. However, the precise employment status of the operatives involved was frequently unclear, even to the operatives themselves. The validation of the data obtained was obviously difficult and the account was undoubtedly sensationalised by the interviewees. In this respect it is perhaps best understood as a story, and as such offers invaluable insights not only into the lived realities of a major construction site but also into the self-identities of the operatives.

The project manager who acted on behalf of Timfix was an individual by the name of Andy Hatton. Andy had been engaged as a 'foreman' specifically to manage this contract and had no previous connection with Timfix. He had been approached by Doug Collins, a site manager with previous experience of working for Timfix. Andy had a reputation as a hard worker and someone who understood complex joinery operations on a large scale. He was approaching 40 years of age and was obviously popular with the men he directed. He had previously owned his own joinery business that had collapsed during the last recession. Andy had been asked to work out the best way of approaching the fit-out contract by Timfix on the understanding that if he came up with a good solution he would be allowed to manage the project and select his own team. He clearly enjoyed his self-employed status, and to all intents and purposes operated as a subcontractor. However, he clearly accepted no contractual risk and seemed to be paid on the basis of submitted time sheets as agreed with Doug Collins, who in contrast seemed to be employed on a direct basis. Doug was by no means a typical site manager and seemed to be a stereotypical English gentleman in his early fifties. He had worked for Timfix before and had the reputation of guiding projects through to completion. Neither Andy nor Doug had had any formal project management training and they certainly had no conception of 'project management' as a discipline. They preferred to see themselves as being in the 'building game'. In fact, they repeatedly invoked the metaphor of 'playing the game' to describe their working lives.

Doug and Andy were the men responsible for the day-to-day working. Timfix were supplying items of prefabricated joinery on a twice-weekly basis and Doug and Andy oversaw the work as it progressed. Timfix's contract director was Jerry Bird, universally referred to as the 'Birdman'. Jerry was an aggressive individual who was based at Timfix's head office in Nottingham. He reported directly to the owner of the company. Timfix's contract not only covered the joinery works, they were also responsible for the installation of kitchen fittings, mechanical services, floor surfaces, suspended ceilings and dry lining. These activities were clearly not within Timfix's domain of experience and all were subcontracted out under the direct supervision of Andy and Doug, who in turn were supervised on site by Greensub employees. Most operatives at this level were only vaguely aware of Natcon as the main contractor as a result of the site hoardings and the initial safety briefing that all operatives were required to attend.

Act 1

Andy Hatton was undoubtedly the motivating force behind the job. His sense of humour was essential to building good relationships with both workmates and managers. He worked hard to keep his immediate 'employees' happy and to ensure that everyone was rewarded fairly. During the research period, there were approximately 100 men involved in Timfix's operation. None of them were Timfix employees, although several of them saw themselves as being employed by Andy Hatton. Most of the men were living away from home and were striving to work as many hours as possible. When the site was running at its peak, this involved seven-day working. At other quieter times many operatives would leave on Thursday evening and return on Monday. Andy habitually recorded them as working for one hour per day longer than they actually did. This was seen to be the way that 'things were done'. However, such practices were not tolerated by the Birdman who descended upon the site at least once a week to check the register against those who were out on site. It seemed to be the case that all operatives were paid by the hour irrespective of productivity, although Andy 'slipped in extra money' to reward those who he felt to be working hard. There was seemingly no attempt to implement any formal bonus scheme on the basis of measured output. When the word spread that the Birdman was about to arrive the site was described as going into overdrive. Men who had been gone for hours would suddenly appear, others would leave their so-called 'skiving holes' desperately trying to appear busy. Andy Hatton was happy to turn a blind eye to such behaviour and clearly had no loyalty to Timfix, despite being largely responsible for allocating their money. Andy clearly had his favourite teams who were paid at a higher rate. This was seemingly negotiated as part of the initial arrangement with Timfix. Doug Collins clearly had little say over these issues, and concerned himself primarily with liaising with Greensub. The men were paid directly by Andy in accordance with what he claimed from Timfix. Tax was deducted at source, but the operatives were not conscious of any contract of employment. Doug Collins was presumably responsible for reconciling what was paid out to Timfix with the milestone payments approved by Greensub, but this was of no concern to the teams of joiners working for Andy Hatton. The discipline of project management simply did not penetrate this far down the project hierarchy. The rhythm of the events was not driven by Natcon, but by the group norms within the work teams.

Act 2

Work on the site routinely started at 7 a.m. Most of the tradesmen lived in pubs and guesthouses within a two-mile radius. Most shared rooms with their workmates. The site canteen opened at 9 a.m. and was invariably full for breakfast at 10 a.m. The teams of joiners were clearly self-regulating in terms of their work rate: there was a recognised 'social norm' that was only adjusted when 'management' appeared:

> The boys working for Andy are Boggy, Jock and Kev. They've been around the block a few times and so are well aware of the fact that you don't go burning yourself out on big jobs like this, pace is all important. As funny as it may seem the pace always picks up when there are managers around, this is all part of the game.

The joiners came from all over Europe. In the initial start-up period they were all British, usually from the North of England but also a small number of Londoners. During the early stages of the job the interviewees frequently complained that they were standing around waiting for materials to arrive.

As the job progressed it became apparent there were not enough qualified joiners to complete the necessary work. This was in the context of a skills shortage across London, whereby tradesmen would move from project to project in search of the most lucrative rates of pay. A further problem for the project in question was that it was due to finish in early December, while most men would seek to position themselves to ensure that they were in work right up until Christmas. In response, Timfix sent a request to the agencies that they should send all available joiners to the site. In the words of one interviewee, this resulted in the arrival of the 'worst bunch of rag tag and bobtail pretenders you have ever set your eyes on'. Ninety per cent of the new arrivals were from Eastern Europe. Nationalities included Lithuanian, Latvian, Polish, Czech and Romanian. The remaining 10 per cent were from Africa, including Ghana, Nigeria and South Africa. Many were engaged by labour-only agencies, although

Andy also had his own contacts with individual 'gangmasters'. The standard of English language varied from excellent to non-existent. As the resource levels grew teams would increasingly be structured around nationalities. Apparent tradesmen were frequently arriving with no tools, and were therefore reliant on being equipped by others. This introduced obvious and immediate tensions.

The extent to which the new arrivals were accommodated depended primarily on their alignment with existing nationalities. With some of the new arrivals it rapidly became apparent that they had no joinery skills. These were either returned to the agency or put to work on unskilled work at a much lower rate of pay. Others managed to camouflage their lack of skills for as long as four weeks. This was achieved by a combination of disappearing at appropriate moments and being carried by teams of compatriots. Some of the workers masquerading as tradesmen had previously held professional positions in their home countries. The wage differentials between Eastern Europe and London were such that an individual would be better off working as a joiner in London than as a doctor in Poland. Accidents frequently went unreported. If an operative had to miss a few days due to injury, his workmates would organise a whip-round to compensate for lost earnings.

Act 3

Notwithstanding the above, it would be disingenuous to suggest that the operatives from Eastern Europe did not include some excellent tradesmen. The informal sorting system meant that it was difficult for unskilled operatives to draw tradesmen rates for any significant amount of time. However, even skilled tradesmen could find themselves working alongside others who attracted different conditions of employment and a higher hourly rate. Nationality was just one determinant in a seemingly unregulated labour market. Counterfeit Inland Revenue registration cards authorising holders to be paid gross were reportedly widely available on the black market in local pubs. Not surprisingly, all the interviewees claimed that their taxation status as subcontractors was genuine. This was invariably a very sensitive area where questioning was not encouraged.

The team spirit within some of the Eastern European groups was frequently cited as exemplary, despite the fact that they tended to be given the most physically demanding jobs and were paid less than their equivalents who were British nationals. It was not at all unusual for the cohorts of Eastern European workers to sing as they worked. Quite often different groups of workers would be singing in different languages in the same area. The majority of these posted workers were sending the majority of their earnings back home to support their families. There was even a suggestion that Timfix and their supporting gangmasters would target operatives whose families were in debt to Mafia crime rings as they represented cheap labour who could more easily be manipulated. Whilst this accusation was at best hearsay, there is undoubtedly potential for direct connections between Eastern European organised crime and the gangmasters who supply labour to London construction sites. Indeed, it would not be stretching credibility too much to suggest that the same individuals could conceivably be involved in prostitution rings.

Act 4

During the last few months of the job there was increasing concern about the quality of the finished work. Partly as a result of pressure from Greensub, Timfix introduced a new finishing foreman, Frank Casper, to oversee the work and to ensure quality. Within a week Frank Casper had a reputation as a hard man. His brief was to ensure that those who were not up to the required standard were dismissed and returned to the agency. His opening comment to one group of joiners was 'you're going to be sick of me by the time this job finishes'. Many joiners were immediately made to feel fearful for their position. Within the first week ten were dismissed from the project. Some men were sacked for reasons of poor workmanship, others for bad timekeeping and some allegedly because Frank Casper took a dislike to them. Given that none of the men were direct employees of Timfix, they had limited rights of employment. The introduction of the new foreman very quickly changed the atmosphere and the perk of the extra hour disappeared. A subtle power game unfolded whereby Andy Hatton, Frank Casper and Doug Collins sought to establish an understanding of their respective positions. After a couple of weeks it became apparent that Frank exercised no authority over Andy and in consequence people became a little less fearsome of him. Given that he still exercised the power to 'sack' people the site remained very alert to his presence. Most people simply sought to avoid him, on the basis that he couldn't sack them if he couldn't find them. Slowly but surely the Spanish practices were reintroduced as the informal system adjusted itself to Frank's presence. Ultimately, everybody understood that Frank could not sack all the joiners because they could not easily be replaced. The completion of the works remained dependent upon Andy Hatton as he was the only person who could depend upon any degree of loyalty from the workforce.

It was during this same period that rumours started to circulate that Timfix was in financial difficulty. A court case was pending addressing a dispute on a previous contract running to several million pounds. Operatives who had been employed through the agencies to satisfy Timfix's demands for joiners began to experience problems with their pay. Many were receiving much less than they were expecting, which caused the better tradesmen to immediately seek employment elsewhere. Others would persevere in the absence of any better opportunities, but morale was generally undermined by these difficulties. It most cases the problems were subsequently rectified and many noticed that the payments became more predictable following a visit by the Birdman. Nevertheless, coupled with the fact that the job was nearing completion, such uncertainties provided a further motivation for operatives to look for opportunities elsewhere. This changing environment was a central factor in limiting the impact of Frank Casper.

Three weeks from completion 50 per cent of the remaining workforce were told they were finished at the end of the week. As it happened all the chosen operatives were employed through a single agency and included the bulk of the Eastern European joiners who had flooded the site at its peak. It seemed to be the case that Timfix were struggling to pay for the labour and that a decision was made that they would be better off with a single large creditor rather than several smaller ones. This meant that Timfix was highly dependent upon those who remained on the job, who included most of Andy Hatton's initial chosen team. Through a combination of force of personality and bribery, Andy motivated this group of men to stick with the task and bring the joinery work package to timely completion.

Postscript

Whilst Andy Hatton finished the job on time, he reportedly funded the last two weeks of work largely from his own pocket. It was important to Andy's personal reputation that the job was finished on time. On completion, Timfix apparently owed him £59,000. Initial efforts to recover the money proved unsuccessful. Rumour has it that he subsequently visited the house of the Birdman with one or two of the 'boys'. Timfix thereafter went into liquidation, but Andy Hatton moved on to the next job working once again as a subcontractor to a subcontractor. The identity of the main contractor would be equally as irrelevant as the discourse of project management. Andy of course knew nothing of project management, but of the 'management of projects' he knew everything. His self-identity has not been shaped by the discourse of project management, but is primarily a product of thirty years of industry change and the associated rise of the enterprise culture. Of particular importance is the shift away from direct employment towards 'supply chain management', labour casualisation and deregulation by means of a period of deliberate government encouragement of self-employment followed by decades of vicissitude. It is interesting to note that although Andy Hatton saw himself as a subcontractor, he had no acceptance of the possibility of making a loss. Many of the men who worked for him were paid by the hour and similarly took no risk. Such factors suggest that they were falsely self-employed and should on the basis of any 'economic reality' test have been on the books. Also of note is the way the men were frequently denied full employment rights, including: protection from unfair dismissal, the right to notice and redundancy pay, statutory sick pay and holiday pay. Perhaps of greatest concern is the development of a transient multi-tiered workforce comprising a myriad of different employment arrangements. 'Human resource management' has no purchase in such circumstances. Whilst Andy Hatton's 'chosen few' may revel in their self-employed status, others have little real choice and end up performing identical jobs on much lower rates of pay. In a previous age, Andy Hatton would probably have been a 'union man', but in today's climate we must all be entrepreneurs. Some would see this as progress. Others would see it as a corrosive cancer that threatens the ability of the construction sector to deliver the built infrastructure upon which a civilised society depends. Even more worrying is the way these divisions subdivide groups by their nationalities.

Concluding remarks

This chapter has demonstrated a significant disconnect between the prescriptive project management literature and the lived reality of the way that the 'management of projects' is enacted. It has been suggested that the link between prescriptive recipes and what happens in practice is much more tenuous than is commonly supposed. It has further been suggested that project management is best understood as a form of discourse that competes for attention with other managerial storylines. Complex socially embedded filters determine which discourses are mobilised by practitioners for the purposes of sense-making in particular situations. First is the requirement that the discourse should have some sense of resonance with an individual's experienced reality. Second is the need for the script to be relevant to an individual's domain of responsibility. Third is the extent to which different discourses reflect those favoured by the dominant power group. Project organisations are the arenas within which these processes unfold over time. The above filters have acted in combination to shape conceptualisations of project management in the construction sector.

The accepted narratives of 'better management' have further been dependent upon 'ideological fit' with the enterprise culture. They have also been responsive to changing contractual arrangements and employment patterns by providing managers with a legitimising narrative. Employee and union member have become 'bad', whereas self-employed subcontractor has become 'good'. This shift in employment patterns is directly reflected in the discourses mobilised by main contractors' managers. Critical path analysis of individual activities becomes irrelevant because project managers are only responsible for administrating subcontracts; they are not responsible for productivity. Supply chain management and partnering become the legitimising discourse that justifies an increasing reliance on outsourcing and the emergence of the hollowed-out firm. Progressively over time, an unfolding interplay between language, action and structure has produced a model of managing projects that bears no resemblance to the sanitised world of the project management literature.

Perhaps the most striking conclusion to be drawn relates to the limited impact of project management discourse on those who populate the lower reaches of the construction project supply chain. Each link in the articulated chain of subcontracts serves to dissipate the message. Project managers working for main contractors can act out whatever project management script they wish, but the influence on those engaged in the physical work of construction is negligible. The self-identities of the workforce are shaped elsewhere. For some, the legitimising narrative is derived from the rhetoric of the enterprise culture. For others, it lies within the gangster-capitalism of post-communist Eastern Europe. But there is little comfort for those who seek evidence of Foucauldian notions of surveillance and control. Construction projects comprise numerous glass cages within glass cages, and the windows become increasingly opaque at each level of subcontract. Control and discipline seem quaintly attractive when compared to the anarchy of employment relationships that resides on many construction projects.

Acknowledgement

Thanks are due to David Clark for his help with the case study material.

References

Alvesson, M. and Deetz, S. (2000) *Doing Critical Management Research*. London: Sage.

Alvesson, M. and Willmott, H. (1996) *Making Sense of Management: A Critical Introduction*. London: Sage.

APM (Association for Project Management) (2000) *Body of Knowledge*, 4th edn. High Wycombe: Association for Project Management Publishing.

Barrie, D.S. and Paulson, B.C. (1991) *Construction Project Management*, 3rd edn. New York: McGraw-Hill.

Briner, W., Hastings, C. and Geddes, M. (1996) *Project Leadership*. London: Gower.

Burrell, G. (1988) 'Modernism, Postmodernism and Organizational Analysis 2: The Contribution of Michel Foucault', *Organization Studies*, 9(1): 221–35.

Burrell, G. (2001) 'Ephemera: Critical Dialogues on Organization', *Ephemera*, 1(1): 11–29.

Cannon, J. (1994) 'Lies and Construction Statistics', *Construction Management and Economics*, 12(4): 307–13.

Cherns, A.B. and Bryant, D.T. (1984) 'Studying the Client's Role in Construction Management', *Construction Management and Economics*, 2(2): 177–84.

CIC (Construction Industry Council) (1996) *Project Management Skills in the Construction Industry*. London: Construction Industry Council.

CIOB (Chartered Institute of Building) (1982) *Project Management in Building*. Ascot: Chartered Institute of Building.

Clark, T. and Salaman, G. (1996) 'The Use of Metaphor in the Client–Consultant Relationship: A Study of Management Consultancies', in C. Oswick and D. Grant (eds), *Organization Development: Metaphorical Explorations*. London: Pitman, 154–74.

DETR (1998) *Rethinking Construction*. London: Department of the Environment, Transport and the Regions.

du Gay, P. and Salaman, G. (1992) 'The Cult(ure) of the Customer', *Journal of Management Studies*, 29(5): 615–33.

Dunford, R. and Jones, D. (2000) 'Narratives in Strategic Change', *Human Relations*, 53(9): 1207–26.

Fairclough, N. (1989) *Language and Power*. London: Longman.

Fournier, V. and Grey, C. (2000) 'At the Critical Moment: Conditions and Prospects for Critical Management Studies', *Human Relations*, 53: 7–32.

Giddens, A. (1984) *The Constitution of Society: Outline of the Theory of Structuration*. Berkeley, CA: University of California Press.

Goffman, E. (1959) *The Presentation of Self in Everyday Life*. Garden City, NY: Doubleday.

Grant, D. and Oswick, C. (1996) *Metaphor and Organizations*. London: Sage.

Green, S.D. (1998) 'The Technocratic Totalitarianism of Construction Process Improvement', *Engineering, Construction and Architectural Management*, 5(4): 376–86.

Green, S.D. and May, S.C. (2003) 'Re-engineering Construction: Going Against the Grain', *Building Research & Information*, 31(2): 97–106.

Harris, F. and McCaffer, R. (2001) *Modern Construction Management*, 5th edn. Oxford: Blackwell.

Harvey, M. (2001) *Undermining Construction*. London: Institute of Employment Rights.

Harvey, M. (2003) 'Privatization, Fragmentation and Inflexible Flexibilization in the UK Construction Industry', in G. Bosch and P. Philips (eds), *Building Chaos: An International Comparison of Deregulation in the Construction Industry*. London: Routledge, 188–209.

ILO (2001) *The Construction Industry in the Twenty-first Century: Its Image, Employment Prospects and Skills Requirements*. Geneva: International Labour Office.

Jackson, B. (2001) *Management Gurus and Management Fashions*. London: Routledge.

Keys, P. (1991) 'Operational Research in Organisations: A Metaphorical Analysis', *Journal of the Operational Research Society*, 42(6): 435–46.

Levy, S.M. (1999) *Project Management in Construction*, 3rd edn. New York: McGraw-Hill.

Lundin, R. and Söderholm, A. (1998) 'Conceptualising a Projectified Society', in R. Lundin and C. Midler (eds), *Projects as Arenas for Renewal and Learning Processes*. Boston, MA: Kluwer, 12–33.

Mangham, I.L. (1990) 'Managing as a Performing Art', *British Journal of Management*, 1: 105–15.

McCloskey, D.N. (1994) *Knowledge and Persuasion in Economics*. Cambridge: Cambridge University Press.

Moore, D.R. (2002) *Project Management: Designing Effective Organizational Structures in Construction*. Oxford: Blackwell.

Morgan, G. (1997) *Images of Organization*. London: Sage.

Morris, P.W.G. (1994) *The Management of Projects*. London: Thomas Telford.

Ogbonna, E. and Harris, L.C. (2002) 'Organizational Culture: A Ten-Year, Two-Phase Study of Change in the UK Food Retailing Sector', *Journal of Management Studies*, 39(5): 673–706.

Pettigrew, A.M. (1997) 'What is processual analysis?', *Scandinavian Journal of Management*, 13(4): 337–48.

Pettigrew, A.M. (1985) *The Awakening Giant*. Oxford: Blackwell.

Pilcher, R. (1992) *Principles of Construction Management*, 3rd edn. London: McGraw-Hill.

Pinto, J.K. (1998) *Project Management Handbook*. Newtown Square, PA: Project Management Institute.

PMI (2000) *A Guide to the Project Management Body of Knowledge*. Newtown Square, PA: PMI.

Powell, W.W. and DiMaggio, P. (eds) (1991) *The New Institutionalism in Organizational Analysis*. Chicago: University of Chicago Press.

Pozzebon, M. (2004) 'The Influence of a Structurationalist View on Strategic Management Research', *Journal of Management Studies*, 41(2): 247–72.

Ritzer, G. (2000) *Sociological Theory*, 5th edn. New York: McGraw-Hill.

Ropo, A., Eriksson, P. and Hunt, J.G. (1997) 'Reflections on Conducting Processual Research on Management and Organisations', *Scandinavian Journal of Management*, 13(4): 331–48.

Sewell, G. and Wilkinson, B. (1992) '"Someone to Watch Over Me": Surveillance, Discipline and the Just-in-Time Labour Process', *Sociology*, 26(2): 271–89.

Shapiro, E.C. (1995) *Fad Surfing in the Boardroom*. Reading, MA: Addison-Wesley.

Spender, J.C. (1989) *Industry Recipes*. Oxford: Blackwell.

Walker, A. (2002) *Project Management in Construction*, 4th edn. Oxford: Blackwell.

Walsh, D.F. (1998) 'Structure/Agency', in C. Jenks (ed.), *Core Sociological Dichotomies*. London: Sage, 8–33.

Weick, K.E. (1979) *The Social Psychology of Organising*, 2nd edn. Reading, MA: Addison-Wesley.

Weick, K.E. (1995) *Sensemaking in Organizations*. Thousand Oaks, CA: Sage.

Winch, G. (1998) 'The Growth of Self-Employment in British Construction', *Construction Management and Economics*, 16: 531–42.

Winch, G. (2002) *Managing Construction Projects*. Oxford: Blackwell.

Woodward, J. (1997) *Construction Project Management: Getting it Right First Time*. London: Thomas Telford.

13

Managing projects in network contexts: a structuration perspective

Jörg Sydow

The fluid and the permanent: considering the contexts of projects

In addition to the more instrumental, allegedly practice-oriented literature, managing projects has been increasingly addressed by organisation studies. This follows earlier attempts to conceive 'projects as organisation' or 'projects as organising' (Sahlin-Andersson, 1992) and to present them as 'temporary systems' (Lundin and Söderholm, 1995). These views, mostly informed by organisation theory, depart from the mainstream, rather technocratic literature on project management in at least two respects. First, instead of emphasising the need for planning and rationality, these views point to the importance of perception, power and process – and, thus, to what really goes on in projects. Second, instead of conceiving projects as islands of planned coordination, they highlight the importance of social context for an understanding of what goes on in projects and how to manage projects (Engwall, 2003).

Emphasising perception, power and process in projects is an obvious outcome of considering the diversity of project contexts. But taking context into consideration is also a necessary implication of more processual accounts of projects and project management (Ekstedt *et al.*, 1999). Whatever the starting point for a more processual *and* context-sensitive analysis of projects and project management, for an understanding of what is really taking place in projects – and thus for any realistic approach to managing projects – it seems of outstanding importance to relate the temporary and fluid, that is, the project, to the more permanent and stable, that is, the organisation, the network and/or the field in which projects are usually embedded. Such a processual *and* context-sensitive approach, however, will only support the development of a more critical, more realistic understanding of project work and project management

252

if based upon a theory that is able to conceptualise the relationship of the fluid and the permanent, to care for process as much as for context, to take into account action as well as structure, and to conceptualise the interplay of more micro and more macro levels of analysis with the project level.

Structuration theory, developed by Anthony Giddens (1984) as a social theory and, in the meantime, amply applied to the analysis of the management of organisations as well as of inter-organisational networks (for example, Ranson *et al.*, 1980; Whittington, 1992; Clark, 2000; Windeler and Sydow, 2001; Pozzebon, 2004), is one of the possible candidates for such an endeavour. This theory, which to my knowledge has been referred to quite often (for example, Ekstedt *et al.*, 1999) but, so far, hardly been used to thoroughly analyse projects and project management (see Bresnen *et al.*, 2004, for a notable exception), qualifies for this endeavour for at least three reasons. First, structuration theory emphasises process without ignoring the importance of structures. Second, it supports a multilevel analysis of praxis, including not only individual actors, but also different levels of social systems and institutions. And, third, it considers social context not as external to, but rather as implied in social practices: context shapes and is also shaped by these practices. In addition, structuration theory is more comprehensive and balanced than most theories, for it highlights the aspects of signification and legitimation of social practices, including project practices, as well as the power and domination that is implied in any (fluid) actions and (permanent) structures.

Instead of presenting structuration theory in a formal way, I will rather apply it to the analysis of producing content in the television industry (for example, movies, soaps, science programming). The empirical insights derive from a two-part study of the German television industry that was carried out from 1997 to 1999 and 1999 to 2001 respectively. Overall, more than 80 semi-structured interviews were conducted with TV producers and editorial and managerial staff of TV stations in particular, but also with economic development agencies, film sponsors, trade union officials and other industry experts, mainly in Germany, but – in order to cover the two largest TV markets in the world – also in Hollywood (Sydow and Windeler, 1999; Windeler and Sydow, 2001; Lutz *et al.*, 2003). The insights from this study are complemented by an ongoing research project which investigates, in significantly more detail, two particular TV movie productions (Sydow and Manning, 2004; Manning, 2005), without, however, ignoring its embeddedness in the context of other projects, the organisations participating in the two projects, and the 'media regions' (Lutz *et al.*, 2003) in which the movies are produced. In the course of this research, 20 additional interviews have been conducted.

In the following I will focus on the inter-organisational embeddedness of projects in what are called 'project networks' – however, without ignoring their embeddedness in other contexts such as single organisations and the wider organisational field (Windeler and Sydow, 2001). From this analysis, which is based upon structurationist thinking as a kind of practice-based theorising (Schatzki *et al.*, 2001), several conclusions will be drawn for managing and researching projects in a more realistic and relevant manner. The main argument of the chapter is that project networks – together with project boundaries and project paths – provide a semi-permanent context that makes managing *inter*-organisational projects easier if not possible. While this organisational form is much supported in this function by the regional or institutional field in which the network is situated, more problematic contingencies may arise from the fact that the networks link not only people, but organisations. Nevertheless, a more reflexive approach to organising these networks of interpersonal and inter-organisational relationships may be desirable, especially since the network – as a social system – exhibits structural properties agents may refer to when coordinating a particular project.

Project networks in the television industry as an illustrative example

Content for television, such as feature films, documentaries and even long-running soap operas, has traditionally been produced in projects. When the Hollywood studio system dissolved (Storper and Christopherson, 1987), the character of these projects altered from predominantly organisational to chiefly inter-organisational. The same occurred many years later in Germany, where the in-house production regime practised by pubic television channels changed to outsourced production preferred by private channels which were franchised by the government in the mid-1980s (Windeler and Sydow, 2001). This then new and now dominant organisational form of content production relies heavily on project networks. This form, together with the project boundaries and project paths that are created and reproduced in project networks as social systems, provides a rather stable context for managing individual projects. At the very least, like other social systems that extend in time and space, they exhibit certain additional structural properties to which agents may more or less reflexively refer in their interactions and which, thereby, are reproduced or changed (Giddens, 1984).

Project networks as an organisational form

Projects in the television industry are usually commissioned by a television channel to a production firm that, in close interaction with channel representatives, coordinates the production process. Apart from the producer and the customer, these projects – depending somewhat upon the type of content produced – embrace authors, directors, cutters and quite a number of other individual entrepreneurs and firms that provide creative or technical services (see Figure 13.1). One or several of these, also depending on the type of content produced, may be more critical for the success of the project than others.

Projects that are carried out by more than one organisation have more recently been of major concern to project researchers coming from an organisation studies perspective. However, apart for some notable exceptions (for example, Dahlgren and Söderlund, 2001; Gerwin and Ferris, 2004), the implication that studying projects

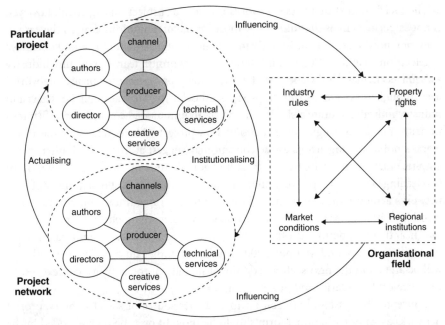

Figure 13.1   Project network as an organisational form
Source: Sydow and Manning (2004)

cutting across the boundaries of a single organisation requires a multilevel approach in order to take into account the contextual embeddedness of these projects has largely been ignored. Such an explicit multilevel approach is made easier by the concept of project network that provides the immediate and often rather stable context for the fluid project – and is itself embedded in the wider organisational field.

While projects have been introduced as temporary systems, these are often contextually embedded in project networks that are 'more than temporary systems' (Sydow and Windeler, 1999). In television, the producer, often in close interaction with the channel representative, selects the members for a particular project from a larger pool of individuals and firms that have been partners in former projects and/or are likely to be partners in future collaborations. This pool does not only 'contain' potential project members, but also project practices that have been applied before and, like 'standard operating procedures' (Cyert and March, 1963) or 'routines' (Nelson and Winter, 1982), are likely to be applied again in future projects. These practices are brought about and eventually institutionalised when present project partners not only, by referring to rules of signification and legitimation, develop shared frames of references, interpretative schemes and norms, but – as a hopefully critical 'success factor' – also draw on resources of domination in exercising (countervailing) power (Giddens, 1984). In turn, the partners of a particular project actualise these practices when they refer to these very structures of the project network when coordinating their project.

The social context that these networks provide for project management, however, is not as permanent as that offered by most formal organisations that, in the case of television production, are most likely to be present as production firms and operators of television channels. While Blair (2001) considers project teams in the film industry as 'semi-permanent', this label may be even more appropriate for project networks, even though these are, as our empirical studies in the German and US television industry indicate, to quite a significant extent an unintended consequence of (intentionally) managing single-content production projects. Moreover, the project network is not as homogeneous as the concept may suggest at first sight. Rather, as the empirical data – especially from our (still ongoing) study of the project networks of two leading German TV production firms – indicate, they consist of a number of sub-networks arranged around the individual producers. In addition, some dyadic relationships within these networks (for example, producer–channel; director–cutter) are significantly more permanent than others, that is, they constitute 'temporary islands of stability' (Sydow and Manning, 2004) in the still rather fluid project networks. As will be argued in the next section, additional stability of the network context results from project boundaries and project paths.

Conceptually, but also with respect to a further source of social stability, project networks as an organisational form should be thought of as being embedded in the wider social context. This kind of context may be well-captured by the concept of 'organizational fields' (DiMaggio and Powell, 1983) that has gained much prominence in recent organisation theory (for example, Anand and Watson, 2004). Organisational fields, 'in the aggregate, constitute a recognized area of institutional life: key suppliers, resource and product consumers, regulatory agencies, and other organizations that produce similar services or products' (DiMaggio and Powell, 1983: 148). The field that a project network operates in provides additional structures, that is, rules of signification and legitimation and resources of domination, which enable, guide and constrain interactions within the project and within the network, including the management of these temporary and more than temporary systems. For instance, in a field that – like a 'project ecology' (Grabher, 2002) – is populated by projects, this organisational form – different to 'networks as form' (Human and Provan, 2000) – will hardly be questioned in terms of legitimacy.

The field concept can be related to either the industry or the region a project network operates in or, as in the case of media regions, to both. Then it captures, for instance, what counts as a viable format (as an industry rule) and who is likely to hold the copyrights (as a property rights issue) for such a format (or a specific programme). Moreover, the field, in Germany as well as in the USA, is characterised by rather oligopolistic demand structures (as a market condition) and, at least in the German media clusters in Berlin, Cologne, Hamburg and Munich, populated by a bunch of regional institutions that support the functioning of this organisational form by providing formal training and financial services, for example (Lutz et al., 2003). However, the organisational field, unlike project boundaries and paths to which I shall turn next, is a source not only of stability, but also of change. One should think, for instance, of the changing audience tastes and fluctuating advertising budgets that are an important source of income for financing TV content production.

Project boundaries and project paths

Project boundaries, like projects, are produced and reproduced via project practices in general and via temporal, task and institutional boundary work in particular. To a large extent, the temporal and task boundaries are the outcome of boundary work as a 'rhetorical activity' (Sahlin-Andersson, 2002). This insight also applies to the production of TV content. For instance, a producer typically explains the task to be accomplished and the time and budget restrictions to be met to other participants and, thus, focuses attention, mobilises action and supports the coordination in and of the project. The boundaries created in the course of these rhetorical activities delimit or decouple the project from its organisational and inter-organisational environment (Lundin and Söderholm, 1995).

Simultaneously, these activities relate the project to its relevant social contexts in the organisation, the network and/or the field. In these communications, the producer, in close interaction with the channel representative, draws not only on rules of signification of the relevant systems, but also on rules of legitimation. For instance, when they explain to financiers why a project or a project network appears to be a suitable form of governance for television production, the producer refers to prevailing views as well as to industry norms indicating why this form is efficient and legitimate. Moreover, they refer to resources of domination in order to communicate this message (and to sanction this activity) in a way that influences the perceptions and the behaviour of the financiers. In this process of rhetoric, the boundaries of the particular project are not completely delimited *ex ante*, but collectively produced and reproduced in the process of daily interactions in which more or less all actors of the project are involved and power plays a significant role.

Alongside project boundaries, 'project paths' (Sydow and Manning, 2004) are likely to emerge out of an interrelated series of projects that are carried out within the framework of a more or less stable project network. Project paths that, like temporal boundaries of projects, emphasise the time context of managing a project, not only exert a binding force out of themselves on the actors involved, but also support learning beyond the single project (DeFillippi, 2001). Actors like the particular producer, the author or the director become affiliated with the series of 'products' and bind themselves and others (for example, in the case of directors, cutters) to the path. The path concept emphasises that time in general and history in particular matter a lot for the managing of projects. In addition, it contains the message that self-reinforcing processes emerge and a certain momentum may buildup that makes quitting or redirecting the path difficult, if not impossible.

Such more or less collaborative path processes are constituted within and, in turn, constitute project networks and contribute a lot to their semi-permanence, including the islands of stability mentioned before. Like these very networks (and the project boundaries), they may be more or less subject to reflexive management. Both TV movie projects we have analysed in significant detail can be interpreted as being part of project paths, since they emerged from and relate to fictional series by the same producer–channel representative dyad. In both cases, the paths are managed quite reflexively by the producers in close interaction with the channel representatives in order to avoid lock-ins for the star actor, the production firm and the channel (Sydow and Manning, 2004).

A practice-based approach to managing projects in network contexts

Studying projects and project management from the practice-based perspective that is offered by structuration theory highlights the fact that agents, in their actual project practices, powerfully and repeatedly refer to structures of the project, the project network, the organisations involved and the wider organisational field. On the other hand, the structures of these very systems, that is, rules and resources in Giddens's jargon, are produced and reproduced by these interactions. That is, social practices are necessarily the focus of such a structurationist analysis that decentres the agent as well as the systems the agents act in – but neglects neither the one nor the other. Rather, and this is the main message of the structurationist concept of the 'duality of structure' (Giddens, 1984), interactions and systems are related by these very practices in a contextually embedded process of production and reproduction. This process, as should be clear by now, can and must be analysed with regard to the interplay of actions and structures in social practices on the one hand and all three dimensions of the social on the other: signification, legitimation and domination. Together with the insight that project networks, project boundaries and project paths balance the temporary and the (more) permanent, this has several implications for managing projects in networked contexts. In what follows, only those implications will be highlighted that concern organising in terms of 'reflexive structuration' (Ortmann et al., 1997) and, thus, the level of reflexivity in managing projects in networked contexts.

Thereby, reflexivity means the constant examination and reformation of practices in the light of incoming information about those very practices and implies that agents 'routinely "keep in touch" with the grounds of what they do as an integral part of doing it' (Giddens, 1990: 36). Although reflexivity is an attribute of all human beings, organising and managing as reflexive structuration go one step further by not only signifying and legitimating the use of resources in particular but reflexively using resources themselves in these processes which (try to) contribute to organisational or inter-organisational reflexivity (Ortmann et al., 1997: 315–17).

Managing project networks: more reflexivity needed!

Projects in the television industry are managed quite reflexively, although – in a similar way to the live entertainment industry (Hartman *et al.*, 1998) and possibly several other project-based industries – classical project management tools and techniques are rarely used. Nevertheless, projects emerge as social systems from project management practices that focus on managing people, building teams, emphasising and controlling timelines, and so on. Despite these activities, the process – like its outcomes – is of course not entirely under the control of those who are in charge of managing the project and coordinating the project network. One reason is that in face of the omnipresent 'dialectic of control' (Giddens, 1984), agents can always act otherwise. Another reason is that, because of unintended consequences and unacknowledged conditions of actions, system structures are, to some extent at least, produced and reproduced behind the back of the coordinator.

This is particularly true with respect to the project networks which, in practice, still seem to be less reflected upon than either the project or the field with its actors, constellations, technologies, regulations and institutionalised practices (Leblebici *et al.*, 1991). Nevertheless, some network-related reflexive practices can be observed in the television production industry.

For instance, some producers try to select and reselect adequate partners in order to maintain 'good' relationships with all other network members, not to mention the commissioner of a programme, that is, the channel representative. In other cases, entire projects are created in order to maintain such good relationships. For instance, in one of the two TV movie productions studied, the film was spun off a series of detective stories and especially developed for the star actor in order to vary his public image and, thus, open up further project opportunities. In the short term, this provides an additional source of income for the production firm and large parts of its project network. In the long run, the actor as well as the producer and the channel, which form a rather stable triad in this case, would certainly profit most, because of consciously building up their reputation by following certain project paths (Sydow and Manning, 2004).

From time to time, producers even acquire or develop projects that allow them to activate 'sleeping relationships' (Hadjikhani, 1996) in order to strengthen an otherwise probably loosening relationship. An even more reflexive approach to managing a project network would result in creating a portfolio of projects that allows the reproduction of network relationships, at least to critical agents, from time to time. At the same time, the coordinator of the project network, that is, the producer in close collaboration with the channel, may develop network-related rules that enhance common understandings and care for redundant resources within the network (Sydow and Windeler, 1999). In any of these cases and some others not mentioned here, the agents refer rather reflexively to the structures of the network, not only to those of the particular project, the organisation or the wider organisational field. However, this still seems to be the exception to the rule of less reflexive management of project *networks*.

These network structures are most likely to be shaped rather reflexively by the practices of the powerful coordinator(s). It is true that, despite the presence of some global players, most production firms in the German as well as in the US television industry are medium-sized. Nevertheless, due to their close collaboration with the channel, they are likely to be the most powerful actors in relative terms. This is also likely to be reflected in the fact that, because of their access to the channel, they are inclined to be the most influential actors in shaping the rules and resources of the network. However, in face of the unintended consequences and unacknowledged conditions of action and, in particular, of the omnipresent dialectic of control, this does not imply that these actors are really able to impose these structures upon other, less powerful network members. Moreover, at least some of them (for example, star actors) are themselves also likely to control a critical resource, though not all of them are of course decisive for the success of the project or even a series of projects.

There are some hints that at least a few powerful production firms have encountered a new level of reflexive network management and started to conceive themselves as coordinators, not only of projects, but also of project networks. One of the producers who coordinates the production of one of the two TV movies under study, for example, has announced a decision to employ more agencies (for example, for actors as well as for script writers). A major interest of the firm in doing so is to simplify its coordinating task by delegating this to other network firms (agencies in this case) and thereby to reduce coordination or transaction costs. Consequently, these agencies are the ones that are likely to build up a pool of potential project partners, to maintain 'good' relationships with them, and/or to activate sleeping relationships, that is, to support the production firm in its reflexive yet distributed management of the entire project network. Thus, this production firm seems to start recognising that the networked context of the project, the temporary system, is semi-permanent and that it is worth paying attention to this web of interpersonal and inter-organisational relationships more strategically. By the way, it is also this firm that started to diversify its content production by reflexively engaging a producer who is familiar with producing for private channels that, at least in Germany, constitute a rather distinct world of production (Windeler and Sydow, 2001).

Thus, there is at the very least some anecdotal evidence that the embeddedness of the project (as a temporary and fluid system) in a more than temporary and stable system makes managing inter-organisational projects easier if not possible and, if reflected upon, may offer additional capacities for organising projects. This is especially the case in a field like television production, where classical project management tools and techniques are rarely, if ever, used and yet projects are finished on time and within a budget.

Managing project boundaries and paths: stick to the level of reflexivity?

If compared to project networks, both project boundaries and, though to a somewhat lesser extent, project paths already seem to attract significantly more attention from producers, acting *de facto* as network coordinators (see Figure 13.2). This higher degree

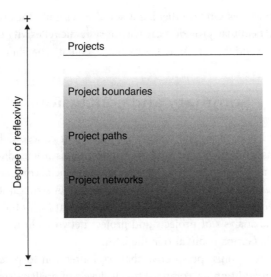

Figure 13.2 Different degrees of reflexivity in managing projects in networked contexts

of reflexivity is not surprising, since most producers care about clarifying project tasks, communicating time and budget constraints, and so forth. Moreover, they think strategically about the path their businesses and that of their major customers may take. One reason among many is that these paths may be closely related to the specific competencies a production firm accumulates when managing projects: 'project capabilities' (Brady and Davies, 2004). And in a project-based industry like television production, these paths are of course triggered by and made up of projects. Despite this significant degree of reflexivity, project paths are not only consciously designed, but may also emerge as a consequence of otherwise motivated actions.

Defining project boundaries and, in particular, creating and maintaining project paths is a complex and very contingent process. Although producers, in close collaboration with channel representatives, seem to be the most powerful agents in this process too, some other creative agents (for example, star actors, directors) and, under specific circumstances, even providers of technical services (for example, special effects) may also have a significant impact upon the definition of boundaries and the course of project paths. Such contingencies and dependencies deserve as much attention as the 'forces' that bind an agent to a particular path. Nevertheless, project paths support managing in a fluid environment that projects, even project networks, offer. But project paths also require managerial attention since the momentum that is characteristic of paths may turn into a lock-in – as implied in the notion of 'path-dependency' (David, 1985).

However, and this is also true with regard to managing project networks more reflexively, reflexive attention and care are certainly *not* to be maximised, especially not for the individual actor. This is so because reflexivity is demanding on agents. And more reflexivity is only possible when 'knowledgeable agents' (Giddens, 1984) are, in some other instances, relieved by standard operating procedures, routines and other highly institutionalised practices. On the other hand, social systems like the project network or the organisational field may provide a capacity of systemic reflexivity that further supports the individual and the corporate agents' management capabilities and capacities.

Summary and conclusions

In this chapter it has been argued that an approach that conceptualises what really goes on in projects (and project networks) must be process-oriented without neglecting structures. In addition, it must be sensitive towards social contexts and be able to address social phenomena on different levels of analysis. A structuration perspective has been proposed as a serious candidate for a theory that fulfils these requirements and applied to the analysis of projects and project networks in the TV production industry, mainly in Germany but also in the USA.

Overall, a structurationist perspective that pays attention to perception, process and power and, in addition, integrates different levels of analysis such as the single project, the project network and the organisational field provides a more complete and realistic – practice-based – rather than an either too optimistic or too sceptical view of the possibilities and limits of managing projects. One reason is that social context is not considered as something external to those interactions, but rather as related to interactions via social practices by which the agents refer to structures of the social systems within which they act. Since these practices produce not only intended, but also unintended consequences, which – as unacknowledged conditions – may be the next sequence of interaction 'behind the back' of even project managers, a somewhat more reflexive management not only of projects, but of their contexts, in this case project networks, may be advisable.

Project networks have been introduced as more than temporary systems that relate the fluid to the permanent, although – as semi-permanent structures – they are likely to be less institutionalised than formal organisations (and more than organisational fields). Project boundaries and project paths, but also stable constellations within these networks, contribute significantly to the relative stability of these structures in a project-based industry. Consequently, these social systems provide agents in projects with (additional) structural properties they may draw upon when managing projects in networked contexts that are very common in the TV industry. Agents, in their management practices, draw upon these structures that make the coordination of projects in these and other project-based industries significantly more likely. Finally, it has been argued – and illustrated by several examples from the field of TV production – that more reflexivity is needed in managing project networks, while a presumably sufficient level of reflexivity has already been achieved in managing project boundaries, and, to a lesser degree, in managing project paths.

Future research on managing projects should extend the contextual focus pursued in this chapter to the field and societal level. Thereby, the embeddedness of these forms in the wider social context and its effects on managing projects and project networks could be clarified. While some studies have already done so (for example, Windeler and Sydow, 2001; Grabher, 2002, 2004; Lutz *et al.*, 2003), the influence of these contexts on project (network) practices (and vice versa) has not yet been scrutinised. Future research should also return to organisational contexts that matter in inter-organisational projects and, at least from a social network perspective, may also be conceived as networked. In addition, more attention has to be paid – on all these levels – to the interplay between powerful acting, communicating and sanctioning, on the one hand, and the structures of domination with structures of signification and legitimation from which these interactions are derived, on the other. At least, this is what a structuration perspective requires.

References

Anand, N. and Watson, M.R. (2004) 'Tournament Rituals in the Evolution of Fields: The Case of the Grammy Awards', *Academy of Management Journal*, 47(1): 59–80.
Blair, H. (2001) ' "You're only as good as your last job": The Labour Process and the Labour Market in the British Film Industry', *Work, Employment & Society*, 15(1): 149–69.
Brady, T. and Davies, A. (2004) 'Building Project Capabilities: From Exploratory to Exploitative Learning', *Organization Studies*, 25(9): 1601–21.
Bresnen, M., Goussevskaia, A. and Swan, J. (2004) 'Embedding New Management Knowledge in Project-based Organizations', *Organization Studies*, 25(9): 1535–55.
Clark, P. (2000) *Organizations in Action*. London: Routledge.
Cyert, R.M. and March, J.G. (1963) *A Behavioral Theory of the Firm*. Englewood Cliffs, NJ: Prentice-Hall.
Dahlgren, J. and Söderlund, J. (2001) 'Managing Inter-firm Industrial Projects – on Pacing and Matching Hierarchies', *International Business Review*, 10: 305–22.
David, P.A. (1985) 'Clio and the Economics of QWERTY', *American Economic Review*, 75: 332–7.
DeFillippi, R. (2001) 'Project Based Learning, Reflective Practices and Learning Outcomes', *Management Learning*, 32(1): 5–10.
DiMaggio, P.J. and Powell, W.W. (1983) 'The Iron Cage Revisited: Institutional Isomorphism and Collective Rationality in Organizational Fields', *American Sociological Review*, 48: 147–60.
Ekstedt, E., Lundin, R.A., Söderholm, A. and Wirdenius, H. (1999) *Neo-industrial Organizing*. London: Routledge.
Engwall, M. (2003) 'No Project is an Island: Linking Projects to History and Context', *Research Policy*, 32: 789–808.
Gerwin, D. and Ferris, J.S. (2004) 'Organizing New Development Projects in Strategic Alliances', *Organization Science*, 15(1): 22–37.
Giddens, A. (1984) *The Constitution of Society*. Cambridge: Polity Press.
Giddens, A. (1990) *The Consequences of Modernity*. Cambridge: Polity Press.
Grabher, G. (2002) 'Cool Projects, Boring Institutions: Temporary Collaboration in Social Context', *Regional Studies*, 36(3): 205–14.
Grabher, G. (2004) 'Temporary Architectures of Learning: Knowledge Governance in Project Ecologies', *Organization Studies*, 25(9): 1491–514.
Hadjikhan, A. (1996) 'Project Marketing and the Management of Discontinuity', *International Business Review*, 5(3): 319–36.
Hartmann, F., Ashrafi, R. and Jergeas, G. (1998) 'Project Management in the Live Entertainment Industry: What Is Different?', *International Journal of Project Management*, 16(5): 269–81.
Human, S.E. and Provan, K.G. (2000) 'Legitimacy Building in the Evolution of Small-Firm Multilateral Networks: A Comparative Study of Success and Demise', *Administrative Science Quarterly*, 45(2): 327–65.
Leblebici, H., Salancik, G., Copay, A. and King, T. (1991) 'Institutional Change and the Transformation of Interorganizational Fields: An Organizational History of the U.S. Radio Broadcasting Industry', *Administrative Science Quarterly*, 36: 333–63.
Lundin, R. and Söderholm, A. (1995) 'A Theory of the Temporary Organization', *Scandinavian Journal of Management*, 11(4): 437–55.
Lutz, A., Sydow, J. and Staber, U. (2003) 'TV Content Production in Media Regions: The Necessities and Difficulties of Public Policy Support for a Project-Based Industry', in T. Brenner and D. Fornahl (eds),

Cooperation, Networks and Institutions in Regional Innovation Systems. Cheltenham: Edward Elgar, 194–219.

Manning, S. (2005) 'Managing Project Networks as Dynamic Organizational Forms: Learning from the TV Movie Industry', *International Journal of Project Management*, 23: 410–14.

Nelson, R.R. and Winter, S.G. (1982) *An Evolutionary Theory of Economic Exchange*. Cambridge, MA: Harvard University Press.

Ortmann, G., Sydow, J. and Windeler, A. (1997) 'Organisation als Reflexive Strukturation', in G. Ortmann, J. Sydow and K. Türk (eds), *Theorien der Organisation*. Wiesbaden: Westdeutscher Verlag, 315–54.

Pozzebon, M. (2004) 'The Influence of a Structurationist View on Strategic Management Research', *Journal of Management Studies*, 41(2): 247–72.

Ranson, D., Hinings, B. and Greenwood, R. (1980) 'The Structuring of Organization Structures', *Administrative Science Quarterly*, 25: 1–17.

Sahlin-Andersson, K. (1992) 'The Use of Ambiguity – the Organizing of an Extraordinary Project', in I. Hägg and E. Segelod (eds), *Issues in Empirical Investment Research*. Amsterdam: Elsevier, 143–58.

Sahlin-Andersson, K. (2002) 'Project Management as Boundary Work: Dilemmas of Defining and Delimiting', in K. Sahlin-Andersson and A. Söderholm (eds), *Beyond Project Management*. Copenhagen: Liser CBS Press, 241–60.

Schatzki, T.R., Knorr Cetina, K. and von Savigny, E. (eds) (2001) *The Practice Turn in Contemporary Theory*. London and New York: Routledge.

Storper, M. and Christopherson, S. (1987) 'Flexible Specialisation and Regional Industrial Agglomerations: The US Film Industry', *Annals of the Association of American Geographers*, 77(1): 104–17.

Sydow, J. and Windeler, A. (1999) 'Projektnetzwerke: Management von (mehr als) temporären Systemen', in J. Engelhard, and E.J. Sinz (eds), *Kooperation im Wettbewerb*. Wiesbaden: Gabler, 211–35.

Sydow, J. and Manning, S. (2004) 'Projects, Paths, and Relationships: Binding Processes in Television Production', paper presented at the SAM/IFSAM VIIth World Congress, 5–7 July 2004, Gothenburg, Sweden.

Whittington, R. (1992) 'Putting Giddens into Action: Social Systems and Managerial Agency', *Journal of Management Studies*, 29(6): 693–12.

Windeler, A. and Sydow, J. (2001) 'Project Networks and Changing Industry Practices – Collaborative Content Production in the German Television Industry', *Organization Studies*, 22(6): 1035–60.

14

Making the future perfect: constructing the Olympic dream

Stewart R. Clegg, Tyrone S. Pitsis, Marton Marosszeky and Thekla Rura-Polley*

Introduction

'How do we deal with it now to avoid it later?'

That question was put by one of the Project Alliance Leadership Team members during the project that frames our reflections in this chapter. In many respects, it is a quintessential management question – how to make the uncertainty attached to the future something that can be dealt with in advance of it occurring – to which there are many, equally quintessential, strategic management answers, the most widely accepted in project management being the collection of management processes described by the Project Management Institute (PMI) as its Guide to the Project Management Body of Knowledge (PMBOK). Essentially the PMBOK is a set of project management tools and processes that span all stages of a project and consider all the major elements that comprise successful project delivery (Duncan, 1996).

In the literature it is generally accepted that there is no explicit theory of project management (Shenhar, 1998; Turner, 1999). Shenhar examines a very broad range of

* We thank members of our research team including Professor Peter Booth and Emma Bowyer. Thank you to Dr John Crawford for his valuable assistance. We also gratefully acknowledge the financial support from the Australian Research Council through the ARC Large Grant and ARC Small Grants Scheme. Most of all we would like to thank members of the NSTP Alliance – their openness, and honesty during interviews and fieldwork over the past three years have proved to be the source of a rich and detailed data set. Finally we would like to acknowledge the journal *Organization Science* and its reviewers for their valuable contribution to an earlier draft, which was published as Pitsis, T., Clegg, S.R., Marosszeky, M., and Rura-Polley, T. (2003) 'Constructing the Olympic Dream: Managing Innovation Through the Future Perfect', *Organization Science*, 14(5): 574–90.

project types in terms of technological complexity and system scope (size and complexity) and concludes that project management has a tenuous conceptual framework. He proposes that project management strategies should be designed to more specifically address the very great differences that exist in project type and complexity. Turner supports this proposition, suggesting that we need to move from adding to the extensive list of tools and techniques that do not take cognisance of the wide variety of project types to developing the theoretical basis of the subject. Reflecting this position, it is not surprising that project management research has been focused on management processes, practices and experience rather than the theoretical underpinnings of the discipline and there is little discussion of theory within the discipline.

It has been recently argued that the practices described in the PMBOK are underpinned by an implicit set of theories (Koskela and Howell, 2002a). First, project delivery has three primary concerns: producing the product, managing internal goals (in relation to factors such as price, quality and so on), and managing external demands (such as customer needs and expectations). Koskela and Howell (2002a) deduce that in the PMBOK a number of implicit theories are assumed. In relation to project delivery it assumes a theory of transformation (Starr, 1966, in Koskela and Howell, 2002a); its theory of management sees it wholly as a matter of planning (Johnston and Brennan, 1996: 372). There is also an implicit theory of communication in relation to project execution, while in relation to project control the PMBOK has an implicit cybernetic model of management control. Recently, researchers have sought to make the theoretical basis for the management of projects less implicit and more coherent (Koskela, 1992; Shenhar, 1998; Turner, 1999; Koskela and Howell, 2002a, 2002b; Bertelsen, 2003; Bertelsen and Koskela, 2003; Macomber and Howell, 2003; Marosszeky, 2003). A broad theoretical framework is proposed by Koskela and Howell (2002a) in terms of the three principle concerns of project management. In relation to the project, the framework of relevant theoretical constructs has been broadened to include interactions within the supply chain in terms of a theory of flows (after Gilbreth and Gilbreth, 1922), external demands are conceptualised in terms of a theory of value creation (Sahlin-Andersson, 1992), and planning is linked to action through the theory of management-as-organising (Johnston and Brennan, 1996: 380), which embraces the realist conceptualisation of organising as a process of seeking agreement between parties (Macomber and Howell, 2003). Finally, in relation to the issue of control, they broaden the relatively simple concept of cybernetic control, which represents the assessment of variance to guide the return to normal, to include the concept of cyclic, stepwise improvement through feedback. They call this the scientific experimentation model, with an emphasis on innovation through learning (Spear and Bowen, 1999) rather than the cyclic process improvement conceptualised earlier in the century for manufacturing processes (Shewhart and Deming, 1939, in Koskela and Howell, 2002a). The framework is summarised in Table 14.1.

While the proposed theoretical framework is certainly an improvement on the accumulated normative injunctions of the PMBOK, it is not much of an improvement when assessed from the contemporary perspectives of organisation theory. It

Table 14.1   Ingredients for a proposed theoretical foundation for project management

Subject of theory		Relevant theories
Project		Transformation
		Flow
		Value generation
Management	Planning	Management-as-planning
		Management-as-organising
	Execution	Classical communication theory
		Language/action perspective
	Controlling	Thermostat model
		Scientific experimentation model

Source: Koskela and Howell (2002a)

remains highly rationalistic, needlessly and unrealistically so, at least from an empirical perspective informed by contemporary organisation theory addressed to the management of large complex projects. Theoretical issues related to a broad raft of organisational concerns are glossed over, especially the fundamentally undecidable context in which so much project work occurs. Complex projects rarely evenly and smoothly apply a rational plan determined beforehand and rolled out as the project elapses. In this chapter we make a contribution to the broader conceptualisation of project goals and execution from a social science rather than an engineering perspective. From a social science perspective, the core issue is the assumption of linear and unbounded rationality underlying the PMBOK: it is both unrealistic and atemporal. In place of the implicit linear conception of time elapsing we wish to substitute a conception that is less means–end rationalistic and more reflexive.

At the core of any project and its management is the concept of the future perfect as an accomplished projection. The central idea is the simultaneity of a notion of something being projected into the future and being thought of at the same time as if it were already completed. The concept of the future perfect is rooted in the philosophy of Alfred Schutz (1967: 61), who defined it as the cognitive process by which an 'actor projects his actions as if it were already over and done with and lying in the past … Strangely enough, therefore, because it is pictured as completed, the planned act bears the temporal character of pastness … The fact that it is thus pictured as if it were simultaneously past and future can be taken care of by saying that it is thought of in the future perfect tense.' While many researchers and authors have adopted Schutz's notion of the future perfect (see Bavelas, 1973; Boland, 1984; Davis, 1987; Hogarth, 1987; Bandrowski, 1990; Langlois, 1990; Leonard-Barton, 1992; Langlois and Csontos 1993; Rollier and Turner, 1994; Schilling, 1998), it was Weick (1969, 1995, 2000) who did most to make Schutz known amongst management theorists. Weick's conception of enactment, for instance, relies on the creation of meaning through action oriented to the future perfect (Schutz, 1967). In the future perfect, the forward-looking projection of ends is combined with a visualisation of the means by which that projected future may be accomplished (Weick, 1979: 198). In this chapter we extend Schutz's key concept from analysis in decision-making, urban planning and organisation theory (Weick, 1969, 1979, 2000; Petranker, 2000) to project management.

It is important to differentiate the future perfect from some other common strategic conceptions that are temporally sophisticated, such as the concept of strategic thinking (Rowe et al., 1986; Lenz, 1987; Ohmae, 1993). Strategic thinking has been presented as a dynamic approach: one that addresses planning's overly rational orientation, and its obsession with extrapolation from past data (Buttery et al., 1999). Scenario planning has also been advocated as a way of achieving more creative strategic thinking (van der Heijden, 1996; Ringland, 1998). Ringland (1998: 2) has defined scenario planning as that part of strategic planning which relates to tools and technologies for managing the uncertainties of the future. Use of future perfect strategy differs significantly from scenario planning. It combines forward-looking projection of ends with a visualisation of the means by which that projected future may be accomplished, as an emergent rather than explicitly scripted strategy. Scenario planning has been explicitly developed for situations of high uncertainty, such as work in the oil industry, where most of the work is done at the planning stages of the project, to instil a vision of what the future 'may' look like in order to create mental maps of how one might deal with variation if it occurs. In one sense, these approaches share some of the rationality of the planning models they criticise. Although they do not extrapolate from past data they extrapolate from past expectations grounded in extensive practice under 'business as usual' conditions. Moreover, they tend to be deeply embedded in competitive frameworks for analysis, rather than those that are collaborative.

By projecting as yet non-existent phenomena into an imagined future, construction projects, in general, offer a prime site for research in the complex organisation of inter-organisational collaboration. Inter-organisational collaboration has been defined as '[a] process through which parties who see different aspects of a problem can constructively explore their differences and search for solutions that go beyond their own limited vision of what is possible' (Gray, 1989: 5). It has been argued that collaboration might operate as a strategic tool for gaining efficiency and flexibility in times of rapid change (Westley and Vredenburg, 1991: 66). Collaboration produces new capabilities for organisations that they could not achieve alone; moreover, it aids organisations in innovating solutions beyond an individual organisation's presently bounded rationality, as well as being a way of spreading risk and pooling resources. Typically, such projects achieve high rates of failure in meeting stated objectives (see Koza and Lewin, 1999; Flyvbjerg et al., 2002). Consequently, how inter-organisational collaborative quality is achieved becomes a significant area for research. It was in seeking to understand, describe and analyse how collaborative quality was able to occur in a project that we began to investigate the future perfect as a strategy.[1] Typically, contractual policing, litigation and arbitration,[2] especially in situations of multiple actors and interests, characterise projects. We discovered a project where these dysfunctional organisational characteristics did not apply, because of innovative organisation.

The structure of the chapter is as follows: first, we identify and elaborate some of the detail of the project; second, we outline the methods that we used in researching the project; third, we move to a discussion of some of the ways in which the actors in the project organisation used future perfect thinking in their everyday management; fourth, we discuss some of the anticipated and unanticipated outcomes that they achieved through doing so, before moving to some conclusions.

The project: fast-tracking for the Olympics

A decision to undertake a major project in the run-up to the Sydney 2000 Olympics was taken as a part of the New South Wales (NSW) Government Waterways Project in May 1997, designed to clean up NSW rivers, beaches and waterways. Cleaning up the waters of Sydney Harbour was seen as a priority for the Olympics in 2000 given that the 'eyes' of the world would be on the city in just over three years.[3] The proposal sought to capture sewerage overflows that occurred during Sydney's subtropical storms, when stormwater backs up the sewage system and overflows into the harbour, bringing in not only raw sewage but also street detritus such as litter, syringes and dog faeces. The main detail of the project was to build approximately 20 kilometres of tunnel in the sandstone under the very affluent areas north of Sydney Harbour.

The project was unique on a number of counts: in its symbolic and social impact; as a major piece of Sydney Olympics infrastructure; in its innovative prefiguring of an increasing use of public/private partnerships; and in the mode of its delivery, without any prior specification of methods, machinery and environmental conditions through detailed prior planning. A global indicative budget was determined for the project, with the possibility of performance on the budget – and a number of other key performance indicators that we will encounter shortly – being linked to returns to the parties involved in the project. If the budget was saved the partners made money; if it was exceeded they lost money. An additional strategic purpose was that the prime partner, Sydney Water, had been under severe public criticism because of outbreaks of *Giardia* and *Cryptosporidium* in its water supply only a few years earlier. As a long-term service provider in Sydney, the client was committed to improve its relationship with the community. This made it imperative that the alliance team shared its commitment to excellent outcomes in non-cost and schedule performance areas, such as community relations, safety and environmental management. Sydney Water believed that this could be best ensured if it participated in the project team through an alliance approach.

At the time of commencement, relatively little was known about the ground conditions and the tunnel had not been designed. Given the tight time frame the availability of tunnel boring machines (TBMs) was critical, as these had to be sourced on subcontract from elsewhere in the world. The first stage of the project, of about

18 months, involved a detailed exploration and design phase. Without this, the contractual risks arising from latent conditions would have been unacceptable to any government client. That made completion in an extraordinarily short period of time vital, obviating against a conventional strategic planning process; instead, a constant process of thinking through the future perfect was implemented. The process comprised imagining a future and then seeking to realise it, subject to constant revision, an approach that seemed inductively to fit Schutz's conception of the future perfect.

The degrees of ambiguity and uncertainty inherent in the project were high because of the deadline, the lack of engineering information, the lack of information about the characteristics of major pieces of technology (the TBMs), and also the characteristics of the communities affected by the project. Because of the more than usual degree of uncertainty the project was to be managed in a unique way. Instead of a tender process, where the entire project has to be specified in advance and those specifications made public for community comment, Sydney Water invited expressions of interest from companies willing to enter an alliance to deliver the project. The specifications were only 28 pages in length (unheard of in conventional construction where the bill of works and associated contractual documents can run into many thousands of sheets). As the project would involve concurrent engineering much of the design was unspecified. Specified in detail were the agreed principles that the partners were to commit to as the means for resolving issues within the alliance. These differed markedly from traditional detailed construction contracts with the prospect of arbitration when agreement broke down. A typical approach to selecting partners for the alliance was followed (Stiles and Oliver, 1998), choosing the partners on the basis of their commitment to the process envisaged.

Having thought of the usual way of doing things, with the usual problems that this might entail, with worst- and best-case parameters, they then set about trying to think of extraordinary ways of creating the desired outcome. The outcome was easily encapsulated colloquially: 'a lot less shit and rubbish in the harbour' and sparkling blue water for the TV cameras covering Olympic sailing and swimming events, as well as, in the long term, less pollution generally for residents and tourists. The detailed design of the tunnel was commenced by the alliance once it was established in early 1998 through first defining a business-as-usual (BAU) case, using conventional scenario-planning approaches: the outcome that would be most likely to occur with the project if they designed and constructed it through traditional planning methods, such as reverse scheduling. But the project partners wanted to do much better than this: they wanted breakthrough innovations. The alliance partners sought to imagine the project, in terms of outcomes that were so good that everyone benefited: the marine life in the harbour (a potent symbol in the project iconography); the residents around the foreshore and under the tunnel route; the local communities with whom they would interact in the process; the Olympics organisers; public works contractors throughout the state of New South Wales; and the employees, contractors and client themselves – the members of the alliance. An innovative approach to organisational collaboration framed their thinking and action.

An innovative approach to organisational collaboration

Management consultants experienced in large-scale construction projects helped design a project culture.[4] The consultancy assumed that the alliance would only achieve its objectives if staff at all levels shared the same values, believed that the project was 'something special', and had only its ultimate success in mind – rather than sectional 'home' organisation interests.[5] They recommended that cohesiveness could be fostered through creating a project culture that was explicitly designed and crafted to encourage shared behaviours, decision-making and values. A list of value statements was produced by the PALT (Project Alliance Leadership Team), which comprised the formal statement of the culture: the two core values were striving to produce solutions that were 'best for project' and having a 'no-blame' culture:

- Build and maintain a champion team, with champion leadership, which is integrated across all disciplines and organisations
- Commit corporately and individually to openness, integrity, trust, cooperation, mutual support and respect, flexibility, honesty and loyalty to the project
- Honour our commitments to one another
- Commit to a no-blame culture
- Use breakthroughs and the free flow of ideas to achieve exceptional results in all project objectives
- Outstanding results provide outstanding rewards
- Deal with and resolve all issues from within the alliance
- Act in a way that is 'best for project'
- Encourage challenging BAU behaviours
- Spread the alliance culture to all stakeholders.

All staff would be expected to think creatively and laterally in order to come up with solutions considered best for this project rather than merely implement second-best solutions known already from previous projects. In this way they sought to instil future perfect thinking in the everyday life of the project. Intricately linked with this 'best-for-project' mentality was the 'no-blame' element: staff would be expected to find solutions to problems rather than to dispense blame. Additionally, every alliance partner committed to making the most appropriate, technically skilled and team-oriented staff available for the project, even if that meant withdrawing them from other projects. Induction workshops were held to ensure that everyone, including subcontractors, understood 'that the alliancing concept means what is best for the project – meaning there might be things I like from my experience but it may not be good for the project ... We have five objectives in the project: time, cost, ecology, safety, and community. We always think of those things, we always challenge ourselves with those things, we are guided by them' (project leader, 1 February 1999).

The project sought to exceed BAU expectations and achieve outstanding results. In order to do this, they were constantly thinking in the future perfect: what would they have to have done to achieve the outstanding performance across the demanding range of indicators to which they had committed? When contrasted with the more traditional construction methods of adversarial exploitation of contractual details for profitable advantage – which are not at all oriented to the future perfect, rather more the future imperfect – and the prospect of their ultimate resolution in arbitration (Clegg, 1975, 1992), then the uniqueness of the project approach can be grasped.

The basis for the contractors and client benefit was a risk/reward calculation. The project agreement provided for a risk/reward regime based on performance compared to project objectives defined in terms of five key performance indicators (KPIs): cost and schedule – no surprises there – but also safety, community and environment – which are not usually part of construction KPIs. There was one non-negotiable performance criterion, the completion of the project for use by the Olympic Games. While the alliance had the responsibility of defining BAU objectives in terms of suitable criteria, there was no precedent for a construction project being assessed against such parameters. To ensure independence, external consultants were engaged to review the benchmarks for the non-cost/schedule criteria that had been developed by the alliance. For each area, performance levels, ranging from poor to outstanding, were defined, with the brief being simply to define outstanding through the future perfect – what would an absolutely spotless report card and review of the project require? The specialist consultants also assessed and reported performance against all criteria regularly throughout the project. Success against the non-cost/schedule criteria was critical for project success both in commercial and overall terms and, as such, this area presented the alliance team with significant risks.

There were positive and negative financial outcomes for performance on each of the objectives in the risk/reward process. Financial rewards were payable on a sliding scale for performance above BAU to outstanding. All objectives, except cost, had a maximum amount. Financial penalties accrued when performance was below BAU and, most importantly, performance in any one area could not be traded off against any other area that was represented by the KPIs. Only outstanding performance against all five KPIs would yield the maximum return; less than this in any one area would diminish that return and adverse performance would put the reward at risk as penalty clauses began to bite. To make the future perfect concrete meant constructing something that could be imagined as already complete and subject to audit. Thus, in each area performance processes and outcomes were constructed on which the project would be assessed.

Methods

Within the case we conducted in-depth qualitative research: we attended every monthly, and later bimonthly, PALT meeting, as well as occasional informal meetings; collated newspaper clippings related to the project; and collected public relations materials issued by the leadership team. In the ethnographic tradition, these archival and published records were collected and analysed, as were local, state and national media articles. We also examined reports from the independent assessors. Thus, over an eighteen-month period, research team members attended all meetings of the PALT. The meetings monitored performance, discussed project-level learning, and sought to solve problems and determine future strategy. As audio taping of meetings was not allowed, a laptop computer was used to record key points. The meeting secretary read these notes, which we supplemented by the minutes, to ensure nothing was taken out of context.[6]

Data analysis

The attendance at all PALT meetings inspired the line of enquiry followed in this study. It became evident that temporal issues were of critical importance to the PALT members. The temporal nature of the data was also an issue consistently highlighted by three independent coders employed to assist in data analysis. It became obvious to us that the uniqueness of the project had created a unique concentration on the temporal aspects in the strategic management of the project. The transcribed interviews and the ethnographic notes were initially analysed using open-coding techniques (Strauss and Corbin, 1990). Principal researchers and research assistants participated in a joint open-coding workshop and specific training sessions in which we employed examples for coding and checking of codes. The qualitative software package QSR NUD*IST Vivo (NVivo) assisted in our coding. We noticed that managers sometimes projected events, actions and behaviour that had not yet occurred into the future as if they had already occurred and were lying in the past. They would then retrospectively plan the actions that would lead to accomplishing that outcome.

The pattern emerging was intriguing and we started to look for other instances. In line with the work of Schutz (1967) and others (Weick, 1969; Rollier and Turner, 1994), we coded such instances as managing by future perfect strategy. We then checked all codes against the final categories, used NVivo to search all documents for the final categories, and collated them in a comprehensive coding data report spanning all interviews and PALT notes. We sorted the report by time of interview or meeting in order to see how management strategies and processes changed over time. Table 14.2 provides excerpts of some of the data coded as future perfect strategy. Each independent coder created such tables, and each coder was required to justify their reason for coding text as they did. To get to future perfect strategy, coding went through three iterations of coding. We did not want to break down text into further codes for fear of moving data too far away from their original meaning (Bansal and Roth, 2000). First-order coding was grouped under the heading of 'time' and paragraphs of text were coded as time if they contained words pertaining to time created from a thesaurus program called WordWeb. Text coded included words like temporal, time, schedule, moment, minute, hour, second, instant, occasion, season, instance,

Table 14.2 Examples of text coded as future perfect strategy

Text	Source	Analysis
Everything we do is difficult because our contract is so bloody different and no one is used to it – for the whole team, it's a very new environment for them. We needed to do more research but we can't, we have no bloody time … so we need to make what we do a way of life, need to make it clear that the bonus can go up and down, make it clear to them what they get when we finish will be bigger than anything they would otherwise get. As long as our outcomes are better than BAU on all our performance indicators …	Project leader, PALT meeting (31 March 1999)	The future perfect strategy requires commitment way beyond the normal if it is to overcome ambiguity and uncertainty. Linking the culture of the project (as a way of life) to the KPIs builds this strategic commitment
We made a number of changes to the tunnel designs, made Scotts Creek tunnel larger because of geotechnical and machinery issues that we couldn't have known in advance. These changes acted as a catalyst to Scotts Creek community's revolt because these changes were never in the plan. But [expletive] they [community] can't keep referring to the plan because just about everything's changed since we made that plan public …	Project manager, PALT meeting (13 March 1998)	This passage reflects the inability to plan strategically for changes to design under future perfect conditions, because there is insufficient information at the outset of planning. Future perfect strategy emerges as changes to plan as information becomes available: the emergence affects stakeholders, such as the community, whose rational expectations are that there is a plan and that the project is 'fleecing' it
[In response to community criticism] … (PD) What are the options? Let's think what's best for project? Now, if the board make a contractual change it has to advise the alliance of this. But the board does not seem keen on spending money to solve a problem that is not objectively there. But we all know the problem will still be there anyway, and, when it is, we won't have the budget to deal with it. So how do we deal with it now to avoid it later? (PL) We need to pre-emptively prepare to meet with other CLCs [Community Liaison Committees] and have people prepared to soak up the abuse and put out fires.	Conversation between project director and project leader, PALT meeting (13 March 1998)	In this passage the respondent recognises that, in reality, in the world of the technically rational engineer, the problem that the community in question is agitating about is not 'really' a problem. But he also knows that it will not go away. So, even though it is not a real problem, it still has to be dealt with as if it were, in the here and now, in order to avoid the problem undermining the future perfect achievements of the project. The CLCs will have to absorb present anxieties to secure future perfect outcomes, rather

Quote	Source	Commentary
(PD) Well I can tell you one thing, if this had been a non-Alliance relationship the decisions would have been made 10 weeks ago to smash through. [Conversation on the below-BAU safety performance] (PD) Culturally, were just not getting there on safety. We can't expect or accept the old 'death a mile' attitude. (PL) You can put in a great safety process, and we have had independent auditors say this is the best project he has ever seen in terms of processes to combat accidents … but if all a team hears is production, production, production what do you expect? Safety and productivity should go together, drive each other! (PD) We need to move fast and have a week-by-week improvement. From now on site supervisors are going to have daily reports on safety scores. I mean it. I want them to have daily reports and they will come back in a month, two months and show me how much they have improved. I want everyone on this, unions, supervisors, contractors, everyone.	Conversation between project director and project leader, PALT meeting (16 June 2000)	than the project crashing through with what it knows is the 'right' technical solution, irrespective of community sentiment In a normal contract a 'death a mile' in a hazardous operation, such as tunnelling, is the usual expectation. The contract is falling behind on delivery. It is important for the future perfect strategy that the culture should not allow anyone to think that safety can be sacrificed for completion. The future perfect has to harness both together, and so management steps are spelt out as to how safety will be managed to achieve this. Both safety and completion are being conceptualised in relation to the future perfect rather than to normalised expectations or existing progress completion on the present project
[On safety and schedule] You know I think we need to ask ourselves what happens when you have two opposing incentive schemes acting as reinforcers. One for safety, the other for schedule! There is a need to link working faster to working safer and I don't think this was addressed. So [project leader] could you please get someone working on that issue?	Project director, PALT meeting (18 January 2000)	In a future perfect world all the KPIs reinforce each other – that they should do so becomes a matter for project culture design
The project team must be perceived to be in front of the game, leading it. Not behind the game. So PALT must assist the project teams to achieve results. We know where we want to be, where we want to go, where we want to finish up. We need to plan the end and work out each step to get there so everything is synchronised. We need ownership over the deliverables at the end of the project. The ultimate product is the built product!	Project leader, PALT meeting (18 January 2000)	Starting from the end state, the imagined future perfect, the project needs to work out what it has to do to get there

(Continued)

Table 14.2 Continued

Text	Source	Analysis
[Discussion on the possibility of not meeting schedule] (PD) Well we will have a practical completion date of October 12 and we are going to meet that practical completion date a month early. So I think we have a good case to show we are doing everything in our power to meet the completion date. (PL) The Olympics will also have an effect upon what we can and can't do. But we were really stuffed around by the government and some people in the community. So what if we claim ... [cut off] (PD) I am uncomfortable in revisiting past decisions that we made and try and change them. So we should look at only current issues and events, and future issues and events and work on that basis only.	Conversation between project director and project leader, PALT meeting (15 August 2000)	The realisation of the future perfect is pre-scribed, literally, as a date. Then the relation between current issues and events and the achievement of this future perfect is fixed by reference to the future perfect rather than its revision because of the exigencies of the here and now
If someone like Sydney Water said, 'change what you're doing', we would do that. But in the meantime, one of the requirements that we entered into, or one of the objectives we entered into, is that we would talk and liaise about these things with the community. We would consult and communicate as we go, but see that objective is now threatening us in meeting our other objectives: costs, schedule, environment, and safety, and particu-larly cost and schedule. So I said to them [the community], we are going ahead, as we've said, and your recourse now is, legal, political, er, you know, you can lobby, try and get things changed through the legal or political processes. You always have those rights; we cannot take those rights away from you, even if we wanted. We think you're going to exercise those rights, so we will not give you the same level of information about what we're doing as we previously have.	Interview with project director about community opposition to tunnel venting (2 August 2000)	The future perfect limits are made evident in their breaching by the community. While the PALT would change the parameters of the design that they have envisaged in response to authoritative input from, for example, Sydney Water, they will not do it for input from the community. The limits of community power and responsibility are made evident when the community breaches the role that the PALT would prefer them to play in the future perfect scenario

clock, period, era, forever, sometimes, continuous, end, start, beginning, stop, now, later, early, tardy and other words and variations of words (for example, late, later, lately). In the second stage of coding, using NVivo, chunks of text were analysed for the conceptual relevance to the notion of future perfect. Text that appeared to be discussing issues as either completed or thrown forward were then isolated. The final stage of coding then isolated all text that had some kind of strategic intent. So text like 'In two weeks from now I'll be lying on a beach laughing about all this community crap' (project manager, PALT, 28 February 2000), while anecdotally amusing, was judged not to be strategic, whereas the text contained in Table 14.2 was judged, by all three independent coders, to be strategic in its intent. By strategic we mean the text related to issues important or integral to the project.

Discussion

Through the future perfect strategy the partners were committed to completing the infrastructure by 31 July 2000. Consequently, project leaders recognised that they had to challenge the normal BAU mentality and behaviour in the construction industry, if they wanted to achieve the optimal outcome. Business as usual normally meant fixing things as one went along: this was a special project needing special behaviour grounded in a specific value – the uniqueness of the project and the excitement that this created for those working on it. The project leaders tried to bring all staff and community members on board by making them excited about the project – 'We need to get them hooked on the excitement of the project' (PALT meeting, May 1999). The excitement that the project leaders felt was in the sheer creativeness of the project, the constant envisioning and revisioning in a future perfect mode, the audacity of their setting themselves much more complex KPIs than was normal, and the returns that excellence would deliver. By focusing on the uniqueness of the process, staff and community could work together to solve any problems. Rather than focusing on inevitable construction problems as sources of profitable variation for their firm, members of the project would work in ways that would deliver whatever was best for the project. This extended to involving the union representatives as vital to the success of the project: they were just as committed to the alliance as management, having shared in the culture workshops that created a common sense of 'governmentality' for the project (Clegg et al., 2002).

The future perfect strategy

When we encountered what we were to term the 'future perfect strategy' in action we found something the existing literature had missed, a proposition we tested by scanning the strategy literature. Mintzberg (1990) presents the relevant schools of thought: in Table 14.3 we demonstrate how they might have been applied to the case,

Table 14.3 Mintzberg's descriptive schools of thought

School	Key features	Relationship to the case	Theoretical added value from present study
Entrepreneurial	Strategy as vision and mission. Key role for leadership is to instil a shared sense of vision and objectives	Established through the PALT. A multiple/ collaborative leadership team unified around the 'best for project' culture (see culture)	Leadership is neither individual nor hierarchical but collaborative and collective. Entrepreneurial strategy lacks detailed explanation of how to ensure shared vision and objectives in inter-organisational collaboration as it presumes unitary managerial prerogative
Learning	Strategy as incremental, developing over time. Organisation learns from its environment and adapts strategy accordingly	Strategy develops through learning from doing with what was available, in conditions of very high uncertainty	In the case of the PALT project, learning was not incremental but a highly accelerated and focused process. Strategising, therefore, was always linked to the projected future (future perfect) and not linked to rational planning
Political	Strategy as negotiation and compromise. Multiple stakeholders, with multiple views	Multiple stakeholders and interests aligned through PALT's commitment to designer culture and risk/reward system. Multiple stakeholders were aligned through an intricate system of KPIs, such as community, ecology, safety, budget, schedule	The political school of strategy generally works with an implicit model of zero-sum power: in order for one party to gain power the other party or parties have to lose power. This is a negative rather than positive conception of power. The PALT worked with a positive conception of power. They explicitly framed the members of the various organisations forming the project in a 'designer culture'. To bind members further, a 'risk/reward' scheme was implemented whereby, through explicit evaluation of the project's performance on the five KPIs, a positive culture of power was created

Cultural	Strategy as shared values and the adherence to the 'way we do things around here'	The creation and use of a designer culture (see Clegg et al., 2002) that made it possible to instil the 'what's best for project' culture. Dispersed across and down the four organisations and to subcontractors through an intricate system of banners, induction workshops, regular informal and formal meetings, incentives, etc.	Instilling the 'what's best for project' culture was complex and done at the early stages of the project, but required careful management throughout the life cycle of the project, as well as an explicit material reinforcement through the relation of risk/reward and KPIs
Configurational	Strategy is crafted, as opposed to planned, and focused on engagement developed through experience and commitment	The configurational school, while it is broadly in line with the approach developed here, does little to provide a theoretic tool for making sense of this project. It assumes that the organisation is unitary and that strategy is an emergent intra-organisational process. Hence it is a perspective difficult to apply to the role of the client and inter-organisational collaboration in project management. Knowing the complexity of strategy and treating it as an emergent process does not remove tension between strategic intent and client expectations, which are inextricably linked in project management	The configurational school assumes that strategy unfolds at irregular intervals, and at different stages, whereas in a complex project management system it is a continuous flow process that is constantly under revision in many loosely coupled situations. And, in the Olympic project, these situations were loosely coupled to neither any formal blueprint nor any set of detailed plans

Source: Adapted from Mintzberg, H. (1994) 'Strategy Formulation: School of Thought', in J.W. Frederickson (ed.), *Perspectives on Strategic Management.* New York: HarperCollins

and the lack of explanatory power that these existing strategy approaches had in accounting for what occurred within the case.

The discipline of collective imagination of a future perfect, framed by the designer culture and bound by the governmental strategies of the KPIs and the risk/reward scheme, tied the loose coupling of the collaboration together, as regularly reported in the monthly PALT meetings. In addition, specific future perfect strategies were routinely used as management devices throughout the project. We were able to identify three specific means of managing through the future perfect strategy. These means included the creative use of strange conversations, the rehearsal of endgames and the practice of workshopping, and the projecting of feelings, concerns and issues. Each of these adds to our knowledge of how the future perfect strategy is possible, and so we elaborate them here.

Strange conversations

It was Karl Weick (1979: 200) who introduced the notion of strange conversations to the management literature, a topic that he took from ethnomethodology. Garfinkel (1967), the founder of ethnomethodology, would often proceed, methodologically, by making conversations strange. For instance, he would instruct his researchers and students continually to interrogate people whom they encountered in quite normal everyday settings, such as the family, or shopping. His general injunction was to ask, 'What do you mean by saying …?' He instructed them to do this to elicit the everyday grounds of routine actions. Garfinkel's point was that deep layers of tacit knowledge supported even the most mundane utterance. Using this form of questioning was one way of breaching the rules of normalcy in order to try and reveal the nature of these tacit assumptions. At the point at which people became angry at the conversational turn then these everyday rules for making sense were breached. Normally, these rules would not be visible – ruptures made the tacit explicit. However, as one of his experiments, written up at length in McHugh (1967), showed, strange conversations could be generated through apparently normal conversational routines. In these experiments he used random assignment of answers to the questions that were asked (the answers were either 'yes' or 'no') by subjects, seeking advice, and unaware of the experimental situation that they were involved in. These responses generated conversational sequences in which the actors desperately sought to minimise the strangeness of the conversations they increasingly entered into, by showing that they were capable of making sense of even seemingly bizarre and contradictory interaction sequences.

We did not have to manipulate our subjects to produce strange conversations, but took our cue from Weick (1979). Weick defined strange conversations as ones where the agenda, process and outcomes were unclear. A great many community meetings were associated with the project: in each of these, the agenda was unclear, the process highly emergent, and the outcomes unknown. In these meetings community members were invited to surface anxieties and make suggestion in relation to the project (almost all of which took place beneath the surface, of which they had little knowledge). What they proposed was often a surprise that, in terms of the rationality of the engineers involved in the project, made little sense: for instance, they were concerned about the visual obtrusiveness of the above-ground works, the noise, mud on the roads, potential loss of access to walk their dogs or for children to play. These were all secondary considerations for the engineers, intent on building the project.

The conversations were initially strange because the premises from which each of the two sides came were so different; initially some tensions occurred in some meetings. But these strange conversations helped to produce creative solutions to many local community relevancies, such as the diagnosis of the aesthetics of the works. One site was diagnosed as 'ugly' in conversations between the project and the community. That the community liaison officers would be addressing aesthetics was not an outcome that had been envisaged prior to these conversations. Often, in the initial meetings, it was unclear what it was that was being discussed, as talk ranged so widely, in terms of the community member's emotional and aesthetic response to the engineering works. In fact, it was often the case that the eventual outcome informed what it was that the conversations had been about: for instance, once the proposal for the concealment and beautification of one of the sites had emerged, then it crystallised as what had been wanted all along, even though, at the outset, this was not clear at all. Later in the project community liaison officers found themselves organising barbecues between community and project members, where more such intriguing conversations occurred.

Endgames and the practice of workshopping

Endgames helped concentrate minds on the future perfect strategy in the project. Endgames occurred frequently, as project completion was enacted in the future perfect. Here is an example that occurred at the January 2000 meeting, when a project leader reminded everybody of the objectives. He said:

> We know where we want to be, where we want to go, and where we want to finish up. We need to plan the end and work out each step to get there so everything is synchronised. We need ownership over the deliverables at the end of the project. The ultimate project is the built product.

As we have made clear earlier in the chapter, it was the absence of the usual project pre-scoping and its incorporation in a complex bill of works that made the project unique. It was designed as the process unfolded – an unfolding that did not always develop according to expectations. For instance, in March 1999, one project leader exclaimed, 'It comes down to we have lost ten weeks but we have only been on the job for 26 weeks!' This particular project leader then complained that suggestions being made on how to deal with the slippage were reactive. The project leaders needed to be more proactive in orientation. He seemed to suggest updating their future perfect planned strategies. Implicitly, he said that they should still project the infrastructure as something that would be built by 31 July 2000. At the same time he suggested that they should plan backwards for the 78 weeks that were left for this particular phase and take into account that they had only accomplished the amount of work budgeted for 16 weeks in the previous 26 weeks. So, while the original planning had been based on 104 weeks, they would now have to plan as if they had never had more than 94 weeks (of which only 78 were now left).[7]

At the August 1999 PALT meeting, where slippage on the completion date was at issue, one of the project leaders used the endgame technique to challenge his colleagues to think in future perfect terms:

> Look, I'd like not to have a stretched target. Where will we really be in 2 or 4 weeks? Think hard about what you want to be judged on. What are those numbers you want to be associated with? You know that this will come back to you. We will ask you, have these forecasts been met? What will you say?

The answer, which was simply 'We can meet it', was clearly not what he had hoped for:

> Don't set a stretched target and miss it. If you cannot meet it, change it now. I mean we are going to have a very serious discussion with government. We will say to them, we need to increase time, increase costs, because you stuffed us up. They will say ok, but cross-examine us first.

He wanted them to project themselves into a future where – as the endgame – government agencies would question them and then think backwards towards the present. How would they cope? How would they feel? He knew that the project would be judged by the outcome and wanted them to think backwards from the outcome. A representative of an indirectly linked organisation, who only attended that one particular PALT meeting, stated this bluntly:

> Well, I can guarantee you PALT members one thing! The Minister will ask what day you will finish, if you are not finishing on the day you said you were going to finish. You will have etched this into stone, on a report and you will be judged on this date!

He was told that there were contingency plans and that working with machinery was, at best, like a lottery. Another project leader also insisted on future perfect thinking at this meeting by asking, 'If we were meeting the Minister tomorrow, what would we say the finishing date would be?' The project leaders responded by agreeing: 'OK, by such and such a date we will have had a risk analysis on schedule done.'

The significance of endgames was that they worked as aids for visualisation of the future perfect and enabled the PALT to focus on the future perfect they were seeking to construct. One of the key techniques used to maintain future perfect focus on the end game was workshopping. When it looked as if the project might run over schedule, the PALT agreed to have a workshop to address the alignment of the five key objectives between headquarters and construction sites (PALT meeting, June 1999).

They agreed that by the time of the workshop, one of the project leaders would have met with the programme managers responsible for the key objectives. He would have discussed the alignment of the overall objectives with those of the particular construction sites. Additionally, he would have codified the learning breakthroughs at each construction site, so that they could identify how they had reached their outstanding achievements. Further, he would have discussed the workshop agenda with management consultants and would have arranged a workshop venue. Once again, the PALT engaged in future perfect strategy.

Projecting feelings, concerns and issues

Although the PALT team were almost all engineers, people with a technical background who were more professionally versed in technical than social construction, there was some explicit recognition of the importance of social construction in one aspect of the PALT meetings. The agenda for each meeting originally contained a section titled 'Projecting feelings, concerns and issues'. We were rather surprised when we first saw this in action: we had not expected such empathetic and social maintenance work from highly professional engineers. Any member could raise anything under this recurring agenda item, with the issue remaining on the agenda until 'it was no longer important or was addressed to the satisfaction of the person who raised the issue in the first place'. The inclusion of this clause was supposed to ensure that future perfect thinking maintained a reality check: if an issue had been constructed in regard to any aspect of the project that was causing concern, then it was reiterated monthly until it was no longer a matter for concern. While some of these feelings, concerns and issues were quite technical – about scheduling and such like – others concerned more complex community relations.[8]

The technique was significant – it ensured that the future perfect agenda was open and democratic in its projections among the top leadership team. It created a space in which emotional aspects of the project could be discussed (Fineman, 1993; Albrow, 1997). Increasingly, the routinised use of the item, which, after a while, became merely a matter for noting rather than action and was then later abandoned, signalled the limits of future perfect thinking when confronted by community matters that were outside project control. It was this that alerted us to the limits of future perfect strategy: a point we will go on to develop in the next section.

Anticipated and unanticipated implications

In this section we wish to focus on some outstanding achievements identified in the use of future perfect strategy, as well as some unanticipated drawbacks. We expected the project to be completed on time, given the people, the PALT organisation, and the careful design of the management approach. Early on in the project, as we saw some of the key KPIs slipping, there was an expectation that the incredibly high goals set may not be achievable and that business as usual would prevail: if this were the case, then the project would end up in an acrimonious wrangle, a normative as well as statistically normal outcome in the industry. In addition, making the project more complex and hazardous, there were issues beyond the control of the project leaders. These included a state election that stirred political resentment in one of the affected communities; the unanticipated collapse of some subterranean rock; the need for more complex tunnel bolting than had been projected; damage to houses due to subterranean movement in another area; and a panic orchestrated about the potential polluting effects of the tunnel venting system. Also, there existed a tight labour market in the pre-Olympic boom conditions prevailing in the NSW construction industry. Finally, after permission had first been granted, there was a refusal to dispose of materials as agreed. Although these factors contributed to the project running late and slightly above cost, it was, nonetheless, a highly innovative and successful project, as we shall see.

Project innovations

Much of the innovation achieved was technical. Because of the time required to source the TBMs, order them, transport them to site and commission them ready for use, the decisions on equipment were made very early, at a stage when relatively little was known about the ground conditions. This was a major risk and created numerous challenges. First of all, once the geo-technical investigations had been completed, an optimisation exercise led to the redesign of the tunnel configuration to ensure safer working conditions in two critical areas where unexpectedly poor conditions would have slowed the project and made the excavation more hazardous. The resulting design accelerated construction, saving some five weeks in the programme. Other tunnel design innovations included raising the tunnel in one area to position it in a more suitable rock formation and extending it in another location to improve the environmental outcomes by extending the catchment area of the overall overflow facility, and an improved understanding of the rock condition enabled the team to reduce the extent of concrete invert lining required. Finally the tunnel configuration was altered because of the timing of equipment arrival and a larger-diameter tunnel was constructed where a smaller one had been envisaged.

A number of design innovations to the operating equipment of the completed facility led to alterations in the design of a treatment plant, two pumping stations and an electrical switch room. This led to savings in buildings and considerable savings in excavation for underground plant rooms. Reductions in excavation had time, cost and safety implications. Related to this area also, modifications in the design of vents led to significant reduction in excavation and enhanced safety.

In a traditional contract, design changes of this magnitude could not have been contemplated without substantial cost renegotiation and probably delay. Also there would have been no motivation for the generation of savings throughout the contract period and it was this aspect of the use of the future perfect – linking it to the outcomes – that, more than anything else, produced the innovation.

There were also a number of significant construction process innovations. An automated laser profiling system (ALPS) was developed to improve the control of excavation with a road header. This led to reduction in over-excavation and hence had efficiency and safety implications. It also reduced the requirement to check the alignment of the excavated surface by survey. The TBMs had to be modified throughout the project in response to changes in ground conditions, all of which were unknown when the project was commenced. There were a number of significant innovations in materials-handling both underground and in the disposal of spoil to an inland reclamation site. Large lengths of continuous conveyor, with the use of booster stations, reduced the need for underground haulage in a number of locations, a shuttle conveyor system was designed for the efficient loading of barges and the use of long-reach excavators for unloading of barges avoided the requirement for wharf strengthening. Also, the TBMs were assembled elsewhere, shipped to Sydney and unloaded on a pontoon barge, avoiding the costly strengthening of wharf structures to carry the load of the TBMs. All of these were excellent examples of future perfect thinking in operation: the innovations were achieved through thinking in the future perfect as to how to hasten time, rather than just doing business as usual.

A number of innovations were motivated by environmental considerations. These included the use of closed water systems and a run-off collection system at one site to ensure that contaminated water did not leave construction sites. In another area the realignment of a tunnel reduced the risk of disturbing contaminated material in a cut-and-cover operation. The construction of a major portal structure for the loading of spoil onto barges reduced visual pollution in a sensitive area and significantly reduced noise emissions. Also an innovative technique effectively eliminated construction noise during the driving of piles in this area.

In terms of overall performance, the use of non-cost/schedule performance measures was innovative in itself. This appears to have been a unique aspect of this project. It placed the alliance team under pressure to perform at a high level across a wider range of performance characteristics than is normally the case on such projects. This forced the management team to maintain its focus across all the areas of performance defined at the outset as being critical by the client, in terms of their everyday accomplishment. None could be glossed over in the interests of expediency favouring construction rate or cost, though these are common compromises made on construction projects. It should also be recognised that this was a project working under extreme time pressure and considerable pressure from the community.

Unanticipated consequences

Tasks 'involving judgement, ambiguity, creativity, and volatility of environment' are especially hard to programme (Keen and Scott-Morton, 1978: 68). Future perfect thinking has been seen as useful for unstructured, non-programmed tasks because the methodologies needed to solve such problem are rarely determinable in advance (Rollier and Turner, 1994). The construction project involved high ambiguity, needed creative solutions, and occurred in a highly volatile environment. Sometimes the solutions developed within a cultural commitment to the future perfect became a part of the problem. For instance, the best-for-project and no-blame culture had been intended to reduce ambiguity, yet sometimes seemed to amplify it. According to a project leader, some members mistook the no-blame aspect of the culture to mean:

> That you couldn't call anybody up on what they hadn't done. That it meant no one could go up to someone and say 'tighten your schedule, you said you would be here at two o' clock. I've structured my day around you being here at 2pm and you arrived at 3pm. I'm losing confidence that you are going to do what you say you're going to do!' ... I think that [no-blame culture] is something Australians find really-difficult to deal with. In Australia it's more like 'Hey, you get lost or something?' ... That happens all the time and is a real problem where there are many parties involved. (18 February 2000)

In Australia there is a phrase that people often use, 'She'll be right, mate', meaning do not worry, do not get angry, there may be a problem but it will be good enough when the project is finished. The 'she'll be right' culture did not map easily onto a project that relied so much on future perfect thinking and proclaimed itself a 'no-blame culture' in order to encourage innovation. It tended to make the need for accountability seem like a way of attributing blame; conversely, for some members, the no-blame culture was seen as just a local version of the 'she'll be right' philosophy.

The best-for-project principle also contributed to problems. Despite its aims, the project had not always employed the best and some of the best left the project to work for other projects or companies. Hence the project leaders were forced to make changes to staffing:

> It was obvious to us that individuals have a lot to do with the achievement of a project. So, you can never get past the issue of people being everything, because they are. But in this project we did not really pick the best people... but I've got no doubts, with the team that we've got there now, if we had that team from the start, we'd be romping it in. I have no doubts about that! (Project leader, 18 February 1999)

In January 2000, problems with the retention of staff were voiced for the first time in a PALT meeting. The best-for-project culture could not keep the best people in a highly mobile labour market. While the culture increased certainty about accomplishing the project on time and budget it also allowed managers to stick to the ethos of strong project commitment as the most appropriate courses of action when it was unlikely that more of the same behaviour would reverse the situation.

> Leader 1: ... So [the project leaders] must assist the project teams to achieve results, show them [the staff] we are committed to the project and its future success.

Leader 2: … We need commitment to the deliverables at the end of the project. The ultimate product is the built product!

Leader 3: We have [team building consultants] – between the PALT and [team building consultants], have we got all the tools we need to get them [staff] all committed?

Leader 1: Well, we can identify all the tools we need.

This exchange during a meeting of the PALT shows the assumption amongst the leaders that commitment to the project and its culture from all staff at all sites would solve problems. Having cast the die for the PALT culture and the alliance method as the way to complete the project on time, on budget and in excess of expectations, the tendency was to attribute setbacks to factors that were not a part of the future perfect projection – how could they be, when this was the solution to problems encountered?

Nowhere was the sense of present difficulties more evident than in managing the social rather than the technical construction of the project, particularly community affairs. At the outset the project team's community liaison process was caught on the back foot. They were not ready for the level of community concern and hostility that they experienced and the project team had underestimated the resources that were required to manage this aspect of the project. The project operated at five sites in most of which its relationship with the community was good; however, at one particular site it had a very poor relationship with the local community. One lesson learned was that it is much more difficult to regain the trust of the community once it has been lost than to capture it and maintain it from the outset, as had been done at other sites which had highly successful outcomes. Project teams cannot afford to under-resource this increasingly critical area, as it is very difficult to recover from a bad start.

The fact that the alliance's performance in community management had an impact on its bottom line empowered the community and perhaps even made community opposition more vocal. However, there was no formal mechanism for community response: in a sense the community had power without responsibility, and this skewed the dialogue in the community's favour. The view of senior management in the alliance was that the community problems would have driven a contractor in a conventional contractual arrangement from the site and led to major cost claims. The structure of the alliance, with its long-term commitment to good community relations on behalf of the client partner, ensured that the alliance had the will, tenacity and hence the flexibility to deal with this issue, even at its most confrontational site.

Lukes (1974) has argued that to exercise power is to be responsible for the consequences. The project gave the affected communities a voice in the design of the project, empowering potential critics with voice, but it did not create responsibility. The PALT imagined that people in the affected localities would exercise their voice in design and engineering choices. Yet some representatives were most concerned about the choices already implicit in the projected design. They would have preferred a completely different piece of infrastructure but were given no space in which to voice their opposition to the framework of choices. People could oppose and propose, as they did when one neighbourhood community council came up with a proposal for the enclosure of one construction site in an aesthetically designed shed. But this was a minor, if costly, change to concede compared with the profound opposition that other communities had to aspects of the project.

In general, residents and local authorities were not involved in the initial deliberations on what kind of infrastructure to build nor charged with any role in the subsequent management of the project. Although empowered to give voice to their frustration, the community was not included in PALT's circuit of management power (Clegg, 1989). For instance, the tight deadline had prevented any community involvement in the initial environmental impact statement. Instead, community concerns were to be incorporated into the concurrent engineering and design: there had been no design parameters 'other than the required outcomes described in the Environmental Impact Statement' (conference presentation, September 1999). However, the community did not understand the underlying concept and had expected a perfectly specified plan; in its absence, their puzzlement became an issue to be managed. As one community liaison officer told us:

> I am not sure about how much they [project leaders] thought about the whole strategy in the early days. That should have been sorted out . . . it was widely misinterpreted by the community. (27 July 1999)

The 'misinterpretation' was such that some communities were satisfied neither with the means nor the ends. Yet the project leaders continued to expect the community to trust them to create an outcome that represented a technical solution to the problem that the project engineers perceived as important: creating a tunnel that would keep stormwater and sewage out of Sydney Harbour. But this was not the concern of the one community that generated most of the community issues: they focused much more on the venting of the storage tunnel as a source of possible pollution. From an engineering point of view the project managers saw no problem – but the community were not engineers and engineering solutions could not convince them. Besides, Sydney Water, the organisation that had brought them *Giardia* and *Cryptosporidium* in their water supply, seemed hardly able to be trusted when it came to matters of pollution control. If community representatives had been involved with the project in a supervisory board these issues might well have been aired explicitly as social – rather than technical – issues at an earlier stage.

Conclusion

Both social and material reality changed in the Olympic project. Materially, a major amenity and piece of infrastructure was developed, while, socially, a shared culture was built to deliver it, around what we came to characterise as a future perfect approach. We developed this interpretation of the management of the project through intensive case study and fieldwork. We then shared our interpretation at one of the last PALT meetings, where we presented an earlier version of this chapter to the members. Indeed, we modified our interpretation as a result of the discussion that this presentation provoked.

Most research (for example, Rollier and Turner, 1994) stresses the quantity and quality of a priori strategies in securing exceptional outcomes. In this project, there were no detailed a priori strategies, other than those constantly reconstructed through the future perfect. Hence, there was no strategic plan other than the frame of the future perfect and the risk/reward scheme that accomplished it. Work was constructed imaginatively on an unfolding basis that continually rescoped the future perfect without reference to any original guiding design but with reference to a set of criteria on which the entire process would be judged. The project occurred despite the stillbirth of that strategic planning usually done by theoreticians, who make decisions early on, based on minimal information, yet lock the process into an inevitable and unquestioned future. Instead, the people who had the greatest opportunity to alter the outcomes were the people who made the strategy up as they went along; normally they would be locked into protecting decisions already made for them through tactics that invariably lead to litigation. Rather than using detailed project scoping and planning to reduce high ambiguity, as is typical of construction (Stinchcombe, 1985), the PALT project leaders sought to reduce it through creating a shared culture that enabled future perfect thinking to flourish in an imaginative process oriented to a broad range of imagined outcomes by which they would hold themselves accountable.

Future perfect thinking worked most smoothly where the planners had most control – that is, control of the technological and material context for future action. When external actors were empowered to question, achieving the future became more difficult. There were pitfalls in allowing for voice but not providing accompanying responsibility that increased the potential for a project to become hijacked. Future research should consider the empowerment of external stakeholders, where such stakeholders have not been involved in the accomplishment of the projected outcome. Further research on future perfect strategy needs to investigate the relationship between voice and responsibility. While project managers may adumbrate a strong culture they should avoid being sucked in by its rhetoric and realise that it does not necessarily incorporate all stakeholders.

Schutz used some simple reflections on everyday life to make some complex analytical points about meaning; Weick built on this by introducing the idea of the future perfect into enactment, and enactment made its way into strategy. In this chapter we have extended these ideas to illuminate the use of the future perfect as an alternative to the traditional approach to construction of contract packaging. The client selected its suppliers on the basis of cultural fit and technical competence rather than price; it then defined its needs in performance terms and empowered the team to develop the best solutions possible. In contrast, in the traditional approach strategic planning is finalised with limited information in advance of the project team being selected and the solution is locked in early, limiting creativity during delivery. It represented a shift of strategic decision-making to the people who can make the difference – a reasoning that underlies the transformation of construction prefigured in this project. Consequently, we think that researchers should spend less time looking at strategic planning and more time researching everyday organisational life because, as the PALT realised, it is rather more in the detail that action unfolds and outcomes are produced – not so much in their a priori documentation and codification, which they couldn't have anyway. The project grew from just 28 pages, with no design and no clauses, other than an injunction to think in the future perfect and create a much cleaner Sydney Harbour, to a project that delivered what it set out to do: on time, only slightly over budget, it made Sydney Harbour sufficiently clean that in July 2002, in an ecologically symbolic representation of the success of the project, three 80-ton whales came into the harbour to frolic under the famous Sydney Harbour Bridge, with the equally famous Opera House behind them.[9] In living memory whales had never been this far into the harbour before: the Olympic dream appeared to have been spectacularly realised.

Notes

1. We began research with questions about how quality was managed; we were sensitized to the importance of the future perfect from discussions monitored in Project Alliance Leadership Team (PALT) meetings. It should be clear that to label it as such was an analytic move rather than one embedded in the everyday experience of the subjects being researched. The concept emerged from an exploration of the mechanisms of 'collaborative quality'.
2. Successful completion of multi-organisational projects rarely involves a very high degree of coherence, unity of purpose and project, even at the management level (Flyvbjerg, 2000). Conflict, ambiguity and lack of common purpose have been much more evident, as past research has demonstrated (Higgin et al., 1966; Clegg, 1975). In these organisational arrangements, despite the recourse to contractual tightness and strict surveillance, control has been extremely difficult to achieve (Stinchcombe, 1985: 25–7).
3. The project client, Sydney Water, completed team selection and concurrently undertook the environmental impact statement (EIS) in record time in the three months between September and December 1997. The government approval for the project was given in late December and the alliance contract was signed in January 1998, leaving the team two years and nine months to complete the project. A five- to seven-year timespan would have been available under normal approaches to contracting. It was evident that normal contracting methodologies would not produce the tunnel on time. While the time for completion was strictly stipulated at the outset, such that it was to be ready for the Sydney 2000 Olympics, along with an approximate budget of (AU) 380 million dollars, these were the only variables stipulated.
4. The authors were at no stage consultants to the project, it should be clear.
5. The detail of this 'designer culture' is examined in more detail elsewhere (see Clegg et al., 2002).
6. It should be stressed that this was only a part of our data collection strategy. Our initial aim in studying the alliance was to study in detail how it managed collaborative quality. To this end we collected qualitative data based on extensive interviews of personnel and observation of meetings and analysed those through open coding techniques assisted through qualitative analysis software. In the initial stages of the research we identified and interviewed individuals in key positions within the alliance. A 'snowball' effect led us to additional people who were information-rich respondents, familiar with the overall collaboration. In the course of the project, after a few months, when opposition to the project became vocal in the local media, we also interviewed key individuals who were affected by the project: government agencies, local councils and community members, both those who supported and those who opposed the project. Twenty-two project team interviews were conducted (with another eight being with external stakeholders); the shortest interview took 90 minutes, the longest five hours. Semi-structured interviews using an established interview protocol were designed to capture differing viewpoints on critical issues relating to collaborative quality. All those involved in data collection followed the same approach: all interviews were attended by a minimum of two and, in some cases, three principal

researchers. Interviews were tape-recorded and subsequently transcribed. Hence, rather than random sampling we used theoretical, purposive sampling (Cooper and Schindler, 1998). Specifically, we used a variant called intensity sampling, a selection of 'participants who are experiential experts and who are authorities about a particular experience' (Morse, 1994: 228).

7. The project was eventually fully commissioned some months later than the pre-Olympic date. However, importantly, the project was certified as operationally available by the due date even though it was not completely finished. If the tunnel had been used at this stage, had the need transpired, it would have meant that some of the physical infrastructure that required decommissioning would have had to be sacrificed by being left in vaults off the tunnel.

8. Over time the list of issues and concerns on the agenda became longer and longer and it became clear that some issues were more noted than addressed, let alone resolved: they were mentioned as a concern at the outset, typically projected into the future, and then the next person's concerns were raised. When the list of issues and concerns became overwhelming, the project leaders, with some limited opposition, decided to delete the recurring item from the agenda, even though many of the issues were still to be resolved – especially those that concerned community relations and the social construction that key players in the community were placing on the issue of the tunnel venting system as a potential source of pollution.

9. Cynics might also want to note that the winter had been very dry so little or no run-off would have occurred anyway.

References

Albrow, M. (1997) *Do Organizations Have Feeling?* London: Routledge.

Bandrowski, J.F. (1990) 'Taking Creative Leaps', *Planning Review*, 18: 34–8.

Bansal, P. and Roth, K. (2000) 'Why Companies Go Green: A Model of Ecological Responsiveness', *Academy of Management Journal*, 43(4): 717–36.

Bavelas, J.B. (1973) 'Effects of the Temporal Context of Information', *Psychological Reports*, 32: 695–8.

Bertelsen, S. (2003) 'Complexity – A New Way of Understanding Construction', paper presented at International Group for Lean Construction 11th Annual Conference, Blacksburg, VA.

Bertelsen, S. and Koskela, L. (2003) 'Avoiding and Managing Chaos in Projects', paper presented at International Group for Lean Construction 11th Annual Conference, Blacksburg, VA.

Boland, R.J. (1984) 'Sense-making in Accounting Data as a Technique of Organizational Diagnosis', *Management Science*, 30: 868–82.

Buttery, E., Fulop, L. and Buttery, A. (1999) 'Networks and Interorganizational Relations', in L. Fulop and S. Linstead (eds), *Management: A Critical Text*. London: Macmillan, 414–63.

Clegg, S.R. (1975) *Power, Rule and Domination: A Critical and Empirical Understanding of Power in Sociological Theory and Organizational Life*. London: Routledge & Kegan Paul.

Clegg, S.R. (1989) *Frameworks of Power*. London: Sage.

Clegg, S.R. (1992) 'Contracts Cause Conflicts', in P. Fenn and R. Gameson (eds), *Construction Conflict Management and Resolution*. London: E and FN Spon, 128–44.

Clegg, S.R., Pitsis, T.S., Rura-Polley, T. and Marosszeky, M. (2002) 'Governmentality Matters: Designing an Alliance Culture of Inter-organizational Collaboration for Managing Projects', *Organization Studies*, 23(3): 317–37.

Cooper, D.R. and Schindler, P.S. (1998) *Business Research Methods*, 6th edn. Boston, MA: Irwin McGraw-Hill.

Davis, S.M. (1987) *Future Perfect*. Reading, MA: Addison-Wesley.

Duncan, W.R. (1996) *A Guide to the Project Management Body of Knowledge*. Newton Square, PA: Project Management Institute.

Fineman, S. (1993) *Emotion in Organizations*. London: Sage.

Flyvbjerg, B. (2000) *Rationality and Power: Democracy in Practice*. Chicago: University of Chicago Press.

Flyvbjerg, B., Holm, M.S. and Buhl, S. (2002) 'Understanding Costs in Public Works Projects: Error or Lie?', *American Planning Association*, 68(3): 279–95.

Garfinkel, H. (1967) *Studies in Ethnomethodology*. Englewood Cliffs, NJ: Prentice-Hall.

Gilbreth, F.B. and Gilbreth, L.M. (1922) 'Process Charts and Their Place in Management', *Mechanical Engineering*, 70(January): 38–41.

Gray, B. (1989) *Collaborating: Finding Common Ground for Multiparty Problems*. San Francisco, CA: Jossey-Bass.

Higgin, G., Jessop, N., Bryant, D., Luckman, J. and Stringer, J. (1966) *Interdependence and Uncertainty: A Study of the Building Industry*. London: Tavistock.

Hogarth, R. (1987) *Judgement and Choice: The Psychology of Decision*, 2nd edn. Chichester: John Wiley & Sons.

Johnston, R.B. and Brennan, M. (1996) 'Planning or Organizing: The Implications of Theories of Activity for Management of Operations', *Omega, The International Journal of Management Science*, 24(4): 367–84.

Keen, P.R. and Scott-Morton, M.S. (1978) *Decision Support Systems: An Organizational Perspective*. Reading, MA: Addison-Wesley.

Koskela, L. (1992) 'Application of the New Production Philosophy to Construction', Technical Report No. 72, Center for Integrated Facility Engineering, Stanford University.

Koskela, L. and Howell, G. (2002a) 'The Underlying Theory of Project Management is Obsolete', Slevin, D., Cleland, D. and Pinto, J. (eds), *Proceedings of the PMI Research Conference*, 2002, 293–302.

Koskela, L. and Howell, G. (2002b) 'The Theory of Project Management: Explanation to Novel Methods', paper presented at International Group for Lean Construction 10th Annual Conference, Gramado, Brazil, UFRGS.

Koza, M.P. and Lewin, A.Y. (1999) 'The Co-evolution of Strategic Alliances', *Organization Science*, 9(3): 255–64.

Langlois, R.N. (1990) 'Bounded Rationality and Behavioralism: A Clarification and Critique', *Journal of Institutional and Theoretical Economics*, 146(4): 691–5.

Langlois, R.N. and Csontos, L. (1993) 'Optimization, Rule Following, and the Methodology of Situational Analysis', in Uskali Mäki, Bo Gustafsson and Christian Knudsen (eds), *Rationality, Institutions, and Economic Methodology*. London: Routledge.

Lenz, R.T. (1987) 'Managing the Evolution of the Strategic Planning Process', *Business Horizon*, 30(1): 34–9.

Leonard-Barton, D. (1992) 'Core Capabilities and Core Rigidities: A paradox in Managing New Product Development', *Strategic Management Journal*, 13: 111–25.

Lukes, S. (1974) *Power: A Radical View*. London: Macmillan.

Macomber, H. and Howell, G. (2003) 'Foundations of Lean Construction: Linguistic Action', paper presented at International Group for Lean Construction 11th Annual Conference, Blacksburg VA.

Marosszeky, M. (2003) 'Managing Construction Process Risks: Production, Safety, Quality and Environment', paper presented at International Group for Lean Construction 11th Annual Conference, Blacksburg VA.

McHugh, P. (1967) *Defining the Situation: The Organization of Meaning in Social Interaction*. New York: Bobbs-Merrill.

Mintzberg, H. (1990) 'Strategy Formulation: Schools of Thought', in J.W. Frederickson (ed.), *Perspectives on Strategic Management*. New York: HarperCollins.

Mintzberg, H. (1994) *The Rise and Fall of Strategic Planning*. New York: Free Press.

Morse, J.M. (1994) 'Designing Funded Qualitative Research', in N.K. Denzin and Y.S. Lincoln (eds), *Handbook of Qualitative Research*. Thousand Oaks, CA: Sage, 220–35.

Ohmae, K. (1993) 'The Rise of the Region State', *Foreign Affairs*, 72: 78–87.

Petranker, J. (2000) 'Knowing the Future: Toward a New Temporality of Change Management', paper presented at the annual meeting of the Academy of Management, Toronto.

Ringland, G. (1998) *Scenario Planning: Managing for the Future*. Chichester: John Wiley & Sons.

Rollier, B. and Turner, J.A. (1994) 'Planning Forward by Looking Backward: Retrospective Thinking in Strategic Decision Making', *Decision Sciences*, 25(2): 169–88.

Rowe, H., Mason R. and Dickel, K. (1986) *Strategic Management and Business Policy: A Methodological Approach*. Reading, MA: Addison-Wesley.

Sahlin-Andersson, K. (1992) 'The Social Construction of Projects. A Case Study of Organizing an Extraordinary Building Project – the Stockholm Globe Arena', *Scandinavian Housing and Planning Research*, 9: 65–78.

Schilling, M.A. (1998) 'Technological Lockout: An Integrative Model of the Economic and Strategic Factors Driving Technology Success and Failure', *Academy of Management Review*, 23: 267–84.

Schutz, A. (1967) *The Phenomenology of the Social World*. Evanston, IL: Northwestern Press.

Shenhar, A.J. (1998) 'From Theory to Practice: Toward a Typology of Project Management Styles', *IEEE Transactions on Engineering Management*, 45(1): 33–48.

Spear, S. and Bowen, H.K. (1999) 'Decoding the DNA of the Toyota Production System', *Harvard Business Review*, 77(5): 97.

Starr, M. (1966). 'Evolving Concepts in Production Management', in E.S. Butta (ed.), *Readings in Production and Operations Management*. New York: John Wiley, 28–35.

Stiles, R.M. and Oliver, J.M. (1998) 'Anecdotes from Alliancing', *New Zealand Petroleum Conference Proceedings*. http://www.med.govt.nz/crown_minerals/1998_pet_conference/stiles/index.html, accessed on 14 September, 2000.

Stinchcombe, A.L. (1985). 'Project Administration in the North Sea', in A.L. Stinchcombe and C.A. Heimer (eds), *Organization Theory and Project Management: Administering Uncertainty in Norwegian Offshore Oil*. Oslo: Norwegian University Press, 25–118.

Strauss, A. and Corbin, J. (1990) *Basics of Qualitative Research: Grounded Theory Procedures and Techniques.* London: Sage.

Turner, J.R. (1999) 'Project Management: A Profession Based on Knowledge or Faith?', *International Journal of Project Management,* 17(6): 329–30.

van der Heijden, K. (1996) *Scenarios: The Art of Strategic Conversation.* Chichester: John Wiley & Sons.

Weick, K.E. (1969) *The Social Psychology of Organizing.* Reading, MA: Addison-Wesley.

Weick, K.E. (1979) *The Social Psychology of Organizing.* 2nd edn. Reading, MA: Addison-Wesley.

Weick, K.E. (1995) *Organizational Sensemaking.* Thousand Oaks, CA: Sage.

Weick, K.E. (2000) Discussion piece presented at the annual meeting of the Academy of Management. Toronto, Canada.

Westley, F. and Vredenburg, H. (1991) 'Strategic Bridging: The Collaboration Between Environmentalists and Business in the Marketing of Green Products', *Journal of Applied Behavioural Science,* 27(2): 65–90.

15

Conflicting rhetorical positions on trust and commitment: talk-as-action in IT project failure

John Sillince, Charles Harvey and G. Harindranath

Introduction

The prevalence of inter-organisational networks (Smith *et al.*, 1995) has placed a huge burden on managers to be effective in negotiating and working with partners (Kanter, 1991). At the same time, it is widely recognised that inter-organisational relationships often fail or exhibit unstable, unpredictable and contradictory features (Inkpen and Beamish, 1997). Yet little theoretical or empirical research has been conducted on the dynamics of inter-organisational negotiating processes (Thompson, 1990; Ring and Van de Ven, 1994; Osborn and Hagerdoorn, 1997). There have been few attempts to describe and explain the social reality of managing across organisational boundaries (Weingart *et al.*, 1990, 1996).

In this chapter, we investigate the role of rhetoric in the negotiation process, responding to the call for more interaction-based studies (Lawler and Yoon, 1995). In particular, we analyse from a rhetorical perspective the failure of an inter-organisational network engaged in a large project. The type of inter-organisational network researched was a consortium, defined as a temporary alliance formed in order to complete a specific project (Lei and Slocum, 1991). A single project thus forms the backbone of any consortium, and the failure of the consortium may in turn threaten the project's chances of success. Political support may decline dramatically if a consortium partner defects from a project (Dutton, 1981; Dutton and Kraemer, 1985).

The more politically sensitive the environment, the more the project and consortium management process come to resemble a state of conflict resolution. According to Lewicki *et al.* (1994), there are three main stages involved in resolving disputes.

294

Initially, parties estimate the costs and value of agreement versus non-agreement. Next they agree on a decision rule for getting to the final outcome. Then they aim for cascading levels of agreement. For example, the cost of non-agreement increases as a result of the sunk-cost effect (Keil *et al.*, 1995). Likewise, the value of agreement would be expected to decrease as technical flaws reach some critical mass, or as political support ebbs away (Sauer, 1993), or as the costs of coordinating a team increase (Currie, 1994). It is in this context that rhetoric assumes significance, as sunk costs, value of agreement versus non-agreement, and internal team-coordination costs can all be minimised or magnified through its application. The position is made more complex and potentially more heated when two or more rhetorical positions are in conflict. Watson (1995), for example, has provided evidence of two coexisting yet conflicting rhetorical positions within the same organisation relating to empowerment on the one hand and control on the other hand. The relevance of conflicting rhetorical positions in this chapter, however, is to show that opposed parties in negotiations deploy rhetoric as a political resource.

Talk-as-action

By itself, talk is viewed conventionally as ineffectual ('only talk') and separate from action ('talk first, act later'). But in recent years there has been an increasing emphasis in the management, organisation studies and communication literatures on processes which combine talk and action into one, more complex unity. Such processes include single-, double- and triple-loop learning (Argyris, 1993; Argyris and Schon, 1978), reflective practice (Schon, 1983), sense-making as reflection on action (Weick, 1995), enactment (Starbuck, 1985) and organisational learning as acted procedure as well as internalised interpretation of those actions (Senge, 1990). This has led to the notion, principally put forward by discourse analysts, of 'talk-as-action', which sets out to establish the intimately connected nature of talk and action, by positing a model which shows the multiple relationships which exist between conversational activity and content, identity, skills and emotions, and action (Grant *et al.*, 1998).

Talk constructs reality

Reality is subjectively understood and interpreted (Weber, 1947), and social interaction leads to a process of socially constructing reality (Berger and Luckmann, 1966). Conversation is a means of constructing that social reality. Two people must put themselves in the other's position, in order to establish a 'reciprocity of perspectives' (Schutz, 1967) through which each can accept the other's reality. Through this process things seen initially as problematic become things seen without deliberative interpretation (Merleau-Ponty, 1962) and thus become 'taken-for-granted', in the 'natural attitude' (Schutz, 1967). Anthropologists have identified means by which societies create boundaries in order to motivate action. Rhetorical justifications for why an action must occur include those of God, money or time (Douglas, 1973). But an important distinction exists between what is 'technical' (and therefore outside the bargaining arena) and the 'social' (which can be negotiated and argued about). To make something seem 'technical' removes it from discussion and renders it taken for granted. The effect of conflict and political processes within projects is to reveal to participants that what they have regarded as undeniably technical aspects are in fact socially interpreted and socially constructed (Sillince and Mouakket, 1997). Examples in the case study analysed below involve concepts like commitment and risk, both of which were treated as technical in many contexts (commitment is often supported by technical props such as deadlines, reports, budgets, rules and procedures; risk is often supported by mathematical and economic theories), but when disagreements emerged they were revealed to be socially constructed.

Talk performs as well as informs

The analysis of utterances has led to their characterisation as 'speech acts' such as promising, requesting, commanding and so on (Searle, 1969), and some have suggested that these are to be understood not only as providing information (a request informs us that the requester wishes us to do something) but also as performing an action (such as when a request warns that anger or retaliation may follow) (Austin, 1962). In the case study below, we will show that talking in a project setting about a new building reassured the building partner in the consortium. Talk thus acted as a 'symbolic action' (Johnson, 1990).

Talk as 'structurational' action

Discourses are also actions in the sense that they create influential social rules and roles which influence individuals' later actions. Ethno-methodological studies have shown that each social situation creates the special context for participants to develop their own rules. For example, inmates in a 'halfway house' for paroled narcotics offenders created their own rules (for example, 'Do not "snitch" to staff') (Wieder, 1974). Usually it is not straightforward as to what is 'right' and 'wrong', what is 'acceptable' and 'unacceptable', because these categories have to be socially negotiated. This process is 'structurational' (Giddens, 1984) because the individual actor or agent is viewed as initiating actions which effect changes in social structure, later constraining action, as within inter-organisational networks (Sydow, 1996; Sydow and Windeler, 1996; Sydow et al., 1998).

This iterative, structurational process is demonstrated in the case study by showing that values and ideas which first appear in discourse later become accepted as constraining rules and roles. Our host organisation, a hospital, wanted long-term collaboration but short-term delay, whereas its consortium partners wanted short-term commitment on a written contractual rather than an unwritten, trusting basis. In some ways, contracts can act as barriers to the creation of trust in inter-organisational networks (Backmann, 2000). Many organisations and industries are using network governance (defined as trust-building measures which avoid formal contractual agreements) to establish working arrangements (Jones *et al.*, 1997). The hospital therefore rhetorically presented the notion of delay and commitment as complementary concepts (both reinforced collaboration) and this constrained the way it dealt with its partners. A primary constraint was that it led to the hospital supporting a loose, tacit collaborative form of commitment (dependent on trust) and rejecting its partners' preference for a legalistic form of collaboration (which depended upon a written contract). The dichotomy is a common dilemma in networks of trust relationships (Smitka, 1994; Liebeskind and Oliver, 2000). The distinction has been defined more narrowly as one between 'arm's-length' and 'obligational' contracting (Whitley *et al.*, 1996: 398).

In order for this collaborative definition to be constructed, several other alternative definitions had to be challenged and discarded. Commitment was viewed in several divergent ways, depending on which point of view was expressed. The consortium and the suppliers defined it in decision terms as the opposite of delay. It was also seen by them as a divisible entity, to be bought in instalments, and it was seen by the hospital as achieving incremental increases in later (and therefore better) technology. It was also seen by the hospital in symbolic terms, as a form of reassurance for its partners.

Talk-as-cognition

Just as talk and action are not separate, Edwards (1997) has argued that talk and cognition are inseparable. People use talk as a means of perceiving, enacting and interpreting the world: the way in which people talk illuminates and constrains the way they view the world. Wallmacq and Sims (1998: 125–6) discuss the case of a woman who had previously started a training company that grew very successfully. Her account of that process is illuminating: 'The firm was becoming too big: there were too many of us, and so we decided to split: I asked my second in command if he would manage the new firm in Luxembourg; he accepted and so that is what we did.' The metaphor conjured up was one of cellular division. But it was not only talk. The metaphor channelled her perception of being marginalised and uncomfortable at losing her power into an ambition to, in the words of one of her employees, 'reproduce her firm by photocopy'. Perceptions and ambition are not only talk – they are also cognition. The cellular division metaphor was thus both talk and cognition.

Interaction processes that induce a negative atmosphere influence the ability to settle disputes (Loewenstein *et al.*, 1989). This was true of the case study: we show below that the way the consortium partners talked to the hospital led it to perceive its partners as 'salesmen ... people who want all the answers now'. This further constrained what the hospital said and lowered its expectation of a long-term and open collaboration on the basis of sharing intellectual capital.

Rhetorical performance

Another intellectual seed for the talk-as-action approach has been ethno-methodology's concern for the pursuit of participants' own categories, the use of participants' resources (everyday rhetorical discourse and rules of thumb) as analytical data, the focus of attention on the dramaturgical notion of 'performance' (Garfinkel, 1967) – which combines talk and action as essential elements – and therefore the interest in breaches, slips and other presentational problems. The talk-as-action approach regards 'the situation of action as transformable' wherein meaning is 'discovered, maintained, and altered as a project and product of ordinary actions' (Heritage, 1984: 132). The actions of 'discovered, maintained, and altered' are deliberately chosen by Heritage to indicate that each is involved in the making of a rhetorical performance.

In our case study, the issue of how well the performance was carried out hinged on conflict between two types of discourse – the hospital talked about trust, whereas its partners talked about risk. This was despite the fact that the hospital was putting up a large amount of money itself and was therefore taking a large financial risk. The same events and facts evoked two opposing reactions. The necessary arguments to span the gulf which existed were not provided. The performance (of agreement, of reconciliation of opposing sets of priorities) was not convincingly carried out. Thus, contrary to the hospital's confident expectation, there was no preexisting agreement. Agreement can only come about as the result of negotiation in which bargaining strength is influenced by the persuasiveness of the performances of individual actors.

The case study

The research focused on a major healthcare project at an acute London hospital trust (WLH) within the UK National Health Service (NHS) employing 1,300 people and with an annual turnover in excess of £55 million. Capital funding of £20 million had become available through a combination of land sales and Private Finance Initiative (PFI) monies for WLH to establish an Ambulatory Care and Diagnostic (ACAD) Centre adjacent to the main hospital. Rapid service delivery and clinical process redesign of the kind proposed had yet to win widespread acceptance amongst UK hospital consultants, to the extent that WLH could claim a UK first, following the lead taken by pioneering centres in Australia, Switzerland and the USA (the Mayo Clinic).

The ACAD Centre required thoroughgoing changes to business and medical processes and social structures because of its focus on rapid throughput, automated scheduling and clinical process control. It also required careful interfacing between new systems and existing hospital operations and information systems. Although the new unit had the advantage of a purpose-designed new building, it was to be sited within a much larger hospital complex and would draw upon existing staff. The new information system had to link with referring doctors in the primary care sector, known in the UK as general practitioners (GPs), the main hospital and other NHS care units, and had to solve complex scheduling problems, enabling a radical reduction of the length of patient stay in hospital. The approach not only required restructuring of working practices but also the widespread application of new technologies, including MRI (medical resonance imaging) scanning and minimally invasive surgery.

The consortium

WLH joined together with a software developer, an equipment manufacturer and a facilities management supplier as a consortium to develop the ACAD Centre. A member of the WLH board, the Director of Contracts and Clinical Facilities, served as project manager and chair of the ACAD Steering Committee, which included the chief executive and chairman, top clinical staff, consortium representatives, the architect for the ACAD Centre and the lead external consultant systems analyst of the software requirements team.

Research design

The authors recorded and transcribed 20 meetings, and received minutes of a further 16 meetings between 11 July 1996 and 14 July 1998. The team collected 127 documents (reports, scenarios and minutes), and carried out a number of semi-structured interviews with participants (a total of 16). These meetings included the ACAD Centre Steering Committee, and meetings of its Clinical Sub-Group (which involved clinicians in reengineering working practices), Design Sub-Group (which commissioned the architects to work up detailed plans for the new building), IS Sub-Group (which commissioned a software team to produce a specification of requirements) and Negotiation Sub-Group (led for WLH by its finance director). In what follows, we focus on the Steering Committee and Negotiation Sub-Group and discussions relating to the partnership between WLH and the consortium. It was within the Steering Committee and the Negotiation Sub-Group that the partners most clearly and explicitly staked out their competing rhetorical positions.

Within any setting in which talk is of primary interest, there will be a set of contrasts and alternatives available to participants (de Saussure, 1974; Josephs, 1995). The approach we took was to identify the 'categories and contrasts ... of situated practices' (Edwards, 1997: 70). These were the constructs which seemed to be appearing and reappearing in transcripts of meetings and interviews. The constructs used to relate to consortium partners involved values that were directly relevant to the management of key relationships. These constructs included delay and commitment, which were at various times associated with different ideas depending on what argument the speaker wished to put forward (Heritage, 1984; Potter and Wetherell, 1987: 137).

Delay versus commitment

One of the main problems that WLH and its consortium partners encountered was that of uncertainty regarding the development of information systems for the ACAD Centre. This held back the consortium and WLH from reaching a legally binding agreement for the development of facilities and infrastructure. Several processes were in motion. One was building design, another information system specification, and yet another redesign of clinical processes and working practices along ambulatory (walk-in, walk-out) lines.

After a fanfare at the launch of the consortium, WLH slowed things down because of uncertainties surrounding the information system design, which in turn had a knock-on effect on physical design of the ACAD Centre:

> The building itself will depend upon what kind of activities information systems can do, such as scheduling, links to GPs, imaging storage and retrieval, tele-medicine, electronic medical records, and whether there is [*sic*] paperless information systems. (Systems Analyst, Steering Group meeting, 31 July 1996)

This did not impress consortium members who wanted to contract with WLH as soon as possible in order to justify devoting resources to the project and begin recovering already sunk costs. The facilities management partner was designated a crucial integrative role in the consortium and became the most accountable and exposed to risk, financial and reputational. This stemmed from having responsibility for activities controlled by others:

> [The facilities management partner] is concerned that they would have to manage and operate a building that was not designed by them. They have reservations about taking the risks involved with the design defects which may arise later. (Director of Contracts, Negotiation Group meeting, 16 August 1996)

This led to a delicate negotiation that put commitment at the heart of a rhetorical process.

Commitment as a rhetorical concept

Organisational commitment has considerable effects on behaviour. It reduces the likelihood of defection from an organisation (Randall, 1990) or a consortium. It is associated with high levels of willingness to share and make sacrifices (Randall *et al.*, 1990). However, commitment is a broad concept about which there are many conflicting interpretations (Randall *et al.*, 1974; Reichers, 1985) and requires specific occasions, settings and images for it to be of convincing value. It is therefore good material for rhetoric.

In the case study, several linguistic devices were used to convince audiences about the need for commitment. For example, one device was to engender a sense of urgency:

> But out-patient activity cannot be ignored. So we have to start work on the Main Hospital issues pretty soon. (Director of Contracts, Steering Group meeting, 3 September 1996)

This illustrates how 'continuance commitment' (Meyer and Allen, 1991) was used rhetorically to emphasise urgency and the need to stick to a timetable and speed of progress. In a second, the costs of not keeping to a plan are made more vivid by the use of a town-planning blight metaphor which makes uncertainty about the future more menacing: plans may be damaged if not implemented quickly:

> Now we have a plan. But we need to act on it now. We should not get caught in a planning blight. (Director of Contracts, Information Systems Group meeting, 2 October 1996)

Delay and commitment recognised as opposites

WLH may have wished to delay the project, but its managers privately admitted that delay and commitment stood in opposition to one another. Contracts were viewed favourably as a means of reducing risk, so it was not the principle of contracting that was at issue but rather the question of when to sign one:

> In order to avoid unnecessary risk, all attendees felt that the master contract date should be set for March/April 1997. (Minutes of Timeout Conference, 25 July 1996)

However, various individuals at WLH privately believed that delay was in the hospital's best interest. They had a repertoire of arguments in favour of delay and against commitment. One was that internally generated uncertainty (because of novel and untried information systems) meant that commitment should be delayed:

> There is uncertainty about information systems, which may lead to not signing the commercial agreement contract. (Director of Contracts, Steering Group meeting, 30 July 1996)

A second reason why WLH favoured delay was that delay meant better technology:

> Signing as late as possible would be better as the technology is changing and we could get the latest. In January 1999 [the ACAD Centre] opens and so between March and November 1997 would be a better period to sign up. (Director of Contracts, private meeting with Chairman, 30 July 1996)

A third reason was to enable users to determine information system requirements:

> We should postpone the master contract of the consortium to March/April '97. All services will then have time to decide what systems they want and so will be able to plan. (Hospital General Manager, Steering Group meeting, 30 July 1996)

A fourth reason was signing early to demonstrate commitment might be penalised financially:

> If you sign too early and want to change then they'll want more money. (Chairman, Steering Group meeting, 30 July 1996)

This body of opinion viewed commitment in pejorative terms, for example, through application of the prisoner metaphor:

> Should the contract be legally binding or non-legally binding? If legally binding then the hospital will be locked into the contract. (Director of Contracts, Steering Group meeting, 12 August 1996)

However, it was not only WLH that wanted to avoid commitment. The software supplier also saw advantage in delay:

> [The software supplier] want some money up front. [The supplier's representative] asked after the Negotiation Group Meeting on the 16th of August. I reassured [him] that they will get the contract. [He] seems more like a salesman and doesn't seem to be interested in a 'partnership' approach. [The software supplier] may not sign a contract until the information system uncertainties are sorted out. It might take at least 12 months. The request for payment came after the [software supplier] person came from the USA and felt unhappy about the information system uncertainties. (Director of Contracts, Steering Group meeting, 19 August 1996)

The other consortium partners had a different view. For them, any delay in signing the final contract or coming to a final and legally binding contract was perceived as a lack of commitment to the consortium on the part of WLH. They were not entirely convinced of the hospital's intentions. For instance, the facilities management supplier, as lead consortium partner, insisted on a so-called 'letter of comfort':

> [The company's] culture makes it difficult for me to convince my company that [WLH] is committed firmly to the deal and to the consortium. A 'letter of comfort' with the Finance Director's signature on it should do the trick. (Facilities Management Consortium Representative, Steering Group meeting, 16 August 1996)

Delay and commitment rhetorically presented as complements

WLH wanted delay but knew that the consortium wanted commitment. Its way of working around this problem was rhetorically to present the two values of delay and commitment as complementary and mutually reinforcing. It offered to progress an outline agreement, so-called Heads of Terms (HoT), while speeding up the erection of the new ACAD Centre building as a tangible sign of commitment to the project. In reaching HoT, the consortium's need for tangible evidence of commitment should be met:

> [The WLH Chairman] recognised the Consortium's need for a firm and timely partnership agreement and it was agreed that binding 'Heads of Terms' would be completed by December 1996 at the latest. (Minutes of Timeout Conference, 25 July 1996)

At the same time, it would be hard to be accused of delaying matters when work on the actual ACAD Centre building was moving on apace.

> Just 3 million out of the £18 million goes to the consortium. So let's concentrate on the building and engineering of [the ACAD Centre] and give the consortium a simple reassurance of their involvement. (Director of Contracts, Steering Group meeting, 30 July 1996)

Another way of simultaneously playing for delay and commitment was to pay for commitment in incremental portions, avoiding any need for trust:

> These options are going to be difficult as now [as consortium members] want to be paid upfront for putting in any further resources. (Director of Contracts, Information Systems Group meeting, 2 October 1996)

This may have been what the consortium wanted, but WLH did not want to play the consortium's game.

Legal and collaborative commitment rhetorically presented as opposites

Appropriation concerns are important in inter-organisational networks (Gulati and Singh, 1998). In this sense, WLH saw commitment in terms of shared aims, the consortium members working together as co-innovators in delivering a novel scheme. Knowledge of how the ACAD Centre worked was seen to represent valuable collective intellectual property, which might be exploited to the full sometime down the line.

The opportunity for shared learning justified a careful and creative approach to all elements of the information systems and clinical process designs, which in turn demanded a long-term and collaborative view of commitment. This collaborative definition of commitment contrasted starkly with the consortium's legalistic contractual view:

> There's tremendous intellectual value for [the consortium] from this project. But they're being front-ended by 'salesmen', led by people who just want all the answers now. [WLH] must think through all the logistics. Solutions will take time. [The consortium] representatives cannot just keep on selling. We are prepared to educate them. (Director of Contracts, Facilities Management Group meeting, 2 September 1996)

Collaborative commitment to shared design work was viewed as reducing risk:

> By being involved with the designers, [the facilities management partner] can be certain that the building will be designed well and that they can then manage it well. (Director of Finance, Negotiation Group meeting, 16 August 1996)

However, this view of commitment was antithetical to a legal, contract-based view of commitment:

> [WLH] feels that the agreements at this stage cannot be made legally binding as it would cause damage to both parties. (Director of Finance, Negotiation Group meeting, 16 August 1996)

The suppliers took the same view about the opposition between legal and collaborative commitment. What differed was that they emphatically wanted legal commitment. Collaborative commitment put them in the position where they depended on parties over whom they had no control, such as the systems analyst developing the information systems requirements document:

> [The facilities management partner] is concerned that [the systems analyst] should get full support from [WLH] as its people have to decide on procedures and this will have implications for how the system performs. (Facilities Management Consortium Representative, Negotiation Group meeting, 16 August 1996)

Even the systems analyst, so supportive of WLH's position in other ways, feared that a lack of contractual clarity would increase the risk of non-delivery:

> Where we have no clarity, we should leave it out of the IT contract. This is because [the software supplier] will get paid for it, but they will not deliver! We know they cannot deliver when there is no clarity. (Systems Analyst, Information Systems Group, 2 October 1996)

A typical argument

The following argument between WLH and the consortium during a Negotiation Group meeting on 27 September 1996 illustrates the differences in perception that existed between the two groups:

> Consortium representative: 'The Heads of Terms agreement is transferring the risk of building design to the Consortium.'

> Director of Finance: 'We are not. But we are all agreed that the building design will affect the way you work. So you are involved in the building design. The HoT in fact only provides an extra channel for you to use, i.e. apart from approaching us, you can approach the builders to express disapproval if you are not entirely happy with the design.'

> Consortium representative: 'But we don't want to do this. If the performance of any equipment is hampered by building design error, we only want to come to you. We do not want to be responsible for this and we do not want to go to the architects.'

> Director of Finance: 'If you are not interested in this, then how different is this deal from a normal tender? [WLH] could actually tender facilities management, equipment and information systems in the normal way. Why are we here then? Why are we negotiating with one consortium – one party? The idea of the deal was that you will share the risk involved.'

> Consortium representative: 'We cannot take any responsibility for building design. This is a significant shift in the deal since April 1996.'

> Equipment supplier representative: 'Our understanding was that [WLH] will come to us with what you need – requirements. And we will provide these.'

> Director of Contracts: 'We thought that we were getting the intellectual input from a world class organisation.'

The disagreement was fundamental and led the WLH to decide:

> Careful analysis of the Consortium submission indicates that ... there is insufficient risk transfer from the [WLH] to the consortium; and there is little evidence of partnership and understanding which will be of prime importance in any on-going relationship over a 5 year period and, potentially, beyond ... the Steering Group is asked to make the following recommendations to the [WLH] Board: that the consortium's final proposal does not satisfy either the hospital's requirements for service and value or PFI requirements for risk transfer; that, accordingly, there is no merit in further negotiations with the consortium; that [WLH] go back to the market and seek a new PFI partnership. (Director of Contracts, Steering Group meeting, 5 August 1997)

Trust as a rhetorical construct

Commitment was therefore viewed in several divergent ways: it was seen in decision terms as the opposite of delay; it was seen as a divisible entity, to be bought in instalments;

it was seen in symbolic terms, to be created by means of reassurance; and it was also seen in psychological terms as the effect of persuasion. Because of these divergent views of commitment, it was important that the parties should trust each other. Indeed, the size of the risks seemed to be a justification for the value of trusting each other. Trust was given the mantle of a saviour in difficult circumstances. What follows is the argument that the greater the risk, the more that trust is needed:

> The issue is trust and the management of risks. There are risks for both sides. But with trust the parties can sort it out. (Chairman, Negotiation Group meeting, 16 August 1996)

The significance of this as rhetoric for a public audience is shown by considering the private scepticism sometimes demonstrated, such as anticipation of the effects of withdrawal of parties from the consortium:

> We don't know the reaction of [WLH] if [the Software Supplier] drops out … [the Systems Analysis Consultant] needs to prepare for risk management by changing the information systems plan which will be tendered out to several solution providers if [the software supplier] jumps off. The plan as of now is not strong enough to meet a tender. (Director of Contracts, Information Systems Group meeting, 2 October 1996)

Company culture used as a rhetorical weapon

Even the fact of being in a company whose culture did not value trust was used as a rhetorical weapon. For example, the facilities management supplier representative argued that it needed full-scale legal commitment because it had no past history as a company of entering into the kind of collaborative arrangements WLH favoured. A past history of suspicion was by sleight of hand transformed from being a problem into being a negotiating strength:

> The company's culture makes it difficult to convince them that [WLH] is firmly committed to the deal and to the consortium. (Facilities Management Supplier Representative, Negotiation Group meeting, 16 August 1996)

Cooption used as a rhetorical weapon

The hospital's rather self-centred view was that it could use cooption, and that it could absorb outsiders into its own concerns without having to commit itself to a formal and binding agreement. Here is the 'success story' of the 'outsider transformed into insider'. The implication is that all consortium partners should allow themselves to become similarly coopted:

> [The systems analyst] works as though he is a '[WLH] director' in charge of IT. That way he gets support from everyone. His voice is the hospital's voice and he understands [WLH] and

NHS [National Health Service] management. (Director of Contracts, Negotiation Group meeting, 16 August 1996)

Rhetorical performance

The following conversation expresses the two opposed discourses – the hospital's discourse of trust and the consortium's discourse of risk. The consortium asked for a 'letter of comfort' which the hospital provided. The WLH chairman sent a letter to the software supplier who wanted to be compensated for the time devoted to the hospital. To the consortium's chagrin, however, this was not possible because WLH wanted all payments to be made for deliverables. The consortium thought that the Heads of Terms placed too much responsibility (coded as 'too much time') on it without any payment:

> Our company feels that the Heads of Terms ought to be 'Heads' of terms and not details. We're spending far too much time negotiating these HoTs rather than having a simple memo of understanding and negotiating the contract itself. (Software Company Consortium Representative, Negotiations Group meeting, 27 September 1996)

To this WLH replied that the details were informatively ('clarity'), not punitively, intended:

> The details are simply to provide clarity to the consortium. Who's going to be responsible for what etc. (Director of Finance, Negotiations Group meeting, 27 September 1996)

A document full of assignments of responsibilities affected the consortium the most because it was the most vulnerable to risks created by its constituent partners being dependent on each other without being able to control each other's work:

> HoTs are not what we expected. It slows a normal 'design and build', which is not what we're here for. We simply need a strategic level document. If HoTs are to be legally binding, then let's sign it but we need more flesh around all the clauses. We need to know exactly what we're in for. We feel that the HoT is transferring the risk off the Building Design Group to us. (Facilities Management Consortium Representative, Negotiations Group meeting, 27 September 1996)

WLH wanted the consortium to negotiate solutions bilaterally with individual partners. This was strongly rejected by the consortium. The disagreement underlined the impossibility of writing a contract to legislate for a situation in which the partners do not trust each other to share risks. Even more dysfunctional was the software supplier's unidirectional 'user states requirements to supplier' model. Again WLH referred to its vision of shared risk by means of collaborative learning and by jointly appropriated discoveries. The answer was combative in a disputatious and negative way:

> We're a strong consortium! And we are in fact going to see another hospital! Can we have some interim consultancy payments – because we are working entirely on speculation? (Software Company Consortium Representative, Negotiations Group meeting, 27 September 1996)

Discussion

The type of institutional relationship influences the need for rhetoric

The need for rhetoric as a means of resolving conflict between discourses depends upon the type of relationship between the parties. There are at least three types of relationship which are relevant here:

1. When the relationship is unbreakable and when there is no room for a smoke-screen (the content is important), as in a courtroom – there must be some legal result which affects both parties – then the result must take account of both of the opposed discourses, either by (a) not accepting one party's account (for example, a guilty verdict) or (b) rhetorically resolving both as a series of puzzles and solutions (for example, contradictory evidence: Pollner, 1974) or (c) attempting rhetorically to make incompatible entities seem compatible (this was attempted unsuccessfully by WLH with delay and commitment in our case study) or (d) telling different stories to different parties (the way in which project organisations sometimes deal with their sponsors and supporters – Brown, 1995; Sillince and Mouakket, 1998 – using withholding, slanting and emphasising of selected information – March and Simon, 1958; Tversky and Kahneman, 1974).
2. When the relationship is unbreakable but the content is relatively unimportant, as in a diplomatic agreement where the fact that there is any agreement is seen as a victory, then an unspecific language can be used to avoid any commitment.
3. If the relationship can be broken and the content is important, as in the present case involving the dissolution of the consortium, there is no need to resolve the differences between opposed discourses.

In this sense, the type of institutional relationship determines the need for using rhetoric. This suggests that organisations (in which individual members have little freedom to go elsewhere) will be rich in rhetoric, whereas in markets and networks, where institutional ties are weaker, there will be less rhetoric.

Talk constructs reality

One of the interesting aspects of the process of socially constructing knowledge was how situations were made to seem unchangeable on the one hand, and the subject of negotiation and therefore changeable on the other, depending on the participant's point of view.

Establishing permanence was pursued in several ways. Here is an example of someone attempting to fix a problem firmly in place, providing a framework (accountability to a named individual) and hence making the situation (the problem of risk) appear acceptable and unproblematic:

> Let's look at the risks. There is the cost of the building overrun, and the risk of the consortium. They are both accountable to [facilities management supplier representative]. (Director of Contracts, Steering Group meeting, 30 July 1996)

This symbolic problem-solving role is also played by quasi-legal (contracts, agreements) or management processes (deadlines, sign-offs):

> A legally binding Heads of Terms agreement by December will sort things out. (Director of Contracts, Negotiation Group meeting, 16 August 1996)

On the other hand, this semblance of calm can be quickly punctured by talk which heightens tension and pinpoints disagreement. This can be achieved by stereotyping and demonising ('they're being front-ended by salesmen') or by strong criticism of competences ('they will not deliver!'), or by emphasising the lack of trust ('we are working entirely on speculation').

Talk performs as well as informs

Warnings and promises do not merely give information to the listener. They also change the situation fundamentally. Warnings strengthen an argument ('outpatients' activity cannot be ignored. So we have to start ... pretty soon'), but they also raise suspicion ('we know they cannot deliver when there is no clarity'). Warnings therefore are a double-edged sword – they inform of impending disaster but also perform an action by ratcheting up the level of suspicion and thus destroying trust ('we're a strong consortium! And we are in fact going to see another hospital!').

Talk as 'structurational' action

WLH rhetorically presented the notion of delay and commitment as complementary concepts (both reinforced the value of the notion of collaboration) and this constrained the way it dealt with its partners in a number of ways. First, this rhetoric failed to reassure the hospital's partners. Accountability for risks was defined by the hospital as accountability of an individual ('Let's look at the risks. They are accountable to...'). But this did not reassure the consortium partners, who were concerned about financial risk at the level of their companies. Second, the reason for delay was internal to WLH (difficulties of sorting out what each speciality wanted) and so had little relevance to the hospital's partners. Third, because WLH believed delay to be beneficial – leading to a better final result – it developed a patronising attitude towards its partners ('we are prepared to educate them'). Because the hospital believed that delay was beneficial, structures were put in place which reinforced that belief and which constrained events. For example, meetings became less frequent, and fewer consortium representatives turned up to them.

The two opposed groups, WLH and the consortium partners, constructed two opposed sets of means–end rules and these acted as a structural constraint, mirroring the rhetorical strategies at play internally within WLH (Mueller *et al.*, 2004). In order to ensure the end of accountability, WLH emphasised the means of individual responsibility and probity, whereas the consortium partners emphasised the risk to each company of financial loss. In order to ensure the end of responsibility to common consortium goals, WLH emphasised the means of sharing (advice, the potential of intellectual capital, risk) whereas the consortium partners emphasised the means of dividing up and modularising responsibilities. To ensure commitment, WLH (the customer) emphasised late deadlines, whereas the consortium partners (the suppliers) emphasised early deadlines. In order to maintain the relationship between the parties, the means advocated by each side were different – long-term versus short-term, non-legally binding versus legally binding, payment for deliverables versus payment up-front, and cooption versus arm's-length. It is important to emphasise that these means–end rules arose naturally out of the conflicting rhetorical positions, and that both sides became locked into their respective positions and were thus constrained by them.

Talk-as-cognition

The way people talk works to constrain the way they think. On the one hand the hospital's view was that the new building design depended on the new information system and this in turn depended on other issues such as scheduling. The chains of dependencies were complex and long and sometimes circular or irresolvable in a short time ('the building itself will depend upon what kind of activities information systems can do … and whether there are paperless information systems'). Inevitably, this kind of talk by WLH created an expectation of patient, slow analysis and development and of giving connectivity its proper weight. The opposite view (that of the consortium) was that connectivity was bad: one of the partners was 'concerned that they would have to manage and operate a building that was not designed by them'.

Rhetorical performance

The crucial reason why the consortium failed, in our view, was that the performance of a unifying rhetoric was not convincing enough. The rhetoric had a number of aspects. The consortium's need for commitment had to be publicly recognised – the fact that the hospital chairman 'recognised the consortium's need for a firm and timely partnership agreement' was indeed specially recorded. There was the attempt by WLH to rhetorically present commitment and delay as complementary (rather than opposed) and as joint preconditions of collaboration, and as financially worthwhile ('there's tremendous intellectual value for the consortium from this project') and to suggest that long-term collaboration is a mark of 'world class' partners. There was the use of a number of linguistic and para-legal devices (letter of comfort, Heads of Terms) with which WLH hoped to satisfy its partners' need for commitment. And there was the support for the symbolic effect of the building work aimed at demonstrating tangible progress ('let's concentrate on the building and engineering ... and give the consortium a reassurance of their involvement').

This performance, though competent, was not sufficiently convincing. There were a number of explanations offered by participants for this failure. For example, one consortium representative said his company's 'culture makes it difficult for me to convince my company that [the hospital] is committed firmly to the deal'. WLH itself individualised the problem as being that its partners were being 'led by people who want all the answers now'.

Implications

It is important to note that the two rhetorical positions were not incommensurate (that is, unrelated and thus containing irresolvable contradictions), because even though they did talk past each other and failed adequately to connect with each other, risk and trust are closely related in inter-organisational networks (Nooteboom *et al.*, 1997; Holm *et al.*, 1999).

Our analysis of the rhetorical positions taken up has relevance for the management of negotiation processes, which have often been treated as a 'black box' by emphasising antecedents and consequences rather than analysing the processes themselves (Pruitt and Kimmel, 1977; Brett *et al.*, 1999). According to Brett (1991), in multiparty negotiations it is important, first, to understand the costs involved in cases where no agreement is reached between the parties. This constitutes the 'information stage' in the negotiation (Mollering, 1997). What will happen in the event of non-agreement? Are the costs of non-agreement the same for all parties? Rhetoric is used to magnify the costs to the other parties of withdrawal but may also result in self-deception (for example, Taylor and Brown, 1988; Tyler and Hastie, 1991). Such perceptual biases – as Lewicki *et al.* (1994) call them – can lead to parties viewing their agreement and non-agreement options inaccurately, overblown rhetoric often leading to an exaggerated sense of power over the negotiations.

According to the negotiation literature (Lewicki *et al.*, 1994: 281–8), the next important step would be to understand how other members of the group understand the decision rule, that is, how are they are going to decide the final outcome. This is where we find problems with the negotiation approach to conflict resolution. As the WLH case shows, the final outcome was not a one-off decision that came suddenly, but was incremental and came in stages through a variety of conversations, that is, through talk.

The next step in complex multiparty negotiations would be to strive for cascading levels of agreement, and building trust in 'small steps' (Smitka, 1994), beginning with what Lewicki *et al.* (1994) term 'a first agreement'. In the case study, the Heads of Terms clearly can be seen as representing such a first step. However, we find again that the conflict resolution literature cannot deal with unexpected changes or perceptions on the part of actors. For instance, although HoT was represented as a first step towards the final contract, and as a sign of commitment, it did not eventually satisfy the consortium partners. What was initially welcomed did not continue to hold the same significance for the partners as negotiations proceeded. Clearly, as they talked about it, the meanings and significance attached to HoT underwent dramatic changes. Thus, what was essentially a first agreement did not succeed in leading on to a second or third agreement; it did not result in cascading levels of agreement because the significance that the consortium partners attached to such an agreement changed as talk occurred. For all practical purposes then, after the initial enthusiasm, the first agreement, as proposed by the conflict resolution model, did not exist, or at best was of minimal significance.

Some other analytical constructs are therefore needed to understand the process. Our main analytical construct has been that of two opposing rhetorical positions, one of trust held by WLH, and one of risk held by the consortium. These two rhetorical positions were resolved by one voice, the consortium's, being silenced by its collapse. The case demonstrates that talk is not 'just' talk, but that it is also action: by the end of the study period, the hospital's collaborative view of commitment (rather than the legal view of commitment espoused by consortium partners) had become the dominant position.

The conflict between rhetorical positions is therefore a manifestation of a power struggle (zero-sum contest), and a resolution (silencing one rhetoric) indicates winning (deciding the power inequality). Luhman (1979) and Hardy *et al.* (2000) have shown the connection between trust and power. This interpretation gives further meaning to the two rhetorical positions investigated here, for surely the trust position is a 'façade rhetoric' (Hardy *et al.*, 2000) of the powerful leader ('trust me, I can do things for you'), whereas the risk position is the rhetoric of the weak follower ('help me, I am afraid'). Coherent rhetorical positions therefore not only contain persuasive elements (appeal for support, establishing plausibility) but also signal negotiating strength. It is significant that a partner's low negotiating strength may not count against them if they are viewed as indispensable, and if their weakness is consistent with what they are arguing.

References

Argyris, C. (1993) *Knowledge for Action*. San Francisco, CA: Jossey-Bass.

Argyris, C. and Schon, D.A. (1978) *Organizational Learning: A Theory of Action Perspective*. Reading, MA: Addison-Wesley.

Austin, J.L. (1962) *How to Do Things with Words*. Oxford: Clarendon.

Backmann, R. (2000) 'Conclusion: Trust, Conceptual Aspects of a Complex Phenomenon', in C. Lane and R. Backmann (eds), *Trust Within and Between Organizations*. Oxford: Oxford University Press, 299–322.

Berger, P. and Luckmann, T.L. (1966) *The Social Construction of Knowledge: A Treatise on the Sociology of Knowledge*. Garden City, NY: Doubleday.

Brett, J. (1991) 'Negotiating Group Decisions', *Negotiation Journal*, 7: 291–310.

Brett, J., Northcraft, G.B. and Prinkley, R.L. (1999) 'Stairways to Heaven: An Interlocking Self-Regulation Model of Negotiation', *Academy of Management Review*, 24(3): 435–51.

Brown, A.D. (1995) 'Managing Understandings: Politics, Symbolism, Niche Marketing and the Quest for Legitimacy in IT Implementation', *Organization Studies*, 16(6): 951–69.

Currie, W. (1994) 'The Strategic Management of a Large Scale IT Project in the Financial Services Sector', *New Technology, Work and Employment*, 9(1): 19–29.

de Saussure, F. (1974) *Course in General Linguistics*. London: Fontana.

Douglas, M. (1973) *Natural Symbols*. London: Pantheon Books.

Dutton, W.H. (1981) 'The Rejection of an Innovation: The Political Environment of a Computer-Based Model', *Systems, Objectives, Solutions*, 1(4): 179–201.

Dutton, W.H. and Kraemer, K.L. (1985) *Modelling as Negotiating: The Political Dynamics of Computer Models in the Policy Process*. Norwood, NJ: Ablex.

Edwards, D. (1997) *Discourse and Cognition*. London: Sage.

Garfinkel, H. (1967) *Studies in Ethnomethodology*. Englewood Cliffs, NJ: Prentice-Hall.

Giddens, A. (1984) *The Constitution of Society*. Berkeley, CA: University of California Press.

Grant, D., Keenoy, T. and Oswick, C. (eds) (1998) *Discourse and Organization*. London: Sage.

Gulati, A. and Singh, T. (1998) 'The Architecture of Cooperation: Managing Coordination Costs and Appropriation Concerns in Strategic Alliances', *Administrative Science Quarterly*, 43: 781–814.

Hardy, C., Phillips, N. and Lawrence, T. (2000) 'Distinguishing Trust and Power in Inter-organizational Relations: Forms and Facades of Trust', in C. Lane and R. Backmann (eds), *Trust Within and Between Organizations*. Oxford: Oxford University Press.

Heritage, J.C. (1984) *Garfinkel and Ethnomethodology*. Cambridge: Polity Press.

Holm, D.B., Eriksson, K. and Johanson, J. (1999) 'Creating Value Through Mutual Commitment to Business Network Relationships', *Strategic Management Journal*, 20: 467–86.

Inkpen, A.C. and Beamish, P.W. (1997) 'Knowledge, Bargaining Power and the Instability of International Joint Ventures', *Academy of Management Review*, 22(1): 177–202.

Johnson, G. (1990) 'Managing Strategic Change: The Role of Symbolic Action', *British Journal of Management*, 1: 183–200.

Jones, C., Hesterly, W.S. and Borgatti, S.P. (1997) 'A General Theory of Network Governance: Exchange Conditions and Social Mechanisms', *Academy of Management Review*, 22(4): 911–45.

Josephs, I.E. (1995) 'The Problem of Emotions from the Perspective of Psychological Semantics', *Culture and Psychology*, 1(2): 279–88.

Kanter, R.M. (1991) 'The New Managerial Work', in J.J. Gabarro (ed.), *Managing People and Organizations*. Boston, MA: Harvard Business School Press, 57–69.

Keil, M., Truex, D.P. and Mixon, R. (1995) 'The Effects of Sunk Cost and Project Completion on Information Technology Project Escalation', *IEEE Transactions on Engineering Management*, 42(4): 372–81.

Lawler, E.J. and Yoon, J. (1995) 'Structural Power and Emotional Process in Negotiation: A Social Exchange Approach', in R. Kramer and D. Messick (eds), *Negotiation and Social Processes*. Thousand Oaks, CA: Sage, 143–65.

Lei, D. and Slocum, J.W. (1991) 'Global Strategic Alliances: Payoffs and Pitfalls', *Organization Dynamics*, 19(3): 44–62.

Lewicki, R.J., Litterer, J.A., Minton, J.W. and Saunders, D.M. (1994) *Negotiation*. Burr Ridge, IL: Irwin.

Liebeskind, J.P. and Oliver, A.L. (2000) 'From Handshake to Contract: Intellectual Property, Trust, and the Social Structure of Academic Research', in C. Lane and R. Backmann (eds), *Trust Within and Between Organizations*. Oxford: Oxford University Press, 118–45.

Loewenstein, G.F., Thompson, L. and Bazerman, M.H. (1989) 'Social Utility and Decision Making in Interpersonal Context', *Journal of Personality and Social Psychology*, 57: 426–41.

Luhman, N. (1979) *Trust and Power*. Chichester: Wiley.

March, J.G. and Simon, H.A. (1958) *Organizations*. New York: Wiley.

Merleau-Ponty, M. (1962) *Phenomenology of Perception*. London: Routledge & Kegan Paul.

Meyer, J.P. and Allen, N.J. (1991) 'A Three-Component Conceptualisation of Organizational Commitment', *Human Resource Management Review*, 1: 61–89.

Mollering, G. (1997) *The Influence of Cultural Differences on the Establishment of Trust Between Partners in Inter-organizational Cooperation*. Working paper, Judge Institute of Management Studies, University of Cambridge.

Mueller, F., Sillince, J., Harvey, C. and Howorth, C. (2004) 'A Rounded Picture is What We Need: Rhetorical Strategies, Arguments and the Negotiation of Change in a UK Hospital Trust', *Organization Studies*, 25: 75–94.

Nooteboom, B., Berger, H. and Noorderhaven, N.G. (1997) 'Effects of Trust and Governance on Relational Risk', *Academy of Management Journal*, 40(2): 308–38.

Osborn, R.N. and Hagerdoorn, J. (1997) 'The Institutionalization and Evolutionary Dynamics of Inter-organizational Alliance and Networks', *Academy of Management Journal*, 40(2): 261–78.

Pollner, M. (1974) 'Mundane Reasoning', *Philosophy of the Social Sciences*, 4: 35–54.

Potter, J. and Wetherell, M. (1987) *Discourse and Social Psychology: Beyond Attitudes and Behaviour*. London: Sage.

Pruitt, D.G. and Kimmel, M.J. (1977) 'Twenty Years of Experimental Gaming: Synthesis and Suggestions for the Future', *Annual Review of Psychology*, 28: 363–92.

Randall, D.M. (1990) 'The Consequences of Organizational Commitment. Methodological Investigation', *Journal of Organizational Behavior*, 11: 361–78.

Randall, D.M., Fedor, D.B. and Longenecker, C.O. (1990) 'The Behavioral Expression of Organizational Commitment', *Journal of Vocational Behavior*, 36: 210–24.

Reichers, A.E. (1985) 'A Review and Reconceptualisation of Organizational Commitment', *Academy of Management Review*, 10(3) 465–76.

Ring, P.S. and van de Ven, A.H. (1994) 'Developmental Processes of Cooperative Inter-organizational Relationships', *Academy of Management Review*, 19(1): 90–118.

Sauer, C. (1993) *Why Information Systems Fail: A Case Study Approach*. Henley-On-Thames: Alfred Waller.

Schon, D.A. (1983) *How Professionals Think in Action*. New York: Basic Books.

Schutz, A. (1967) *Collected Papers*. Den Haag: Nijhoff.

Searle, J.R. (1969) *Speech Acts: An Essay in the Philosophy of Language*. London: Cambridge University Press.

Senge, P.M. (1990) *The Fifth Discipline: The Art and Practice of the Learning Organization*. New York: Doubleday.

Sillince, J.A.A. and Mouakket, S. (1997) 'Varieties of Political Process During Systems Development', *Information Systems Research*, 8(3): 1–30.

Sillince, J.A.A. and Mouakket, S. (1998) 'Divisive and Integrative Political Strategies in the IS Adaptation Process: The MAC Initiative', *European Journal of Information Systems*, 7: 46–60.

Smith, K.G., Carroll, S.J. and Ashford, S.J. (1995) 'Intra and Inter-organizational Cooperation: Toward a Research Agenda', *Academy of Management Journal*, 38(1): 7–23.

Smitka, M.J. (1994) 'Contracting without Contracts', in S.B. Sitkin, B. Sim and R.J. Bres (eds), *The Legalistic Organization*. London: Sage, 91–108.

Starbuck, W.H. (1985) 'Acting First and Thinking Later', in J.M. Pennings (ed.), *Organizational Strategy and Change*. San Francisco, CA: Jossey-Bass.

Sydow, J. (1996) 'Inter-organizational Relations', in M. Warner (ed.), *International Encyclopaedia of Business and Management*, Vol. 3. London: Thompson, 2360–73.

Sydow, J. and Windeler, A. (1996) 'Managing Inter-firm Networks: A Structurationalist Perspective', in C.G.A. Bryant and D. Jary (eds), *Anthony Giddens – Critical Assessments*, Vol. 4. London: Routledge, 455–95.

Sydow, J., van Well, B. and Windeler, A. (1998) 'Networked Networks: Financial Service Networks in the Context of Their Industry', *International Studies of Management and Organization*, 28: 43–65.

Taylor, S.E. and Brown, J.D. (1988) 'Illusion and Well-being: A Social–Psychological Perspective on Mental Health', *Psychological Bulletin*, 103: 193–210.

Thompson, L. (1990) 'Negotiation Behavior and Outcome: Empirical Evidence and Theoretical Issues', *Psychological Bulletin*, 108: 515–32.

Tversky, A. and Kahneman, D. (1974) 'Judgement under Uncertainty: Heuristics and Biases', *Science*, 185: 1124–31.

Tyler, T. and Hastie, R. (1991) 'The Social Consequences of Cognitive Illusions', in M. Bazerman, R. Lewicky and B.H. Sheppard (eds), *Research on Negotiation in Organisations*, Vol. 3. Greenwich, CT: JAI Press, 69–98.

Wallmacq, A. and Sims, D. (1998) 'The Struggle with Sense', in D. Grant, T. Keenoy and C. Oswick (eds), *Discourse and Organization*. London: Sage.

Watson, T.J. (1995) 'Rhetoric, Discourse and Argument in Organizational Sense Making: A Reflexive Tale', *Organization Studies*, 16(5): 805–21.

Weber, M. (1947) *The Theory of Social and Economic Organization*, (eds and trans. A.H. Henderson and T. Parsons). Glencoe, IL: Free Press.

Weick, K.E. (1995) *Sensemaking in Organizations*. London: Sage.

Weingart, L.R., Hyder, E.B. and Prietula, M.J. (1996) 'Knowledge Matters: The Effect of Tactical Descriptions on Negotiator Behavior and Outcomes', *Journal of Personality and Social Psychology*, 70: 1205–17.

Weingart, L.R., Thompson, L.L., Bazerman, M.H. and Carroll, J.F. (1990) 'Tactical Behavior and Negotiation Outcome', *International Journal of Conflict Management*, 1: 7–31.

Whitley, R., Henderson, J., Czaban, L. and Lengyel, G. (1996) 'Trust and Contractual Relations in an Emerging Capitalist Economy: The Changing Trading Relations of Ten Large Hungarian Enterprises', *Organization Studies*, 17(3): 397–420.

Wieder, D.L. (1974) 'Telling the Code', in R. Turner (ed.), *Ethnomethodology*. Harmondsworth: Penguin.

16

Sense-making as a process within complex projects*

Chris Ivory, Neil Alderman, Ian McLoughlin and Roger Vaughan

Introduction

Conventionally, the project management literature has been dominated by rationalistic and prescriptive assumptions representing the problem of project management in terms of the need to effectively plan, communicate and evaluate to ensure the achievement of predicted outcomes – in short, a focus on efficient and effective project *organisation*. As such, project management theory, and the associated tools and techniques prescribed to ensure its realisation in practice, have been based upon classic twentieth-century principles of management control – principles which have elsewhere been progressively abandoned in large swathes of management theory, if not practice, as we have moved into the twenty-first century.

In contrast, sense-making is a well-established perspective in strategic management and organisation studies, but to date has had little impact on the analysis of project management theory and practice (Thomas, 2000). In general this approach is less concerned with the identification of specific forms of organisation to suit particular circumstances or tasks and more with the process of *organising* itself: that is, the means by which organisation is continually enacted and accomplished (Weick, 1979).

* The project was funded by the joint research council Innovative Manufacturing Initiative Learning Across Business Sectors programme, through UK Economic and Social Research Council grant no. L700257003. We are particularly grateful for the support of Clarke Chapman Ltd, Northumbrian Water Ltd and ALSTOM Transport Ltd and the time and contributions of their staff to the project. The views expressed in this chapter are the responsibility of the Newcastle University research team and are not necessarily endorsed by the collaborating companies. We would also like to thank Richard Badham, Ross Wotherspoon and Camilla Niss for their comments on earlier versions of this chapter. Earlier versions of this chapter were presented at the 'Making Projects Critical' workshop in Bristol, April 2003, and the IRNOP VI Conference, Finland, August 2004, and the helpful comments of reviewers and participants of these meetings are also acknowledged. The chapter is a much extended version of an earlier paper published in the *International Journal of Project Management* (2005), 23(5): 380–5.

In this chapter we draw on the sense-making perspective and additional concepts to explore the possibility of an alternative explanation of the twists and turns of project experience in the context of a specific project. The illustrative example draws on a study of the Pendolino high-speed tilting train (dubbed by some in the industry the Pendolino Britannico), developed by ALSTOM Transport for the West Coast Main Line franchise operated by Virgin Trains. An analysis of this project suggests that insights from the sense-making literature provide a way of understanding some of the activities and decisions that were observed during the project and the way in which the different perspectives of the various actors and stakeholders in the project were interpreted and reconciled.

Coping with complexity in projects

Traditional project management

The traditional view of project management is a rationalistic perspective that views it as a process of planning, monitoring, controlling and coordinating the activities and resources that are needed to achieve the goals of a project. Project management is seen as 'a method for solving complex organizational problems' (Söderlund, 2004: 183) and represents a form of organisation for dealing with projects, usually defined in terms of uniqueness and time-limitedness, and within clearly defined parameters of cost and quality (for example, Buchanan and Boddy, 1992: 8). This project management process is one based on a prescribed set of tools and techniques as encapsulated within the Project Management Body of Knowledge (PMI, 2000) and a plethora of project management textbooks (for example, Turner, 1993; Meredith and Mantel, 1995; Maylor, 1999).

For straightforward projects this toolkit is undoubtedly helpful, indeed may well be sufficient. However, it is clear that a conventional rationalistic framework for project management does not equip the project manager to cope with projects displaying additional complexity in terms of technologies or organisational networks and increased levels of uncertainty, as the high level of failure reported in the literature (for example, Morris, 1994) and in the press (recent high-profile examples being the Millennium Dome or the Scottish Parliament Building and the Beagle 2 expedition to Mars) testifies. One problem with the traditional project management approach is that it is predicated on 'the nostrum of "On time, on budget and to specification", [which] is perhaps not able to encapsulate the complexity that is modern project management' (Whittaker, 2000: 135). Whittaker suggests that as projects develop to involve more than just manual activities or the creation of physical artefacts, adherence to the triad of time, cost and quality does not always equate with ultimate project success. Fundamentally, the basic assumptions underpinning the traditional approach can be seen to be flawed in the face of growing complexity.

'Complex' projects have been defined by Williams (2002: 58–9) in terms of the dimensions of structural complexity and uncertainty. Structural complexity is derived from the interaction between the number of elements which make up the project and the interdependence of these elements. Uncertainty is derived from the lack of clarity and agreement concerning project goals and the means to achieve goals. The result is that project elements interact in complex and unpredictable ways and undermine attempts to manage them using a rationalistic project management framework.

Service-led projects

In this chapter we are concerned with what we suggest represents an emerging form of complex project. These are what we term 'service-led' projects (Alderman *et al.*, 2002) where the whole rationale for the project, the demands for innovation, the supporting infrastructure and the long-term service component are driven by the client's business strategy and objectives for a new or enhanced service to its own customers. Project-based product/service delivery of this form represents a new source of potential competitiveness and there is evidence that this is leading to a variety of organisations reorientating their business to focus on the design and delivery of 'integrated solutions' (Maylor, 1999: 17; Davies *et al.*, 2001). Moreover, the significant revenue streams increasingly occur in the service component or the operations phase, rather than in the manufacturing or capital good delivery phase. This implies an extension to the normal conception of the project life cycle. Such projects are nowadays typical of industries such as power generation, railway rolling stock and offshore oil and gas exploitation, and also form a fundamental part of, for instance, the UK government's Private Finance Initiative, extending to facilities such as hospitals and highways.

Service-led projects introduce a new realm of project complexity as the number of stakeholders in the project increases considerably as a range of different actors, agencies and institutions have to be enrolled in the project in order to deliver the complete service-enhanced package for the client over time. Project management becomes a task not only of managing the project team within the contracting organisation, but also of managing wider intra- and inter-organisational teams, supply chains and other relationships, and the pattern of interactions between these different agents becomes more complex. Moreover, the project involves not just the combination of manufacturing/construction and service provision, but the recognition of a new 'vision' or objective for the project, which is driven by the downstream service delivery rather than the need for a new technology or artefact. This 'vision' has therefore to be communicated, understood and legitimated across a wide range of organisational contexts and interfaces.

The limitations of the conventional approach to project management readily become apparent. As Söderlund (2004) points out, the contextual, situated nature of individual projects means that the basic premise that all projects can be treated the same, with a universal project management approach and the selective use of techniques from the project management toolkit, is problematic. Precisely because projects have an element of uniqueness, and because the complexity leads to emergent properties, alternative perspectives are needed to help project managers make sense of this complexity and to equip them to deal with emergent problems and crises and the need to manage meaning within the project network. One of these perspectives is that of sense-making.

Sense-making in projects

The notion of sense-making derives from a rich set of academic antecedents concerned with cognition in sociology and social psychology in particular (for a comprehensive review see Walsh, 1995). Sense-making is a phenomenological concept (Schutz, 1967) concerned with processes of enactment (Weick, 2001). It represents a viewpoint that sees organisations not as fixed objective entities, clearly delimited by organisational charts and management hierarchies, but as variable and multiple representations of reality that are 'constructed during human sensemaking activities' (Gephart, 1978: 557). From this viewpoint, not only are organisations socially constructed, but so too are the environments within which they exist (Smircich and Stubbart, 1985). Through sense-making meanings are 'created (both in social interactions as well as in interactions with artefacts and nature), deconstructed, negotiated and elaborated' (Czarniawska-Joerges, 1992: 33). This can be achieved through discourse understood here in terms of language, conversation and texts, and sense-making is thus the process through which the 'intersubjective or cultural world is constructed or produced' (Gephart, 1993: 1469).

Sense-making is a well-established perspective in strategic management and organisation studies and although it has had less impact on the analysis of project management theory and practice (Thomas, 2000) it is certainly beginning to make its presence felt in critical approaches to project management. In general, sense-making is less concerned with the identification of specific forms of organisation to suit particular circumstances or tasks and more with the process of organising itself. Writers on sense-making have concerned themselves with this process in the context of the organisation and the activities of managers within the organisation, such as through leadership (Smircich and Morgan, 1982). However, it is only a short step to considering this as something that takes place in the context of a complex project. We contend that complex projects provide an ideal context in which to consider sense-making because these are occasions that give rise to multiple perspectives and understandings that arise from the multiple stakeholders, extensive organisational networks established to deliver project outcomes, and different 'communities of practice' (Wenger, 1999; Garrety et al., 2004) that need to be accommodated. A sense-making perspective is well-adapted to an analysis of how projects are enacted. 'Self-organising' agents within a project network may organise themselves in accordance with different senses of what the project is about or what is required in terms of project delivery.

The diversity of project stakeholder requirements, it may be suggested, will inevitably lead to quite different perspectives on the project, its objectives and its meaning for the different organisations, communities and individuals involved. This will lead to different discourses or 'narratives' (Boddy and Paton, 2004) reflecting different interpretations of what the project represents. Boddy (2002) suggests that these competing views of a project will be more prevalent in projects where there is a high degree of novelty, rapid change, changing goals, many external linkages and resulting pressures of uncertainty, urgency and the need to integrate (Turner and Muller, 2003). These are precisely the attributes of service-led projects of the type we are interested in: the long time frame of the operations phase adds to the uncertainties inherent in the project; the (often conflicting) needs of additional stakeholders may place more pressure on meeting the client's delivery schedule; and integration extends beyond the notion of systems integration to incorporate the integration of many sub-projects or interrelated areas of activity within the project (Alderman *et al.*, 2002).

The different discourses within the project process arise as a result of individuals and communities attempting to 'make sense' of this unfamiliarity and complexity. The point stressed by Weick (1993) is that there are multiple interpretations of this (project) reality which are all plausible and the discourses and narratives highlight the sense-making process. Project participants have to make sense of their experience of the project in order to provide a basis for action. Thus, according to Thomas (2000: 42), 'a sense-making focus on project management directs us to look at the processes of action and interaction that enable individuals to make sense of organizational activities and to act'. Sense-making therefore runs counter to traditional approaches to 'project management' as it points to the emergent (and often divergent) aspects of organising.

In this view of projects as an emergent phenomenon, effective project management depends upon the alignment of the sense-making activities of project participants in such a way that major 'communication failures' do not take place. Project managers have to pay attention to the meanings that the project and its objectives have for the different participants. These meanings are encapsulated in the different project narratives. 'Narratives deal with the politics of meaning, i.e. how meanings are selected, legitimized, encoded, and institutionalized' (Patriotta, 2003: 351). Through this process project participants become aligned around particular visions or understandings of the project. Others have argued that it is also appropriate to make the distinction between sense-making as 'taking sense' and the act or process of 'sense-giving' (see, for example, Gioia and Chittipeddi, 1991). There will be some actors who will attempt to promote a particular project narrative in support of their objectives (sense-giving) and others who are attempting (initially at least) to understand the new context in which they have to operate (sense-taking).

An acceptance of sense-making also suggests that whatever management controls are in place, the discourses weaving together that process are subject to continual development. Audiences, as well as narrators, through applause, refusal, editing and so on, contribute to the ongoing formation of narratives and discourses (Czarniawska-Joerges, 1997). This may come through user input, but other influences are just as likely (internal sponsors, finance controllers and so on). Such a process clearly has the potential to divert projects from their intended goals and carefully crafted discourses can have potentially powerful shaping effects on project actors and projects in terms of the sense that is made of the project. As Doolin notes, 'Discourses ... act upon the subjectivity of individuals ... constraining certain ways of thinking and acting, while opening up others' (2002: 379). Drawing on Bourdieu's (1991) work *Language and Symbolic Power*, Atkinson (1999) argues that language can be seen as setting the boundary of the debate, and thereby the possibilities for action, by determining what can and what cannot be discussed. Ultimately, already dominant groups will be better able to create shared meanings which suit their construction of reality (Rhodes, 2000). The unequal opportunities created by numerous unequal power relations are likely to abound in most contexts where variable interpretation is possible, and sense-making, because it is interactive by nature, gives rise to struggles for control at all levels (Marshall and Rollinson, 2004).

A framework for understanding sense-making in projects

Drawing on concepts from symbolic interactionism, Garrety and Badham (2000) and Wotherspoon (2001a, 2001b) provide potentially useful frameworks for understanding the emergent and sense-making nature of projects and the critical role of alignment of sense-making at key points if a project is to progress. Whilst these frameworks have been applied in the context of the engineering design process and the development of technological systems, our contribution is to extend them to the consideration of complex service-led projects, where there may be significant technology development, but this is not the primary driver, nor the ultimate outcome from the perspective of the project's client. The following concepts drawn from this work will be applied to the case of a specific complex service-led project reported below:

- *Trajectories*: the course of development of a phenomenon – for example, project, technology – over time. Critically trajectories are not driven by a 'technical inner logic' but rather reflect the social actions and interactions which 'contribute to this evolution' (Garrety and Badham, 1999: 279). Of importance here is the notion that the project is not a fixed entity. The lengthened time frames of service-led projects increase the degree to which the project as it is understood evolves. Indeed, as we shall illustrate, changes to the external environment of the project may alter the original conception and rationale of the project.
- *Social worlds* are domains of 'shared commitments and beliefs about what is important' as evidenced by the 'action and discourse' of actors whose interactions both create trajectories but also seek to influence and shape their future development (Garrety and Badham, 1999: 280; also Wotherspoon, 2001a: 6). Complex service-led projects not only bring together disparate groups of actors, but also require the management of the discourses that emerge from their

interactions both internally within their 'community of practice' and through interaction with other groups of actors.

- *Boundary objects* provide the means through which a trajectory (or multiple trajectories) can 'develop in a meaningful direction' by providing a basis upon which actors from different social worlds can achieve a common understanding despite their differing interests and perceptions (see Garrety and Badham, 1999). Garrety and Badham make a distinction between primary and secondary boundary objects. The former are the material artefacts around which the project is organised. The latter are other 'physical or abstract entities that facilitate and enable communication and action across social worlds' (for example, contracts, operating procedures, project methodologies) (Garrety and Badham, 1999: 280–1).

Whilst there are some terms and concepts here that are shared with other perspectives, notably Actor Network Theory (ANT) (Latour, 1987; Callon, 1992), the approach adopted is not that of 'following' the central actors in the project network as in ANT (where an empirical emphasis has focused attention on the project manager and the way they perform the project (Blackburn, 2002)). Instead it is one of examining the emerging multiple discourses and interpretations of the project and its requirements as a means to identifying where dissonance in the sense-making of different project participants occurs and the ways in which this can impact negatively on the achievement of the project outcomes that ultimately are designed to meet the needs of the client and its business plan.

Translating the temporal components of Wotherspoon's framework to the familiar project life cycle introduces the following concepts of seeding, negotiation and accomplishment as distinct phases through which a project may be considered to proceed:

- *Seeding*: where the concern is the definition and formulation of the basic project idea – what we would see as the key process of defining the project itself as a boundary object. In this phase an eclectic variety of trajectories of sub-component technologies are present without 'specifically established bonds or relationships with one another'. Their inclusion in the project is determined 'through their compliance, at least in appearance' with 'conditions of the obligatory passage point that marks the juncture between seeding and negotiation phases' (Wotherspoon, 2001a: 6–7). In complex projects this seeding phase can be quite extended and incorporates activities such as tendering, contract negotiation, feasibility assessments and so on. Project participants will have a view or 'model' of the project that reflects previous experience. Complex service-led projects introduce new social worlds and new expectations. The project space is therefore quite extensive at this stage.
- *Negotiation*: where interaction is focused around the detailed specification and design of sub-elements of the project and their integration into the artefact(s) which constitute the project as a whole. Here we would see secondary boundary

objects as identified by Garrety and Badham playing a key role in enabling actors in different social worlds to establish common understandings. To the extent that such actions and interactions are facilitated and enabled, project sub-component trajectories which are loosely related will 'develop more individual detail and stronger interrelationships with one another' to the point where 'linkages align with the sub-component trajectories' such that 'a synthesised technology enters the accomplishment phase' (Wotherspoon, 2001a: 7). Here the term 'negotiation' is not used in the conventional sense of contract negotiation, but reflects the core of the activities of project delivery (the generic project business process of riding the project life cycle in Winch (2000)), during which time there will be many conflicting design, resource and implementation issues to be resolved.

- *Accomplishment*: where interaction is focused on negotiating consensus across social worlds concerning the 'final form' or 'relatively stabilised' form of a project and its constituent elements (for example, do sub-elements supplied to the contractor meet the specification and synthesise with those elements from other suppliers; does the delivered project meet the client's expectation and perform in accordance with external regulatory requirements such as health and safety and so on?).

Wotherspoon's framework thus provides an alternative way of categorising the stages in the project process that specifically focuses on processes of negotiation, narrative and sense-making that permeate all projects, but are especially critical to the emergent form of complex projects. Figure 16.1 provides a schematic representation of the three phases of a project when sense-making may be seen to occur as a result of the social interactions and narratives that arise. *Project seeding* can be seen as a phase when a multiplicity of possibilities or trajectories are aligned through the creation of the primary *boundary object* – the principal artefact delivered by the project. *Project negotiation* is a phase in which selected trajectories are influenced and shaped in a manner which enables them to be integrated together into something approaching the final form of the delivered project; the extent to which this occurs being contingent upon the facilitating and enabling character of secondary boundary objects. Finally, *project accomplishment* is the phase in which negotiation occurs over the 'final' delivered project. However, in the context of the kind of complex projects in which we are interested, this notion of 'accomplishment' needs to be seen as a potentially highly attenuated pattern of interaction over time.

A key additional concept which enables us to understand how the development of a project is influenced by actors from different social worlds is provided by the notion of *design boundaries*. These are a product of 'meaningful social interaction between actors from different social worlds' and 'the resultant design boundaries reflect the hidden agendas and power struggles that often occur within the design process' (Wotherspoon, 2001a: 7). In the context of complex projects the notion of 'design boundaries' may be

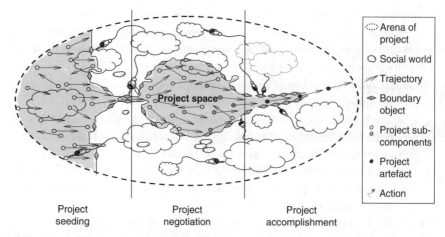

`<·::·>`	Arena of project
`○`	Social world
`↗`	Trajectory
`◆`	Boundary object
`○̥`	Project sub-components
`•`	Project artefact
`↶`	Action

Project seeding	Project negotiation	Project accomplishment

Figure 16.1   Phases in project sense-making
Source: Adapted from Wotherspoon (2001a: 5)

too limited. We therefore suggest that the notion of 'project boundaries' is more appropriate to delimit the 'space' within which project activities are deemed to occur. The project boundary delimits the 'project space' as depicted in Figure 16.1.

We contend that complexity arises in the sense-making experience of project management in these types of projects because there are multiple sources of significant discontinuities which give rise to the need for sense-making by different actors and social worlds (customers, clients, contractors, suppliers, financiers, engineering and other technical disciplines). In long-term complex projects such discontinuities are particularly marked, for example, by the particular issues of translating customer requirements into project specifications, detailed specifications into design freezes, and the translation of designs into 'working' artefacts and systems beyond the capital to the service phase of the project. In such contexts, project management may be construed as the process by which what we term 'sense-making discourses' are brought into communication with each other to evolve the most satisfactory solution to all the stakeholders. In practice such an intention is likely to be contested, negotiated and the outcome emergent.

We therefore focus on the clash and interplay of the discourses that arise from different sense-making activities. A focus on competing sense-making discourses also allows us to open up some of the taken-for-granted assumptions which are embedded in design – and indeed, to follow those discourses back to social groups that might otherwise have remained hidden. 'Successful' discourses are those which are durable enough to survive the transition from one phase to another until they are ultimately 'inscribed' in the project artefact (Akrich, 1992).

The implication for project management in the context of complex projects is that it is best seen as a form of *organising* (Packendorff, 1995), concerned to clarify what is required and when, in the face of unfolding actions, events and so forth (Thomas,

2000: 35). This stands in contrast to the conventional view of project management as a form of *organisation*: that is, a structure for planning, controlling and evaluating the relatively one-off and short-term activities that constitute projects. We go on to illustrate these principles in the interpretation of a specific complex project that exhibited the service-led complexity characteristics described above.

The Pendolino Britannico: an illustrative case

Our empirical illustration is drawn from a project involving detailed case studies of three long-term engineering projects. We focus here on some of the aspects of one of these projects: ALSTOM Transport's contract to design, manufacture and maintain high-speed tilting trains for the West Coast Main Line (WCML), operated by Virgin Trains. The original 12-year contract with Virgin Trains was worth £1.2 billion (1.8 billion euros). Of this figure £592 million was accounted for by the rolling stock with the remainder taken up by the service provision. ALSTOM Transport is the main contractor, developing the Italian Pendolino (the high-speed tilting train) for use on the West Coast Main Line (WCML) to become the UK's first 140-mph tilting train. This was a project incorporating high levels of risk and uncertainty and exacting performance targets. It entailed a significant reorganisation of the manufacturing facility at the Washwood Heath plant in Birmingham in order to meet the requirement for a fast rate of production through the creation of an assembly line layout in the factory, contrasting sharply with the railway industry's traditional and more familiar 'coach-building' approach. The project also featured an enhanced design process based on functional co-location within an award-winning open-plan design studio.

The principal method of research was by extensive and detailed interviews with key actors in each project network. A multidisciplinary team of researchers with backgrounds in engineering, management, economics, economic geography and sociology conducted the research. At least two members of the team attended each interview. Each interview was also recorded and later transcribed for distribution and discussion amongst the research team and for verification by the respondent. The process began with senior managers and other staff engaged on the project within the collaborating organisations. Through these internal interviews, other key actors were identified and the research used a 'snowball' approach whereby each respondent was asked to identify key contacts, collaborators or other actors (or did so in the course of telling the story of the project) and these individuals were then approached for interview and the process repeated until the network was sufficiently delineated to provide a coherent picture of the project. In this process a complete picture of the project network was built up covering the supply chain, the client and intermediaries that were involved in the project. The research also used the mechanism of inter-company workshops to explore key issues arising from the shift to a long-term project perspective and the discourses associated with them.

Seeding: the origins of a project

Typical of projects emerging in a post-privatisation world is the fact that new types of client are appearing, many of which are entering the industry from very different backgrounds, the entry of bus or airline operators into the rail market being a case in point. In comparison to the former nationalised British Rail, these clients, whilst still concerned with the 'technical details' of the project and the technology embodied in the train, typically addressed through the intermediation of professional technical consultants, pay much more attention to the service element – the service provided by the new train operator to its own customers, the travelling public.

For many of these new train operators, such as Virgin Trains, their social world is based around the organisation's brand image and the desire to deliver a completely new experience of rail travel. This was encapsulated in the bid by Virgin for the WCML franchise, described by the railway press in June 2000 as 'breathtaking in its boldness' (Modern Railways, 2000: xxiv). Accordingly, the project was defined in terms of Virgin's business plan for the franchise and its vision for the future of rail travel.

The discourses driving the trajectory of the project were reflected in the nature of the specification to ALSTOM for the new rolling stock. A new type of discourse replaced the traditional 'engineering-led' discourse that would have dominated in the days of British Rail, when most of the basic design would have been carried out by British Rail engineers and rolling-stock manufacturers invited to tender against this specification. Virgin's discourses could be interpreted as, first, one centred around the notion of 'passenger experience', a service concept, not a technological concept. This concept related to the internal environment of the train and the services provided to the passenger. These included systems for handling at-seat ticketing and reservations, a requirement for entertainment systems, provision of retailing opportunities and the creation of a particular ambience.

A second discourse centred around the requirement not for a specific number of trains, but for reliable 'seat miles'. In other words, Virgin wished to procure the service, not the product. ALSTOM Transport as the train manufacturer is therefore required to deliver the requisite number of trains to the platform each morning to allow Virgin to fulfil its obligation to the Strategic Rail Authority for the number of daily diagrams agreed in the WCML franchise. This is a discourse reflecting the long-term service provision aspect of the project rather than a technically driven one.

As we have articulated elsewhere (Alderman *et al.*, 2003), one of the major implications of complex projects of this type is that the contractor has to understand the client's requirements, which, as the example shows, may be expressed very differently from traditional capital delivery projects. As an integral part of the 'passenger experience' discourse, Virgin interacted with ALSTOM through a document known as the 'Red Book'. This represented in essence an aspirational design, comprising, amongst other things, a series of visual images that capture what it is the client wants the train to look like and (just as importantly) what it should not look like. For a client such as

Virgin, achieving the right image through the passenger experience is impacted more by dirty toilets than by power supply characteristics.

The Red Book was thus an important mechanism for managing the process of conveying this narrative and represents a secondary boundary object in the context of our model. Design engineers faced with the Red Book did not find it easy to identify the design implications of images of, for example, clean and unclean toilets. This method of specifying the customer's requirements was new to them. Interpreting the Red Book was therefore an important aspect of the process by which ALSTOM, its designers and subsequently its suppliers, 'made sense' of the project and the client's requirements.

Negotiation: the vision meets engineering and economic realities

If the seeding phase is about making sense of the customers' requirements, the negotiation phase is when the detailed design activity in any complex project takes place and these requirements become embodied in the artefact. In our studies it was possible to see how the design boundaries became more rigid and defined as detailed technical specifications were produced to implement the basic concepts and visions within the Red Book and to meet the performance requirements for the Pendolino. This process reflected the interplay of the different discourses at work within the project.

In this phase of the project ALSTOM translated Virgin's reliability discourse into a discourse about 'design for maintainability' (Ivory et al., 2003). One of the implications of the types of long-term service-led project that we have been studying is that once the manufacturer takes on the long-term responsibility for the reliability and availability of their product there are strong economic imperatives to ensure that the costs of maintenance are minimised. In these types of project the major revenue streams and associated profits typically accrue during the operations phase.

During the negotiation phase a wider range of different actors, both within ALSTOM and from other external organisations, were involved in the detailed design of the train. Potentially then, the different social worlds that came together in this activity could have been a source of disjuncture and discontinuity for the project. In particular, ALSTOM had to reconfigure the motivations of different stakeholders in the project in order to make 'design for maintainability' a key driver in the design and innovation process. To do this ALSTOM reorganised itself, creating an internal customer in the form of West Coast TrainCare (WCTC), which is the lynchpin of ALSTOM Transport's maintenance of the Virgin Trains WCML fleet. WCTC is also the signatory on the contract with Virgin Trains for the Pendolino train sets. Thus, WCTC, rather than the train builder, is perceived by Virgin to be the service provider and it is from WCTC that it takes delivery of the trains (and to whom it will apply liquidated damages if they prove unreliable). By making the maintenance staff effectively the 'customer' for the train, the design for maintainability discourse is placed centre stage.

The disjunctures between discourses, however, can be seen in terms of the perceived conflict between this new discourse and the traditional engineering design discourse, which was frequently referred to by respondents. This is encapsulated in the basic design heuristic 'big and strong' that has historically dominated railway engineering thinking. Engineers clearly made sense of project requirements in a way that reflected their previous relationship with the nationalised British Rail.

> They were the engineer not us, and basically you made the design fit around exactly what they asked for.

It was suggested that *'engineers find the adjustment difficult'* in moving away from a performance-led discourse about train design towards the needs of the maintainability discourse. In the past, of course, these issues of looking after the train once it was in service would have become the responsibility of the client (British Rail). For engineers working on the design of the train, therefore, engaging with the new discourse was not straightforward. There remained a distance between the design process and the processes and problems that accompany the 'doing' of maintenance. As was clearly recognised within WCTC, reliability can be specified in a contract and can be incorporated into a design, but the notion of 'maintainability' is more problematic:

> 'Maintainable' – what does that mean to someone who has never been in a maintenance depot?

This issue was recognised and ALSTOM ensured that designers spent time in the train-care centres developing an awareness of maintenance problems, through a programme of two-week visits, including time on the night shift.

The urgency that characterises projects manifested itself in the very demanding delivery schedule stipulated by Virgin, driven by the length of the franchise. Time was therefore of the essence and the project team effectively had the challenge of as much as halving the time a contract of this magnitude might have conventionally taken to deliver. Again, it was suggested that this sense of urgency was not always appreciated by those steeped in the traditional *modus operandi* of railway engineering design. One respondent, commenting on his colleagues in the engineering function at ALSTOM, caricatured the engineering viewpoint as:

> We build fantastic trains – if they are late they are late.

The maintainability discourse was also affected by a financing discourse, driven by the rolling-stock company (ROSCO) that will actually own the trains and is providing the finance – Angel Trains. Here longevity is the key issue, since the financing model is dependent on the trains having an acceptable residual value at the end of the franchise, when they will be still less than halfway through their expected operating life (Vale, 2000). Angel Trains, as the rolling-stock owner, also has a voice in the design process based on this discourse around residual value.

Suppliers also had to engage with the design for maintainability discourse. ALSTOM Transport's procurement team has been careful to ensure that 'maintainability' has been clearly specified to suppliers. Suppliers to the WCML contract must state the life-cycle costs of all equipment on a standard pro forma. For maintainability, ALSTOM Transport also stated fixed time limits within which individual items must be made accessible for maintenance. It was also recognised by WCTC and ALSTOM Transport that suppliers should be involved earlier in the project. 'Reliability conferences' were set up to encourage their input. There have also been changes in the deployment of finance. Money, once set aside for penalty payments, was redeployed to help improve train life-costs by funding technology solutions developed through the reliability conferences. The 'design for maintainability' message was reinforced through the use of financial penalties and rewards associated with reliability performance.

There were many new suppliers to the Pendolino project, partly reflecting the novelty of the project objectives. For such suppliers, making sense of the context of the project and the particularities of the industry they sought to supply into was essential. One supplier commented:

That has been the biggest learning curve for me – understanding trains … why, how; the history behind things.

Part of this learning came about through conversation and dialogue with the assembly line and shop-floor workers at ALSTOM as well as with the design and procurement teams.

Another illustration of the dissonance or conflict between senses and understandings of the project and its requirements is provided by the following statement made by a member of one of the project procurement teams:

At the end of the day what is the passenger interested in? He [sic] is buying a ticket to travel, he is not buying the vehicle … finish is money.

Here the respondent was directly comparing a car owner with a rail passenger. Traditionally, in the rail industry, tolerances have been much greater than in, for example, the automotive or aerospace industries. In the harsh environment of the train, fine tolerances add significantly to cost. For this respondent, it did not make sense to do this. For the client, however, wide tolerances contributed to poor or unattractive finish, ill-fitting features, unsightly joins and so on. From the perspective of passenger experience such things are to be avoided as they have a deleterious effect on the overall ambience and visual impression of the train environment. For the client, and thus for senior management at ALSTOM, it made perfect sense to put more effort into resolving such issues. The resolution of these disjunctures comprised an important aspect of the negotiation that took place as the design was firmed up and the Pendolino moved from mock-up to pre-series and finally to the production line.

Accomplishment: the end of the story(ies)?

The character of long-term service-led projects, with their extended operations/maintenance phase, suggests that accomplishment will be an attenuated and continuous activity, in contrast to the conventional project life cycle that sees accomplishment in the handover to and acceptance of the project output by the client. At this point in time it might be suggested that in the case of the Pendolino, the entry of the trains into passenger service only represents accomplishment for a handful of the social groups involved in the project. For the train maintainer (WCTC) and the many suppliers that have given long-term performance guarantees, the project continues to unfold. It is only once the trains enter service that WCTC will discover whether they are as reliable and maintainable as the discourse intended they should be.

We have argued elsewhere (Alderman *et al.*, 2002) that long-term service-led projects exist interdependently with a volatile environment. Recent events, notably the collapse of Railtrack and the failure to complete the planned upgrade of the WCML, have meant that the original vision and discourse about the passenger experience have had to be modified, because the trains will not be able to run at the specified top speed of 140 mph. As Chris Green, Chief Executive of Virgin Trains, is reported to have said: 'our greyhound will have to be content with being a labrador' (Modern Railways, 2004: 65). The notion of what constitutes accomplishment in the Pendolino project is therefore having to be redefined for reasons beyond the control of either the contractor or the client in this instance.

Discussion

Managing in the context of sense-making

The Pendolino project illustrates the application of a number of different tools or methods of sense-making or sense-giving on the part of managers and staff at ALSTOM and its partners in the project network. The use of these mechanisms is not unproblematic, however. For example, some suppliers complained that they only saw those parts of the Red Book directly relating to their area of activity. Their ability to make sense of the overall project requirements was hampered (perhaps) by not having access to the complete picture. This restriction was justified in terms of intellectual property protection, but clearly as a mechanism for sense-making it had its limitations in terms of conveying the meanings of the project down the supply chain.

The leadership mode of sense-giving was reflected in a number of actions occurring within the project. On some occasions Richard Branson himself 'was mobilised' through high-profile PR visits to the factory complete with photo and press calls. The novelty and challenge of the project were also effectively conveyed through Virgin's predilection for the naming of locomotives, with one of the earliest Pendolinos being given the moniker *Mission Impossible*. The ultimate success of the project was

subsequently reflected in the naming of the last train to move down the ass
as *Mission Accomplished*.

The design studio was not just a means of providing a co-located multi
work environment, but was also a symbolic feature of the project with (initi
banners hung on its walls promoting the urgency of the project and its imp
flagship development and as a motivator of those staff working in the stud
these were all deployed by management as sense-giving tools. For many
however, it was clear that preexisting discourses were too well entrench
have had much impact. Subsequently, when design issues emerged over a
interior and senior management realised that the organisation of the pro
ated additional and unforeseen complexities, swift action was taken t
identified shortcomings in project structure and the banners were quicl

The reliability conferences were also a mechanism not just for promou..
ation within the supply chain, but also for helping suppliers to make sense of the pic
ject requirements for reliability and maintainability since the operational phase of the
project and the revenue streams flowing from this relied on achieving a high degree of
reliability, much of which was incumbent on the performance of components and
subsystems provided by the supply chain. The meaning and implications of these
requirements were not fully understood by all suppliers at the outset.

Emergence in complex projects

It is clear from the discussion of accomplishment above that the emergent nature of
complex projects requires adjustments to the meaning ascribed to the project by the
various actors involved. Because the Pendolino was part of a much wider undertaking
with a variety of different stakeholders, the range of meanings and senses of the project held by the various parties will have created a multiplicity of interpretations of the
project, not just within ALSTOM and its supply chain, but also amongst the various
rail industry bodies and other key partners such as Virgin, Angel Trains, the Strategic
Rail Authority and so on. The challenge for those managing or attempting to manage
the project is to find some way of creating a degree of shared meaning as understood
by these stakeholders. This sharing of meaning will almost certainly be partial, but an
appreciation of the key drivers and features of the project that relate to the needs of
the client and its business plan will prevent many of the more blatant disjunctures
that could otherwise arise.

Project managers need mechanisms for bringing stakeholders together to share discourses and to ensure that they are exposed to the central discourses that define the
meaning of the project for the client and other key players. This will at least create
some chance of sense being made of a very complex set of project requirements.
Although sense-making is retrospective the demands of long-term service-led projects create the need for it to be projected forward in time to reflect on anticipated situations in order to affect design decisions made in the present. Sense-making in this

context is a process of creative understanding of a new phenomenon rather than the analysis of the known, although it can also be a way of understanding 'the known' differently. Understanding the implications of future service (maintainability) requirements in terms of the immediate problem of how to design the Pendolino is one of the aspects of this prospective sense-making.

Managerial action is, however, constrained by the relative power wielded by different groups of actors in the project. The extent to which actors can be motivated to make sense of a particular discourse will be affected by the degree of resistance to that discourse. This can be seen with the relative power of the engineering design community within the rail industry. They are widely regarded, and regard themselves as a body of experts and, as Marshall and Rollinson (2004) show, the label 'technical expert' can lead to some discourses achieving wider acceptance than others. Economic power on the part of specific suppliers led to resistance to some of the requirements ALSTOM attempted to place on them. The supplier of the aluminium flooring had to be replaced, because it would not accept, and could not be compelled to accept, the need to change the way it supplied its product in line with the project's discourses.

Conclusion

We have argued in this chapter that complex projects of the type discussed represent an almost continuous stream of discontinuities in the flow of experience of the actors involved. This brings about the process of sense-making by them as they struggle to come to terms with what is happening or is likely to happen and evolve effective responses. The sense made is framed partly by the discourses deployed by the different actors and social worlds which reconstruct problems and constrain actions taken. The analysis of the Pendolino Britannico project highlights the inadequacies of a conventional rationalistic approach to project management. The challenge for project management can be seen in terms of the selection of cues used to direct attention to some overarching 'project discourse' in an attempt to mediate the more sectional discourses.

Whilst sense-making has probably always been implicitly recognised as what project managers actually do, by examining the need to make sense at an appropriately high level, as well as at a detailed engineering and manufacturing level, we see the need for a meta discourse to be constructed for a project that can, for example, encompass the client's business aspirations and the suppliers' worlds in order to deliver a successful project. More effective project management in such circumstances will require project managers to focus on the 'management of meaning' by providing 'interpretative frameworks'. This echoes the call of Daft and Weick (1984: 294) for managers to 'take seriously their role as interpreters'. These frameworks will need not only to be better able to bring about degrees of consensus between competing and potentially competing discourses within projects, but also to effectively align the activities of sense-giving and sense-taking. In the case of complex projects, the multiplicity of novel dimensions, the differences, the newness, the discontinuities in project concept and so forth have led us to argue that they constitute a particularly fruitful opportunity to explore the way in which the notion of sense-making may help to untangle the project management challenge in a new way.

References

Akrich, M. (1992) 'The De-scription of Technical Objects', in W. Bijker and J. Law (eds), *Shaping Technology/Building Society: Studies in Sociotechnical Change*. Cambridge, MA: MIT Press.

Alderman, N., McLoughlin, I.P., Ivory, C.J., Thwaites, A.T. and Vaughan, R. (2003) 'Trains, Cranes and Drains: Customer Requirements in Long-Term Engineering Projects as a Knowledge Management Problem', in M. von Zedtwitz, G. Haour, T. Khalil and L. Lefebvre (eds), *Management of Technology: Growth through Business, Innovation and Entrepreneurship*. Oxford: Pergamon Press, 331–48.

Alderman, N., Ivory, C.J., Vaughan, R., Thwaites, A. and McLoughlin, I.P. (2002) *The Project Management Implications of New Service-Led Projects*, Working paper, *Proceedings of the British Academy of Management Conference*, London, 9–11 September.

Atkinson, R. (1999) 'Discourses of Partnership and Empowerment in Contemporary British Urban Regeneration', *Urban Studies*, 36(1): 59–72.

Blackburn, S. (2002) 'The project manager and the project-network', *International Journal of Project Management*, 20: 199–204.

Boddy, D. (2002) *Managing Projects: Building and Leading the Team*. Harlow: FT Prentice Hall.

Boddy, D. and Paton, R. (2004) 'Responding to Competing Narratives: Lessons for Project Managers', *International Journal of Project Management*, 22: 225–33.

Bourdieu, P. (1991) *Language and Symbolic Power*. Cambridge: Polity Press.

Buchanan, D.A. and Boddy, D. (1992) *The Expertise of the Change Agent*. Reading: Prentice Hall.

Callon, M. (1992) 'The Dynamics of Techno-economic Networks', in R. Coombs, P. Saviotti and V. Walsh (eds), *Technological Change and Company Strategy: Economic and Sociological Perspectives*. London: Academic Press.

Czarniawska-Joerges, B. (1992) *Exploring Complex Organizations*. London: Sage.

Czarniawska-Joerges, B. (1997) *Narrating the Organisation: Dramas of Institutional identity*. Chicago: University of Chicago Press.

Daft, R. and Weick, K. (1984) 'Toward a Model of Organisations as Interpretation Systems', *Academy of Management Review*, 9: 284–95.

Davies, A. with Tang, P., Brady, T., Hobday, M., Rush, H. and Gann, D. (2001) *Integrated Solutions: The New Economy Between Manufacturing and Services*. Falmer: SPRU, University of Sussex.

Doolin, B. (2002) 'Enterprise, Discourse, Professional Identity and the Organisational Control of Hospital Clinicians', *Organization Studies*, 23(3): 369–90.

Garrety, K. and Badham, R. (2000) 'The Politics of Socio-technical Intervention: An Interactionist View', *Technology Analysis and Strategic Management*, 12(1): 103–19.

Garrety, K., Robertson, P.L. and Badham, R. (2004) 'Integrating Communities of Practice in Technology Development Projects', *International Journal of Project Management*, 22: 351–8.

Gephart, R.P. (1978) 'Status Degradation and Organisational Succession: An Ethnomethodological Approach', *Administrative Science Quarterly*, 23: 553–81.

Gephart, R.P. (1993) 'The Textual Approach: Risk and Blame in Disaster Sensemaking', *Academy of Management Journal*, 36: 1465–514.

Gioia, D.A. and Chittipeddi, K. (1991) 'Sensemaking and Sensegiving in Strategic Change Initiation', *Strategic Management Journal*, 12: 433–48.

Ivory, C., Thwaites, A. and Vaughan, R. (2003) 'Shifting the Goal Posts for Design Management in Capital Goods Projects: "Design for Maintainability"', *R&D Management*, 33: 527–38.

Latour, B. (1987) *Science in Action: How to Follow Scientists and Engineers Through Society*. Cambridge, MA: Harvard University Press.

Marshall, N. and Rollinson, J. (2004) 'Maybe Bacon Had a Point: The Politics of Interpretation in Collective Sensemaking', *British Journal of Management*, 15: 71–86.

Maylor, H. (1999) *Project Management*, 2nd edn. London: FT/Pitman.

Meredith, J.R. and Mantel, S.J. (1995) *Project Management: A Managerial Approach*. New York: Wiley.

Modern Railways (2000) *West Coast Route Modernisation*. *Modern Railways* Special Report, June.

Modern Railways (2004) 'Pendolino Surge', *Modern Railways*, July: 65.

Morris, P.W.G. (1994) *The Management of Projects*. London: Thomas Telford.

Packendorff, J. (1995) 'Inquiring into the Temporary Organization: New Directions for Project Management Research', *Scandinavian Journal of Management*, 11: 319–33.

Patriotta, G. (2003) 'Sensemaking on the Shop Floor: Narratives of Knowledge in Organizations', *Journal of Management Studies*, 40: 349–75.

PMI, (2000) *A Guide to the Project Management Body of Knowledge*. Newton Square, PA: PMI Publishing.

Rhodes, C. (2000) ' "Doing" ' Knowledge at Work: Dialogue, Monologue and Power in Organizational Learning', in J. Garrick and C. Rhodes (eds), *Research and Knowledge at Work*. London: Routledge, 217–31.

Schutz, A. (1967) *The Phenomenology of the Social World*. Evanston, Ill: Northwestern University Press.

Smircich, L. and Morgan, G. (1982) 'Leadership: The Management of Meaning', *Journal of Applied Behavioural Science*, 18: 257–73.

Smircich, L. and Stubbart, C. (1985) 'Strategic Management in an Enacted World', *Academy of Management Review*, 10: 724–33.

Söderlund, J. (2004) 'Building Theories of Project Management: Past Research, Questions for the Future', *International Journal of Project Management*, 22: 183–91.

Thomas, J. (2000) 'Making Sense of Project Management', in R.A. Lundin and F. Hartman (eds), *Projects as Business Constituents and Guiding Motives*. Norwell, MA: Kluwer Academic Publishers, 25–43.

Turner, J.R. (1993) *The Handbook of Project-based Management*. London: McGraw-Hill.

Turner, J.R. and Muller, R. (2003) 'On the Nature of the Project as a Temporary Organization', *International Journal of Project Management*, 21: 1–8.

Vale, J. (2000) 'The Procurement, Financing and Leasing of Advanced Tilting Trains for Virgin Rail Group's Use on Britain's West Coast Main Line', *Studies in Leasing Law and Tax 2000*. Colchester: Euromoney Institutional Investor plc, 20–5.

Walsh, J.P. (1995) 'Managerial and Organizational Cognition: Notes from a Trip Down Memory Lane', *Organization Science*, 6: 280–321.

Weick, K.E. (1979) *The Social Psychology of Organizing*, 2nd edn. London: McGraw-Hill.

Weick, K.E. (1993) 'Sensemaking in Organizations: Small Structures with Large Consequences', in J.K. Murnigham (ed.), *Social Psychology in Organizations: Advances in Theory and Research*. New York: Prentice-Hall (reprinted in Weick, 2001).

Weick, K.E. (1997) 'Enactment Processes in Organizations', in B. Staw and G. Salancik (eds), *New Directions in Organizational Behavior*. Chicago: St Clair (reprinted in Weick, 2001).

Weick, K.E. (2001) *Making Sense of the Organization*. London: Blackwell.

Wenger, E. (1999) *Communities of Practice: Learning, Meaning and Identity*. Cambridge: Cambridge University Press.

Whittaker, J. (2000) 'Reflections on the Changing Nature of Projects', in R.A. Lundin and F. Hartman (eds), *Projects as Business Constituents and Guiding Motives*. Norwell, MA: Kluwer Academic Publishers, 133–41.

Williams, T. (2002) *Modelling Complex Projects*. London: Wiley.

Winch, G. (2000) 'The Management of Projects as a Generic Business Process', in R.A. Lundin and F. Hartman (eds), *Projects as Business Constituents and Guiding Motives*. Norwell, MA: Kluwer Academic Publishers.

Wotherspoon, R. (2001a) 'An Ethnographic Study of Engineering Design', paper delivered at Asia-Pacific Researchers in Organization Studies (APROS) conference, Hong Kong Baptist University, Hong Kong, December.

Wotherspoon, R. (2001b) 'Janus: The Multiple Faces of Engineering Design', PhD thesis, Department of Management, University of Wollongong, New South Wales.

Afterword:
making the management of
projects critical

Peter Morris

I have been asked to give a response to the foregoing chapters, to provide a view from someone who, as both an academic and a practitioner, has been deeply interested for many years in trying to understand and explain how to manage projects effectively.

I work a lot with managers, as a consultant, researcher and teacher, and I know well how they struggle to deliver projects successfully. In this sense I am unashamedly managerial. I share with them the desire to perform better and look to concepts and practices to help in doing this. Many senior people in many walks of life are very serious about creating the right managerial conditions to ensure that capital expenditure projects, for example, or product development projects or organisational change programmes are set up and delivered effectively and efficiently. And many people involved in such efforts are, on a day-to-day basis, challenged to wonder how to do so better. There is clearly a strong instrumental rationality character – a 'design, regularity and control' bias, as Cicmil and Hodgson put it in the Introduction – to this approach. (Dare I yet say: to this 'discipline'?) I know too well, however, that projects are implemented by people, and when people become involved, perception, communication, agenda, power and a whole raft of similar issues come into play and begin to change the 'design, regularity and control' intent of managers.

There is a classic example. Many if not most oil and gas companies spend billions of dollars a year undertaking projects. Most see project management as a core organisational competence. Several would think of themselves as pretty good at it. Some continue to experience difficulties, however, and most are interested in improving their performance. Most therefore perform inter-firm, inter-project benchmarking. The benchmarking data show clearly, it is claimed, that certain 'Value Improving Practices' will, if applied, lead to better-performing projects. Yet, and this is the interesting point, most of these companies have real difficulty in getting their people to take note of, internalise and apply these practices. It is the same often with lessons learned: most such companies now perform 'lessons learned' reviews but most similarly have a hard time in getting people to pay attention to the points, let alone internalise and apply them so that the organisation actually does better. The point is, there *are* established practices and principles for managing projects in these major corporations; there is serious intent to apply them and do better; but there are still difficulties in application, most revolving around people issues.

The editors and contributors to this book are absolutely right therefore to follow the Scandinavian School and others in bringing a more sociological perspective to the study of the management of projects. Hence, even from a managerial perspective [*sic*], one looks forward to a series of essays like this with pleasure and anticipation.

This though is not a book aimed especially at providing managers with insight on how better to manage projects. The chapters' first concern is, as the editors quite reasonably make clear, 'to open up new research trajectories', and to do so by adopting a critical social theory perspective. How useful it seems to be from a manager's perspective is what I want to address. For Hodgson and Cicmil, the book's overriding concern may be said to be to understand better 'what happens when people call something a project'. This I would contrast with my own more managerialist interest which I shall be reflecting here of understanding what competency (knowledge, skills, behaviours, and probably experience) you need to manage projects effectively.

Some contributors would express caution or perhaps even distaste or astonishment at such a seemingly theoretically naive position. Green, for example, accuses project management of being both overtly managerial (theoretically sterile) and simultaneously largely unconcerned with the reality of implementation success, at least in construction. I stand my ground. As I shall argue in conclusion – indeed, right the way through this chapter – it all depends on what you mean by projects and project management (precisely the questions the book sets out to explore, of course, as is set out at the beginning of the Introduction). Green clearly has a very operational view of project management, which is why I suspect he is so unsympathetic towards it. I aim for a more inclusive, contextual, view. This is the perspective offered, I believe, by the 'management of projects' framework (Morris, 1994; Morris and Pinto, 2004), as is reflected for example in the Body of Knowledge developed by the Association for Project Management (APM, 2000, 2006).

The model of project management

The social theory is rich, but the model of project management put forward in many of the chapters in this book generally is not. Most take the *PMBOK Guide* (PMI, 2004) as *the* formal model of project management. On the face of it this is not unreasonable: it is the model of the largest professional society.[1] Yet it is simplistic, and has been criticised as such (Morris, 2001; Williams, 2004). More sophisticated models, such as the

Association for Project Management's (APM, 2000, 2006), the International Project Management Association's (Caupin *et al.*, 1998) or the Japanese (ENAA, 2001), are rarely if ever mentioned, nor is there any reference to the British Standard, BS6079-1 (2002), or to ISO 10006 (2003), let alone to PRINCE2 (OGC, 2002) (except in the Introduction) or to *Managing Successful Programmes* (OGC, 2003), nor to any other of the well-known national standards such as those of NASA, the US Department of Defense (DOD), or the Ministry of Defence (MOD). The *PMBOK Guide*, I would suggest, has little real academic credibility as a representation of what project management is, however popular the PMI and its certification programmes are. It is just a portion of the bigger picture (Morris, 2001; Morris and Pinto, 2004). Criticising this model with all the weight of modern deconstructionism or critical theory is totally valid but hardly fair to project management as a practice.

Similarly the argument has moved on well beyond Kerzner's works, or even Frame's and Meredith and Mantel's, all of which are good introductory primers; using these as the totem of best project management practice is only to be attacking easy targets. Unlike, say, Turner's works (Turner, 1993, 1995; Turner and Simister, 2000), they are not really seen as representing a fuller statement of the discipline (see the reviews in *Project Management Journal* (2003) 34(4): 59, and *International Journal of Project Management* (2004) 22: 603–4).

It is not that the points don't need making, but too often the criticism seems almost to subvert the intention of those trying to articulate and formalise our understanding of how best to manage projects, rather than to critically understand how we can better represent what we do know. There is a fine line in critical theory between subversion and understanding and I am not sure it isn't sometimes crossed in one or two of these chapters.

Some authors do indeed make attempts to portray the reality of managing projects – Clegg *et al.*, Green, Ivory *et al.*, Linde and Linderoth, Nocker, Sillince *et al.*, Smith – and this is really helpful. Interestingly none draw a picture of project management resembling the *PMBOK Guide*. Indeed, Smith positively ends up making exactly the points made in *The Anatomy of Major Projects* (Morris and Hough, 1987) and *The Management of Projects* (Morris, 1994): that projects need to be managed in their context; that context shapes their management challenge; that the factors which often most influence the chances of success or failure are often not even recognised in the *PMBOK Guide* model; and that, most importantly, managers can influence and in places directly shape these contextual forces.

These are insights which totally inform the Association for Project Management's Body of Knowledge (which is only mentioned in passing by Hodgson and Cicmil and, as far as I can see, by no one else); have been made by the two leading studies of major projects published since *The Anatomy of Major Projects*, namely those by Flyvbjerg *et al.* (2003) and Miller and Lessard (2000) (the former is only mentioned once, the latter not at all); and are central to the modern understanding of, and interest in, programme management (which is never discussed). (Similarly, there are newer references to data on project success and failure: Crawford (2002) and Cooke-Davies (2004), for example, are relevant.)

There is, in short, an overwhelming sense that intellectually too much of the book has been addressed at a simplistic model of project management – one which, while promoted by the PMI, is not by the other professional associations or by the more serious writing in the field, nor is it a framework used by many of the more experienced practitioners.

Projects as forms of adhocracy or instrumental rationality

The aim of the book is wholly valid and interesting. I understand and empathise with the interest of social scientists in investigating 'what happens when people label something a project': projects (and programmes) are real organisational phenomena, giving rise to distinctive managerial challenges and behaviours. And there *are* some real theoretical issues. A very good one, for example, well-made in several chapters, is the apparent conflict between the view, expressed by Toffler (1970), Mintzberg (1979), Nonaka and Takeuchi (1995) and others, of projects as *ad hoc*, loose, flexible structures on the one hand, and as fine examples of process-driven and control-focused instrumental rationality (Weber, 1949) on the other – a very telling point which I feel is never quite resolved but allowed to lie as a smoking gun leaving us scratching our heads. There is an answer, I believe, but it goes to the heart of asking what we mean by projects and project management.

As both BS6079 (2002), the *PMBOK Guide* (PMI, 2004) and the APM Body of Knowledge (2006) point out, projects can be, and are, thought of in terms of both the product development project life cycle and the 'Initiate–Plan–Control–Execute–Close-Out' project management process. And project management can be, and is, thought of as either the management of the overall project as it moves through its product development cycle (the view of the discipline most likely to be found in the general public's conception) or as it moves between stage gates (as recommended in PRINCE2 for example). In the early stages of the project product development life cycle – Concept, Appraise, Define and so on – the project will typically be in a more creative, innovative mode than later, as the design becomes firmed up and options are closed down. In other words, there is a move, in the language of Burns and Stalker (1961), from a predominantly organic phase to a mechanistic one. Even within the early organic stages there will, of course, be control, but this is normally more periodic – at design reviews, risk reviews, periodic status reports, quality reviews and so on. Once the delivery parameters are established, the mode shifts and the control becomes much tighter. Interestingly just about everyone in this book ignores the product development basis to the definition of projects and its implications for the way management is carried out on the project (though Nocker and Clegg *et al.* give examples of how a contextual, interpretive perspective may be useful in the early stages of requirements definition and project planning which I shall return to).

The second point concerns how tightly project management practices should be applied. The *PMBOK Guide* itself is quite clear that it does not expect all the practices contained within it to be applied all of the time. It is up to the project management team to decide which practices should be applied and how rigorously. Davies and Hobday (2005), building on the work of Burns and Stalker (1961) and Seeley-Brown and Duguid (1995), make this point very eloquently in the case of IT project management, as do Linde and Linderoth in this book. (Crawford and Pollack (2004) discuss this in the context of soft systems methodology.) Too often project management is caricatured as being too control-orientated, mechanistic and limiting ('enclosure, partitioning and ranking' creating rigidities and blinders (Thomas)), but some rules, some control, are necessary. Freedom needs some constraints, as many writers have pointed out (not least Vickers in relation to control theory in *Freedom in a Rocking Boat* (1970)). Projects are, after all, truly about delivery; there are often truly important, big things at stake – money, careers, responsibilities, even lives: some rules and control *are* necessary. But this doesn't mean that freedom to innovate and be creative is proscribed. The issue, as Linde and Linderoth show, is how firmly to apply the project management practices and when to ease off. The answer, I would suggest, is to understand the practices sufficiently well to know when they need *not* be applied.

Emergence and prescription

Another chestnut is whether projects are invented or found, and perhaps therefore how robust our knowledge about how to manage them can be. Much is made of projects and project management being contextual. (As Green says, 'context is important in shaping practice; and practice is important in shaping context'.) Surely this general point is largely accepted by now. The *PMBOK Guide* implies as much; the fifth edition of APM Body of Knowledge states it explicitly. And projects are indeed invented, as is the language of stages and stage gates, of the roles and tools and techniques that go with them. But once engineered they have meaning and reality. The meetings happen, even if individual actors' views of them may vary (Sydow). The critical realist sees nothing wrong in trying to abstract rules and knowledge from such socially constructed reality (Hacking, 1999).

Bresnen and Ivory *et al.* make much of emergence and sense-making but neither refer to the modern concept of programme management (OGC, 2003): Thiry (2004) has argued cogently in my view that in programme management the emergent, sense-making and organisational learning attributes are dominant features at the programme level with a parallel and simultaneous directional, control-oriented focus at the project level.

Chia's 'being–becoming' distinction (1995) is undoubtedly useful, however. In projects, managers, engineers and others are after all engaged in inventing the future (*pace* Clegg). As Sydow puts it, project teams are creating trajectories into the future. (Miller and Lessard (2000) have this as a central skill of project teams.) Linehan and Kavanagh explore the 'being–becoming' dichotomy very fairly: one has empathy with their position that both operate in managers' lives. ('Our argument is not so much that one ontology is superior to the other, but that each is necessarily partial…'.) Weber's instrumental rationality *is* a dominant mode in much of managing projects, but this does not mean that we are not operating within a social construct that is always in a state of both interpretation and becoming. Nocker points out how people can manage projects creatively while still managing them in terms of instrumental rationality, though Bresnen puts well the tensions that this can cause. Molloy and Whittington suggest that project management tools and techniques can be helpful in bringing an objective reality to change situations which inevitably involve actors having multiple perspectives, though Green is more negative.

A good example of the practical results of managing a project simultaneously both as being and becoming, as rationally instrumental and creative, is the challenge of adequately and appropriately communicating requirements – requirements defined as a construction of negotiated meanings (Nocker) or as sense-making (Ivory *et al.*) – an insight too often completely ignored by the systems engineering community (Johnson, 2003). (Though interestingly, the Pendolino train, the 'product' realised from the Red Book vision document, used in Ivory *et al.*'s case study, failed to perform to its operating requirements!) Sillince *et al.* take a similar tack in their account of how the manner of talking – for example, rhetoric – shaped people's perception of trust and commitment and how this adversely influenced the negotiations for a new medical facility. Many managers of projects will be familiar with this situation.

Bodies of knowledge and professional knowledge

The Foucault observation that history shapes the way we see a discipline (as indeed ourselves) is important: obvious in itself – after all history is heavily about interpretation – the observation is clearly the more telling the closer one gets to discussing science. But here again we are in danger of stubbing our toes on issues that surely have already been well-aired. Is project management a science? Is management? In addressing these issues, I find both the Hodgson and Cicmil and Thomas chapters to be slightly unreal. (As Griseri has remarked (2002), deconstructionism is not naturally empathetic to attempts at building structures of knowledge!)

Hodgson and Cicmil suggest that 'mainstream project management reflects an enduring theme of management theory: the belief that its study is analogous to natural science', a view which, they contend, leads to the 'naturalisation of "the project" as a taken-for-granted object [reified] through the institutionalisation of standards'. This naturalisation of the project becomes both the focus and *raison d'être* of project management, they contend. The imputation is that project management, and those who aim to establish professional bodies of knowledge in it, are philosophically naive. Some may be but not nearly as awkwardly as Hodgson and Cicmil contend ('the elevation of universal, abstract rationality over embodied and reflexive rationality'). Let us look at this from the project management professionals' side.

The goals of the professional societies are not, I believe, unreasonable – 'to identify and describe that subset of [knowledge within the profession of project management] that is generally accepted … applicable most of the time, and [of which] there is widespread consensus about their value and usefulness' (PMI, 2004: 3) – a view which Hodgson and Cicmil actually do not dispute (see the section on 'Reach or scope' in Chapter 2). Reification of socially interpreted knowledge is surely quite acceptable (Lave and Wenger, 1991). To be sure, there is a lot that can be, and is, criticised about PMBOK, and sometimes language, and intent, does get carried away, but my reading of Hodgson and Cicmil's position is that it wilfully paints the professional societies into an extremist, naturalist position which neither the PMI nor the other project management professional societies would really recognise. Some of Hodgson and Cicmil's criticisms are indeed fair, but would be even more so if *always* believed. (The problem is that all kinds of statements are made by all kinds of people in this area.) Caution does indeed have to be exercised in using the term 'standards' – but these are really guides, not mandatory requirements. And for heaven's sake, compliance *is* important. Yes, a lot of project management is quite necessarily technicist and control-oriented. But as I've said, rules are needed: there's often a lot at stake in achieving a successful outcome, and it's not always just about money (for example, safety). In the end the thrust of their criticisms is diminished by being hung on an over-engineered presentation of project management as naturalism when in reality the *PMBOK Guide*, APM BOK, and most serious authors take some mix of either the Linehan and Kavanagh view that there can be simultaneously coexisting ontologies, or a more critical realist (and perhaps interpretivist) view that there is some version of reality out there but that this is interpreted by the observer(s), recognising the contingent and contextual reality of what is being observed.

Similarly Thomas, while rightly pointing out the dangers of project management commodification, and tellingly making the point that project management techniques were foisted on the US defence industry in the 1960s, ignores the early work that was done on organisational behaviour factors by NASA and others in the 1960s (Morris, 1994: 106), positioning it in the late 1970s and quoting DeMarco and Lister as implying that what work there had been wasn't empirically based. Much was (for example, Gemmill and Wilemon, 1970; Gemmill and Thamhain, 1973; Thamhain and Wilemon, 1975), though, sure, there could have been more of it, and subject to greater critical scrutiny. And here again there is the danger of using other theorists' precepts to characterise project management, as in this postmodernist colouring: 'The process of managing a project … is associated with a belief in linear progress, absolute truths, the rational planning of ideal social orders, and the commodification of knowledge and production' – with then a reference given to Harvey's *The Condition of Postmodernity*. To the best of my knowledge I can think of no project managers who would sign up to this.

Theory-based truth

As so often, what one gets from so much of this critical theory approach is a sense of theory in search of evidence, more or less precisely what Thomas is accusing project management of. 'If projects are central to human, let alone organisational, existence, how did we survive so long without the concept?' To turn the tables, for how long could managers survive with the theories paraded here?

Clegg *et al.* is an interesting example, for here we have theory espousing managerialism: the Sydney tunnel project apparently worked out its management strategy as it went along. Again, I suspect, sadly, an oversimplification. The basic management set-up is highly reminiscent of the BP Andrew project (Knott, 1996): essentially the core supply chain was involved on an alliance basis explicitly charged with setting and reaching 'stretch targets' using a profit- (and, unlike Andrew, loss-) sharing formula. Interestingly, *pace* the becoming/being, interpretive debate, external facilitation played a major part in setting these targets on Andrew – 'thinking the unthinkable' – and in achieving workable solutions. Human involvement is clearly seen here as critical to formulating management strategies and technical solutions. Yet Clegg *et al.* pass this over to propose instead a reflexive, means–end model of management as the tunnellers worked out what to do next over the 'traditional' linear and unbounded rationality model where management tactics flow from established project strategy.

As before, there's some truth in this but not, I suspect, the whole truth. Of course there was a strategy, if only to choose the route, in deciding on the form of supply chain relationships, in building up the budget and schedule, and in selecting the range of KPIs (not nearly as unusual as Clegg *et al.* claim, as any reference to construction best practice websites will show (Morris, 2004a)). What I find interesting, as an engineer, is that the influence of the nature of tunnelling as a form of technical work flow on management, *à la* Woodward (1958), is not brought out. Tunnelling is largely linear and, notoriously, is underground: you never quite know what you are going to encounter until you get there. (Like the future but worse!) To a significant extent it forces a staged and strongly practical approach to management planning. Sillince *et al.* in fact explore the way 'socio-' (talking) factors influence the understanding of 'technical' issues in their discussion of the specification of an IT system, as discussed earlier – which bears back on the being/becoming debate discussed above.

Much is made of the postmodern, deconstructionist perspective on power and gender. Gender is important but most project managers I know are awake to this by now: most male project managers positively welcome female appointments, at all levels. Power receives substantial analysis. Marshall makes the interesting observation that most project management texts only consider power as a tool or technique. Virtually none treat it critically. However I find the disciplinary perspective raised by Lindgren and Packendorff, Nocker and Thomas less telling practically than the discussion of what project management practices and tools are imposed. As I've already pointed out, people on projects genuinely *do* need to be controlled, to some extent, most of the time, otherwise targets may be missed, but to position this as 'control over the workers' and reporting as 'confession' (Thomas) seems unnecessarily wide of the mark. Lindgren and Packendorff's essay ends up feeling that we are just trapped in capitalism. Maybe we are, but does this tell us 'what happens when people label something a project', let alone 'what competence we need to manage projects effectively'? Power *does* exist in organisations, and organisations are not necessarily the worse for it; and this is not necessarily at odds with creativity or adhocracy (Marshall).

As we've seen, Sillince *et al.* show how important commitment and trust are to making project management work satisfactorily. In a similar vein Marshall and Thomas raise the interesting issue of how the views of those in power can impose techniques, and it is clear that this influences the competencies people believe they need in order to manage projects effectively. There is still much debate within the project management community over the benefit of adopting earned value, for example: not everyone sees the professional project management societies as 'colonising powers', however, to quote the Introduction – though some within the community indeed do. And Thomas is quite right to point out the resistance of industry to many of the practices promulgated by DOD in the 1960s. She omits the interesting point about PERT, that Vice Admiral Raborn, the US Navy Program Manager for Polaris, promoted it as much for its PR and symbolic value in securing funding support as for its practical, control benefits, which Sapolsky reports were in any case disappointing (Sapolsky, 2003; Morris, 1994); and the congruent point that with the US Supersonic transport, the USAF-dominated focus on such tools led the programme's managers completely to miss the importance to the programme of stakeholder opposition, which of course in the end proved fatal (Horwitch, 1982; Morris, 1994). Green extends this further showing, fairly I believe, how narratives set managerial agendas, as does Thomas.

Green extends his narratives-driven critique to claim that project management has missed the boat in construction, by which he must mean building and civil engineering for, as we saw at the outset of this chapter, it is core to process engineering (aka construction engineering) (Morris, 2004a). He then goes on to make an extended analysis of construction firms as 'hollowed out', denuded of an employee labour force, blaming this partly at least on the rise of project management. His comments are telling and the substantive issues raised should not be ignored, but apart from the obvious inconsistency of whether or not project management is or is not a potent force in today's construction industry, the validity of his criticism again comes down to what view one entertains 'the management of projects' to be. Green clearly sees the term as a 'linguistic shuffle', merely reaffirming 'an instrumental tools and techniques' approach. The intent rather is far from this: it is that the discipline has to embrace all that is needed in order to define, develop and deliver projects successfully (Morris and Pinto, 2004).

Marshall's observations of the power of contracts is spot on. Power does force certain practices to be observed, but this is common in many branches of management. It doesn't necessarily mean that the techniques or practices are in themselves bad or good. (Sydow's observation that TV doesn't use formal project management tools yet still completes projects on time in budget is interesting. The *PMBOK Guide* wouldn't argue with this though. As we've already seen, the *PMBOK Guide*, in good contingency fashion, allows the project management team to choose which practices to deploy – 'interpretative flexibility', as Bresnen reminds us.)

Several chapters stress the importance of networks in addition to key actors in projects in shaping project goals (Linde and Linderoth) and in embedding learning (Sydow, Bresnen). Bresnen takes this further by discussing how learning from projects will often become expressed in routines (Nelson and Winter, 1982), an observation also made by Sydow, but that these then become difficult to adapt and hence pose constraints on organisational learning. He goes on to discuss the challenges this also represents in training, career development and other HR practices. All this rings true.

Linehan and Kavanagh make the point that process-based knowledge refers more to how things should be done; though contextual and constructed, this allows for abstraction of good practices more readily than knowledge of substantive decision-making which is generally even more contextual. I reached a similar conclusion, as illustrated with the way project management deals with risk management, by arguing:

> It is the process-based knowledge that largely forms the base of project management's gen-eralisable rules. It would be naïve to maintain that these are to a degree also not context dependent, but they are more generalisable than the substantive knowledge of the context-specific situations that sit above these basic [project management] process 'good practices'. The difference is not quite one of normative, positivist rules versus constructivist insights but rather one of stratification (Bhaskar, 1978, 1998; Outhwaite, 1987). (Morris, 2004b)

Conclusion: whose reality do you critique or support, and why?

As I write this I am sitting on a train going into UCL. I am sure in my own mind that my mental models are cogent. Two people next to me, however, are complaining about all the jargon and procedural terminology of their new (Turnbull-inspired) risk management practices! 'Knowledge always implies a knower', as Linehan and Kavanagh quote Seeley-Brown and Duguid!

Levels of knowledge and thinking about the management of projects vary hugely but the leading practitioners and writers, I believe, will not be as dismayed by most of what is stated here as many critics might imagine. Much of the difficulty arises around:

- definitions of projects (emergent, invented, but then designed and prescribed; dealing with the non-normal – the 'unique undertaking' – in a normal manner (via the life cycle and other project management practices))
- definitions of project management (*PMBOK Guide* or one of the many more sophisticated models)

- questions of levels of flexibility of application of 'best practices' (the false picture of rigid, mandatory standards against a more flexible application which is what in fact the project management bodies of knowledge recommend).

But then again, that is precisely the debate the editors wished us to have. They are to be congratulated therefore on a thoroughly good discussion!

There is real insight in these chapters. When I take issue it's often not in the fundamental point being made but in the level of detail, or sweep of assertion. Meanwhile, I am acutely aware that my own perceptions of what constitutes the reality of project management are, even if cogent, inevitably biased and imperfect – they are just that: my own socially constructed perceptions, albeit based on well-documented evidence.

Personally, I have a broader view of managing projects, one that sees projects as defined principally by the activity of effectively and efficiently managing the product as it develops through the project life cycle (Morris, 1987, 1994, 2004). But there is validity and substance in all views which see things differently. Certainly the *PMBOK Guide* needs enlarging in scope, and many of the criticisms of Thomas, Hodgson and Cicmil and others of its model of project management are right, as I have argued elsewhere (Morris, 2001). I just wish more of the academic community would follow those like Packendorff and me who argue for a bigger picture of the practice, as represented for example by the APM BOK (2006), the IPMA *Competence Baseline* document (Caupin *et al.*, 1998), or the Japanese P2M BOK (ENAA, 2001), or by texts such as Turner (1993, 1996), Turner and Simister (2000), Miller and Lessard (2000), Flyvbjerg *et al.* (2003), Prencipe, Davis and Hobday (2003), and Davies and Hobday (2005).

Projects *are* important. They are recognised as established means of effecting capital investment, new product development and organisational change. They offer a blend of instrumental rationality with reflective, social knowledge. Their processes and structures are invented but are then imposed so that their goals can be achieved as efficiently and effectively as possible. People managing the development of the project, or programme, as it evolves do so generally following some set of best practices – practices which have been collected by communities of practitioners and then formalised as well as they are able. These communities know that their knowledge is contextual. They know that not all the practices need to be applied all the time. (They explicitly say so.) Certainly the way the human and social dimension interacts with these rules is critical to their effectiveness. But then this is true of all management.

Note

1. The Project Management Institute (PMI) has 200,000 members worldwide as of late 2005, the nearest competitor being the UK's Association for Project Management (APM) which is a tenth of its size.

References

APM (Association for Project Management) (2000) *Body of Knowledge*. High Wycombe: APM.
APM (Association for Project Management) (2006) *Body of Knowledge*. High Wycombe: APM.
Bhaskar, R. (1978) *A Realist Theory of Science*. Sussex: Harvester Press.

Bhaskar, R. (1998) *Possibility of Naturalism*. Atlantic Heights, NJ: Humanities Press.

BS 6079-1 (2002) *Guide to Project Management*. London: BSI.

BS ISO 10006 (2003) *Quality Management Systems – Guidelines for Quality Management in Projects*. London: BSI.

Burns, T. and Stalker, G.M. (1961) *The Management of Innovation*. Oxford: Oxford University Press.

Caupin, G., Knöpfel, H., Morris, P., Motzel, E. and Pannenbäcker, O. (1998) *ICB IPMA Competence Baseline*. Zurich: International Project Management Association, available at http://www.ipma.ch

Chia, R. (1995) 'From Modern to Postmodern Organizational Analysis', *Organization Studies*, 16(4): 579–604.

Cooke-Davies, T.C. (2004) 'Maturity and Measurement', in D.P. Slevin, D.I. Cleland and J.K. Pinto (eds), *Innovations: Project Management Research 2004*. Newton Square, PA: Project Management Institute.

Crawford, L. (2002). 'Profiling the Competent Project Manager', in D.P. Slevin, D.I. Cleland and J.K. Pinto (eds), *The Frontiers of Project Management Research*. Newton Square, PA: Project Management Institute, 151–76.

Crawford, L. and Pollack, J. (2004) 'Hard and Soft Projects: A Framework for Analysis', *International Journal of Project Management*, 22(8): 645–54.

Davies, A. and Hobday, M. (2005) *The Business of Projects*. Cambridge: Cambridge University Press.

ENAA (Engineering Advancement Association of Japan) (2001) *P2M: Project and Program Management for Enterprise Innovation*, available at http://www.enaa.or.op.jp

Flyvbjerg, B., Bruzelius, N. and Rothengatter, W. (2003) *Megaprojects and Risk: An Anatomy of Ambition*. Cambridge: Cambridge University Press.

Gemmill, G.R. and Thamhain, H.J. (1973) 'The Effectiveness of Different Power Styles of Project Managers in Gaining Project Support', *IEEE Transactions on Engineering Management*, May 38–43.

Gemmill, G.R. and Wilemon, D.L. (1970) 'The Power Spectrum in Project Management', *Sloan Management Review*, 12(4): 15–25.

Griseri, P. (2002) *Management Knowledge: A Critical View*. Basingstoke: Palgrave Macmillan.

Hacking, I. (1999) *The Social Construction of What?* Cambridge, MA: Harvard University Press.

Horwitch, M. (1982) *Clipped Wings*. Cambridge, MA: MIT Press.

Johnson, S. (2003) 'Systems Integration and the Social Solution of Technical Problems in Complex Systems', in A. Principe, A. Davies and M. Hobday (eds), *The Business of Systems Integration*. Oxford: Oxford University Press.

Knott, T. (1996) *No Business as Usual*. London: BP.

Lave, J. and Wenger, E. (1991) *Situated Learning: Legitimate Peripheral Participation*. Cambridge: Cambridge University Press.

Miller, R. and Lessard, D.R. (2000) *The Strategic Management of Large Engineering Projects*. Cambridge, MA: MIT Press.

Mintzberg, H. (1979) *The Structuring of Organizations*. Englewood-Cliffs, NJ: Prentice-Hall.

Morris, P.W.G. (1994) *The Management of Projects*. London: Thomas Telford.

Morris, P.W.G. (2001) 'Updating the Project Management Bodies of Knowledge', *Project Management Journal*, 32(3): 21–30.

Morris, P.W.G. (2004a) 'Project Management in the Construction Industry', in P.W.G. Morris and J.K. Pinto (eds), *The Wiley Guide to Managing Projects*. Hoboken, NJ: Wiley.

Morris, P.W.G. (2004b) 'The Validity of Knowledge in Project Management and the Challenge of Learning and Competency Development', in P.W.G. Morris and J.K. Pinto (eds), *The Wiley Guide to Managing Projects*. Hoboken, NJ: Wiley.

Morris, P.W.G. and Hough, G.H. (1987) *The Anatomy of Major Projects*. Chichester: Wiley & Sons.

Morris, P.W.G. and Pinto, J.K. (eds) (2004) *The Wiley Guide to Managing Projects*. Hoboken, NJ: Wiley.

Nelson, R. and Winter, S. (1982) *An Evolutionary Theory of Economic Change*. New York: Cambridge University Press.

Nonaka, I. and Takeuchi, H. (1995) *The Knowledge-Creating Company*. New York: Oxford University Press.

OGC (Office of Government Commerce) (2002) *Managing Successful Projects with PRINCE 2*. Norwich: The Stationery Office.

OGC (Office of Government Commerce) (2003) *Managing Successful Programmes*. Norwich: The Stationery Office.

Outhwaite, W. (1987) *New Philosophies of Social Science: Realism, Hermeneutics, and Critical Theory*. New York: Macmillan.

PMI (Project Management Institute) (2004) *A Guide to the Project Management Body of Knowledge*, 3rd edn. Newtown Square, PA: Project Management Institute.

Prencipe, A., Davies, A. and Hobday, M. (2003) *The Business of Systems Integration*. Oxford: Oxford University Press.

Sapolsky, H. (2003) 'Inventing Systems Integration', in A. Prencipe, A. Davies and M. Hobday (eds), *The Business of Systems Integration*. Oxford: Oxford University Press.

Seeley-Brown, J. and Duguid, P. (1995) *Diffusion of Innovations*, 4th edn. New York: Free Press.

Thamhain, H.J. and Wilemon, D.L. (1975) 'Conflict Management in Project Life Cycles', *Sloan Management Review*, 17(3): 31–50.

Thiry, M. (2004) 'Program Management: A Strategic Decision Management Process', in P.W.G. Morris and J.K. Pinto (eds), *The Wiley Guide to Managing Projects*. New York: Wiley.

Toffler, A. (1970) *Future Shock*. New York: Random House.

Turner, J.R. (1993) *The Handbook of Project-Based Management*. London: McGraw-Hill.

Turner, J.R. (1995) *The Commercial Project Manager*. London: McGraw-Hill.

Turner, J.R. and Simister, S.J. (eds) (2000) *Gower Handbook of Project Management*, 3rd edn. Aldershot: Gower.

Vickers, G. (1970) *Freedom in a Rocking Boat*. Harmondsworth: Pelican.

Weber, M. (1949) *The Methodology of Social Sciences*. New York: Free Press.

Williams, T. (2004) 'Assessing and Building on the Underlying Theory of Project Management in the Light of Badly Overrun Projects', paper presented at the PMI Research Conference, London, 2004.

Woodward, J. (1958) *Industrial Organization: Behaviour and Control*. Oxford: Oxford University Press.

Name index

Subject index

355